LAW AFTER GROUND ZERO

Edited by

John Strawson

London • Sydney • Portland, Oregon

First published in Great Britain 2002 by
The GlassHouse Press, The Glass House,
Wharton Street, London WC1X 9PX, United Kingdom
Telephone: + 44 (0)20 7278 8000 Facsimile: + 44 (0)20 7278 8080
Email: info@cavendishpublishing.com
Website: www.cavendishpublishing.com

Published in the United States by The GlassHouse Press, Cavendish Publishing
c/o International Specialized Book Services,
5824 NE Hassalo Street, Portland,
Oregon 97213-3644, USA

Published in Australia by The GlassHouse Press
c/o Cavendish Publishing (Australia) Pty Ltd
45 Beach Street, Coogee, NSW 2034, Australia

© Cavendish Publishing Limited 2002
Reprinted with amendments 2004

The GlassHouse Press is an imprint of Cavendish Publishing Limited

British Library Cataloguing in Publication Data
1 Human rights 2 International law
3 War on terrorism, 2001 – influence
I Strawson, John
341.4'81

Library of Congress Cataloguing in Publication Data
Data available

ISBN 1-904385-02-8

1 3 5 7 9 10 8 6 4 2

Printed and bound in Great Britain

To
Michael Wilson

Acknowledgments

I would like to thank the School of Law at the University of East London for encouraging me with this project, and especially Fiona Fairweather for her support. The contributors have been painstaking in their work and yet unfailingly quick in responding to tight deadlines. All at Cavendish have been endlessly helpful and always available. Ruth Massey has been patience itself and unsparing in her time and attention. Without Beverley Brown this book would not have appeared.

John Strawson
August 2002

Contributors

Bill Bowring, School of Law, Government and International Relations, London Metropolitan University

Anthony Carty, Division of Law, University of Derby

Costas Douzinas, School of Law, Birkbeck College, University of London

Peter Fitzpatrick, School of Law, Birkbeck College, University of London

Keith Hayward, Department of Social Policy, Sociology and Social Research, University of Kent

Jacqueline Ismael, Department of Social Work, University of Calgary

Tareq Ismael, Department of Political Science, University of Calgary

Rafiq Latta, Petroleum Argus

David Meltzer, School of Law, University of Kent

Qudsia Mirza, School of Law, University of East London

Wayne Morrison, The External Programme for Laws, University of London

Siraj Sait, School of Law, University of East London

John Strawson, School of Law, University of East London

Rhiannon Talbot, School of Law, University of Newcastle upon Tyne

Kim Van Der Borght, School of Law, University of Hull

Ali Wardak, Department of Humanities and Social Sciences, University of Glamorgan

Contents

PART I
LAW'S FIRST STRIKE

PART 2
THE GROUND OF RIGHTS

PART 3
GROUND ZERO'S PROSPECTS

Transliteration of Arabic terms

Note: the transliteration system adopted in the text is based broadly on the system adopted by the International Journal of Middle East Studies.

Al Qa'ida	the organisation, meaning 'the base'
Qur'an	literally, 'the book'
Sunna	traditions of the Prophet contained in canonical collections, a source of Islamic law
Ijtihad	independent legal reasoning, a source of Islamic law
Shari'a	Arabic term for Islamic law, literally, 'the path'
Usul al fiqh	Islamic jurisprudence, literally, 'the roots of law'
Hidaya	literally, 'a guide', a key law text of the Sunni school
Sunni	the largest group of Muslims
Shi'a	the second largest group of Muslims
Jihad	literally, 'effort or struggle'; has legal significance in Islamic international law as military action – not be translated as 'holy war'
Siyar	Islamic international law
Siyassa	Islamic public law
Huddud	literally, 'limits/boundaries' (pl); singular 'had': category of fixed penalties
Hijab	veil
Qanun	law or a norm of law
Al haq	also law but conveying right, as in the French *droit*; sometimes used as 'right'
Hukum	plural of haq, meaning 'rights'
Ijma	consensus, a source of Islamic law
Qiyas	analogical reasoning, a source of Islamic law
Ibadat	rules of religious devotion
Maslaha	public interest
Muamalat	rules of social interaction
Qiwama	difference between the sexes
Ulama	jurists

Abbreviations

ATCS	Anti-Terrorism, Crime and Security Act 2001 (UK)
ATA	Afghan Transitional Authority
DFLP	Democratic Front for the Liberation of Palestine
GATT	General Agreement on Tariffs and Trade
ICC	International Criminal Court
ICJ	International Court of Justice
IDF	Israel Defense Forces
IZL	Irgun Zvai Leumi, National Military Organization, also known as the Irgun
MK	Member of the Knesset (Israel)
NCIS	National Criminal Intelligence Service (UK)
PA	Palestinian Authority
PIRA	Provisional Irish Republican Army
PKK	Kurdish Workers Party (Turkey)
PLO	Palestine Liberation Organisation
SEATO	South East Asia Treaty Organisation
SOE	Special Operations Executive (UK during World War II)
TA	Terrorism Act 2000 (UK)
UNRWA	United Nations Relief and Works Agency for Palestinian Refugees in the Near East
UNSCOP	United Nations Special Commission on Palestine
USA-PATRIOT Act	Uniting and Strengthening of America to Provide Appropriate Tools Required to Intercept and Obstruct Terrorism Act, 2001 (USA)
WTC	World Trade Center (New York)
WTO	World Trade Organization

Introduction
In the name of the law

John Strawson

In some ways, September 11 has returned law to Ground Zero. The attacks on New York, Washington and Pennsylvania appear to have disturbed legal cultures. International law has been revealed as feeble, constitutional law as insecure, while human rights law has become negotiable. Law's apparent stable edifice has been exposed as being as fragile as our world order. International legal doctrines, treaties and constitutional texts seem superseded by the political expediency of alleged international and national security concerns in the face of terrorist threats. The Bush Administration in the United States speaks about law as if we were at a new foundational moment at which existing legal norms and institutions are either irrelevant or questionable. *Law after Ground Zero* explores the legal responses to September 11 from the United Nations, national legislatures, governments, the media and other scholars. It confronts the dangers and opportunities for law at this new juncture against the background of discussions about international law, Islam, human rights, Afghanistan and the Middle East.

This book brings together analyses of different elements of debates taking place in international and national law in the context of George Bush's and Tony Blair's 'war against terrorism'. The essays in this book offer strikingly diverse approaches reflecting the sometimes radically different theoretical standpoints of the authors. The contributors not only come to this book from different political backgrounds but also work across several disciplines – political science, jurisprudence, sociology, criminology, war studies, international relations, Middle East studies, in addition to law. This demonstrates the significance that law, one thought of as marginal, has become more significant and requires serious attention.

Order and outlaws

One shared concern is with the rhetoric of the outlaw that became such a common image in political discourse soon after the attacks. It became apparent that Al Qa'ida and their Taliban original backers were not the only outlaws. As military action began, and as national legislation in the United States and the United Kingdom demonstrated, migrants and asylum seekers, Muslim communities, individuals from the Middle East, as well as a designated group of states, were put on notice that they were candidates for 'outlaw' status. President Bush exemplified this in his speech announcing the Afghan war: 'if any government sponsors the outlaws and murderers and killers of innocents, they have become outlaws and murderers themselves.'[1] Undoubtedly, Bush intended outlaw to convey the sense of being opposite to law, yet within American popular culture significantly the term evokes the image of the rogue pitted against a precarious and fragile legal order.

The idea of the outlaw goes to the heart of modern law's foundational exclusions, first in the state and then with the development of international law through the agency of colonial conquest.[2] While the state was based on the distinction between citizen and non-citizen, international law from the 17th century developed a world

---

1 George Bush, Address to the Nation, 7 October 2001.
2 See Fitzpatrick, 1992 and 2001.

order divided between sovereign states and subject peoples based on the distinction between civilised and uncivilised nations. The results of this history still remain in the Statute of the International Court of Justice, where Article 38 speaks about one source of international law as being 'general principles of law recognised by civilised nations'.

Human rights discourses seek to attach rights to the human being irrespective of citizenship or origins.[3] However, human rights discourses as conscious narratives are relatively new and, despite the West's claims to their pedigree and practice, there is only a tenuous commitment to human rights within national and international law. As Bush demonstrates, the exclusionary impulse is very strong. Indeed, in the name of protecting the human rights of the victims of Ground Zero, thousands of civilian casualties are permitted in Afghanistan, mass killings of prisoners of war at Qalia Janhi are not investigated and, highly symbolically, Al Qa'ida and Taliban detainees were held in shackles at Guantanamo Bay.

The Middle Eastern and Muslim origins of the perpetrators of the attacks placed all Middle Easterners and Muslims at the margins of human rights. The register of exclusion is established through connection to terrorism. Bush pointed the finger to ask which side such people and states were on: 'Afghanistan is just the beginning. If anyone harbors a terrorist, they're a terrorist. If they fund a terrorist they're a terrorist and if they house a terrorist they're terrorists.'[4] Paul Wolfowitz, Deputy Secretary of State, explained exactly what this meant for American policy after the fall of Kabul in November 2001: 'We are going to continue pursuing the entire Al Qa'ida network,' he said, 'which is in 60 different countries and not just Afghanistan ... This is a campaign against all the global terrorist networks and the states that support terrorism.'[5] As states were named – Iran, Iraq, North Korea, Libya, Syria, Sudan and later Cuba[6] – the United States' calls for 'regime change' became a mantra of the new order.

In the United States there was an assumption that international law justified its response. Indeed, sustenance for this came from the key United Nations Security Council Resolutions that had linked the response to the 'terrorist attacks' of September 11 to 'the inherent right of individual and collective self-defense'.[7] These resolutions conveyed the unmistakable message that the United States was a victim of an attack that threatened international peace and security and that it was entitled to respond to such attacks by the use of force.[8] In this way, the United States' interests and international objectives appeared to become one. At the same time, from the legal point of view, the resolutions appeared to grant 'terrorist attacks' the status of an 'armed attack' by a state – the trigger for the self-defence justification under Article 51 of the United Nations Charter.[9] This has undoubtedly nourished the United States' current obsession with renegotiating its international legal relations. This allegedly new unilateralism on the part of the United States encompasses withdrawing from the Kyoto Protocol on global warming, not ratifying the Rio Pact on biodiversity, withdrawing from the Anti-Ballistic Missile Treaty, questioning the Geneva Conventions, opposing the ban on land mines, opposing new proposals to strengthen the biological weapons convention and completely opposing the establishment of the International Criminal Court. To this

---

3 See Douzinas, 2000.
4 See above, n 1.
5 Paul Wolfowitz (CBS *Face the Nation*, 28 November 2001).
6 See John R Bolton, US Under-Secretary of State, *International Herald Tribune*, 28 November 2001.
7 See United Nations Security Council Resolutions 1268 (2001) and 1273 (2001).
8 See Murphy, 2002.
9 See Byers, 2002.

long list must also be added the Bush Administration's campaign to justify a war against Iraq.[10] In these developments the United States' unilateral policy is clothed in the language of international co-operation. However, in a return to the heyday of European colonialism in the 19th century, the United States is the sole arbiter of international good.[11]

It is ironic that as the year since September 11 has progressed, the United States' view of international law has become increasingly out of step with the rest of the world, including its allies.[12] The rejection of the International Criminal Court has become a central aspect of United States foreign policy.[13] The DeLay Act gives the Administration powers to cut off military aid to states that do not enter into agreements with the United States to prevent the prosecution of United States citizens before the Court. Indeed, the law also permits a US government to use military means to free any Americans that might be detained by the Court.[14] This suggests, perhaps, that the power of the United States is more elusive than is often claimed. Despite appearances, the United States is unable to influence international institutions and thus attempts to place itself outside them. In a curious way, the United States becomes a kind of outlaw itself.

Within the United States domestic sphere, security interests have produced far-reaching legislation, equipping the government with extensive powers of search, seizure and detention without trial. Under the grandiose title of 'Uniting and Strengthening of America to Provide Appropriate Tools Required to Intercept and Obstruct Terrorism Act' – whose acronym is the USA-PATRIOT Act – a matrix of international and domestic law was constituted in which concerns for security were introduced at the expense of human rights.

The huge legal edifice created to protect civilians from terrorism has been aimed mainly against migrant communities in the United States. Since September 11 thousands have been detained without trial and very few have ever been prosecuted, none for offences related to terrorism.

September 11 reveals a moment of infinite fragility for international order.[15] The shocking consequences of the attacks and, in particular, the collapse of the Twin Towers have led to exaggerated claims about the strength of the Al Qa'ida network. Yet, the terrifying results of their actions should not be allowed to obscure the reality that this action was undertaken by 19 men armed only with knives and box cutters. Their other attributes were a ruthless disregard for human life, the ability to fly planes at large buildings and to read airline schedules. Strangely, these attributes have been said to be sophisticated, requiring planning by a complex organisation. Indeed, within days, the United States Administration, from President Bush down, began to suggest that Al Qa'ida might have access to nuclear or chemical weapons. This indicates much about the insecurities of the most powerful state on the planet. It is as if power is retained by exaggerating the strength of your opponent.

When it proved difficult to find direct evidence linking Al Qa'ida to weapons of mass destruction the Administration turned to Saddam Hussein for assistance. As Iraq might have weapons of mass destruction and is still acting in defiance of the United Nations, the United States government argued, Iraq could be in a position to supply them to Al Qa'ida. This new amalgam neatly brought Iraq into the

---

10 See Vagts, 2001.
11 See Koskenniemi, 2001.
12 See Francis Fukuyama, 'The West may be cracking', *International Herald Tribune*, 9 August 2002.
13 Although there are many American voices that take a different position. See Scheffer, 2001–02.
14 See Elizabeth Becker, 'US warns backs of tribunal may lose aid', *International Herald Tribune*, 12 August 2002.
15 See also Halliday, 2001; Scraton, 2002; Booth and Dunne, 2002.

framework of the war against terrorism. The Bush Administration attempted to turn Iraq into an immediate threat to the United States and the plans for military action began. The prospects of action against Iraq have, however, revealed serious differences across the United States political spectrum, including government circles, and have not proved popular among the allies. Indeed, it is the questionable legal basis for military action that has dominated much of the debate.

The talking up of Al Qa'ida as powerful played into the hands its leader, Osama bin Laden, who proved a consummate public relations expert when he released his extraordinary videotape to be broadcast worldwide. Bin Laden seized the opportunity to speak on behalf of the Muslim world and to challenge the United States in a twisted version of *jihad*. This was a gang leader used to speaking to hundreds transformed into a mass communicator. His bloodcurdling threats to the West and to Jews fed the insecurity that September 11 had bred, licensing the United States government to warn of the imminent danger of further outrages. Indeed, at regular intervals government officials, from Cabinet members, Governors to the FBI, have issued notice to the public to be vigilant. In the autumn of 2001 this threat seemed to materialise when letters containing anthrax were sent to legislators and some parts of the media. Several people died and more became ill. However, mysteriously, the letters stopped and the government buried the issue. Extraordinarily, the FBI, CIA and the powers under the USA-PATRIOT Act failed to identify the criminals and the government failed to explain why.

In the intervening months, only two Al Qa'ida suspects have been detained for attempting new actions. Richard Reeves, known as the shoe bomber, was overpowered on a transatlantic flight as he tried to set light to his shoe in full view of passengers and crew. His shoes did contain explosives and he could have caused a terrible tragedy. Then the arrest of Joe Padilla was hailed by Attorney-General, John Ashcroft as a major advance and it was claimed that he was planning to use a 'dirty' nuclear device to attack major United States cities.[16] It was later revealed that the evidence against Padilla consisted of the fact that he had surfed the internet under 'explosives' and had visited a nuclear website.[17] Neither of these two individuals, both with backgrounds of criminal activities, both of whom had converted to Islam in prison, appeared to signal a sophisticated or powerful organisation. If Al Qa'ida did possess weapons of mass destruction it seems curious that these have remained unused – when set against the hatred for the United States and the West revealed in Osama bin Laden's statements and television appearances.

Internationally, the repercussions have been most marked for the Palestinians. It appears that, in the absence of Al Qa'ida, the present Palestinian suicide bombers have sustained the reality of the threat. The lethal and inhuman campaign by Palestinian fringe groups against Israeli civilians in Israel and the occupied territories, however, is hardly comparable to September 11. Yet the Israeli government's success in winning the Bush Administration's approval for linking Arafat to the 'war against terrorism' has drastically worsened the human rights situation in the occupied territories. The re-occupation of most of the West Bank, the Israeli military campaign and the curfews and checkpoints imposed on the civilian population have created child malnutrition, medicine shortages and mass unemployment. The only reasonable solution to the conflict, the creation of a viable sovereign Palestinian State, has become hostage to our post-September 11 times.

---

16 There is some disquiet even amongst the right in the US as to the role of Ashcroft, post-September 11; see Neil A Lewis, 'Conservatives uneasy about Ashcroft's zeal',' *International Herald Tribune*, 25 July 2002.

17 See Tony Allen-Mills, 'Spectre of dirty bomb fades', *The Sunday Times*, 16 June 2002.

In Europe, although there were initially similar reactions to those in the United States, enthusiasm waned as the Bush Administration focused almost exclusively on the implications of September 11 for the American position in the world. Nonetheless the moment was seized to enact similar anti-terrorist legislation. In almost all cases this was accompanied by measures to toughen immigration and asylum laws and procedures. These moves have been accompanied by the rise in support for anti-immigrant parties at elections. In Denmark, the Netherlands and France this has had a dramatic effect on the political system. In each case the September 11 sub-text that Islam is the threat has been consciously mobilised against Muslims. In this way an elision is made between Al Qa'ida and Muslim communities.

Overall, the speed with which international and national human rights provisions have been set aside in the interests of security has been instructive.[18] It is as if the sacrificing of human rights will ward off terrorism. Certainly, the intertwining of law with national security is not new. What may be more pronounced is the aggressive manner in which it has been done. The fragility of international order is thus doubly revealed: not only in the ability of small groups to strike terror in powerful societies, but also in those societies' weak attachment to human rights values. Legal discourse has also found it difficult to deal with the characteristics of terrorism. It has vacillated between defining September 11 as a crime or an act of war – and at the same time pondering whether or not this distinction has significance.

Law's first strike

The first part of the book situates law's responses to September 11 as a necessary legitimising accompaniment to military might. Bill Bowring's survey of international law since the mid-1980s links a sense of disappointment with the way that positive doctrines of law work with a sensitivity to the impossibility of the mission of law in current world order. He reminds us of the debates that surrounded the bombing of Libya in 1986, the Kuwait crisis, and Kosovo intervention. These events and the discourses of international law that they produced are connected to the war in Afghanistan. He believes that 'international law been dragged through the mire'. The question of his title, 'the degradation international law?', neatly places his piece in the space that Koskenniemi charts between utopia and apology.[19]

Costas Douzinas offers us a glimpse of a new order through a subtle re-telling of the West's story of just war. He plots the doctrine of just wars through Greek philosophy and the Crusades to its recurrence within modernity. Douzinas delivers the just war in postmodern form that rests on a 'moral-legal order' although increasingly freed from constraint by the possession of overwhelming force and the erosion of territorial sovereignty. Obscured with the rise of apparently collective security organisations in the 20th century, the League of Nations and the United Nations, the just war doctrine nonetheless remained a significant subliminal force that re-surfaced at the end of the cold war. His discursive history is an unsettling account of the secretion of national interests within international legal and human rights discourses. He urges us to act in the debate on the character of the period for,

---

18 See Mary Robinson, 'After September 11: human rights are still as important as ever', *International Herald Tribune*, 21 June 2002.
19 Koskenniemi, 1989, 1990.

if the current globalising trajectory continues, 'the principle of just wars will have finally won, in the proclamation of an endless peace without justice'.

Peter Fitzpatrick focuses our attention on the way in which the apparent universalism of human rights and freedom is imbricated with exclusionary moments in both philosophical and political discourses of the West. As he argues, the phrase 'enemy of freedom' effortlessly falls from the lips of George Bush as he instantiates the universal in the parochialism of American necessity. The pursuit of these enemies – what Fitzpatrick calls 'an eliminable rump' – destroys the notions of universal freedom and common humanity, as the Other is placed beyond reach.

Anthony Carty is shockingly forthright in the introduction to his chapter: 'double standards are an integral part of the ideology of democracy and the rule of law.' However, Carty is not concerned with a point by point exposure of these double standards but, rather, uncovers the methodology of classical Western international law and demonstrates how ideas about sovereignty, freedom and human rights are incorporated within a discourse of national security and doctrines of war. He elucidates his visits to Cicero, Kant and Hobbes through an intriguing discussion of the International Court of Justice's judgments in the *Nuclear Weapons* case and the *Lockerbie* cases, the subsequent Camp Zeist case against Al Megrahi, and the United Kingdom's pursuit of its ex-intelligence operative, Shayler. Carty deftly moves between international legal doctrine, municipal law and the United Nations Security Council as he makes his case that these discourses themselves are 'quite simply terrorist' as they originate from sanctifying the possession and use of nuclear weapons.

The ground of rights

The second part of the book focuses on the way in which legal norms and discourses have been mobilised since September 11 to destabilise rights. Kim Van Der Borght and I use Cuba to demonstrate how the United States has developed its international legal method to elide American security interests with international peace and security. The comprehensive legal consequences of the four-decade-old embargo of Castro's Cuba are heralded in the Helms-Burton Act 1996. This national legislation not only has international reach through extending United States courts' jurisdiction over any national dealing or trafficking in American nationalised property; at the same time, the Act's provisions for regime change prefigure the post-September 11 Bush Administration's demands for regime change in Iraq and Palestine. Van Der Borght and Strawson argue that United States theory and practice of international law allocates to itself the universal representation of justice, democracy and human rights.

David Meltzer addresses the laws of war as he investigates the relationship between crime and terrorism. He questions the implications of the United States using the language of war and terrorism at the same time. In rooting his discussion of the laws of war in military practices since the Second World War, he allows us to imagine Al Qa'ida as an irregular armed group. If Al Qa'ida is indeed such a force, then its members are bound by the laws and customs of war and as such can be liable for grave breaches. Ironically, he argues that the United States could gain greater flexibility by embracing the law of war than in treating the 'war against terrorism' as a police action.

Siraj Sait's essay on international refugee law is the first of several to turn attention to the Middle East. He continues the theme of the exclusionary character of international law through an examination of the manner in which the world's largest refugee community is placed outside the framework of the United Nations

Convention on Refugees. The marginalisation of the Palestinians in international law is too rarely commented on. As Sait develops this theme, the implications of George Bush's preferred choice of either being with the United States or against it become dangerously clear. Those who are perpetually excluded from world order do not vanish but necessarily nourish dreams of freedom on the margins of legality. In some instances this produces violent reactions. As Sait graphically explains, 'post-September 11 the suicide bombers from refugee backgrounds become a potent symbol of the postmodern outlaw'.

In the aftermath of September 11 women in the Muslim world, particularly under the Taliban, became the symbol of Islamic oppression, a sign of fundamental differences between East and West – thus restaging a familiar moment of colonialist Orientalism and obscuring the engagements that have occurred between Western feminism and indigenous feminist movements in the Muslim world. In an essay that maps the historical links between the development of Islamic feminist movements and Western feminism, Qudsia Mirza's main focus, however, is contemporary Islamic feminist discourse, particularly the emerging interpretive methodologies of scriptural exegesis that have reinvigorated the reformist project within Islam. But, she argues, internal critique is needed in order to challenge the essentialist construction of women within both Islamic orthodoxy and Western feminist discourse. This is at the heart of an increasing theoretical divergence between Islamic feminist discourse and Western feminism. By interrogating both Islamic and Western feminist discourse, Mirza offers a fresh and dynamic conjoining of the two which goes beyond the sterile binary divides.

Rhiannon Talbot assesses the British counter-terrorism legislation passed rapidly after September 11. The Anti-Terrorism, Crime and Security Act has been certified by the British Home Secretary, David Blunkett as being compatible with the European Convention on Human Rights, yet many of its provisions have been widely criticised for curtailing civil liberties. The Act increases police power, affects the rights of asylum seekers and migrants and generally increases all forms of surveillance. Talbot is interested in the way in which such curtailments of civil liberties rarely increase the effectiveness in defeating terrorism. She argues that this Act stands in a chain of anti-terrorist legislation enacted in haste that tends to become a permanent feature of the legal environment.

Ground Zero's prospects

The third part of the book looks at the disturbances that Ground Zero has provoked in legal cultures. Keith Hayward and Wayne Morrison re-work the narratives of crime and war. They see September 11 as both a real and a symbolic event. Hayward and Morrison track the way in which dealing with violence provokes contradictions in the state, itself founded as the monopoly of violence, and through which it offers protection to its citizens. The insecurities created by September 11 underline a fundamental sense of unease created by crime in postmodern societies. George Bush's 'war against terrorism' thus joins those other wars of dubious success, against crime and drugs. Hayward and Morrison speculate that September 11 becomes 'an exemplar of a new world order of risk' that the United States might opportunistically seize in order to consolidate its supremacy.

The events of September 11 are intimately connected to the Middle East. The hijackers were Egyptian and Saudi nationals and their alleged motives related to American military and political presence in the region. Tareq Ismael and Jacqueline Ismael address this connection, noting that in the United States the 'subscripts of public discourse are that Islam and the Arabs are the true causes of terrorism'. They investigate the way in which American academics continue to contribute to the idea of American civilisation as besieged by an inhumane, homogenised Islamic Arab world. Ismael and Ismael show how the work of scholars such as Samuel Huntington, Bernard Lewis and Fuad Ajami legitimise a public discourse in the media that popularises United States foreign policy to the Middle East. These discourses, for example, provide the essential context for current American policy on Iraq as Saddam Hussein becomes linked through the 'axis of evil' with Osama bin Laden.

Rafiq Latta turns to what he calls the 'dramatic deterioration' of the Palestinian-Israeli conflict since September 11. Israel's refusal to abide by the timeframe of the Oslo Agreement for a permanent status treaty by 4 May 1999, and its massive expansion in Israeli settlements in the West Bank, were already features of the crisis before September 2001, also the anniversary of the second intifada. However, as Latta points out, the period since September 11 has seen an escalation of the occupation as the Israeli response to the Palestinian suicide bombings. Ariel Sharon seized on September 11 to equate Israel's security situation with that of the United States. In this amalgamation, Sharon demonises Yasser Arafat as another Osama bin Laden by claiming that the Palestinian Authority is a terrorist organisation. Yet there is no evidence to link Yasser Arafat or the Palestinian Authority to the suicide bombings against Israel. Nonetheless, what Latta calls the 'Sharonisation' of United States policy towards the Middle East, which resulted ultimately in George Bush's 24 June 2002 speech, made the creation of a Palestinian state conditional on the removal of Yasser Arafat. Despite the adoption of United Nations Security Council Resolution 1397 (2002) calling for the creation of two states, Israel and Palestine, Palestinian self-determination appears another victim of September 11.

Afghanistan, unlike Palestine, appears to have seen a fundamental change of political fortune since September 11. The rapid dispatch of the Taliban regime through a combination of United States air power and Northern Alliance ground forces armed with US weapons and US dollars has seen the ascent to power of Hamid Karzai. Ali Wardak explains the Afghan aspect of the transfer of power in his instructive essay on the role of *jirga* in the process. The *loya jirga* that consecrated Karzai as President in June 2002 was the supreme expression of a traditional system of power and dispute settlement in the country. As Wardak explains, a *jirga* is a gathering of people that represents the community at a variety of levels, from the village to the nation. In some form such organisations appear common to all Afghanistan's linguistic and cultural groups. United States support for the *loya jirga* is an interesting example of an attempt to mobilise local legitimation for Western policies. However, as Wardak's essay makes clear, it is also significant that non-Western systems of pluralism and consultation can make such an impression on the world stage. It offers the prospect of cultural interchange in place of the 'clash of civilisations'.

John Strawson continues this theme in his discussion of how the English press dealt with Islamic law after September 11. Tony Blair's speeches became peppered with quotations from the Qur'an as he argued that the attacks were contrary to Islam and Islamic law. This Western attempt to differentiate between competing streams of Islamic jurisprudence does open a small fissure in the 200 year old Orientalist edifice that has constructed Islamic law as necessarily backward, unchangeable and cruel. It offers an interesting public space in which contested views of controversial topics such as *jihad* can be heard.

Law's end

Writing in the American Journal of International Law, Tom Farer warns his readers that, in the wake of September 11, the bounds of normative restraints may have been broken. The actions of Al Qa'ida and the responses to them challenge the system of international legal relations carefully crafted in the second half of the last century. He concludes:

> Once the frame of order is broken, we can reasonably anticipate increasingly norm-less violence, pitiless blows followed by monstrous retaliation in a descending spiral of hardly imaginable depths. The Israeli experience could well prove a microcosmic anticipation of the global system's future in this scenario. To sustain its occupation of desired land filled with people it did not desire as fellow citizens, Israel's government coped with increasing resistance by slipping from the normative restraints on a state's tools for safeguarding its security. Collective punishment, hostage taking, escalatory reprisals, riot control with live ammunition, assassinations, and torture combated a resistance that descended the scale of means from occasional violence and demonstrative acts to unrelenting assault on Israeli civilians. Imagining ourselves in the fire-veined darkness on the West Bank of Jordan, we may then picture on a larger stage the possible results when the frame of order breaks.[20]

Law after Ground Zero is offered as a contribution to this necessary debate about the relationship between law and human rights in an insecure global society. In doing so this collection indicates that Farer's bleak prospect is not the only possible outcome of September 11. The new period has also presented us with opportunities to review and reflect on legal culture, especially international law, constitutional law and human rights. Significantly, this also extends to Islamic law – and, I would suggest, by implication to other non-Western legal systems too. In challenging so much in the international legal order, President Bush may inadvertently have broken the spell of modern law. What had appeared so fixed has now been consciously transformed into a contested arena. September 11 and its aftermath may also mark a critical moment in the decline of the mystique of the United States. Despite its overwhelming military power, it appears more vulnerable and less assured than before. The United States may have the power to destabilise the legal order but perhaps no longer has the capacity to impose its future.

Law after Ground Zero also offers an alternative to the picture of a 'clash of civilisations'[21] so pressed on us all in the aftermath of September 11. The complexities of international society, including multi-national states, mass migration, regional and international groupings, means that 20th century stereotypes no longer work well. Cultural borrowing is as common as cultural confrontation. The rise in interest in Islam after September 11 as seen, for example, in the best-seller status awarded to the Qur'an in many traditionally non-Muslim countries. The discussions in this collection of Islamic law and traditional legal institutions in Afghanistan underline the implications this has for law.

The aftermath of September 11 seems to have created a new space in which to think about legal theory and practice. *Law after Ground Zero* places critical issues on the agenda. There needs to be recognition, however, that great effort will need to be made if we are to go beyond the limitations of our postcolonial world in developing a legal order which reflects the equal contributions of our diverse legal cultures.[22] September 11 has served to highlight how Western law has become the dominant model at both national and international levels. Colonialism bequeathed to the world's states legal systems, civil law and common law stamped with race, gender

---

20 Farer, 2002, p 354.
21 See Huntington, 1993.
22 See Darian-Smith and Fitzpatrick, 1999.

and the class discriminations of the European occupying power. International law emerged with colonialism and sought to legitimise conquest, slavery, ethnic cleansing, genocide and racism. In this process other systems of law became subordinate or were excluded. The legitimacy of current world order is compromised by this past. While we should not be held hostage to it, we do need to recognise it in shaping the new contours of legal discourse. This intricate task involves re-locating privileged positions gained by political and military power but dressed as law. The West's responses to September 11 demonstrate that the shallowness of its human rights culture does not grant it the podium to lecture the world on democracy and the rule of law.

Iraq Postscript: March 2004

The theme of his book is the new prominence that law has been accorded in the post-September 11 world. International law in particular has assumed front page news as the 'war against terrorism' was widened to the war against Iraq. The simple question 'was the war legal?' has become a major political issue internationally and particularly in Britain. In February 2003, millions of people marched against the war in many parts of the world, convinced that any conflict would be illegal unless it had the support of the United Nations. A year after the war, Tony Blair's government is being asked to produce the legal grounds for the war. Its coyness in resisting the publication of the opinions of the Attorney-General, Lord Goldsmith and Professor Christopher Greenwood only fuel the popular belief that the war was of dubious legality. After the Hutton Inquiry into the death of the weapons inspector David Kelly and the new inquiries in both the United States and Britain on the quality of intelligence on Iraq's (apparently missing) weapons of mass destruction, the public is highly sceptical of its political representatives. Yet, for the Bush and Blair administrations, the war against Iraq was said to be a necessary step to rid the world of a key player in the terrorist infrastructure.

While the public want to believe in an international law that is wedded to justice – as the contributors to this book show – all too often international law has been used to legitimate government actions. Indeed international law's origins lie in developing doctrines that justify sovereigns' right to use force. In the case of the war against Iraq, the United States and Britain argued that Saddam Hussein's refusal to co-operate with the United Nations Security requirement to eliminate and to demonstrate the elimination of all weapons of mass destruction constituted a threat to international peace and security. The danger came, they said, following September 11 in that Iraq's suspect regime might pass such weapons to terrorist organisations such as Al Qa'ida. Then there would be the prospect of biological, chemical and even possibly nuclear attacks by terrorists, which would make the destruction of the Twin Towers appear minor. In an attempt to create fear in the public mind, the British and American governments used so-called intelligence reports to show that Saddam Hussein had links to Al Qa'ida and other terrorist groups and that he had chemical and biological weapons and was attempting to acquire nuclear capacity – the latter based on discredited British intelligence but still used by George W Bush in his State of the Union speech before the war.

During the autumn of 2002 the United Nations Security Council adopted Resolution 1441, which appeared to give Iraq some time to comply with UN requirements before facing 'serious consequences'. However, carefully scripted into the resolution was a re-worded version of the earlier resolution that had authorised the use of force against Iraq in 1990 over the invasion of Kuwait. Resolution 1441 says, 'recalling that its Resolution 678 (1990) authorized Member States to use all necessary means to uphold and implement Resolution 660 (1990) of 2 August 1990 and all subsequent resolutions to 660 (1990) and to restore international peace and security in the region'. This slight redrafting of the 1990 resolution appears to insert into Resolution 1441 the right of member states themselves to decide whether or not UN Security Council resolutions have been 'upheld and implemented' and to take 'all necessary means' to do so. As a result, Britain and the United States wrested the authority of the Security Council for their action. This neat argument may have a legal nicety about it but it is unlikely to prove attractive to the public.

Since the launch of the war against terror, both the United States and Britain have been keen to heighten tensions about the terrorist threat. As a result, small gangs have been elevated to powerful actors in international relations. This has justified major curtailments of human rights and scandals such as the Guatanamo Bay prison camp. Indeed, Al Qa'ida has been active and the atrocities have continued: Bali, Riyadh and Istanbul. However, all have been on the pattern of September 11, using elementary conventional weapons. It now appears that the threat from Saddam Hussein was also played-up. The work of the UN weapons inspectors indicates that Iraq had not had any of the banned weapons since 1991. What is clear, however, is that Saddam Hussein did behave as if he did still have them. His obstructive behaviour was possibly a ploy to warn the Iraq opposition, his neighbours and the West. In this he may in part have been the author of his own downfall.

The international public is faced with deceptions and exaggerations on all sides. Answers about the legalities of many of the aspects of the 'war on terror' are demanded on many fronts. The new popular interest in international law does, however, offer the prospect of a movement for a new international legal order where its doctrines and institutions can make an acquaintance with justice.

John Strawson
March 2004

References

Booth, Ken and Dunne, Tim (eds) (2002) *Worlds in Collision: Terror and the Future of Global Order*, Basingstoke and New York: Palgrave

Byers, Michael (2002) 'Terror and the future of international law', in Booth, Ken and Dunne, Tim (eds), *Worlds in Collision: Terror and the Future of Global Order*, Basingstoke and New York: Palgrave

Darian-Smith, Eve and Fitzpatrick, Peter (eds) (1999) *Laws of the Postcolonial*, Ann Arbor: University of Michigan Press

Douzinas, Costas (2000) *The End of Human Rights*, Oxford: Hart

Farer, Tom J (2002) 'Beyond the Charter frame: unilateralism or condominium?' 96(2) AJIL 359

Fitzpatrick, Peter (1992) *The Mythology of Modern Law*, London: Routledge

Fitzpatrick, Peter (2001) *Modernism and the Grounds of Law*, Cambridge: CUP

Halliday, Fred (2001) *Two Hours That Shook the World*, London: Saqi Books

Huntington, Samuel P (1993) 'Clash of civilizations?' 72 Foreign Affairs 22

Koskenniemi, Martti (1989) *From Apology to Utopia: The Structure of International Legal Argument*, Helsinki: Finnish Lawyer's Publication Company

Koskenniemi, Martti (1990) 'The politics of international law' 1(1–2) EJIL 4

Koskenniemi, Martti (2001) *The Gentle Civilizer of Nations: The Rise and Fall of International Law 1870–1960*, Cambridge: CUP

Murphy, Sean D (2002) 'Terrorism and the concept of armed attack in Article 51 of the UN Charter' 43(1) Harvard International Law Journal 41

Scraton, Phil (2002) *Beyond September 11: Anthology of Dissent*, London and Sterling: Pluto

Scheffer, David J (2001–02) 'Staying the course with the International Criminal Court' 47 Cornell International Law Journal 47

Vagts, Detlev F (2001) 'Hegemonic international law' 95(4) AJIL 843

PART I

Law's First Strike

Chapter 1
The degradation of international law?

Bill Bowring

Introduction

Some years ago, Tony Carty wrote of *The Decay of International Law*.[1] In a prescient passage, he argued that 'Official argument is, inevitably, confined to one-sided assertions of legal principle which it is thought are likely to appeal, along with many other "non-legal" factors, either to a domestic audience or to particular allied powers. Attempts to "persuade" the adversary are exceptional. Legal doctrine tries to carry the discourse further to precisely this stage. It has nothing to lose but its reputation for integrity'.[2]

Following the US and UK response to the events of September 11, critics like David Chandler instead proclaim the 'degradation' of international law. It is hard to argue with his conclusion that 'International law is no longer accepted as a legitimate curb on the use of force by Western powers, while coercive intervention by Western powers against other states is increasingly legitimised through the framework of "international justice" ... The gap between "justice" and what is "legal" has led to the degradation of international law rather than to its development'.[3]

This essay is an attempt at reflection on what has befallen the law, and at resolution of the question of whether law and power can once again be brought into a relationship in which there is a perspective for justice. I say 'once again', since it is contended here that the development of international law during the 'cold war' was, for reasons which are entirely democratic, progressive and humane.

My starting point is a ghoulish metaphor, a macabre prelude to what follows. Although this essay comprises a tragedy in three acts – Iraq (starting in 1991), Serbia (starting in 1999) and Afghanistan (starting in 2001) – my starting point is 1986, when an act of vengeance and a chilling prophecy could encourage the delusion that history is simply a vicious circle. It is also noteworthy that none of the three disasters I describe has achieved closure. Each continues to wreak vengeance, in part at least through the law of unintended consequences, a law which applies with remorseless lack of irony to the United States especially.

A further element of counterpoint is added by an ironical, and perhaps unfair, accompaniment: the words of the most sunny optimist, the normative liberal par excellence, the true believer in the legitimacy of norms and rules in international law, Thomas Franck.[4]

This essay focuses primarily on scholarly writings concerning the three events noted above. I bear in mind Hilary Charlesworth's forthright critique of the development of international legal scholarship through the examination of 'crises',[5] and plead guilty. Nevertheless, Charlesworth herself suggests that 'One way forward is to refocus international law on issues of structural justice that underpin everyday life. What might an international law of everyday life look like?'.[6] One

---

1 Carty, 1986.
2 Carty, 1986, p 115.
3 Chandler, 2002, p 158.
4 Franck and Patel, 1991; Franck, 1999; Franck, 2001.
5 Charlesworth, 2002.
6 Charlesworth, 2002, p 391.

purpose of the present analysis will be to seek to show how both international human rights, and international law, of which the former is a sub-set, may be vindicated when understood not as a discourse in which a 'degraded vision of the social world' serves to 'sustain the self-belief of the governing class',[7] but as a product of and catalyst of real struggles.

Not least, this essay seeks to corroborate Michael Byers' position, reflecting on the decade of forceful measures against Iraq: 'Although law is necessarily the result and reflection of politics, law nevertheless retains a specificity and resistance to short-term change that enables it to constrain sudden changes in relative power, and sudden changes in policy motivated by consequentially shifting perceptions of opportunity and self-interest.'[8] This is especially the case if law is the result and reflection not only of power, but of struggle and resistance: that is perhaps how law itself can offer resistance.

Vampires

If international law has been degraded, it has also been violated; but violated with its full, enthusiastic participation. The three exemplary uses of armed force against Iraq, Serbia and finally Afghanistan appear as three acts in a tragedy of intimate deception, a macabre vampire-bride relationship between law and power. The three stages can be described as follows. First, *consummation*, when law and power, freed by the end of the cold war, seemed set for the longed-for happy alliance; second, *seduction*, when power sought from law invasion of its means of creation, international custom; third, *rejection*, when power, having taken and ravished the law, turned its back and walked away.

Antonio Cassese, in his first reaction to the US response to September 11, identified another vampirish activity, the reproduction of vampires through the poisoned bite. 'In sum, the response to the appalling tragedy of 11 September may lead to acceptable legal change in the international community only if reasonable measures are taken, as much as possible on a collective basis, which do not collide with the generally accepted principles of that community. Otherwise, the road would be open to the setting in of that *anarchy* in the international community so eagerly pursued by terrorists.'[9] That is, stated less politely, terrorism has bred terrorism; its victim, its own sworn enemy, is only too willing, it turns out, to repeat the cycle of death and destruction.

Some positive international law

On one matter this essay adopts a resolutely positivist, black-letter approach. I have in mind the plain words of the UN Charter, taken together with the hard-won state practice and *opinio juris* concerning the use of force, the 'inherent' right to self-defence, and especially the slippery doctrine of 'anticipatory' self-defence.[10]

Since 1945 it has been an unambiguous principle of international law that the United Nations has, with one strictly limited exception, a monopoly of the use of

---

7   Chandler, 2002, p 235, citing Malik, 1996, p 105.
8   Byers, 2002b, p 35.
9   Cassese, 2001b, p 1001.
10 In his *International Law* (2001a), Antonio Cassese reviews practice and *opinio juris*, and concludes, 'In the case of anticipatory self-defence, it is more judicious to consider such actions as *legally prohibited*, while admittedly knowing that there may be cases where breaches of the prohibition may be justified on moral and political grounds and the community will eventually condone them or mete out lenient condemnation' (pp 310–11).

force in international relations. This is the effect of Article 2(4) of the UN Charter, which prohibits 'the threat or use of force against the territorial integrity or political independence of any State, or in any other manner inconsistent with the Purposes of the United Nations'.

All UN members are strictly bound by this Article – the UN Charter is a binding treaty. Indeed, the UN was established to prevent a repetition of the horrors of World War II.

Only the United Nations Security Council, acting under Chapter VII of the Charter, is entitled to 'take action by air, sea, or land forces as may be necessary to maintain or restore international peace and security' (Article 42). The Security Council may, as in the case of the Gulf War, delegate the execution of such action to states or groups of states. But it must do so expressly, and must remain in charge.

The only exception to this principle is contained in Article 51 of the UN Charter: the right of self-defence if an armed attack occurs against a Member of the United Nations. Customary international law, which long pre-dates the UN,[11] makes it clear that self-defence warrants only measures which are proportional to the armed attack and necessary to respond to it. This principle, and the status of the doctrine of self-defence as customary law independent of the UN Charter, was confirmed by the International Court of Justice in *Nicaragua v US* in 1986.[12] Furthermore, Article 51 also states that self-defence may be used only until the Security Council has taken measures necessary to maintain international peace and security.

While it is accepted, and indeed urged, that the Security Council, its composition and its role are in need of democratic reform, and its dispositions with regard to the existence of a threat to or breach of international peace and security ought to be subject to review by the International Court of Justice, the Security Council itself is in need of protection. In Quigley's phrase, it is in danger of becoming a 'helpless hostage'.[13] He points, with substantial incriminating evidence, to the following:

> Four categories of situations have arisen that reflect the Security Council's inability to fulfil its functions properly as a result of United States dominance. First, in 'threat to the peace' situations, the United States has asserted dubious facts before the Security Council, and the Council has acted as if those facts were true, without investigation. Second, the United States has at several times acted purportedly on the basis of powers granted by the Security Council, but in fact outside any powers actually granted. Third, the United States has convinced the Security Council on several occasions to authorise it to take military action unilaterally rather than under Council control. Fourth, the United States has, by use of its veto power, blocked the Security Council from dealing with the United Nations' longest standing territorial dispute, that over Israel-Palestine.[14]

Quigley's words were prophetic; the Israel-Palestine conflict is the inescapable foundation, playing the roles of cause and effect, in propaganda and in reality, to the events of September 11, and the war in Afghanistan.

Yet it may be argued, with hindsight, that the UN system – itself the result of compromise between the First and Second Worlds, the capitalist and communist systems – acquired its most important concepts and juridical content through the process of de-colonisation. It is no accident that the principles of state sovereignty and non-interference, brought to life by the hard-won legal right of peoples to self-

---

11 See the *Caroline* case (1837) 29 British and Foreign State Papers 1137; 30 British and Foreign State Papers 195–96.
12 *Nicaragua Case* [1986] ICJ Rep 14. See also the UK response to the 1982 Falklands/Malvinas invasion as a necessary and proportionate act of self-defence: Byers, 2002a, p 406.
13 Quigley, 1999–2000.
14 Quigley, 1999–2000, p 130.

determination, became the main source of legitimacy for the United Nations as a focus for the aspirations of new states and aspiring peoples.

The start of a vicious circle – the bombing of Libya

The late 1980s were a turning point in the fate not only of the (former) USSR, but of international law as a potential source of protection from strong states. In 1986 the United States lost the case brought against it in the International Court of Justice by Nicaragua.[15] And on 15 April 1986 the United States attacked five targets in Libyan territory, having sought and obtained the agreement of Margaret Thatcher for the use of the UK as a staging post for its bombers. Not only for the purpose of this essay, the events of 15 April 1986 serve as an awful warning for what took place on 11 September 2001. As was recognised at the time, the civilian deaths in Tripoli and Benghazi, if scaled up from the tiny population of Libya to the huge population of the United States of America, would have represented a strike on New York and Washington causing at least tens of thousands of innocent victims. Neither international law nor justice can countenance an eye for an eye, violence for violence. But the action of the United States in April 1986 was at the very least an awful harbinger, and perhaps one of the causes, of the events of September 11.[16]

However, the purpose of this section is to recall the prophetic words of Paust, writing shortly afterwards.[17] It should be noted at once that Paust was not writing to condemn the United States; far from it. His conclusion was in essence a premonition of Kosovo and Afghanistan. 'Indeed, if the state dominated system did not recognise that the use of force is permissible when reasonably necessary to defend fundamental human rights, such a denial would inexorably demonstrate its own illegitimacy.' At first sight, of course, this is a non sequitur, but we will let that pass. More interesting is the path of Paust's reasoning and the demonstration he offers of the iron consistency of US policy with regard to international law.

Paust starts with the now forgotten 'Schultz doctrine', enunciated on 15 January 1986, before the bombing of Libya. George Schultz, then US Secretary of State, stated in a speech at the National Defense University: 'It is absurd to argue that international law prohibits us from capturing terrorists in international waters or airspace, from attacking them on the soil of other nations even for the purpose of rescuing hostages, or from using force against states that support, train and harbor terrorists or guerillas.' He added: 'A nation attacked by terrorists is permitted to use force to prevent or pre-empt future attacks, to seize terrorists, or to rescue its citizens, when no other means is available.'[18]

Paust contrasts this assertion with the near unanimous (the US abstained) condemnation by the UN Security Council of Israel's use of force in 1985 against the PLO in Tunisian territory. The Security Council condemned this action as a 'flagrant violation of the Charter of the United Nations, international law and norms of conduct',[19] and the 'sincere condolences over the loss of life of its citizens' were extended to the Government of Tunisia by Ambassador Vernon Walters, when explaining US abstention.[20]

---

15 *Nicaragua Case* [1986] ICJ Rep 14.
16 It is worth noting that the UN Security Council condemned the attack as a violation of the UN Charter. The vote was 9:5:1, with the US, UK, France, Australia and Denmark voting no, and Venezuela abstaining.
17 Paust, 1986.
18 The speech is reprinted at 25 ILM 204 (January 1986).
19 UN Doc S/RES/573 (4 October 1985), vote 14:0:1, also 24 ILM 1740 (November 1986).
20 US Mission to the UN, Press Release No 106(85), 4 October 1985.

For Paust, '[o]ne is left necessarily then with the following set of questions: is it permissible under international law to attack terrorists on the soil of another nation without the consent of such a nation-state? Indeed, is it permissible to attack states that support, train, or harbor terrorists?'.[21]

Having reviewed the UN Charter, the 1970 Declaration on Principles of International Law, and the many authoritative condemnations by a wide range of scholars – two full pages of footnotes – of both pre-emptive and retaliatory reprisal actions, Paust concludes: 'For this reason, implementation of the "Schultz doctrine" by the use of pre-emptive or retaliatory use of force would place the United States in violation of international law and must be opposed.'[22]

Paust clearly did not wish to adopt a position which would give the US no response to terrorism. He therefore considered that 'situations may arise when the use of force is reasonably necessary to assure an overall serving of the purposes of the Charter', when the United Nations machinery is not functional.[23] However, he added that 'circumstances would have to be compelling and the actual use of force would have to be reasonably necessary and proportionate and not otherwise involve an impermissible targeting of individuals or objects'.[24]

This essay argues that the law of self-defence is very much more tightly circumscribed. Indeed, a central focus of this analysis will be the legal justifications – if any – offered by the US and UK with respect to their actions against Iraq, Serbia and Afghanistan respectively. What was offered with respect to Libya? Paust points out[25] that shortly after the bombing raid the US made 'confused' – an understatement – references to several wildly differing claims of justification of the attack. First, it was said that force had been used as a reprisal action or retaliation for a prior (10 days previously) terrorist act in Berlin – the death of an American serviceman in an explosion at a nightclub.[26] Secondly, force had been 'mainly a signal to Colonel Qadhafi to cease terrorist acts'.[27] Thirdly, the US intended to intimidate the elite Libyan guard relied on by Qadhafi.[28] Fourthly, it believed that it was carrying out pre-emptive self-defence.[29] Fifthly, the action was self-defence against ongoing attacks on United States nationals and embassies abroad.[30] Paust demolished each of these comprehensively. He concluded – and put it mildly – that the US action was 'highly suspect' under international law.[31]

This confusion – or rather negligent disdain – as to justification in international law looks remarkably like the arguments concerning Afghanistan.

---

21 Paust, 1986, p 714.
22 Paust, 1986, p 719.
23 Paust, 1986, p 721.
24 Paust, 1986, p 722, also citing Paust, 1983, pp 307, 310.
25 Paust, 1986, pp 729–30.
26 See 'US calls Libya raid a success', *New York Times*, 16 April 1986.
27 See 'US aides deny attack is start of an escalation', *New York Times*, 16 April 1986; and Ambassador Vernon Walters' statement to the UN Security Council on 15 April 1986, 'to deter future terrorist acts', reprinted in (1986) 80 AJIL 633.
28 See 'Choose targets to fuel coup against Qadaffi, Schultz says', *New York Times*, 16 April 1986.
29 Ronald Reagan, 'We have done what we had to do', *Washington Post*, 15 April 1986; also Legal Adviser Abraham Sofaer testified before a House subcommittee that the US 'military action in self-defense ... in order to pre-empt and deter' Libya and 'to conduct a military strike ... in its own territory falls within the specific terms of' the War Powers Resolution: (1986) 80 AJIL 636. Sofaer defended the constitutionality of the actions taken against Libya on two grounds: (1) Presidential power to use force in self-defence; and (2) implicit approval by Congress through appropriations.
30 'US defends raids before UN body', *New York Times*, 16 April 1986; and statements of Ambassadors Okun and Walters before the UN Security Council, 14–15 April 1986.
31 Paust, 1986, p 732.

The Gulf War – consummation

Now we come to the apparent consummation – or so it seemed to the enthusiasts of the time – of international law, in 1991. Remember that only three years passed between the Libya raid and the fall of the Berlin Wall in October 1989. The USSR itself was about to collapse in ignominy. Moreover, preparation for the new events at the theoretical level was timely indeed. Thomas Franck's *The Power of Legitimacy Among Nations* appeared in 1990.[32] Not, of course, as a consequence, on 2 August 1990 Iraq invaded Kuwait, and – after a remarkably lengthy pause – on 29 November 1990 the UN Security Council adopted Resolution 678.[33] This Resolution appeared to mark the end of the stifling of the Security Council, so much a feature of the cold war. The system appeared to be about to come into its own.

In part, the delay was caused by the need to win the near-unanimous vote (China was not present) which the United States wanted. In order to win Soviet support for the vote, the United States, according to news reports, agreed to help keep the three Baltic republics out of the November 1990 Paris summit conference,[34] and pledged to persuade Kuwait and Saudi Arabia to provide the USSR with the hard currency it desperately needed; they did so,[35] though only shortly before its demise.

It will be recalled that Resolution 678 '[a]uthorises Member States co-operating with the Government of Kuwait ... to use all necessary means to uphold [the earlier resolutions] and to restore international peace and security in the area'. For the first time since Security Council Resolution 84 of 7 July 1950,[36] recommending unified military action against North Korea, military action was taken with the approval of the Security Council.

Thomas Franck and Faisa Patel were unambiguous in their response to these events. 'The UN System seems politically to be developing the capacity to substitute police enforcement for vigilante violence ... Now, surely, is the time to embrace, to encourage, the new policing system before settling forever for sovereign wars of self-proclaimed self-defence.'[37]

However, there were a number of cogent criticisms at the time.[38] Eugene V Rostow commented that 'Except for the word "authorises", the resolution is clearly one designed to encourage and support a campaign of collective self-defence, and therefore not a Security Council enforcement action'.[39] Burns H Weston went further, questioning the legitimacy of the Resolution and the action which followed.[40] For him, this had four aspects. First, the indeterminacy of the legal authority of Resolution 678; secondly, in the great-power pressure diplomacy that marked its adoption; thirdly, in its wholly unrestricted character; and, finally, 'in the Council's hasty retreat from non-violent sanctioning alternatives permissible under it'.[41]

The Security Council held no meetings on the Gulf crisis between 29 November 1990, when Resolution 678 was adopted, and 14 February 1991, when it met in secret session to discuss the political aspects of the end of the war. On 3 April 1991

---

32 Franck, 1990.
33 See (1990) 29 ILM 1565.
34 Apple, 1990.
35 Freidman, 1990.
36 SC Res 84, 5 UN SCOR (Res & Dec) at 5.
37 Franck and Patel, 1991, p 74.
38 See also Glennon, 1991; Caron, 1991; Damrosch, 1991; Meron, 1991.
39 Rostow, 1991, pp 508–09.
40 Weston, 1991.
41 Weston, 1991, p 518.

the Security Council adopted Resolution 687,[42] Iraq accepted it on 6 April, and the Security Council declared it to be in effect on 11 April.

In one respect, the Security Council did in fact set itself a new precedent; this was indeed to be a new era for the authorised use of force. Christine Gray points out that, since *Operation Desert Storm*, the Security Council has authorised member states to take action in Somalia (1992), Yugoslavia (from 1992), Haiti (1994), Rwanda (1994), the Great Lakes (1996), Albania (1997), the Central African Republic (1997) and Sierra Leone (1997) – as well as Kosovo in Resolution 1244 and East Timor under Resolution 1264: '… it has not concerned itself with identifying a legal basis for such authorisations beyond a general reference to Chapter VII of the UN Charter.' All were internal conflicts, with the debatable exception of the former Yugoslavia.[43]

But Resolution 687 did not bring about any closure in respect of the war against Iraq. Early in 2002 the *European Journal of International Law* devoted a whole issue to 'The impact on international law of a decade of measures against Iraq'.[44]

Operation Desert Storm was soon followed by *Operation Provide Comfort* by the USA, UK and France in protection of the Kurds of Northern Iraq in April 1991.[45] Part of the justification for this was that the action was taken 'in support of Resolution 688', ignoring the fact that this Resolution was not adopted under Chapter VII, and did not authorise the use of force. In January 1993 the USA and UK carried out attacks on Iraqi missile sites in the no-fly zones. The Secretary General of the UN argued that this action was mandated by the Security Council according to Resolution 678, because of Iraq's violation of the ceasefire resolution.[46] Gray points out that the Secretary General never reverted to this argument, and it has been criticised for arrogating to individual states powers which belong to the Security Council.[47]

Very similar justifications were used to justify *Operation Desert Fox* in December 1998, in response to Iraq's withdrawal of co-operation with UN weapons inspectors. This operation, which lasted four days and four nights, saw the use of more missiles than used in the whole of the 1991 crisis. The UK and US referred to Security Council Resolutions 1154 and 1205 as providing the legal basis for use of force. As Gray points out, these Resolutions had been passed under Chapter VIII, but made no express provision for the use of force.

As Mary Ellen O'Connell points out, the first of the post-cold war sanctions regimes was that imposed on Iraq.[48] On 6 August 1990, a few days after Iraq's invasion of Kuwait, the Security Council adopted Resolution 661, which imposed a comprehensive ban on trade and financial transactions with Iraq. Resolution 666 expanded the economic sanctions, but with exceptions for humanitarian considerations. In Resolution 670 of 1991, air links were prohibited. In 1995, the Security Council, 'concerned by the serious nutritional and health situation of the Iraqi population', passed Resolution 986 – 'food for oil'. Nevertheless, the sanctions remain in force. Karima Bennoune, former Legal Adviser at Amnesty International, expresses the view of many critics of economic sanctions against Iraq: '… these sanctions appear to have been relatively useless in undermining the power of the

---

42 SC Res 687, (1991) 30 ILM 846.
43 Gray, 2002, pp 3–4.
44 (2002) 13(1) EJIL.
45 Malanczuk, 1991; Franck, 1995, pp 235–36.
46 Weller, 1993, p 741.
47 Gray, 2002, p 12.
48 O'Connell, 2002, p 67.

Iraqi regime and on the other hand have had an apocalyptic effect on the population of Iraq.'[49]

Indeed, the contradiction between Robin Cook's objectives set out on 12 May 1997,[50] that British foreign policy should contain 'an ethical dimension', and this Iraqi policy, among others, led to the abandonment of the so called 'ethical foreign policy', and its replacement in early September 2000 by the objective of making 'Britain strong in the world'.[51] Williams notes the sustained criticism which has emerged from a variety of groups opposed to British support for sanctions against Iraq despite repeated attempts by ministers to defend the government's record.[52] But Williams says nothing about the war against Serbia.

The war against Serbia – seduction

On 24 March 1999, after the breakdown of the Rambouillet negotiations over the fate of Kosovo and the Kosovars, *Operation Allied Force* was launched. This was the start of a 78 day bombing campaign.[53] As Biddle points out, NATO won: not surprising, when it is considered that the combined population of NATO's 19 countries exceeded Serbia's 11 million by a factor of 65; NATO's defence budget was 25 times larger than Serbia's entire economy; and its armed forces outnumbered Serbia's by 35 to 1.[54]

In many ways, the war against Serbia provided the bridge between the wars against Iraq and Afghanistan. 'Even as NATO bombs fell on Belgrade, US and British aircraft were continuing their sustained (if nearly invisible) war on Iraq, one that expended more than 2,000 bombs and missiles in 1999 alone – not nearly the number used in Kosovo but still a sizeable show of force. And the 2000–01 campaign in Afghanistan was both a clear descendant of and a reaction to the military model unveiled in Kosovo.'[55] In his review for Foreign Affairs, Biddle makes no mention at all of international law, or of the United Nations.

The argument that the bombing was necessitated by the need to avert humanitarian disaster – a new law of humanitarian intervention – had such moral appeal that critics of the action were few, at least in Northern Europe. There were exceptions. Michael Byers and Simon Chesterman responded polemically on 19 April 1999: 'Nato's unilateral intervention in the Balkans has frightened Russia, isolated China, and done little to help the million or so Kosovars in whose name Serbia is being bombed. Its principal achievements may be to ensure the death of the "new world order" famously heralded by George Bush after the liberation of Kuwait in 1991, and to destroy an institution that has helped to prevent international wars for over half a century.'[56]

It is not surprising that Thomas Franck pointed out one of the crucial differences between the Gulf War and the Kosovo War – the distinction between 'mitigation and justification. Neither the US Department of State nor NATO seriously attempted to justify the war in international legal terms'.[57] He was forced to this

---

49 Bennoune, 2002, p 252.
50 Cook, 1997.
51 Williams, 2002.
52 Williams, 2002, p 59, citing Herring, 2002.
53 See Murphy, 2000.
54 Biddle, 2002, p 138.
55 Biddle, 2002, p 139.
56 Byers and Chesterman, 1999.
57 Franck, 1999, p 859.

conclusion by Bruno Simma's unanswerable critique[58] of the war's legality. Franck responded:

> ...while UN authorisation of collective military action did break new ground, there was little new about armed response to outright aggression. Resolution 1244, on the other hand, endorses the deployment of collective (regional) armed force to counteract, not aggression, but gross violation of humanitarian law and human rights ... There is, however, another notable distinction between resolutions 687 and 1244. The former established an international regime for Iraq wrought by the triumph of the Security Council-authorised forces. The latter imposed a regime on Yugoslavia after a campaign by NATO that the United Nations had not authorised. Although the Council had previously invoked Chapter VII and 'stresse(d)' the need for a 'negotiated political solution', it had stopped short of authorising NATO to bring about the results it later embraced in Resolution 1244 ... This has made it hard to disagree with the disquieting conclusion of Professor Bruno Simma ... that NATO's military action was in breach of international law.[59]

The main issue, however, was whether the actions of NATO, especially the United States, had the effect of bringing about, in record time, a new creative development in customary international law through state practice and *opinio juris*. That is, did the imperative – as presented by NATO – of averting a humanitarian disaster in Kosovo, namely the genocide or at any rate ethnic cleansing of Kosovars by the Serbs, trump the provisions of the UN Charter prohibiting the use of force? This was the issue highlighted in Rwanda in 1994, when it appeared that Bernard Kouchner's doctrine of a *droit et devoir d'ingérence* was the main justification for the French intervention, *Operation Turquoise*, approved *ex post facto* by the Security Council.[60]

The debate was conducted primarily in the pages of the *EJIL*. Bruno Simma was answered by Antonio Cassese, whose principled position on the question of anticipatory self-defence has been noted above. Cassese submitted two anguished essays.[61] In answer to the question of whether international law was moving towards a new customary law of 'forcible countermeasures' in response to humanitarian disaster or gross and massive violation of human rights, Cassese argued that if such a new law was indeed developing, then practice and *opinio juris* could at the most justify measures taken only in extreme circumstances, where the intervenors had a reasonable subjective opinion that only prompt intervention could avert disaster, and only then until the Security Council could take control.

Most remarkably, the Independent Commission on Kosovo,[62] comprising such progressive luminaries as Hanan Ashrawi, Richard Falk, the Russian diplomat Oleg Gordievsky, and chairman Richard Goldstone, came to the conclusion that the intervention was 'illegal but legitimate'.[63] For Jack Donnelly, this displays 'tension' – but is 'entirely appropriate'.[64] David Rieff is much less kind in his assessment: he describes the Report as 'the wishful thinking of eminent persons'[65] – in other words, of 'the great and the good of the international social-democratic establishment'.[66] He makes the valid, for me, point that '[s]tates in the poor world oppose the intervention in Kosovo because they continue to believe that sovereignty remains

---

58 Simma, 1999.
59 Franck, 1999, p 858.
60 Bowring, 1995.
61 Cassese, 1999a; Cassese, 1999b.
62 Independent Commission on Kosovo, 2000.
63 Independent Commission on Kosovo, 2000, p 4.
64 Donnelly, 2002, p 101.
65 Rieff, 2002.
66 Rieff, 2002, p 111.

the best protection against foreign hegemony'.[67] More controversially, he argues that '... such interventions, no matter how disinterested, or wrapped up in the mandate of the UN or new international law, are colonising enterprises'.[68] He is especially opposed to the 'human rights understanding of the world', because it is 'curiously indifferent to history'.[69] Thomas Weiss, on the contrary, applauds the Commission's Report, and contends that '[h]umanity, or the sanctity of life, is the only genuine first-order principle for intervention. The protection of the right to life, broadly interpreted, belongs in the category of obligations whose respect is in the interest of all states. All others – including the sacred trio of neutrality, impartiality and consent, as well as legalistic interpretations about the desirability of UN approval – are second-order principles'.[70]

Legal scholars have not failed to notice the political imperatives which law was made to serve. Christine Gray points out that Kosovo is another instance (following Rwanda, Albania and Haiti) of the desire for legitimacy which influenced the USA, the UK and other NATO states in claiming a Security Council basis for their use of force in Kosovo.[71] She adds:

> It is no longer simply a case of interpreting euphemisms such as 'all necessary means' to allow the use of force when it is clear from the preceding debate that force is envisaged: the USA, UK and others have gone far beyond this to distort the words of resolutions and to ignore the preceding debates in order to claim to be acting on behalf of the international community.[72]

Christine Chinkin used an article in the *AJIL* itself to aim the most succinct and deadly criticism of the Kosovo War:

> Finally the Kosovo intervention shows that the West continues to script international law, even while it ignores the constitutional safeguards of the international legal order ... All these incidents serve to undermine the Charter on an ad hoc selective basis without providing clear articulation of the underlying principles, or even assurance of future acceptance by those who currently espouse them. The case of Kosovo may have highlighted the continuing chasm between human rights rhetoric and reality. It does not resolve the way this can be bridged.[73]

The doyen of American international lawyers, Louis Henkin, was, however, quite firm as to the international law: '... the law is, and ought to be, that unilateral intervention by military force by a state or group of states is unlawful unless authorised by the Security Council.'[74] Jack Donnelly, while conceding that this was the view of most commentators, added that 'the moral arguments for humanitarian intervention should not be ignored'.[75] His argument is that '[w]hen faced with a conflict between legal and moral norms, political considerations, rather than a corrupting influence, ought to weigh heavily in decisions to act and in judgements of such actions'.[76]

Nevertheless, Thomas Franck finally permitted himself an optimistic conclusion, in line with his theories of legitimacy and fairness in international law:

---

67 Rieff, 2002, p 116.
68 Rieff, 2002, p 117.
69 Rieff, 2002, p 118.
70 Weiss, 2002.
71 Gray, 2002, p 8.
72 Gray, 2002, p 9.
73 Chinkin, 1999, p 846.
74 Henkin, 1999.
75 Donnelly, 2002, p 101.
76 Donnelly, 2002, p 103.

A final lesson of Kosovo is that, in the end, the United Nations – albeit disdained and circumvented – again became an essential facilitator in ending the conflict. It is not the only forum for the exercise of creative, sustained multilateral diplomacy, but it remains a resilient and irreplaceable one.[77]

However, as with the war against Iraq, the war against Kosovo has had continuing and perhaps unintended consequences.

First, the legitimacy of both the International Criminal Tribunal for the Former Yugoslavia and the European Court of Human Rights has been called into question. The Prosecutor of the ICTY refused to contemplate a prosecution of responsible persons in NATO states for alleged violations of humanitarian law during the bombing of Serbia.[78] And on 12 December 2001 the Grand Chamber of the European Court of Human Rights found the applications of a number of Serbian civilian victims (represented by US and UK lawyers, including Professor Françoise Hampson of Essex University) of the NATO bombing of the Belgrade TV station on 23 April 1999 to be inadmissible.[79] These apparently one-sided results, no doubt highly satisfactory for the NATO states, have provided ammunition for Slobodan Milosevic in his own trial at The Hague.

Secondly, the legal status of Kosovo, whether as a continuing part of Serbia, as an autonomy of some description or as a fully independent entity, remains unresolved. The character of the UN administration, first under Bernard Kouchner (see above) as Special Representative of the Secretary General of the UN, now Hans Haekerrup, has been a source of considerable concern. The UN military presence, KFOR, and the civil administration, UNMIK, operate with effective immunity from legal challenge in ordinary courts. Only the Ombudsperson Institution in Kosovo, led by the former member of the European Commission of Human Rights, Marek Antoni Nowicki, has been able to challenge a number of disturbing phenomena.

Thus, in April 2001 he was obliged to challenge the incompatibility with recognised international standards of the scope of the grant of immunity to KFOR and UNMIK in their institutional capacities.[80] In June 2001 he found that 'deprivations of liberty imposed under "Executive Orders" or any other form of executive instruction, decree or decision issued by the Special Representative … do not conform with recognised international standards'.[81] He found that any such deprivation of liberty and the absence of judicial control over deprivations of liberty imposed under Executive Orders violated Article 5 of the European Convention on Human Rights.

The elections of 17 November 2001 and the election of Nexhat Daci as President of the Kosovo Assembly, under the Constitutional Framework for Provisional Self-Government, gave rise to hopes that the rule of law might in future be obeyed. But when the question of the entry of the Federal Republic of Yugoslavia, the FRY, arose

---

77 Franck, 1999, p 860.

78 Final Report to the Prosecutor by the Committee established to Review the NATO Bombing Campaign Against the Federal Republic of Yugoslavia (2000) 21:4–7 HRLJ 257.

79 Application No 52207/99, *Vlastimir and Borka Bankovi, Ivana Stojanovi, Mirjana Stoimenovski, Dragana Joksimovi and Dragan Sukovi against Belgium, the Czech Republic, Denmark, France, Germany, Greece, Hungary, Iceland, Italy, Luxembourg, the Netherlands, Norway, Poland, Portugal, Spain, Turkey and the United Kingdom.*

80 Special Report No 1 of 26 April 2001 'On the compatibility with recognised international standards of UNMIK Regulation No 2000/47 on the Status, Privileges and Immunities of KFOR and UNMIK and their Personnel in Kosovo (18 August 2000) and on the Implementation of the above Regulation', at www.ombudspersonkosovo.org/doc/spec%20reps/spec%20rep1_summary.htm.

81 Special Report No 3 of 29 June 2001 'On the conformity of deprivations of liberty under "executive orders" with recognised international standards', at www.ombudspersonkosovo.org/doc/spec%20reps/spec%20rep3_summary.htm.

in March 2001, the Ombudsperson wrote that the current status of Kosovo as an international protectorate outside the jurisdiction of FRY 'is to place Kosovo completely outside the purview of any international human rights monitoring and/or judicial mechanisms, where it will remain for the conceivable future'.[82]

Thus, as with the war against Iraq, the war against Serbia has led to a continuing denial, by the United Nations itself, of fundamental human rights. In this way, not only is the legitimacy of the Security Council challenged, but the reputation and integrity of the United Nations itself is undermined by its own actions.

The war against Afghanistan – rejection

One of the more extraordinary responses to the aftermath of September 11 has been the article by Jamie Shea, NATO Director of Information, and voice of NATO during the war against Serbia.[83] Ethics, for Shea, is the content of Article 5 of the Washington Treaty, invoked by the 'Alliance' on 12 September. 'The acceptance of such shared destiny is at the heart of ethics in international security policy, for it makes opting out or neutrality in the face of the new, transnational terrorist threats much more difficult to justify.'[84] He makes no mention of international law, or any relation between ethics, law or rights.

There is, however, every reason why we should ask why the US and UK did not seek the explicit authority of the Security Council, which alone should be able to decide questions of pressure, sanctions, or the use of force.

It is noteworthy that the two Security Council Resolutions, 1368 (2001) of 12 September 2001 and 1373 (2001) of 28 September 2001, while reaffirming the right of self-defence contained in the Charter, do *not* authorise any use of force, the bombing or any other – unless one accepts the arguments of Byers, set out below. Indeed, Resolution 1373 deals mostly with preventing the financing of terrorism. In his well known statement of 8 October 2001 (published on the UN home page), Secretary-General Kofi Annan said:

> Immediately after the 11 September attacks on the United States, the Security Council expressed its determination to combat, by all means, threats to international peace and security caused by terrorist acts. The Council also reaffirmed the inherent right of individual or collective self-defence in accordance with the Charter of the United Nations. The states concerned have set their current military action in Afghanistan in that context.

Also on 8 October, the President of the UN Security Council, Richard Ryan (Ireland), issued a press statement following a meeting called at the request of the USA and UK to inform Security Council members regarding the military action. According to him, the UK and US permanent representatives made it clear that 'the military action that commenced on 7 October was taken in self-defence and directed at terrorists and those who harboured them', and stressed that every effort was made to avoid civilian casualties. It appears that the members of the Council were 'appreciative' of the presentation made by the US and UK, but were deeply concerned about the humanitarian situation in Afghanistan.

Thus, it is clear that the Security Council neither endorsed nor authorised the military action, it merely noted that it is taking place, with a justification of self-defence. The Secretary-General's careful formulation is particularly interesting.

---

82 Letter from Marek Antoni Nowicki to Bruno Haller, Secretary General of the Parliamentary Assembly of the Council of Europe, 11 March 2002, at www.ombudspersonkosovo.org/reports_other.htm.

83 Shea, 2002.

84 Shea, 2002, p 76.

Michael Byers notes that there were at least four possible legal justifications for the use of force against Afghanistan: Chapter VII of the UN Charter (for example, Iraq), intervention by invitation (for example, Grenada), humanitarian intervention (for example, Kosovo), and self-defence. 'It is significant that the US relied solely on the last justification.'[85] However, Byers takes the view that Resolution 1373 contains language – buried away in the provisions on freezing terrorist assets – that arguably constituted an almost unlimited mandate to use force. Thus:

The Security Council ...

Acting under Chapter VII of the Charter of the United Nations ...

2   Decides also that all States shall ...

   (b)   Take the necessary steps to prevent the commission of terrorist acts, including ...

According to Byers, 'it provides better evidence of a Chapter VII authorisation than either the "material breach" argument used to justify the no-fly zones in Iraq, or the "implied authorisation" argument used to justify the 1999 Kosovo intervention'.[86] He notes that in future China or Russia could invoke Resolution 1373 and block any attempts to clarify or rescind it – which would explain why it was adopted unanimously. Byers' conclusion, while more measured in tone than his *LRB* piece in 1999, contains an equally stark warning: 'The events of 11 September have set in motion a significant loosening of the legal constraints on the use of force, and this in turn will lead to changes across the international legal system. Only time will tell whether these changes to international law are themselves a necessary and proportionate response to the shifting threats of an all too dangerous world.'[87]

It is plain that the Security Council would indeed have abdicated all authority and responsibility if it had really issued such an unlimited and unrestricted permission to use force. But the reality is even less appealing. The Security Council, and, in effect, the whole of Charter and customary law on the use of force and self-defence, have been jettisoned in the name of the war against terrorism. Once again Thomas Franck has articulated the likely reasoning of the Bush Administration. The *AJIL* has as usual witnessed a fierce exchange of contrary views[88] between Jonathan Charney and Thomas Franck. While Charney argues strongly that the Security Council could and should have remained involved, Franck's conclusion takes his own position several steps closer to a repudiation – contrary to his previous positions – of the role of the Security Council altogether: 'As a matter of law, however, there is no requirement whatever that a state receives the blessing of the Security Council before responding to an armed attack. Were this not so, how many states would deliberately agree to subordinate their security to the Council's assessment of the probity of the evidence on which they based their defensive strategy of self-preservation?'[89]

Finally, Slavoj Zizek makes the obvious but vitally important point:

Is today's rhetoric not that of a global emergency in the fight against terrorism, legitimising more and more suspensions of legal and other rights? The ominous aspect of John Ashcroft's recent claim that 'terrorists use America's freedom as a weapon against us' carries the obvious implication that we should limit our freedom in order to defend ourselves.[90]

---

85   Byers, 2002a, p 401.
86   Byers, 2002a, p 402.
87   Byers, 2002a, p 414.
88   Charney, 2001; Franck, 2001.
89   Franck, 2001, p 843.
90   Zizek, 2002.

This foreboding has been expressed also by the dedicated liberal Jack Donnelly:

> First, anti-terrorism, whether good or bad, is not humanitarian intervention. There are many different forms of evil in the world for which we have developed different international legal norms and political practices. Second, I am doubtful that the international political world has been radically transformed. But, third, to the extent that it has, the consequences (for national and international) human rights are likely to be negative. More generally, appalling as these events were, it would be a further tragedy if they diverted (already scarce) international attention and resources away from more important and widespread moral and humanitarian concerns such as malnutrition, grinding poverty, genocide, pervasive repression, systematic political misrule, and the regular indignities and human rights violations that most people suffer daily in most of the contemporary world.[91]

Thus, the rejection of international law has as its corollary the undermining of the safeguards of domestic law.

Human rights – the villain of the piece?

For Chandler, more debatably, the villain of the piece is human rights ideology, or at least the version of human rights propounded by Geoffrey Robertson QC.[92] But what is at stake is not, as Chandler seems to suggest, the baleful influence of the ideology and discourse of human rights, undermining the gains of international law. I would like to adopt his more persuasive arguments set out in *New Left Review*:

> The 1945 settlement, preserved in the principles of the UN Charter, reflected a new international situation, transformed by the emergence of the Soviet Union as a world power and the spread of national liberation struggles in Asia, the Middle East and Africa ... sovereign equality was given technical recognition in parity of representation in the General Assembly and lip-service to the principle of non-interventionism, setting legal restrictions on the right to wage war.[93]

What is at stake is the decisive 1945 break with the Westphalian system, a new order of law which has been held together by the principle of sovereign equality. As he argues, it is 'not sovereignty itself but sovereign equality – the recognition of the legal parity of nation-states, regardless of their wealth or power – which is being targeted by the new interventionists. Yet such equality has been the constitutive principle of the entire framework of existing international law and of all attempts, fragile as they may be, to establish the rule of "right" over "might" in regulating inter-state affairs.'[94]

Conclusion

International law has certainly been dragged through the mire. Consummation followed by seduction and then rejection is a squalid and pitiful sequence. Of course, scholars should have known better: they should not have greeted the apparent apotheosis of Security Council control in 1990 with such enthusiasm, knowing as they did the contempt with which the UK and US treated the United Nations and its mechanisms in 1986. The purported creation of new custom in 1999, to justify the bombing of Serbia, was inevitably followed by the rejection of the Security Council and of the UN itself following September 11. Any deployment of the rhetoric of human rights since 1991 has now been decisively undermined by the

---

91 Donnelly, 2002, p 105, note 1.
92 Robertson, 2001.
93 Chandler, 2000, p 58.
94 Chandler, 2000, p 55.

reality of UN administration in Kosovo (and Bosnia). Thus, it is wrong to argue, as does Chandler, that human rights are in some way responsible for what has befallen international law.

Instead, there is an uncompleted project to hand. As argued above, the UN and its principles and mechanisms came to life and acquired content during the period of decolonisation. The issues of global social justice which fired the campaigns for the rights to self-determination and development have not left the agenda. The question before the great majority of the world's population is how to reclaim the United Nations.

References

Apple, RW (1990) 'Summit in Europe: east and west sign pact to shed arms in Europe' *New York Times*, 20 November

Bennoune, Karima (2002) 'Sovereignty vs suffering? Re-examining sovereignty and human rights through the lens of Iraq', in 'Symposium: the impact on international law of decade of measures against Iraq' 13(1) EJIL 243

Biddle, Stephen (2002) 'The new way of war? Debating the Kosovo model' May–June Foreign Affairs 138

Bowring, Bill (1995) 'The *"droit et devoir d'ingérence"*: a timely new remedy for Africa?' 7 African JICL 493

Byers, Michael and Chesterman, Simon (1999) 'Has US power destroyed the UN?' 21(9) *London Review of Books*

Byers, Michael (2002a) 'Terrorism, the use of force and international law after September 11' 51 ICLQ 401

Byers, Michael (2002b) 'The shifting foundations of international law: a decade of forceful measures against Iraq', in 'Symposium: the impact on international law of decade of measures against Iraq' 13(1) EJIL 21

Caron, David D (1991) 'Iraq and the force of law: why give a shield of immunity?', in 'Agora: the Gulf crisis in international and foreign relations law' 85 AJIL 89

Carty, Anthony (1986) *The Decay of International Law: A Reappraisal of the Limits of Legal Imagination in International Affairs*, Manchester: Manchester UP

Cassese, Antonio (1999a) *'Ex iniuria ius oritiur*: are we moving towards international legitimation of forcible countermeasures in the world community?' 10(1) EJIL 23

Cassese, Antonio (1999b) 'A follow-up: forcible humanitarian countermeasures and *opinio necessitatis*' 10(4) EJIL 791

Cassese, Antonio (2001a) *International Law*, Oxford: OUP

Cassese, Antonio (2001b) 'Terrorism is also disrupting some crucial legal categories of international law' 12(5) EJIL 993

Chandler, David (2000) 'International justice' 6 NLR 55

Chandler, David (2002) *From Kosovo to Kabul: Human Rights and Humanitarian Intervention*, London: Pluto

Charlesworth, Hilary (2002) 'International law: a discipline of crisis' 65 MLR 377

Charney, Jonathan A (2001) 'The use of force against terrorism and international law', in Editorial Comments, 95 AJIL 835

Chinkin, Christine M (1999) 'Kosovo: a "good" or "bad" war?' 93 AJIL 841

Cook, Robin (1997) 'British foreign policy', Locarno Suite, Foreign and Commonwealth Office, London, 12 May

Damrosch, Lori Fisler (1991) 'Constitutional control of military actions: a comparative dimension', in 'Agora: the Gulf crisis in international and foreign relations law' 85 AJIL 92

Donnelly, Jack (2002) 'Genocide and humanitarian intervention' 1(1) JHR 93

Franck, Thomas M and Patel, Faisa (1991) 'UN police action in lieu of war: "the old order changeth"' 85 AJIL 63

Franck, Thomas M (1990) *The Power of Legitimacy Among Nations*, New York: OUP

Franck, Thomas M (1995) *Fairness in International Law and Institutions*, Oxford: OUP

Franck, Thomas M (1999) 'Lessons of Kosovo', in Editorial Comments, 'NATO's Kosovo intervention' 93 AJIL 857

Franck, Thomas M (2001) 'Terrorism and the right of self-defense', in Editorial Comments, 95 AJIL 839

Freidman, T (1990) 'Mideast tensions: how US won support to use Mideast forces. The Iraq Resolution: a US-Soviet collaboration – a special report' *New York Times*, 2 December

Glennon, Michael J (1991) 'The Constitution and Chapter VII of the United Nations Charter' 85 AJIL 74

Gray, Christine (2002) 'From unity to polarisation: international law and the use of force against Iraq', in 'Symposium: the impact on international law of a decade of measures against Iraq' 13(1) EJIL 1

Henkin, Louis (1999) 'Kosovo and the law of "humanitarian intervention"' 93 AJIL 826

Herring, E, 'Between Iraq and a hard place: a critique of the British government's narrative on UN economic sanctions' 28(1) Review of International Studies 39

Independent Commission on Kosovo (2000) *The Kosovo Report: Conflict, International Response, Lessons Learned*, New York: OUP

Kaldor, Mary (2002) 'A response', in 'A symposium on Kosovo' 1(1) HRJ 129

Malanczuk, Peter (1991) 'The Kurdish crisis and allied intervention' 2 EJIL 114

Malik, K (1996) *The Meaning of Race: Race, History and Culture in Western Society*, London: Macmillan

Meron, Theodor (1991) 'Prisoners of war: civilians and diplomats in the Gulf crisis', in 'Agora: the Gulf crisis in international and foreign relations law' 85 AJIL 104

Murphy, Sean D (ed) (2000) 'NATO air campaign against Serbia and the laws of war', in 'Contemporary practice of the United States relating to international law: international criminal law' 94 AJIL 690

O'Connell, Mary Ellen (2002) 'Debating the law of sanctions', in 'Symposium: the impact on international law of a decade of measures against Iraq' 13(1) EJIL 63

Paust, Jordan J (1983) 'Conflicting norms of intervention: more variables for the equation' 13 Georgia JICL 305

Paust, Jordan J (1986) 'Responding lawfully to international terrorism: the use of force abroad' 8 Whittier L Rev 711

Quigley, John (1999–2000) 'The United Nations Security Council: Promethean protector or helpless hostage?' 35 Texas ILJ 129

Rieff, David (2002) 'On the wishful thinking of eminent persons: the Independent Commission's *Kosovo Report*', in 'A symposium on Kosovo' 1(1) HRJ 111

Robertson, Geoffrey (2001) *Crimes Against Humanity: The Struggle for Global Justice*, revised edn, London: Penguin

Rostow, Eugene V (1991) 'Until what? Enforcement action or collective self-defense?', in 'Agora: the Gulf crisis in international and foreign relations law' 85 AJIL 506

Shea, Jamie (2002) 'NATO – upholding ethics in international security policy' 15(1) Cambridge Review of International Affairs 75

Simma, Bruno (1999) 'NATO, the UN and the use of force: legal aspects' 10(1) EJIL 1

Weiss, Thomas (2002) 'Instrumental humanitarianism and the *Kosovo Report*', in 'A symposium on Kosovo' 1(1) HRJ 121

Weller, Mark (ed) (1993) *Iraq and Kuwait: The Hostilities and their Aftermath*, Cambridge: CUP

Weston, Burns H (1991) 'Security Council Resolution 678 and Persian Gulf decision making: precarious legitimacy', in 'Agora: the Gulf crisis in international and foreign relations law' 85 AJIL 516

Williams, Paul (2002) 'The rise and fall of the "ethical dimension": presentation and practice in New Labour's foreign policy' 15(1) Cambridge Review of International Affairs 53

Zizek, Slavoj (2002) 'Are we in a war? Do we have an enemy?' 24(10) *London Review of Books*

Chapter 2
Postmodern just wars: Kosovo, Afghanistan and the new world order

Costas Douzinas

A new ideal has trumped on the world stage: human rights. It unites left and right, the pulpit and the state, the Minister and the rebel, the developing world and the liberals of the West. After the collapse of communism, human rights have become the morality of international relations, a way of conducting politics according to ethical norms. According to international lawyer Ann-Marie Slaughter, a new world order has emerged which is 'not only anchored by liberal democracy but ... is a genuinely liberal democratic order'.[1] This order is founded on 'judicial equality, the constitutional protection of individual rights, representative government and market economics based on private property rights'.[2] Jurgen Habermas too has argued that we are faced with a choice between a Kantian pacific cosmopolitanism and a regressive and aggressive loyalty to one's tribe, which will bring us to the edge of catastrophe.[3] The victory of the West means that the ideological controversies of the past have given way to general agreement about the universality of Western values and have placed human rights at the core of international law. The geopolitical framework of the new millennium is liberal internationalism. Its signs are everywhere.

In humanitarian wars, military force has been placed in the service of humanity; economic sanctions have been repeatedly imposed unilaterally and multilaterally, allegedly to protect nations and people from their evil governments;[4] politics are being criminalised through the increased use of domestic and international courts; finally, human rights and good governance clauses are routinely imposed by the West on developing countries as a precondition for trade and aid agreements. Human rights are the fate of postmodernity, the fulfilment of the Enlightenment promise of emancipation and self-realisation, the ideology after the end, the defeat of ideologies, the ideology at the 'end of history'.

And yet many doubts persist. The record of human rights violations since their ringing declarations at the end of the 18th century, after WWII and again since 1989, is quite appalling. If the 20th century was the epoch of human rights, their triumph is, to say the least, something of a paradox. Our era has witnessed more violations of their principles than any previous, less 'enlightened' one. Ours is the epoch of massacre, genocide, ethnic cleansing, the age of the Holocaust. At no point in human history has there been a greater gap between the North and the South, between the poor and the rich in the developed world or between the seduced and the excluded globally. No degree of progress allows us to ignore that never before, in absolute figures, have so many men, women, and children been subjugated, starved, or exterminated on earth.

---

1   Slaughter, 2000, p 235.
2   Slaughter, 1992.
3   Habermas, 1997, p 130.
4   Petman, 2002.

It is this paradox of the triumph of humanitarianism drowned in human disaster that this essay explores. The first part discusses the history of the idea of just war and charts its mutation into our recent humanitarian wars. The second argues that while human rights and humanitarianism offer a moral gloss to the economic world order under construction, war remains the highest expression of sovereign power and has contributed towards the reassertion of the principle of sovereignty. The final part concludes that the concept of humanity, in its universalist or communitarian versions, is too indeterminate and cannot act as a normative resource. Wars on behalf of humanity tend to support its opposite, sovereignty.

A short history of just war

Throughout history, people have gone to wars and sacrificed themselves at the altar of religion, empire nation or class. Religious and secular leaders know well the importance of adding a veneer of high principle to low ends and murderous campaigns. This is equally evident in Homer's *Iliad*, in Thucidides' chilling description of the Athenian atrocities at Melos and Mytilene, in the chronicles of the crusades and in the films about the Gulf War and Somalia.

The ability of kings and generals to present their side's war as morally justified and their opponents' as evil – combined with the lack of a moral arbiter who could sift through conflicting rationalisations – has made the just war one of the hardest moral mazes. For the warring parties there is nothing more certain than the morality of their respective causes, while for observers there is nothing more uncertain than the rightness of the combatants' conflicting moral claims. The wars, tortures, forced migrations and other calculated brutalities which make up so much of recent history have for the most part been carried out by men who earnestly believed that their actions were justified, and, indeed, demanded, by the application of certain basic principles.

It is against this background of moral undecidability that we must examine the history of the morally justified or 'just' war. The concept of the *bellum justum* appeared first in Rome and meant that war was initiated and conducted according to certain formalities. Legal formalities such as the issuing of the *jus fetiale*, a demand for just satisfaction which if unmet led to formal declaration of war, complemented religious practices like the taking of the auguries before battle. Their observance guaranteed that the war would be blessed by gods and good fortune. A combination of a sacral, religious function and legal regulation formed the ancient structure of war and is still with us today.

But it was the early Church that first developed a consistent theory of just war in an attempt to serve Caesar without abandoning fully its pledges to God. From the earliest theologico-political attempts at determining the morality of war, an apparent distinction between ends and means appeared. A war is just if it is initiated for and pursues the right ends; it is fought justly if its conduct follows certain religious, customary or positive rules of engagement which restrain its excesses. The distinction was presented formally as that between the *jus ad bellum* (the lawful initiation of war) and the *jus in bello* (the lawful conduct of war). For Augustine, one of the early Church Fathers, the just war is designed to restore the violated moral order, to redress a moral wrong. The element which allowed a war to be blessed, therefore, was its *justa causa*. As a result, medieval theology became preoccupied with the justice of the cause and neglected the means used. The divine duty to punish infidel and evil-doer made the prosecution of war limitless. It justified the unremitting violence of the Crusades, the genocidal attacks on the indigenous people of the newly discovered lands and, later, the atrocities of the religious wars which, conducted on both sides in the name of the true faith, knew no limit in their attempt to annihilate the morally degraded enemies.

The emergence of the *Jus Publicum Europaeum* in the 17th and 18th centuries secularised the idea of the just cause and made the initiation and conduct of war part of international law.[5] The medieval debates had assumed that only one of the warring parties could have the just cause, as it would be contradictory for both parties to pursue a just cause at the same time. The theologians determined the justice of the cause from God's all-seeing perspective. Lawyers have always fancied themselves as a priesthood and as messengers of a higher truth, but even they could not claim God's omniscience. International law abandoned the search for a universal standard of justice and recognised that sovereign states could determine their own cause for going to war. A subjective concept of justice developed, under which both parties could validly believe in their just cause.

The early modern theory of the just war is the clearest sign of the emergence of a system of relations based on sovereign states – those states being demarcated by clear and recognised territorial boundaries. The law of war, one of the earliest components of international law, disassociated the idea of just war from its *justa causa* and related it to a just enemy, defined as an external sovereign, a foe who shares all the attributes of statehood at the formal level. For secular Europe, after the Treaty of Westphalia, a war between sovereigns is just because the combatants are formally equal actors (*hostes aequalitur justi*). Once the European inter-state system is conceived as one amongst the formally equal sovereigns of territorial states, then the invocations of moral justifications for war become redundant as it is the sovereign's decision that decides the justness of the cause. Indeed, the principle that war must be accounted just on both sides is absolutely necessary if any type of restraint is to be introduced into its conduct.

Emphasis was now placed on the development of a detailed *jus in bello*, legal rules of proportionality and discrimination to regulate the conduct of war without overburdening the parties with excessive concern for the collateral damage of their action. The principle of proportionality attempts to adjust the means and scope of military action with its legitimate objectives, while discrimination presents war as an intrinsically limited activity which must be directed only at legitimate targets. But such a regulation of military conduct presupposed that the warring parties were formally equal. A sense of minimum faith, of trust in the enemy, was necessary if restraints were to be successful. Indeed, the term 'just war' became a pleonasm, as all wars amongst sovereigns were considered formally just. As a result, international lawyers abandoned the attempt to classify and abolish war in order to minimise its impact, and for this reason Kant accused them of being 'miserable comforters'. For Kant, who reinvented the idea, reason condemns war and a sovereign not prepared to abandon the warring state of nature of international relations in favour of the promised peaceful cosmopolitan order is an unjust enemy.[6] This rather pious position was adjudged extremely dangerous by Carl Schmitt, for whom Kant was a judge of heresy and a theologian rather than a lawyer. According to Schmitt, Kant's cosmopolitan teachings anticipated the (feeble) attempts in the 20th century (and one could add the much more successful attempts in the 21st) to impose morality on international relations.[7]

---

5   Schmitt, 1950.
6   'Idea for a universal history from a cosmopolitan point of view' and 'Towards perpetual peace: a philosophical sketch', in Reiss, 1986, pp 164–74.
7   Schmitt, 1950, Chapter III.

But while the war between homogeneous Christian sovereigns became regulated and limited, this 'normalisation' was grounded on its exception, namely, a crucial difference that separated the Europeans from the rest of the world. War was conducted differently between Europeans and non-Europeans, as indeed among Europeans outside continental Europe. In the war against savages, the *jus in bello*, premised on a society of homogeneous Christian sovereigns, did not apply. In a related development, the concept of the 'enemies within' emerged. These are political and social forces which challenge the internal *ordre publique*, but are not worthy of respect and constraint since they have no sovereign status. They were reduced to the condition of bandits, terrorists, rebels, infidels to the claims of sovereign statehood.

This internal faultline led to the distinction between war, civil strife and police action. It is impossible, however, to draw the line by distinguishing the character of hostilities. Indeed, while Plato had written that it is an abominable outrage for either party in civil strife to ravage the lands or burn the houses of the enemy – something acceptable in war – modernity, with its religious and ideological fervour, has reversed the situation. War is partly regulated while civil war has no limits. Rebels are treated as absolute enemies, ripe for elimination, or as targets of boundless police action and criminal sanctions which conceal their political nature. One could argue that the distinction between war and police action indicates the way in which the sovereign posits itself towards the law.

The early modern undermining of the theological conceptions of the good or the just meant that the absolute power of sovereignty, the *raison d'état*, replaced the morality of ends. In modernity, the idea of the end belongs exclusively to the sovereign, and war is the ultimate expression of the sovereign end. By declaring and waging war, the sovereign accomplishes its nature in absolute opposition to another sovereign, something acknowledged by the gradual decline of the *jus ad bellum*. The decision to go to war is the sovereign decision *par excellence*, the exception and suspension of law, and as such the confirmation of the sovereign in his majesty. As Karl von Clausewitz, the paramount theorist of modern warfare, put it, 'war is an act of force which theoretically can have no limits'.[8] In this sense, there is no act of violence, cruelty or brutality that falls outside the conduct of war, 'for the logic of war simply is a moral thrust toward moral extremity'.[9] If war is the ultimate expression of the sovereign power to decide and impose the exception to the law and to act in excess, the *jus in bello*, the lawful conduct of law, is a concession by the sovereign and an implicit contract between the warring parties. *Inter armes silent leges* stated the classical maxim; its essence was confirmed in the limited and voluntary acceptance of restraints by the European powers. The suspension of law in the declaration of war, as much as its acceptance in the form of the law of war, was a confirmation of the paramount brilliance of sovereignty.

Modern war, beyond its immediate aims, has always had the further end of accomplishing the sovereign's proper essence. The two new types of war created by modernity, the war of independence and the war of liberation, fully upheld sovereign right: the first, modelled on the American War of Independence, confirms the sovereign order by aiming to create a new sovereign. The second, modelled on the French Revolution, claimed to uphold the natural rights of humanity but ended up with the Napoleonic campaigns and the creation of the French empire. Revolutions and wars of liberation were supposed to create a new type of logic that transcended the sovereign order. But the people's war emerged and entered its

---

8   Clausewitz, 1976, p 76.
9   Walzer, 1977, p 23.

museum phase at the same time. War has remained the highest expression of sovereignty and has formed the foundation of most state sovereigns and their legal systems. Despite attempts to conceal the link, war is the father of law.

The law understands its debt to war, it knows that its foundation is drowned in violence and that the laws of war exist by virtue of a sovereign exception. Police action, on the contrary, appears to give law back its normality; policing appears as war according to law, a war that takes place when the sovereign voice is silent and civil strife can potentially challenge the sovereign. But sovereign action and policing cannot be easily distinguished. Their links have been extensively discussed by Walter Benjamin[10] and Carl Schmitt. As Giorgio Agamben, commenting on their work, put it:

> ... whereas the sovereign is the one who, in proclaiming a state of emergency and suspending the validity of the law, marks the point of indistinction between violence and law, the police operate in what amounts to a permanent 'state of emergency'. The principles of 'public order' and 'security', which the police are under obligation to decide on a case-by-case basis, represent a zone of indistinction between violence and law perfectly symmetrical to that of sovereignty.[11]

War and police action are both at the limit of law: the first projects sovereign power in its momentary epiphany while the latter carries within it the permanent potential of sovereign exception. Their difference lies elsewhere: while war exemplifies sovereign choice, police action – the war of law – operates within limits set elsewhere, between the first principle of law's violent foundation and the final ends always decided in sovereign decisions. Indeed, the idea of law becoming sovereign, of war in the name of humanity so that lawful peace would replace war, would have to wait until our postmodern just wars.

The 20th century changed the main elements of this picture somewhat. After the World Wars, the desire not just to control but to prevent and outlaw war led to a return of a substantive *jus ad bellum*. A crucial count in the Nuremberg indictment was for Nazi crimes against peace. Indeed, Justice Jackson started his address to the tribunal by stating that he had the 'privilege of opening the first trial in history for crimes against the peace of the world'. Nuremberg introduced the principle that planning and waging a war of aggression constituted a crime in international law. Building on this beginning, the UN Charter established a distinction between aggressive and defensive or unjust and justified wars, upon which the Security Council's right to impose sanctions rests. But at the same time, the post-World War II order was based on the inviolability of sovereignty. The principle of non-intervention in the internal affairs of states schizophrenically accompanied the claims to universal justice implicit in the definition of just wars and in the international treaties of human rights that characterised the post-War order. As we know, the attempt by international lawyers to codify the idea of crimes against peace was unsuccessful and has been abandoned. But the apparent failure of lawyers and diplomats to create a detailed legal definition of (un)just war, a double-edged sword for the major powers, has been compensated by the emergence of the much more extensive moral order of human rights and humanitarianism, an order from which the West can easily exempt itself from criticism.

---

10 Benjamin, W, 'Critique of violence', in Benjamin, 1978.
11 Agamben, G, 'The sovereign police', in Massumi, 1993, p 62.

The new world order

The willingness of Western powers to use force for apparently moral purposes has become a central (and worrying) characteristic of the post-cold war settlement. Kosovo was the first war of the new world order formally conducted in the name of the postmodern just cause, human rights. If the Kosovo war established the parameters of a new type of limited independence for those outside the circle of friends and satellites of the major powers, it also sketched out the evolving map of a world order no longer based on the nation-state or traditional sovereignty.

We can detect four central characteristics of this emerging order. First, it is a moral-legal order, in which human rights provide the justification for the new configuration of political, economic and military power and the just cause for war. Secondly, it concentrates overwhelming material force (economic, technological and military) and, as a result, the importance modernity has placed on the regulation of means suffers. Thirdly, we witness the gradual abandonment of the territorial principle of modern sovereignty and the substitution of boundless space for the circumscribed place, or locus, of the nation-state. And, finally, the action against those resisting the new order takes the form of a police operation which aims to prevent, deter and punish criminal perpetrators rather than political opponents. Conversely, the enemies of the new order have often willingly adopted the role of the terrorist assigned to them, of the great criminal who reverses moral principles in the name of a different and higher morality. By committing atrocious acts of terror in the name of religion or justice, the enemies perversely confirm both the moral nature of the new order (the justice of ends) and its preoccupation with efficiency (the destructive effectiveness of means). Let me examine them briefly.

Throughout the Yugoslav campaign constant emphasis was placed on their moral purpose and on the immoral, indeed inhuman, nature of the Serbs. The controversial historian, Daniel Goldhagen, for example, claimed that 'the majority of the Serbian people, by supporting or condoning Milosevic and his policies, have rendered themselves legally and morally incompetent to conduct their own affairs (sic) and a presumptive ongoing danger to others. Essentially their country must be placed in receivership'.[12] Another commentator, Barry Buzan, stated that people have the government they deserve and, when a government promotes policies inconsistent with basic human rights, then 'the war must and should be against both government and people'.[13] The invidious idea of collective responsibility of a whole people for the actions of their leaders was not lost on the military. A few weeks after the start of the war, General Michael Short told journalists that hitting civilians was necessary for success. His tactic was going to be 'no power to your refrigerator. No gas to your stove, you can't get to work because the bridge is down – the bridge on which you held your rock concerts'.[14] The unjust enemies of the new order must be punished paradigmatically in order to establish the moral authority of the new military humanism.

Moral differentiation is supported by a second factor which is closer to the calculations of force. When overwhelming military inequality characterises the warring enemies, the inferior opponent is no longer considered a *justus hostis* and becomes the object of suppression, normally reserved for the enemy within. The powerful considers his superiority as an indication of moral righteousness. Moral argument and force support each other harmoniously and the distinction between

12 *The Guardian*, 29 April 1999.
13 Buzan, 1999–2000.
14 *The Observer*, 16 May 1999, p 15.

just ends and just means disappears. In the postmodern morality/force amalgam, morality exists if it is effective and military action is moral if it succeeds.

Overwhelming force and technological superiority characterised the Kosovo and Afghanistan campaigns. Michael Ignatieff concluded that the Kosovo war was fought by:

> ... no more than 1,500 NATO airmen ... in VTC conference rooms, using targets flashed up on a screen, and all that a commander like Clark ever saw of the rush of battle was the gun camera footage e-mailed every night on secure internet systems to his headquarters in Belgium.[15]

The extensive use of technology aimed at reducing casualties has been hailed as a sign of the humanisation of warfare. Technology is presented as the bloodless substitute for the absence of heroism that characterised the Western warrior.[16] But certain crucial distinctions should be made. The everyday technology of the internet and the advancement of 'smart bombs', non-lethal warfare, stealth aircraft and satellite surveillance should not disguise the fact that war is the technology of the sovereign and its technologisation is part of the wider turning of the world into technology. According to Jean-Luc Nancy, 'there is no "question of technology" in general, that is, a question put to technology or its subject and involving criteria that do not belong to it. War-with-missiles is neither better or worse than war-with-catapults; it is still a question of war'.[17] Indeed, the emphasis placed on the 'marvels' of military technology displaces the key questions of its ends and of war-as-manifestation of sovereign power into a discussion of means and, in doing so, abandons the most crucial aspect of the problem.

Similarly, the celebration of the new humane and victimless wars conceals the strict hierarchisation of the value of life, the putative foundation of all lists of human rights, evident in Kosovo and Afghanistan. In Kosovo, the bombers flew at extremely high altitudes, which put them beyond the reach of anti-aircraft fire, and used smart bombs and stealth technology. The tactic was successful and NATO forces concluded their campaign without a single casualty. But there were serious side-effects too: total air domination did not stop Serb atrocities. Ethnic cleansing intensified and the worst massacres of Albanians occurred after the start of the bombing campaign. If the declared war aim was to 'avert a humanitarian catastrophe', it failed badly. Secondly, the high flight altitudes of the bombers increased significantly civilian 'collateral damage'. Civilians were killed in trains and buses, in TV stations and hospitals, in the Chinese embassy and other residential areas. The most grotesque incident was the killing of some 75 Albanian refugees whose ragtag convoy was hit repeatedly, because, according to NATO, tractors and trailers cannot be easily distinguished from tanks and armoured personnel carriers at an altitude of 15,000 feet.

From Homer to this century, war introduces an element of uncertainty: the possibility that the mighty might lose or suffer casualties. Indeed, according to Hegel, the fear of death and defeat gives war its metaphysical value, by confronting the combatants with the negativity that encircles life and helping them to rise from their everyday, mundane lives towards the universal. In this sense, the Kosovo campaign was not a war but a type of hunting: one side was totally protected while the other had no chance of effectively defending itself or counter-attacking. But a war in which a soldier's life is more valuable than those of many civilians cannot be moral or humanitarian. In valuing an allied life at hundreds of Serbian lives, the

---

15 Ignatieff, 2001, p 111.
16 Coker, 2001.
17 Nancy, 2000, p 116.

foundational human rights claim that all are equal in dignity and enjoy an equal right to life was comprehensively discredited.

The largely undefended bombardment of Yugoslavia and Afghanistan is the ultimate sign of the military superiority, but is also symbolic of the boundlessness of a new type of power not constrained by geographical boundaries and state frontiers. It is not coincidence that the first wars of the new order were air campaigns, as was the attack on Manhattan and the Pentagon – the 'first war' of the 21st century, according to President Bush. While modern sovereignty was bound to place, the new order is both modelled on the openness of space and uses the air as its most appropriate conduit. It is organised horizontally alongside planes of activity that bear no relation to the constraints that earth places on human activity. The limits of state action were decided by pragmatic calculations: Rwanda did not have much strategic, political or economic interest, as was the case with Afghanistan after the Soviet defeat. But that was a miscalculation, we are now told. No area of the globe can be abandoned, since the new, integrated order can be disturbed by activities in its most remote reaches. When politics are sacrificed at the altar of morality and masquerade as police action, a sense of permanent crisis with recurring emergencies becomes necessary and dominant. Moral principle necessarily diverges from the messy world of social, political or ethnic conflict and creates the context, the justification and the potential for permanent military action. As we have been told, the war against terrorism has no time limits.

Finally, these characteristics have turned our recent wars into policing operations against criminals and bandits. This became undeniably clear when huge pressure was put on the new Belgrade regime to surrender Milosevic to the Hague tribunal, in violation of the constitution, in return for large sums in aid; a practice that reminds us of the rewards and bounties offered for the arrest, 'dead or alive', of great criminals. Indeed, all recent wars involving the United States have been characterised by a 'posse' mentality, the declared aim of which was to arrest some evil person who violated the universal moral codes for selfish, cruel or mad ends. Noriega in Panama, Mohammed Aideed in Somalia, Sadam Hussein in Iraq, Milosevic in Yugoslavia, Osama bin Laden are the master criminals, personifications of evil, a tactic that can often backfire. The attacks on America had all the characteristics of an evil reversal of the new order. A painful lesson from September 11 is that its enemies, themselves the keepers of another truth and the enforcers of a different morality, have adopted the role of criminals and are comfortable in their designation as terrorists. When politics becomes policing and policies moral action, some political opponents willingly take on the rogue roles assigned to them and bring to atrocious completion the caricatures of their motives and 'evilness'. Indeed, the terrorists used passenger airliners as manned and guided missiles. By doing this, they adopted and reversed the globalising principle that the most symbolic strike and most effective punishment of enemies is delivered from the air.

These developments have led a number of commentators to conclude that a new imperialism is emerging on the world stage. On the right, this is a welcome prospect and the main worry is that, while the Americans have the resources, they might not 'have the guts to act as a global hegemon and make the world a more stable place'. Indeed, for historian Niall Ferguson, the West should accept its new civilising and stabilising mission and honestly admit that 'globalisation is a fancy word for imperialism, imposing your values and institutions on others'.[18] Similarly,

---

18 Ferguson, 2001.

Robert Cooper, a key British foreign policy adviser, has called for a return to old imperial principles:

> The challenge to the postmodern world is to get used to the idea of double standards. Among ourselves [in the West], we operate on the basis of laws and open co-operative security. But when dealing with more old-fashioned kinds of states outside the postmodern continent of Europe, we need to revert to the rougher methods of an earlier era – force, pre-emptive attack, deception, whatever is necessary to deal with those who still live in the nineteenth century world of every state for itself. Among ourselves, we keep the law but when we are operating in the jungle, we must also use the laws of the jungle.[19]

On the left, Michael Hardt and Antonio Negri have documented and denounced the emergence of a new type of Empire which, unlike European imperialism, extends a decentred and deterritorialising apparatus of rule that incorporates the entire globe within its open frontiers.[20] There is no space to address these pressing issues here; whether recent events mark a return to old imperialism or the appearance of a new hybrid form, there is little doubt that the world moral order joins the premodern attack on the uncivilised infidel with modern police action in the powerful image of the postmodern just wars.

Let me conclude this part. War and just war have been important strategies through which sovereignty has come to existence and has been put to work. War is also a central element of the Western symbolic, of the way in which the West has conceived its existence, territory and importance. War brings states to life: literally as most states have been the outcome of war or revolution, metaphorically by energising nations, and metaphysically by raising them to the universal. But this type of war, a war that pits sovereigns against each other and in so doing underpins the structure of sovereignty, had been retreating from the Western stage for some 50 years. It was first suspended in a cold war and now in the war against terrorism, wars that do not follow the traditional ways of war. Globalisation drained the nation-state, we are told, networks replaced the sovereign, the rule of law and international institutions drew attention to elements of sovereign action exempt from violence and force. Power has allegedly dissolved in legal rules, sublimated in administrative procedures. The state has accepted voluntarily a degree of self-control, and has adopted the barely sovereign role of regulative, juridical and social administrator. Indeed, over the last 20 years, as many commentators in the West celebrated as mourned the passing of war and attributed many of our social ills, from hooliganism and drug abuse to the crisis of the family and masculinity, to the absence of fighting.

But war has now returned triumphantly to our symbolic space, in the Gulf, in Kosovo, in Afghanistan, possibly again in Iraq. It has returned, in a mixture of warlike fantasies, in police action and law. The lack of epic achievements by heroic warriors is filled with technological marvels, which have turned the war into spectacle. We felt a little cheated when the Afghan war finished so quickly. The West had been prepared by the media and the military for a long and hard campaign, the outcome of which was conveniently predetermined but whose conduct would bring together the symbolic of war and victory with the imaginary of spectacle. It was presented as a celebration of the bravery of fighting and the brilliance of technology, in other words of sovereign action, something the West had been lacking for a long time.

---

19 Cooper, 2002.
20 Hardt and Negri, 2000.

It is not surprising, therefore, that war on behalf of human rights appears to have re-legitimised a certain image of sovereignty. We see this everywhere: in the repeated American disregard for the UN; in the celebration of military hardware as the acme of sovereign technology and national prowess; in the statement of President Bush that whoever is not with us is with the terrorists; in the patriotic fervour of the American public and the hitherto marginal argument that America should accept openly and cherish its imperial role; finally, in the insistence that American prisoners be treated and tried according to American law while all others, including British and Australian nationals, under the indistinct jurisdiction on Guatanamo Bay, neither American nor non American nor anything else. One could call this indistinction, the jurisdiction of the non-nation state, a non-sovereign jurisdiction, in other words the jurisdiction of humanity.

But is the return of war a sign of the sovereignty of old, or have the Aristotelian good and Kantian cosmopolitanism replaced the principle of sovereignty? Still today – and forever, I would hazard – the decision to go to war is in form and force a sovereign decision. When a state speaks on behalf of the rights of man and uses them to start war, this is still a sovereign decision and leads to an increase in its sovereignty. More generally, the universal is always placed at the service of the particular as it is the particular that enunciates the universal. The enunciating particular can place itself towards the universal in two positions. It can attach an opt-out clause to the universal, for which the United States acts as the prime spokesperson, or it can arrogate to itself the exclusive power to lay down the definitive interpretation of the universal. The Americans follow both: the former when they denounce the universal jurisdiction of the new International Criminal Court; when they declare that they are no longer bound by the 1969 Vienna Convention on the Law of Treaties, under which a country that has signed a treaty cannot act to defeat its purpose, even if it does not intend to ratify it;[21] finally, when they state that under no circumstances will any American be tried by it. The latter when they declare, despite the unanimous view of international lawyers, that their interpretation of the Geneva Conventions is the only valid interpretation and the Taliban prisoners are designated not as war prisoners but under the novel category of 'unlawful combatants'. Universalist morality claims to muster agreement about the content of its prescriptions. As human rights become the *lingua franca* of the New Times but are unable to eliminate conflict, one expects that the formal struggle will revolve predominantly around the authoritative interpretation and effective application of human rights.

The continuous references to humanitarianism, therefore, indicate that our recent wars are a return to the premodern idea of just war conducted according to the modern protocols of police action. Humanitarian wars return us to sovereignty and to the ancient link between the sacred and the legal. The *jus ad bellum*, the power to declare war and carry it out as policing, is the reassertion of sovereign brilliance against the complacency of accountants and lawyers. It may be that this is a new type of imperial sovereignty, or just the ghost of old sovereignty, which needs the spectacle of war to convince us that it has not passed away in networks of economic, cultural and political governance. The *jus in bello* has been replaced by the efficiency and sophistication of technology. Finally, the *justa causa*, humanity and its rights, becomes the new sacred order in a disenchanted world. To hazard a prediction, the universalisation of human rights rather than pacifying conflict may

---

21 One of the last acts of the Clinton presidency was to sign the ICC Treaty, something resented by President Bush, who has devised various stratagems to prevent its application. Britain, on the other hand, in a rare sign of independence and despite objections by military figures, accepted the treaty.

lead to its increase. The reason for that should be sought in the wider context in which the moral order operates.

Global moral and civic rules are the necessary companion of the universalisation of economic production and consumption, of the creation of a world capitalist system. Over that last 20 years, we have witnessed, without much comment, the creation of global legal rules regulating the world capitalist economy, including rules on investment, trade, aid and intellectual property. Robert Cooper has called it the voluntary imperialism of the global economy. 'It is operated by an international consortium of financial Institutions such as the IMF and the World Bank ... These institutions ... make demands, which increasingly emphasise good governance. If states wish to benefit, they must open themselves up to the interference of international organisations and foreign states.' Cooper concludes that 'what is needed then is a new kind of imperialism, one acceptable to a world of human rights and cosmopolitan values'.[22] The critics, Negri and Hardt, agree with Cooper's diagnosis but find no grounds for celebration: 'Although the practice of Empire is continually bathed in blood, the concept of Empire is always dedicated to peace – a perpetual and universal peace outside of history.'[23]

We can find certain historical parallels between the new world order and the emergence of early capitalism. The legal system developed first the rules necessary for the regulation of capitalist production, including rules for the protection of property and contract, the development of legal and corporate personality, and only later did civic rules emerge, mainly with the creation of civil and political rights, which led to the creation of the modern subject and citizen. These rules gave the man of the classical declarations the legal tools and public recognition necessary to flee his traditional ties, and organise his activities according to a calculation of interest borne by the institution of rights.

Similarly today, the universalisation of morality follows the gradual unification of world markets. The values and rules of the new 'voluntary imperialism' are supplied by the various conventions on human rights, by moral and civic regulations and directives which prepare the individual of the new order, a world citizen, highly moralised, highly regulated but also highly differentiated materially, despite the common human rights that everyone enjoys from Helsinki to Hanoi and from London to Lahore. As economic practices and legal rules and conventions become increasingly standardised and globalised, a unified ethics, semiotics and law become the new *lingua franca*. But while human rights appear to be universal and uninterested in the particularities of each situation, their triumph means that they will soon become tools in political conflict, undermining their claim to universality. The common reference to values will not stop their polemical use, as the Milosevic trial clearly indicates.

The universalism of rights was invented by the West but will be now used by the South and East to make claims on the distribution of the world product. The recent converts to universal values are led to believe that improvement of domestic human rights will strengthen their claim against world resources. Milosevic was extradited to the Hague for a few hundred million dollars in aid to Serbia and the new Afghan regime is promised a few more million if they police the new order effectively. Aid agreements routinely impose privatisation, market economics and human rights and appear to promise an inexorable process of economic equalisation between East, South and West.

---

22 Cooper, 2002.
23 Hardt and Negri, 2000, p xv.

As we know from our Western histories, formal liberties cannot be contained in their formalism for too long. Soon the workers with the vote and the freedom of speech will demand the income and resources to make their newly-found freedoms real, they will ask for the material preconditions of equality. Lecturers in China and farmers in India will demand to earn as much as those in London or France, something that can only be done through a substantial reduction of the Western standard of living. But the (implicit) promise that market-led, home-based economic growth will inexorably lead the South to Western economic standards is fraudulent. Historically, the Western ability to turn the protection of formal rights into a limited guarantee of material, economic and social rights was based on huge transfers from the colonies to the metropolis and extremely favourable demographic conditions. Western policies on development aid and third world debt, and American policies on fuel pricing, gas emissions and defence spending indicate that reverse flows are not politically feasible. When the unbridgeability of the gap between the missionary statements on equality and dignity and the bleak reality of obscene inequality becomes apparent, human rights, rather than eliminating war, will lead to new and uncontrollable types of tension and conflict. Spanish soldiers met the advancing Napoleonic armies shouting 'Down with Freedom'. It is not difficult to imagine people meeting the 'peacekeepers' of the New Times with cries of 'Down with human rights'.

The metaphysics of humanity

In conclusion, a question left suspended for much of the discussion must be addressed. Even if our new wars seem to indicate a return of sovereignty, could man or humanity ever become the new sovereign in the way that Habermas and the new cosmopolitanism evangelise? A war or police action on behalf of global humanity puts the ends of man into play. But what are they? Let me turn briefly to the metaphysics of humanity. Can we define its meaning?

Humanism believes that there is a universal essence of man, and this essence is the attribute of each individual who is the real subject. As species existence, man appears without differentiation or distinction in his nakedness and simplicity, united with all others in an empty nature deprived of substantive characteristics except for his free will, reason and soul, the universal elements of human essence. This is the man of the rights of man, someone without history, desires or needs, an abstraction that has as little humanity as possible, since he has jettisoned all those traits and qualities that build human identity. A minimum of humanity is what allows man to claim autonomy, moral responsibility and legal subjectivity. At the same time, he who enjoyed the 'rights of man' was a man all too man: a well-off, male heterosexual, white, urban citizen who condenses in his person the abstract dignity of humanity and the only real rights, those given by the law of the nation-state. Indeed, one could write the history of human rights as the ongoing and always failing struggle to close the gap between the abstract man, who is supposed to have all these rights and has none, and the concrete citizen, who is the only beneficiary of rights.

While human rights belong supposedly to all human beings on account of their humanity, it is citizenship that turns people into human beings by protecting their so-called eternal or inalienable rights. The nation-state comes into existence through the exclusion of other people and nations. The modern subject reaches her humanity by acquiring political rights, which guarantee her admission to the universal human nature, by excluding from that status those who do not have such rights. Our humanity is predicated on what citizenship excludes, it presupposes the absence of aliens, whose existence is evidence of the universality of human nature but whose exclusion is absolutely crucial for the creation of concrete personality, in other words citizenship. The alien is not a citizen. He does not have rights because he is not part of the state and he is a lesser human being because he is not a citizen. One is a human being to greater or lesser degree because one is a citizen to a greater or lesser degree. The alien is the gap between man and citizen; between human nature and political community lies the moving refugee.

It is this crucial distinction between humans who are supposed to have all these rights but who have none and citizens who have the rights created and protected by the state that defines the reaction of state and law when faced with refugees. They are treated not as subjects but as the subject's contrary or opposite, either as non-subjects or as objects. If they are objects, they are not human beings – and therefore they are not entitled even to the minimum requirements of life, such as food, shelter, clothes, a refuge; this happens daily as they are chased away, kept from our borders lest they engage the law in responsibility. If they are non-subjects, they have no rights or entitlements; the law owes them nothing, their survival is at the discretion of state benevolence or private philanthropy. The 'bare necessities of life' offered reluctantly against the fear of destitution and death are not a recognition of their humanity but an advertisement of the humane nature of the law, always liable to cancellation.

The 'non-humans', the 'vermin' of older and more recent concentration camps, the potential of world annihilation by nuclear weapons, recent developments in genetic technology and robotics indicate that even this most banal and obvious of definitions is not definite and conclusive. Humanity's mastery, like God's omnipotence, includes the ability to redefine who or what counts as human and even to destroy itself. From Aristotle's slaves to designer babies, clones and cyborgs, the boundaries of humanity have been shifting. What history has taught us is that there is nothing sacred about any definition of humanity and nothing eternal about its scope. Humanity cannot act as the *a priori* normative principle and is mute in the matter of legal and moral rules. Its function lies not in a philosophical essence but in its non-essence, in the endless process of redefinition and the continuous but impossible attempt to escape fate and external determination.

Today, the debate about the meaning of humanity as the ground normative source is conducted between universalists and cultural relativists or communitarians. The universalist claims that all cultural value and, in particular, moral norms are not historically and territorially bound but should pass a test of universal consistency. As a result, judgments which derive their force and legitimacy from local conditions are morally suspect. But, as all life is situated, an 'unencumbered' judgment based exclusively on the protocols of reason goes against the grain of human experience, unless of course universalism and its procedural demands have become the cultural tradition of some place; and the US would be a prime candidate. The counter-intuitive nature of universalism can lead its proponent to extreme individualism: only I, as the real moral agent or as the ethical alliance or as the representative of the universal, can understand what morality demands. Moral egotism easily leads to arrogance and universalism to imperialism: if there is one moral truth but many errors, it is incumbent upon its agents to impose it on others. What started as rebellion against the absurdities of localism ends up legitimising oppression and domination.

Cultural relativism, and communitarianism, is potentially even more murderous, because it has privileged access to community, neighbourhood and home, the places where people are killed, abused and tortured. Relativists start from the obvious observation that values are largely context-bound and use them to justify atrocities against those who disagree with the oppressiveness of tradition. But the cultural embeddedness of self is an unhelpful sociological truism; the context, as history, tradition and culture, is malleable, always under construction rather than given and unchanging. History does not teach anything; it is historians and journalists, intellectuals and politicians, academics and ideologues who turn historical events into stories and myths and in so doing construct ways of seeing the present through the lens of the past.

Kosovo and Rwanda are good examples of this process. It was only after Milosevic withdrew Kosovo autonomy in 1994 and declared that it would remain forever in the Yugoslav state, as the cradle of the Serb nation, that Serb oppression started and the KLA, the Albanian Liberation Movement, became active. The fratricidal nationalism which took hold of the two communities was created and fanned by the respective power-holders. This process was even more evident in Rwanda. The genocide there was not committed by monsters but by ordinary people who were coaxed, threatened and deceived by bureaucrats, the military, politicians, the media, intellectuals, academics and artists into believing that killing was necessary to avoid their own extermination at the hands of their victims. The tribal rivalry between Hutus and Tutsis was redefined, fanned and exaggerated to such a point that the 'action' became eventually inevitable.

In Kosovo, Serbs massacred in the name of threatened community, while the allies bombed in the name of threatened humanity. Both principles, when they become absolute essences and define the meaning and value of culture without remainder or exception, can find everything that resists them expendable. Both positions exemplify, perhaps in different ways, the contemporary metaphysical urge: each side has made an axiomatic decision as to what constitutes the essence of humanity and follows it, like all metaphysical determinations, with a stubborn disregard of opposing strategies or arguments. They both claim to have the answer to the question 'what is human value?' and to its premise 'what is [a] human?', and take their answers to be absolute and irrefutable. Universalism then becomes an aggressive essentialism, which has globalised nationalism and has turned the assertiveness of nations into a world system. This is the morality of nihilism, for which no values exist outside those of disconnected individuals. Community, on the other hand, is the condition of human existence, but communitarianism can become the even more stifling morality of mythology. When the supposed opponents become convinced about their truth and the immorality of their demonised opponents, they can easily move from moral dispute to killing. At that point, all differences disappear. From the position of the victim, the bullet and the 'smart' bomb kill equally, even if the former travels a few yards only from the gun of the ethnically proud soldier, while the latter covers a huge distance from the aircraft of the humanitarian bomber.

The individualism of universal principles forgets that every person is a world and comes into existence in common with others – that we are all in community. Being in common is an integral part of being self: self is exposed to the other, it is posed in exteriority, the other is part of the intimacy of self. My face is 'always exposed to others, always turned toward an other and faced by him or her never facing myself'.[24] Being in community with others is the opposite of common being or of belonging to an essential community. Most communitarians, on the other hand, define community through the commonality of tradition, history and culture, the various past crystallisations whose inescapable weight determines present possibilities. The essence of the communitarian community is often to compel or

---

24 Nancy, 1991, p xxxviii.

'allow' people to find their 'essence', its success is measured by its contribution to the accomplishment of a common 'humanity'. But this immanence of self to itself is nothing other than the pressure to be what the spirit of the nation or of the people or the leader demands, or to follow traditional values and exclude what is alien and other. This type of communitarianism destroys community in a delirium of incarnated communion. A solid and unforgiving essence, be it that of nation, class, tribe or community, turns the 'subjectivity of man into totality. It completes subjectivity's self assertion, which refuses to yield'.[25] Community as communion accepts human rights only to the extent that they help submerge the 'I' into the 'We' all the way till death, the point of absolute communion. As the French philosopher Jean-Luc Nancy puts it, this attitude is catastrophic because 'it assigns to community a *common being*, whereas community is a matter of something quite different, namely, of existence inasmuch as it is *in* common, but without letting itself be absorbed into a common substance'.[26]

Rational morality and cultural identity express different aspects of moral experience, and their comparison in the abstract is futile. When a state adopts 'universal' human rights, it will interpret and apply them, if at all, according to local legal procedures and moral principles, making the universal the handmaiden of the particular. The reverse is also true: even those legal systems which jealously guard traditional rights and cultural practices against the encroachment of the universal are already contaminated by it. All rights and principles, even if parochial in their content, share the universalising impetus of their form. In this sense, rights carry the seed of dissolution of community and the only defence is to resist the idea of right altogether, something impossible in the global capitalist world. Developing states which import Hollywood films, Big Macs and the internet import also human rights willy-nilly. The claims of universality and tradition, rather than standing opposed in mortal combat, have become uneasy allies whose fragile liaison has been sanctioned by the World Bank.

What are the stakes in the debate? Postmodern mass societies and globalisation increase existential anxiety and create unprecedented insecurity about life prospects. In this climate, the desire for simple life instructions and legal and moral codes with clearly defined rights and duties becomes paramount. Codification transfers the responsibility of deciding ethically to legislators and moralists, to false sovereigns and fake tribes. In our over-legalised world, rules and norms discourage people from thinking independently and discovering their own relation to themselves, to others, to language and to history. The proliferation of human rights treaties and the mushrooming of legal regulation are part of the same process, which aims to relieve the burden of ethical life and the anxiety or, in Heidegger's terms, the 'homelessness' of postmodern humanity. International human rights law promises to set all that is valuably human on paper and hold it before us in triumph: the world picture of humanity will have been finally drawn and everyone will be free to follow his essence as defined by world governments.

From our perspective, humanity cannot act as the *a priori* normative principle, nihilistic or mythological, and is mute in the matter of legal and moral rules. Its function lies not in a philosophical essence but in its non-essence, in the endless process of redefinition and the necessary but impossible attempt to escape fate. Humanity has no foundation and no ends, it is the action of groundlessness. But if humanity has no ends, it can never become sovereign, and war fought in its name will always be pseudonymous. If rights express the endless trajectory of a nihilistic

---

25 Heidegger, 'Letter on humanism', in Heidegger, 1993, p 221.
26 Nancy, 1991, p xxxvii.

and insatiable desire, humanity's only sacred aspect is its ability to endlessly sacrifice in order to re-sacralise the principle of sovereignty as terrible and awe-inspiring or as its slightly ridiculous simulacrum. At this point the new sovereign will have achieved its end and could even gradually wither away as humanity will have come to its final definition. But this would also be the withering away of humanity. The principle of just war will finally have won, in the proclamation of an endless peace without justice.

References

Agamben, G (1993) 'The sovereign police', in Massumi, Brian (ed), *The Politics of Everyday Fear*, Minneapolis: University of Minnesota Press

Benjamin, W (1978) 'Critique of violence', in *Reflections*, Jephcott, E (trans), New York: Schocken

Bohman, J and Lutz-Bachmann, M (eds) (1997) *Perpetual Peace: Essays on Kant's Cosmopolitan Ideal*, Cambridge, Mass: MIT

Buzan, B (1999–2000) 'The conduct of war' 7(1) Bulletin of the Centre for the Study of Democracy 2

Clausewitz, K von (1976) *On War*, Howard, M and Paret, P (eds), Princeton NJ: Princeton UP

Coker, C (2001) *Humane Warfare*, London: Routledge

Cooper, R (2002) 'The new liberal imperialism' *The Observer*, 1 April

Ferguson, N (2001) 'Welcome the new imperialism' *The Guardian*, 31 October

Fox, G and Roth, B (eds) (2000) *Democratic Governance and International Law*, Cambridge: CUP

Habermas, J (1997) 'Kant's idea of perpetual peace, with the benefit of two hundred years' hindsight', in Bohman and Lutz-Bachmann, 1997

Hardt, Michael and Negri, Antonio (2000) *Empire*, Cambridge, Mass: Harvard UP

Heidegger, Martin (1993) 'Letter on humanism', in *Basic Writings*, Farrell Krell, D (ed), San Francisco: Harper

Ignatieff, M (2001) *Virtual War*, London: Vintage

Massumi, B (ed) (1993) *The Politics of Everyday Fear*, Minneapolis: University of Minnesota Press

Nancy, J-L (1991) *The Inoperative Community*, Minneapolis: University of Minnesota Press

Nancy, J-L (2000) *Being Singular Plural*, Stanford: Stanford UP

Petman, J (2002) 'Fighting the evil with international economic sanctions', in *2002 Finnish Yearbook of International Law* (forthcoming)

Reiss, H (ed) (1986) *Kant's Political Writings*, Cambridge: CUP

Schmitt, C (1950) *Der Nomos der Erde in Volkerrecht des Jus Publicum Europaeum*, 1997 edn, Berlin: Ducker & Humblot

Slaughter, A-M (1992) 'Law among liberal states: liberal internationalism and the Act of State doctrine' 92 Columbia L Rev 1909

Slaughter, A-M (2000) 'Government networks: the heart of the liberal democratic order', in Fox and Roth, 2000

Walzer, M (1977) *Just and Unjust Wars*, New York: Basic

Chapter 3

Enduring right
Peter Fitzpatrick

Not only can man's being not be understood without madness, it would not be man's being if it did not bear madness within itself as the limit of his freedom.[1]

Among the more outrageous claims Baudrillard makes in *The Melodrama of Difference*, there is one which aptly invokes extremities.[2] To the geographical extremity of the Alakaluf people of Tierra del Fuego, Baudrillard would add an existential one. 'They call themselves "Men" – and there were [for them] no others'; and so, '[i]n their singularity, which could not ever conceive of the Other, the Alakaluf were inevitably vanquished', in effect exterminated, by 'the Whites'.[3] Yet, he goes on, 'who can say that the elimination of this singularity will not turn out, in the long run, to be fatal for the Whites too? Who can say that radical foreignness will not have its revenge – that, though effectively conjured away by colonial humanism, it will not return … dooming them to disappear themselves one day in much the same way as the Alakaluf'.[4] Although Baudrillard offers little more than eloquent assertion evidencing this intimated fate, by the work's end it has become inexorable and imminent. If we were to question the position of surpassing perception which enables Baudrillard so encompassingly to know the Alakaluf, then, consistently, we should likewise question the complete assurance with which he knows the Occident and its terminus.[5] With the Occident, however, the evidence, if inevitably inadequate, is somewhat more dense. The evidential strand now pursued in this chapter concerns a pure and primal humanity, a completeness of being, arrogated by the Occident through claims to the 'human' of human rights and to the freedom embedded in their assertion, the particular focus here being the sharpened salience assumed by these rights and this freedom in the aftermath of the 'events' of September 2001.

That combination of rights and freedom is found in an origin attributed to human rights: the 'declaration' and elevation of universal rights, 'rights of man', in the French and 'American' revolutions.[6] Much criticism has been directed at how such universal rights have been tied to the formation of particular national societies or tied to particular social relations. An example of the latter would be the intimate association between the subject of such rights and capitalist economic relations, most pointedly those of the 'free' market. There was also a coeval emergence of modern Occidental right and its subject. The 'man' of this right and the 'political society' of this man were formed in a constituent negation of the savage 'other'.[7] The ensuing civilized being was one of a global significance, ever able to bring effect to a world without necessarily being affected by it. Consistently with that, rights could be found in the contained or inert savage only to the extent allowed by

---

1   Lacan, 1989, p 215.
2   Baudrillard, 1993.
3   Baudrillard, 1993, p 135.
4   Baudrillard, 1993, p 135.
5   For such a line of questioning see Baudrillard, 1987.
6   Douzinas, 2000, Chapter 5.
7   Fitzpatrick, 1992, Chapters 3 and 4.

such an enlightened being.[8] The constitution of human rights in variants of such exclusion persists.[9]

Yet that very constitution of human rights itself demanded an inclusion within the universality of the human. This inclusiveness of human rights is now prominently marked in their more recent explicitly international or 'global' manifestations – 'international human rights is the world's first universal ideology'.[10] So, as well as the imperious, and imperial, assertion that comes with human rights as exclusionary and as self-regarding, there is a responsive regard to the other and a sharing in a commonality of the human. As a component of their legality and as ideology, this inclusive dimension of human rights counters the dimension of self-regarding exclusion, but not entirely so. With the finitely human the two dimensions are inseparable, and what 'counts' is the quality of their combining. For the Occident, the self-regarding and excluding dimension could, and did, imperially extend by subordinating the other-regarding and inclusive dimension to itself.

Of late, this subordination has taken on a new explicitness. The putatively globalised economy sustaining the free market – along with the resurrected belief that the good of all is ensured in the self-regarding assertion of each – now seeks to absorb human rights as its instrument. It does so, for example, by attaching human rights to 'conditionalties' binding nations in loan, aid and trade agreements. Bringing matters closer to the immediate concern of this collection, an instance was provided in March 2002 when George W Bush announced a large increase in foreign 'aid', including 'extra help for countries that agree to respect human rights and reform their economies'.[11]

Even closer to that concern, there is another mode of assertion coming to assume a similar relation to human rights, that of war. This may seem at first a strange conjunction since, in the aspiration and ethos of the Universal Declaration of Human Rights, human rights were set against the modality of war. Yet from the start there was ambivalence here, in that the Declaration retrospectively rendered the preceding 'world' war one for human rights. The conjunction becomes closer with the recent 'human rights war' in the Balkans, a type of war prefigured in the 'humane intervention' of the Gulf War. The facility with which war and the market can combine with human rights suggests a significant compatibility. What provides much of this combining force, I will now argue in the refracted light of the 'events' of September 2001, is a particular kind of freedom and its paradigm exercise by certain actors.

To come to the point, this is an idea of freedom as immune to its effects. It is a self-sufficing freedom, complete in and of itself – an 'enduring freedom', to borrow an accessible phrase. What will be brought to bear here is a contrary idea of freedom once offered by Nietzsche and since amplified in empathic thought, of which more shortly. For Nietzsche, 'freedom is measured ... by the resistance which has to be overcome, by the effort it costs to stay *aloft*'.[12] Such freedom is an affective 'superiority over him who must obey'; it entails a readiness 'to sacrifice men to one's cause', and, when 'viewed more closely' in the setting of liberalism, it is a 'war *for* liberal institutions'.[13] The notion of freedom against which Nietzsche inveighs is one of a freedom which is quasi-transcendent and universal, yet one which is also

---

8   Eg Westlake, 1971, pp 47, 50–51.
9   Fitzpatrick, 2001, pp 207–12.
10 See Wilson, 1997, p 10.
11 Denny and Black, 2002, p 13.
12 Nietzsche, 1968, p 92 – his emphasis.
13 Nietzsche, 1973, p 30 – his emphasis.

possessed of a sealed immanence, of an enwrapped completeness.[14] It is, for instance, the freedom espoused by Arendt when, with an apt resonance, she declares that 'we [that is, all of "us"] hold human freedom to be a self-evident truth', an 'axiomatic assumption'.[15] As such, this freedom is not only the well-spring of 'practical' or 'political' action but also its validation.[16] But – Nietzsche again – 'the raising' of such an idea always involves a 'breaking' and a 'sacrifice'.[17]

When the raised is instantiated, when it is enclosed in particularity, there is an inexorable exclusion and sacrificing of others – of those who are 'other' to that emplacement of universal freedom. That exclusion, in turn, takes on an irreducible intensity because those excluded others, being beyond a universal good, can only 'be' absolutely and chasmically beyond. They can only be 'enemies of freedom', as George W Bush put it in his address to the Congress of the United States on 20 September, and this is why they 'hate us'.[18] They are, he would add, 'hateful of freedom' itself, 'jealous of our way of life', a way of life founded on freedom.[19] Yet, being universal, that good also extends incipiently to them. Here an apt rhetorical charge is provided by the British Prime Minister. The clarion call that was his speech to the annual Conference of the Labour Party on 2 October 2001 would spread the 'values of democracy and freedom round the world', and would bring into the fold 'the wretched ... those living in want and squalor from the deserts of northern Africa to the slums of Gaza, to the mountain ranges of Afghanistan: they too are our cause'.[20] This extension is not offered even remotely in a spirit of mutual adjustment. It is the extension of a sovereign community which can be with or 'tolerate' others within an unencumbered freedom and without change to its 'normal' position. In all, yet another variant of the frustrated algebra impelling the Occident's universal – the impossible combining of exclusion with inclusion. This is not exactly 'wanted dead or alive', to borrow another presidential *aperçu*, but rather 'wanted dead and alive'.

From what position can 'the lords of humankind' thus bestride such an ambivalent world? How can universal arrogation be conjoined with particular location? Transposing this second question to human rights, we could also ask how the 'human' of human rights can be encompassed, set about, made containedly present, yet still be the encompassing, surpassing human. How could such a quality of the human be definitively instantiated? Any particular instantiation as an operative human right is immediately revealed as contested and uncertain (we are, after all, only human), backed by different efficacies of force and representation, subject in its very formulation to broad discretions and derogations. So instantiated, the right in question could no longer be held as transcendingly pure, as a deracinated ideal, but would be revealed as ever contingent and varying, and as constituently including some people and excluding others. There have been

---

14 It could be countered that characteristic notions of 'liberal' freedom are inherently qualified in the recognition that freedom is tied to responsibility. Freedom is constrained when there are pertinent obligations to others or when its exercise would do 'harm' to others. These constraints, however, constitute *a posteriori* qualification which is not allowed to disturb freedom's primal efficacy. What the qualification involves is a consequential calculation, one aimed not infrequently at softening the effect of the initial free assertion or aimed at securing its acceptance. Qualification of this kind would serve to sustain rather than disabuse claims to the prerogative possession of a 'self-evident' freedom.
15 Arendt, 1993, p 143. For resonance becoming direct attribution, see Arendt's identification of such freedom with the US revolution: Arendt, 1973, Chapter 4.
16 Arendt, 1993, pp 143, 151.
17 Nietzsche, 1956, p 228.
18 Roy, 2001, p 1.
19 Berman, 2001, p 2.
20 Shannon, 2001, p 3.

necessary expedients in which this arrogation of the universal and its particular location have been conjoined as, for example, inescapable fact, or as natural, or as a racialised prerogative, but the most prominent expedient in the current situation is that of the exemplar.

With this expedient, a universal value or ideal is concentrated in the particular through an exemplar conceived in Occidental or national terms. The very purchase on the universal becomes folded into and even a property of this exemplar. So, the 'human' of human rights is realised in the exemplar where it becomes factually placed and palpable, yet where it remains universally elevated and a repository of human rights as juridical norm. Those outside the range of the completeness of this fusion of fact and norm can only ever be somehow less-than-human. As such, they provide a structured transgression of human rights and endow the vacuity of these rights with content as that which is thus transgressed against.

Such exemplarity, being intrinsically exemplary of the universal, imports that solipsistic extremity attributed by Baudrillard to 'the West'. Intimations generated by the September events abound. For example, 'anti-Americanism' can be countered by promoting a more adequate picture of the United States and its deeds.[21] The examplar, then, need only hold fast to what it is. Donald Rumsfeld, when 'asked what he would call a victory in America's new war, ... said that if he could convince the world that Americans must be allowed to continue with their way of life, he would consider it a victory'.[22] This enduring exemplarity has also to be more than held, for with it comes the responsibility, the burden, the 'mission', the destiny, of making the value or the ideal 'truly' universal.[23] This is a surpassing responsibility *for* the other, for bringing the other into sameness, not a responsibility *to* the other. And so the British Prime Minister, in that same speech to his party, could call 'us' not just to benevolent action but also to force of arms and, in responding to both calls, we would 'reorder the world around us', all in the name of that selfsame world.[24] Such calls can only be absolute – 'let there be no moral ambiguity'.[25] If they were anything less, if such calls were explicitly contingent or delimited, or ambiguous, the exemplar could no longer appear as the carrier of the universal.

That exorbitant position can hardly be a pacific one. Not only is there an oppositional exclusion of others in its very constitution but, with the universalist imperative that the same others be included, it ensures that the relation to them is an engaged confrontation. This unsettled combining of inclusion with exclusion is an extraversion of the irresolution within the exemplar itself. The modern universal cannot be endowed with enduring content in some quondam reference beyond. Nor can such content form within such universal, for to come to the universal from within is never to encompass or be able to hypostatise it. In short, the bringing of the universal into a determinate, and determinant, particularity can never be something irenically set. The particularity of its instantiation will itself be continually subject to dissipation. In the result, the position of exemplarity does have constantly to be 'held', self-evidently or otherwise. To achieve this there has to be some responsive regard to the chaos of possible effect that ensues from an orientation towards, and from within, the universal. That responsiveness, in turn, has to combine with a bringing of the chaos of effect into order. Summarily, with its embracing of the universal, the position of exemplarity brings possible effect into

---

21 See Owen, 2001, p 2.
22 Roy, 2001, p 2.
23 Derrida, 1992.
24 Williams, 2001, p 21.
25 Williams, 2001, p 21.

relation with the particular and, in the same moment, its universalised elevation of the particular rejects what is found unfitting.

An attuned mechanism of exemplarity can be instanced in the 'war on terrorism' – a war 'to realize the freedom that we have taken for granted up to now', according to George W Bush.[26] With its vacuity of content and range, its pervasive incipience and pall, this war not only accommodates indefinite effect but also generates specific 'targets' of exclusion.[27] It also takes the idea of a human rights war to something like its ultimate extent. That is, the exemplary espousal of human rights along with the values taken as sustaining them – values of civilisation, freedom and democracy – are operatively combined with their extension throughout the globe through the waging of war on those who are deemed opponents in terms of a protean 'terrorism'.

This is a new type of imperial war. It does draw on elements of older types of war, but cannot be reduced to any of them. Although the present 'war on terrorism' took fitful justification as the response of a sovereign state to unjustified aggression, and it has been oriented potentially towards states which 'harbour terrorists', it is not at all confined in this way and as yet overt war has been directed against organisations which are not recognised states, or are purportedly not considered to be such.[28] Yet, if the present war is not a more traditional war as between sovereign states, neither is it simply that more figuratively labelled 'war' – the war on drugs, the war on crime – where concentrated action is directed against a type of transgression, and military means are not supposed to assume a predominance. Nor can the present war be assimilated to the 'world' wars of the 20th century, for those wars were still limited in aim and geography, and the current conflict asserts a freedom of action that accepts no geographical bounds and advances aims of an expansive, even eschatological kind. Although conducted by particular nations, it is a war that takes the globe as its field of ever incipient battle, and it is waged in the name of a globalised humanity. Yet, further, if in its extensive and extensible range this is a global war, a war for the sovereignty of a global community, it is still not, at least in its self-constitution, akin to some ultimate civil war within or for that community, since the enemy is typically presented as something at the end of history, an eliminable rump.

If, then, the imperiously free assertion of human rights has oriented them towards absorption within war, and within the market, is there now anything of human rights that is distinctively other-regarding, that would extend towards a humanity or universality surpassing a self-regarding appropriation of human rights by its supposed exemplars? If my argument is accepted, the human of human rights cannot be contained by the particular or the instantiated. Humanity as universal can only be approached from within, and from that orientation such humanity extends ever beyond any fixity of position, exemplary or otherwise. Adhering in this way to the commonality of the human necessarily involves a responsive regard to the other, a regard cast beyond any positioning. And such a self-surpassing orientation is intrinsic to the juridical in human rights.

---

26 Tisdall, 2001, p 11.
27 It is a war well-fitted in this way to the professed policy of the United States of 'full-spectrum dominance', which translates as 'the ability of US forces operating alone or with allies, to defeat any adversary and control any situation across the range of military operations', and these operations would also include 'amorphous situations like peacekeeping and noncombat humanitarian relief' (Garamone, 2002).
28 The Taliban were either not treated as the government of a sovereign state or were treated as an illegitimate regime.

That point can be confirmed in a series of stark contrasts. In one of his many pronouncements on the limits of a 'legalist approach', the doyen of progressive international lawyers, Richard Falk, asserts the futility of setting up an international tribunal to deal with the attacks on the United States since it would be doubtful whether such a tribunal could impose the death penalty – particularly doubtful having regard to widely accepted human rights – and it would thence be 'impossible to persuade the United States government to empower such a tribunal'.[29] Another contrast intrudes with the purposive holding of people at Guantanamo Bay beyond the range of the now pale precursors of human rights found in the Constitution of the United States. To the same people the rights in the Geneva Conventions are to apply only to the extent allowed by the government of the United States. It is then but an imperceptible step to the complete abandonment of law and legal values. So, a distinguished 'professor of law' in the United States has now 'come to recognize the limits of the law', a law which can be trumped by 'exigent circumstances'.[30] Operatively, enemies in the war are to be denied 'moral equivalence'; impartial 'legal' modalities are found inadequate for dealing with them; those being held who have not been tried yet are routinely described by the highest of United States officials as 'illegal' and 'killers' – the list could go on, and doubtless will.[31]

---

29 Falk, 2001, p 12.
30 Glennon, 2002, pp 12, 19.
31 See eg the Rumsfeld news conference at
  www.defenselink.mil/news/Nov2001/t11132001_t113nb.html and MacAskill, Norton-Taylor and Borger, 2002, p 4. For the continuing discussion see eg Dworkin, 2002.

References

Arendt, H (1973) *On Revolution*, London: Penguin

Arendt, H (1993) *Between Past and Future*, New York: Penguin

Baudrillard, J (1987) *Forget Foucault*, Dufresne, N (trans), New York: Semiotext(e)

Baudrillard, J (1993) 'The melodrama of difference', in *The Transparency of Evil: Essays on Extreme Phenomena*, Benedict, J (trans), London: Verso

Berman, M (2001) 'Waiting for the barbarians' *The Guardian: Saturday Review*, 6 October, p 2

Denny, C and Black, I (2002) 'US and Europe boost aid to poorest countries' *The Guardian*, 15 March, p 13

Derrida, J (1992) *The Other Heading: Reflections on Today's Europe*, Brault, PA and Naas, M (trans), Bloomington: Indiana UP

Douzinas, C (2000) *The End of Human Rights: Critical Legal Thought at the Turn of the Century*, Oxford: Hart

Dworkin, R (2002) 'The trouble with tribunals' XLIX *New York Review of Books* 10

Falk, R (2001) 'Ends and means: defining a just war' *The Nation*, 29 October, p 11

Fitzpatrick, P (1992) *The Mythology of Modern Law*, London: Routledge

Fitzpatrick, P (2001) *Modernism and the Grounds of Law*, Cambridge: CUP

Garamone, J (2002) 'Joint vision 2020 emphasizes full-spectrum dominance', American Forces Press Service, 2 June

Glennon, M (2002) 'Terrorism and the limits of law' XXVI *The Wilson Quarterly* 12

Lacan, J (1989) *Écrits*, Sheridan, A (trans), London: Routledge

MacAskill, E, Norton-Taylor, R and Borger, J (2002) 'UK dilemma over treatment of captives' and 'What will happen to the prisoners?' *The Guardian*, 18 January, p 4

Nietzsche, F (1956) *The Genealogy of Morals*, in *The Birth of Tragedy and the Genealogy of Morals*, Golffing, F (trans), New York: Doubleday

Nietzsche, F (1968) *Twilight of the Idols*, in *Twilight of the Idols and The Anti-Christ*, Hollingdale, RJ (trans), Harmondsworth: Penguin

Nietzsche, F (1973) *Beyond Good and Evil*, Hollingdale, RJ (trans), Harmondsworth: Penguin

Owen, D (2001) 'A world of difference' *The Guardian: G2*, 11 October, p 2

Roy, A (2001) 'The algebra of infinite justice' *The Guardian: Saturday Review*, 29 September, p 1

Shannon, R (2001) 'History lessons' *The Guardian: G2*, 4 October, p 3

Tisdall, S (2001) 'Cool but confident welcome for victory' *The Guardian*, 7 December, p 11

Westlake, J (1971) 'John Westlake on the title to sovereignty', in Curtin, PD (ed), *Imperialism*, London and Basingstoke: Macmillan

Williams, H (2001) 'The danger of liberal imperialism' *The Guardian*, 4 October, p 21

Wilson, RA (1997) 'Human rights, culture and context: an introduction', in Wilson, RA (ed), *Human Rights, Culture and Context: Anthropological Perspectives*, London: Pluto

Chapter 4
The terrors of freedom: the sovereignty of states and the freedom to fear

Anthony Carty

Introduction

The question of whether human rights and the rule of law will survive September 11 was decided centuries ago, when Western societies opted for the path of agnostic liberalism. Individual human rights have always been protected against the backdrop of a 'barbarians without' mythology. Double standards are an integral part of the ideology of democracy and the rule of law. It is no accident that arch-critics of American political culture such as Noam Chomsky and Gore Vidal base their 'self-critique' of their society in terms of its shortfalls in legal standards, including international law. They pinpoint the lawlessness of the states leading the international community.[1] This is not simply the rather vague, even if easily substantiated, argument that these states themselves resort to terrorist activities (such as covert assassinations or indiscriminate bombings). It is, more particularly that they disregard the letter of international law and thereby create a climate in which general resort to lawlessness is inevitable.

Point scoring against the US and the UK at the level of individual infractions is necessary, but it can be left to competent investigative journalists. Instead, in this essay it will be asked, in terms of international legal history, whether liberalism as such can be compatible with objective international order. The main purpose of the essay is to demonstrate that 'the terrors of liberalism' have been recognised by 'mainstream' international lawyers for a very long time. Once this is appreciated, it can be seen most clearly how little there is which is new in Western reactions to Al Qa'ida, Osama bin Laden and Islamic fundamentalism. It is only to be expected that the human rights of the enemy should be disregarded, that innocents are caught with the 'guilty' and that the war against terrorism is self-destructive. There is a tediousness about the obviousness of such point scoring. What needs to be explained is the inevitability of such behavior.

The classical international law tradition

In his magisterial introduction to international law, *The Law of Nations*, Brierly quotes at length the French international lawyer Albert de Lapradelle on the significance of Vattel, whose text, *Le Droit des gens,* published in 1758, is usually regarded as the standard founding statement of modern international law. The Frenchman praises Vattel for having written in advance of the events which the book represents, the principles of 1776 and 1789, of the American and French Revolutions. Vattel is credited with projecting onto the plane of the law of nations the principle of legal individualism. Vattel has written the international law of political liberty.[2]

---

1   Chomsky, 2001; Vidal, 2002.
2   Brierly, 1963, pp 39–40.

Brierly comments astutely that the survival of the 'principles of legal individualism' has been a disaster for international law. The so-called natural independence of states cannot explain or justify their subjection to law and does not admit of a social bond between nations. Vattel has cut international law from any sound principle of obligation, an injury which has never been repaired.[3]

It could be said that there is nothing in the critical legal studies movement about the law relating to the use of force that has not already been said most clearly by Brierly in relation to Vattel. Brierly's views are worth repeating precisely because statements about Anglo-American *unilateralism*, however worthy and true, are statements of the obvious which do little to advance understanding. Focus will be on Brierly's critique of Vattel on the use of force, since it is most relevant.

Vattel makes each state the sole judge of its own actions, accountable for its observance of natural law only to its own conscience.[4] This reduces natural law to 'little more than an aspiration after better relations between states'.[5] For instance, by necessary law (natural law) there are only three lawful causes of war: self defence, redress of injury and punishment of offences. By the voluntary law (effectively the positive law, based on consent) each side has, we must assume, a lawful cause for going to war, 'for Princes may have had wise and just reasons for acting thus and that is sufficient at the tribunal of the voluntary law of nations'.[6]

Liberalism, human rights and national security

Brierly's obvious critique of the subjectivism of liberalism itself must affect the whole ideology of human rights. Liberalism places the individual at the centre of legal concern. At the same time, it says, meaninglessly, that his interests are limited by the needs of the security of the state and democratic order as adjudged by the officials of the state (even if they are judges), whether at a national or an international level. No objective standard exists for the application of human rights.

This paradox in liberalism, its inexorable compromise with the brutality of the security state, has been exposed by Richard Tuck in his book, *The Rights of War and Peace, Political Thought and the International Order from Grotius to Kant*. Tuck's central thesis is that the radically subjective world of the liberal can only be marked by fear. As Tuck puts it, the primary source of conflicts outside of civil society are epistemic in character. It is not that persons are spontaneously aggressive. They are fundamentally self-protective and only secondarily aggressive. It is the differing judgments which people make, which themselves arise from the fact that there is no objective standard of truth, which makes people secondarily aggressive. So, concludes Tuck, 'it is the fear of an attack by a possible enemy which leads us to perform a pre-emptive strike on him and not, strictly speaking, the desire to destroy him'.[7]

Hobbes should be seen as the culmination of a humanist tradition which has always been tied to a *reason of state* tradition, with its implication that fear, whether objectively justified or not, is a legitimate basis for aggressive war. For this school, the idea that there could be objective justifications for war is illusory. The rhetorical and sophist tradition of humanism, coming from Cicero, has to be distinguished from the Aristotelian and Stoic tradition. The medieval Christian practice of interpreting Cicero and others as only permitting war in defence of one's immediate

---

3 Brierly, 1963, p 40.
4 Brierly, 1963, p 38.
5 Brierly, 1963, p 38.
6 Brierly, 1963, p 39.
7 Tuck, 1999, p 130.

safety is rejected. Hobbes himself is part of the alternative tradition which came into international law through Gentili, one of his teachers, a positivist who rejected the concept of just war in favour of neutrality as to the justice of war.[8] Freedom of conscience and reason of state have kept company at least since this time.

The connection between freedom of conscience and state positivism is fully exposed in Hobbes. He is the most explicit exponent of the thesis that the state has to be omnipotent in the making of laws and the final arbiter of any dispute where there is no agreement as to how a supposed norm is to be applied. As all laws have need of interpretation, the idea of law must be subordinated to the question of who interprets it. Whether the authority within the state is democratic, aristocratic or monarchic does not matter. The essential point is that the power it has be 'an Absolute Sovereignty'.[9]

This leaves the European international law tradition with a concept of the state that is incompatible with any overarching, binding notion of law. The Sovereign of a Commonwealth, for Hobbes, cannot be subject to civil laws. He states the problem of the binding nature of law which is recognisable in 19th and 20th century debates about obligation in international law:

> ... For having a power to make and repeal lawes, he may when he pleaseth, free himself from that subjection, by repealing those Lawes that trouble him ... Nor is it possible for any person to be bound to himself; because he that can bind, can release ...[10]

So this Western liberal world is one in which the individual person is epistemically imprisoned and which (s)he has to overcome if (s)he is to reach out to recognise the other person beyond the frontiers of fear and ambition so lucidly constructed by Hobbes.

The connection between Hobbes and modern international legal order can be seen clearly through the great figure of the liberal Enlightenment, Immanual Kant. His vision of world peace has led directly to the United Nations. It is by accepting a Hobbesean anthropological vision that Kant is driven to conceive of international peace in terms of a coercive confederation of states which is, to a considerable extent, reproduced in the UN Charter. Some formulation of overwhelming force is the only option from within the Hobbesean vision. Tuck develops this as his central argument about Kant, as the pinnacle of the European Enlightenment tradition. 'As Kant says in *The Metaphysics of Morals*, "For a lawful condition to be established ... it must subject itself to a public lawful external coercion ...".'[11] Tuck quotes Kant, from the *Critique of Pure Reason*: '... As Hobbes maintains, the state of nature is a state of injustice and violence, and we have no option save to abandon it and submit ourselves to the constraint of law ...'[12]

The explanation for this grim picture of the powerful state is simple. It is the shadow side of freedom of conscience. Kant believes that 'individual men, peoples and states can never be secure against violence from one another, since each has its own right to do *what seems right and good to it*'.[13] In other words, there is built into the liberal international order a contradiction. Subjectivity in the assessment of one's obligations and the capacity to enforce one's subjective views means that international order requires a coercive mechanism to overcome difference.

---

8   Tuck, 1999, pp 138–39.
9   Hobbes, 1968, pp 556–57.
10 Hobbes, 1968, p 313.
11 Tuck, 1999, p 202.
12 Tuck, 1999, p 213.
13 Tuck, 1999, p 208, quoting again from *The Metaphysics of Morals*.

A neo-Kantian theory of contemporary international legal order

The bravest attempt to reconcile democracy and consent with an effective, ie coercively obligatory, international order has been made by Hans Kelsen. The systemic rigour of his thought enables us best to pinpoint the lacunae in that order which the events post-September 11 merely show up once again.

How can there be a legal order in which there are no institutions for the interpretation of law which are independent of states and, furthermore, no mechanisms of enforcement? Kelsen recognises that if international law is to have credibility as a legal order, it must integrate the fact of war into its interpretative framework. If war is to be evaluated from a juridical perspective, it can only be as a sanction that international law furnishes against violators of the law. Kelsen claims that international law does this.[14] Only where a state has suffered an aggression – a violation of its rights – has it a discretion to enforce its rights. In this sense, war is legally objectified.

However, the lack of an independent instance that can verify objectively whether there has been a violation of law remains. Yet Kelsen believes that this difficulty can be overcome. The liberal motive is present in so far as all law must have a democratic foundation in consent. If legal subjects are to be allowed, within an admittedly primitive or decentralised system of law, to use force, this can only be in terms which are clearly agreed in advance by the legal community. There is also need for a system of obligatory jurisdiction that would issue judgments that an executive would be required to implement. Otherwise, one is trapped in the fiction of speaking of states that decide to use force to revenge a violation of their rights, when in fact they are merely taking the law into their own hands.

Nonetheless, it is crucial to such a theory of law, in its democratic aspect, that its corpus must consist of a complete system of general principles which can be applied effectively by a judiciary to concrete situations. Hence, the court will not have to say that with respect to the issue being adjudicated, states have not consented to the development of rules limiting their freedom (sovereignty), with the consequence that the court has to declare that there is no law in place covering the dispute before it. In other words, liberal democracy, in its formal sense, cannot look to courts to overcome the deficiencies in the corpus of rules of international law.

Yet international law is generally known to be a rather incomplete system of law. So Kelsen argues that the application of a general norm to a concrete case is by its very nature an individualisation of the norm. That is to say, the exiting rule of law should be seen as a framework of several different rules. By choosing one of them, the law applying organ excludes the others and thus creates, for the concrete case, a new law.[15] The conclusion which Kelsen, draws from this argument is that there is a difference only in degree and not in nature between the creation and application of law.[16] In this way, the structural weakness of international law – the absence of a density of rules on very specific problems or issues confronting states – can be overcome through the judiciary. Hence democratic theory need have no problem with a creative role for the judiciary. In fact, this argument about the nature of law is only a variant of the Hobbesean view that the law is Who interprets it. There is no avoiding the fact that it transfers the problem of legitimacy to the judiciary. While

---

14 Kelsen, 1920, pp 264–65.
15 Kelsen, 1957, p 18.
16 Tournaye, 1995, pp 43–44.

the profession of international lawyers may welcome this, the question remains whether the judiciary can and will accept the responsibility.

Even if Kelsen's argument is accepted, there is still the question of enforcement. Court judgments should be the starting points for action by an international executive, the Security Council, which states are obliged to obey. Yet the UN Charter does not tie the Council in any way either to decisions of the International Court of Justice or even to international law. This issue became acute in the *Lockerbie* case (see below). There is clearly nothing to oblige the Council to consider any question in an impartial or quasi-judicial fashion. The Charter foresees a perfect independence of the Court and the Council. Yet the effect of the virtually total outlawing of the use of force – the outcome of Articles 2(4) and 51 of the Charter – is that an individualised sanction for a violation of the law (self-help or unilateralism) is excluded. Yet it is not replaced with an equally definite collective sanction. In other words, the liberal ideal of law has to be institutional (ie, it does require some authority to state what is the law and to enforce what it says) and yet it is not able to provide the institutional framework to qualify as law. It does not automatically interpret actions as legal or illegal or guarantee security. Nor does it impose sanctions automatically.

So, it is simply not realistic to expect that states will refrain from enforcing their rights individually whenever they consider them violated. Yet it has to be a minimum condition of a legal order that it can characterise acts of violence either as illegal or as sanctions against illegal behaviour. Where international law does not have an objective way, independent of states themselves, of distinguishing between delicts and sanctions, it cannot qualify as law.

If Kelsen would like to say that we have to suppose that each state decides for itself whether it has been injured and whether the injuring state should incur sanctions, nothing is being said about the reasons which a state has to give for considering itself injured. The feeble level of explanation that is usually required of, or obtained from, an individual state means that it is impossible for an observing third state to distinguish the 'delinquent' from the 'sanctioner'. This is because it is not possible to follow a rule on one's own. The idea of a rule relies on a common explication of the existence and content of the rule. Yet there is no adjudicative process which could guarantee this.[17] Nor, since the Enlightenment, can there be recourse to 'objective reason' or to natural law.

Court adjudication of national security cases: the legality of nuclear weapons, the Lockerbie case, and Regina v Shayler (HL)

The implication of a Hobbesean view of authority in international relations is that there is little to be expected from the possibility of an independent judiciary. Judges are, in any case, state appointees, whether at the national or international level. Even if an individual judge is independent in spirit, the power of a state apparatus in relation to an individual judge can only be overwhelming where the state considers that its national security is at issue. This is, in fact, reflected in judicial interpretations of the meaning of the concept of national security. The power of the state has, further, huge implications in terms of the access of the judiciary to the facts that could form the basis of an objective decision. A court is not necessarily in any better a position to extract information from individual states than is a political body such as the Security Council.

---

17 Pfersmann, 1993, pp 788–89.

1   The Legality of Nuclear Weapons case

In this case, the International Court of Justice decided that, while the threat or use of nuclear weapons would be generally contrary to the rules of international humanitarian law:

> In the view of the current state of international law, and of the elements of fact at its disposal, the court cannot conclude definitively whether the threat or use of nuclear weapons would be lawful or unlawful in an extreme circumstance of self-defence, in which the very survival of a state would be at stake.[18]

Here is precisely an opportunity for the Court to interpret and apply general principles to a particular case. However, it preferred, perhaps correctly in terms of democratic theory, to accept the absence of state consent to a particular rule. This is, in effect, to accept a non-*liquet*, or, to fall back on Vattel's principle that what a state considers necessary for its defence is a matter for its conscience. The British judge, Higgins, dissenting, following a line similar to Kelsen, said that it was precisely the function of the judge to apply general principles relating to self-defence and humanitarian behaviour to develop an answer. Judges can elaborate the meaning of principles of general application in a particular case. The judge should decide between competing norms, for instance the practice of states relying on nuclear deterrence and rules that exclude indiscriminate and mass destruction.[19]

The question is whether this means that she should or can do any more than follow her own conscience. Higgins herself says that one has to remember that it is the physical survival of peoples which is at stake. She effectively comes down on the side of a right of self-defence, based upon the right of subjective assessment of the danger posed by 'the other'. The reason is that we live in a decentralised (read: anarchic) world in which we simply cannot be sure of the intentions of our neighbours, 'the others'. In her own words, some states choose not to be parties to non-proliferation treaties, 'while other non-parties have declared their intention to obtain nuclear weapons; and yet other states are believed clandestinely to possess, or to be working shortly to possess nuclear weapons'. What follows, from a liberal perspective, is a modest expression of opinion. '...It is not clear to me that either a pronouncement of illegality in all circumstances of the use of nuclear weapons or the answers formulated by the court best serve to protect mankind against the unimaginable suffering which we all fear ...'[20]

The liberal conscience experiences uncertainty and fear, but never a guilt rooted in critical self-reflection. Who invented the nuclear weapons and first used them? Whatever the past might yield, we need only indulge our anxieties fed by our self-imposed isolation from 'others'. Our liberal judges will inevitably reflect the epistemic limitations of Western liberalism. The anxiety about national security is due, paradoxically, to the fact that a subjective appeal to conscience, at an individual moral level, comes also with an authoritarian view of political authority. A liberalism which has banished threat and danger to beyond the borders of a strong and aggressive state needs a powerful force to guard its frontiers also against dissent from within.

2   The Lockerbie case

The two significant aspects of the *Lockerbie* case (*Libya v UK and US*) which deserve mention are (1) the interference of the Security Council, in particular the UK and the US, in the operations of the International Court of Justice in the case which Libya

---

18 *Legality of the Threat or Use of Nuclear Weapons* [1996] ICJ Rep 66, p 80; (1996) 35 ILM 809.
19 *Ibid*, ILM, p 937.
20 *Ibid*, ILM, p 938.

brought against these two states, and (2) the further tendency of the Security Council to undertake judicial functions. These aspects serve to stress that at the international level notional divisions of constitutional powers (executive, legislative, judicial) will be overwhelmed by the power of individual states.

It is well known that UNSC Resolution 748 (1992) imposing sanctions on Libya was adopted on 31 March, when Libya had already brought an action to the International Court under Article 14 of the Montreal Convention, including a request for interim measures. The Court was obliged to accept the principle that the UN Charter had priority over individual conventions of international law.[21] It has been well argued that it is very questionable whether the conduct of the Security Council is compatible with the UN Charter.[22] Whatever the merits of the Libyan regime, it is not surprising that it should refute the imputations of terrorism made against it and that it should offer to have the matter adjudicated peacefully before the International Court of Justice. The reasoning of the Security Council only makes sense if one supposes that it has already decided the guilt of Libya, that it is a terrorist state, deprived of the basic legal right to have the question of its guilt adjudicated by an International Tribunal, which it was willing to do. The Charter requires, in Article 36(3), that issues of a legal character normally be submitted to the Court. The issue is more obviously a matter of assessing the evidence of responsibility for criminal acts (a state instigating terrorism through its agents) than it is a question of determining a threat to international peace and security, given that the controversy is about a past event.

3 The Camp Zeist case

It is difficult to argue, in the present space, the merits of the evidence upon which Al Megrahi was convicted, but one may note agreement that there is no direct evidence linking him to the terrorist act of planting a bomb on the Pan American plane. Instead there is supposed to be an accumulation of circumstantial evidence which is, in the end, taken to provide proof of guilt beyond a reasonable doubt. In the present writer's view, the most troubling parts of the evidence are the following. The case containing the bomb was supposed to have been placed unaccompanied on a flight in Malta. This fact was later to be combined circumstantially with the fact of Al Megrahi's presence in Malta just before the flight. Of the placing of the baggage on the plane, the Court said that if the bag was launched from Malta's Luqa airport, the method by which this was done was not established by the Crown. The Crown could not point to any specific route whereby the luggage could have been loaded. The Court accepted that the practices of reconciling baggage to passengers and engaging in repeated head counts of passengers and boarding cards at the airport 'seem to make it extremely difficult for an unaccompanied and unidentified bag to be shipped on a flight out of Luqa'.[23]

Al Megrahi's connection with the incident is based upon supposed evidence that he made a purchase of clothing in Malta shortly before the incident and that he made an unexplained trip to Malta the night before the flight which supposedly carried the case with the bomb. On the evidence of the shopkeeper witness, Mr Gauci, identifying Al Megrahi, the Court gave a remarkable judgment. It considered that the witness:

---

21 *Lockerbie Case (Interim Measures)* [1992] ICJ Rep 3, pp 3 and 114.
22 Remiro Brotons, 2002, p 7 for the arguments which follow.
23 *HM Advocate v Al Megrahi (No 4)* [2001] GWD 5; [2001] WL 14966 (HCJ); [2001] WL 14966 (HCJ); aff'd [2002] JC 99; [2002] GWD 11 (HCJ Appeal).

... himself felt that he was genuinely correct in picking him [Al Megrahi] out as having a close resemblance to the purchaser, and we did regard him as a careful witness who would not commit himself to an absolutely positive identification when a substantial period had elapsed. We accept of course that he never made what could be described as an absolutely positive identification, but having regard to the lapse of time it would have been surprising if he had been able to do so. We have also not overlooked the difficulties in relation to his description of height and age ...[24]

The accused had also been issued with a passport under a false name by the Libyan authorities, known as a coded passport. The Court said that there was no evidence as to why this was issued to him. It was used in 1988 only on the night of 20/21 December on a flight to Malta, leaving the next day to go back to Tripoli. The other occasion on which he came to Malta – on 7 December 1988 – he had travelled on his own passport.[25] The comments of the Court are quite extraordinary:

... There is no apparent reason for this visit, so far as the evidence discloses. All that was revealed by acceptable evidence was that the first accused and the second accused paid a brief visit to the house of Mr Vassallo at some time in the evening, and that the first accused made or attempted to make a phone call to the second accused at 7.11 am the following morning. It is possible to infer that this visit under a false name the night before the explosive device was planted at Luqa [?], followed by his departure for Tripoli the following morning at or about the time the device must have been planted, was a visit connected with the planting of the device. Had there been any innocent explanation for this visit, obviously this inference could not be drawn ...[26]

All that can be added to these remarks was that the second accused was found not guilty, making any association of the first accused with him meaningless in terms of the prosecution.

It seems clear that the world of terrorist trials is as mysterious as any metaphysical reflection on the nature of the universe. A judge can only decide a matter by following his conscience. Reading the judgment, the present author does think it conceivable that the accused was guilty. He would feel a little uncomfortable about screaming at the judges that they had taken leave of their senses. However, one does not 'feel oneself' to be in the presence of deliberations which have a professional character.

In what is widely regarded as a very authoritative critique of the trial, *Cover-Up of Convenience*, Ashton and Ferguson comment on the feelings of the judges in the following blistering terms. While the authors accept that the alternative explanations of the bombing are equally conjecture, they object that the Court is asking the world to believe the following scenario. Al Megrahi, a supposed airline security expert, had chosen to dispatch a bomb from an airport that not only carried out explosive checks on passenger baggage, but also physically counted the bags to be stored in the hold, to ensure that they matched the number recorded by the check-in counter. By putting the explosive on a plane to Frankfurt, rather than a direct flight to London, he ensured that the bag would be handled by more airports and Pan Am staff. Earlier, Al Megrahi had bought the clothes for the bomb-carrying suitcase in a manner that was bound to attract attention to himself, and had left the labels in the clothes, thereby maximising the possibility of their remains being traced back to the place of purchase. He had then colluded in the preparation of a bomb incorporating a timer that was not only impractical for the task in hand, but also, to the best of his knowledge, was supplied exclusively to Libya by a manufacturer with whom he had close personal ties. 'In short, the judges had

---

24 *Ibid.*
25 *Ibid.*
26 *Ibid.*

accepted that one of the greatest terrorist feats of all time was carried out by one of the most reckless and stupid terrorists of all time.'[27]

The main purpose of this argument has been, consistently, that the parameters of the Enlightened liberal concept of the rule of law and of international law is fundamentally flawed by the radical subjectivity of the individualism which it is supposed to uphold. Therefore, the aspects of the extraordinary *Camp Zeist Lockerbie* case which are stressed concern the subjectivity of the assessment of the presence of terrorists, not to speak of the uncertainty of anticipating a risk of terrorist acts. However, more bitter comments about the case do, if true, support the general argument of the essay about the possibilities of law among states where issues of national security are in play within a liberal enlightened framework. Koechler presents two points as decisive: the presence of political officials of the United States and Libya in the proceedings to the point where the independence of the Court appeared to be compromised, and the persistent withholding of evidence from the Court.

He comments that two state prosecutors from the US Department of Justice were seated next to the prosecution team and appeared to control which documents were released to the Court. There were cables in connection with a Libyan CIA double agent which were only partially released to the Court. Finally, the Lord Advocate stated officially that substantial new evidence had been received from an unnamed foreign government in relation to the case. The content of this information was never released. And the requested specific documents were never provided from a unnamed foreign government. Koechler comments: 'Amid shrouds of secrecy and "national security" considerations, that avenue was never pursued, although it was officially declared as being of major importance for the defense case ...'[28] This is a reference to the alternative conjecture that the bombing was done at the instigation of Iran in retaliation for the shooting down of an Iranian airliner by the US. It was carried out by an alliance of Syrian proxy groups in which a Palestinian group was to the fore and Hizbollah played an important role. Iraq's invasion of Kuwait meant that from August 1990 it became important not to upset the post-Gulf War applecart. So, only after 1990 did the 'fingering' of Libya begin.[29]

4   *Regina v Shayler*

The *Shayler* case clarifies another aspect of the relationship between the National Security State and human rights. Shayler published articles in *The Mail on Sunday* on 24 August 1997 in which he alleged that there had been UK security service plots to kill the President of Libya and various other malpractices. He did this on the basis of material he obtained as a member of the secret service, although he published it after he had resigned from the Service. He was prosecuted under the Official Secrets Act 1989, which contained an absolute prohibition on members or former members of the secret service disclosing any information for whatever reason, excluding any public interest defence. The Act provided a very elaborate system of internal review to which a dissatisfied member of the Service could have recourse, including judicial review of the refusal of his superiors to act on his complaint or to allow him to disclose information.

Shayler himself made no use of any of the internal remedies available to him. So, it is difficult to see how he could not be guilty of an infraction under the 1989 Act. However, the interest of the case is the reasoning of the judges in the House of

---

27 Ashton and Ferguson, 2001, p 357.
28 Koechler, 2001, paras 4–7.
29 Ashton and Ferguson, 2001, pp 360–61.

Lords. This indicates that there are probably no circumstances in which any member of the security services would have any reasonable prospect of preventing illegal behaviour by the secret service despite the presence of internal appeal procedures and judicial review. The decision of the House of Lords is all the more important in that it appears to provide a convincing case that it has given full weight to the impact of the European Convention on Human Rights and that it is only following the usual European practice.

The House of Lords refers to the reasoning underlying the legislation (the 1989 Act). All disclosures by members of the secret service are especially damaging because they carry an obvious added credibility. They will reduce public confidence in the secret service's ability to behave effectively and loyally. Any trial procedure which had to consider the material disclosed would be bound to damage the processes whereby the information had originally been obtained. Such a trial would assist terrorism. The secret service would lose its usual option of leaving all statements about its activities unconfirmed, whether true or false.[30]

In other words, it is the rule of law/the judicial process which is itself incompatible with the demands of national security, even in a democratic state. The policy of the legislation is that any attempt to insert a public interest defence would make it impossible to achieve clarity in the law.[31] The judicial comment on the Act is that a defendant cannot show that it was in the national interest to disclose the information. Nor may a jury so find.[32] The judiciary does have a responsibility, if a matter comes up for review, to engage in a balancing act. It must apply a principle of proportionality that is more liberal than the traditional common law ground for judicial review. The difficulty is that there is thought to be no way of 'balancing' the following consideration. In the words of Lord Bingham:

> If the information or document were liable to disclose the identity of agents or compromise the security of informers, one would not expect authorisation to be given. If, on the other hand, the document or information revealed matters which, however scandalous or embarrassing, would not damage any security or intelligence interest or impede the effective discharge by the service of its very important public functions, another decision might be appropriate ...[33]

These are precisely the terms in which the executive usually refuses to take political bodies into its confidence. The irrelevance of the idea of law is made clear where Lord Bingham goes on to repeat the advantages of excluding a public interest defence. 'Otherwise detailed facts concerning the disclosure and the arguments for and against making it would be canvassed before the court and the cure would be even worse than the disease ...'[34]

Another judicial comment appears to be more critical of the 1989 Act. Lord Hope remarks that the defect of the Act is that it does not identify the criteria that officials should bear in mind when taking decisions as to whether or not a disclosure should be authorised.[35] However, the tone of the judgment is once again in favour of the state. The scheme of the Act, the possibility of internal authorisation, subject to judicial review, is appropriate. Lord Hope's reasoning is particularly interesting in the light of the comments which have been made of the *Camp Zeist* case. What the public interest requires is, effectively, anybody's guess, given the fallibility and

---

30 *R v Shayler* [2002] UKHL 11, 21 March, HL, Lord Bingham; [2002] All ER 47.
31 *Ibid*.
32 *Ibid*, p 20.
33 *Ibid*, p 30.
34 *Ibid*, p 36.
35 *Ibid*, Lord Hope, p 71.

finitude of the human condition. That is why we need *Leviathan*. In Lord Hope's own words:

> However well intentioned he or she may be, a member or former member of the security or intelligence services may not be equipped with sufficient information to understand the potential impact of any disclosure. It may cause far more damage than the person making the disclosure was ever in a position to anticipate. The criminal process risks compounding the potential for damage to the operations of these services, if the prosecution have to prove beyond a reasonable doubt the damaging nature of the disclosures ... And it has to be borne in mind that a successful prosecution will do nothing to remedy the damage that a disclosure of security or intelligence information may have caused. Damage already done may well be irreparable, and the gathering together and disclosure of evidence to prove the nature and extent of the damage may compound its effects to the further detriment of national security ...[36]

It is quite clear from all of the judicial pronouncements considered in this section that judges – who are, after all, state officials – cannot engage in a balancing of human rights considerations against those of national security. These issues invariable involve considerations that are, by the nature of the thing, beyond their grasp because they do not have access to all possible information. Hence, they will always *feel* that, in the circumstances, they have to accord the state authorities the benefit of the doubt.

Conclusion

It remains only to stress that there should be no cause for surprise if the Coalition against Terrorism, in particular the US and the UK, do not see the need to submit their actions to the rule of law.

The Taliban government of Afghanistan refuse to hand over Al Qa'ida suspects and Osama bin Laden in the absence of substantial proof, which is normal in extradition proceedings. The US and the UK convoke the Security Council merely to inform it of the steps they are taking under the cover of the inherent right of self-defence, recognised by Article 51 of the UN Charter. Their explanation to the Council is that they are undertaking actions to prevent and discourage renewed attacks against them. This form of military force is quite simply reprisal, prohibited under the UN Charter.[37]

A central plank of the attack directly against the Government of Afghanistan, the Taliban, is that they harboured and were therefore directly responsible for the activities of Al Qa'ida. Yet the possible complicity of the Taliban is not enough in terms of international law to invoke the legal argument of a right of self-defence against armed attack. For instance, the precedent was not internationally accepted when Israel bombed PLO quarters in Tunis in 1985 and Israel was expected to compensate Tunisia. The US did not veto a Security Council Resolution calling for this. Furthermore, in *Military and Paramilitary Activities in and against Nicaragua*,[38] the International Court of Justice also affirmed, in 1986, that the notion of armed attack, which activates Article 51, cannot include mere assistance to rebels in the form of supplying arms and logistic assistance.[39]

The argument against the legality of the attack on Afghanistan is simply that the concept of self-defence has a definite technical meaning which is being misused. It is a transition stage between the suffering of an attack and an institutional coercive

---

36 *Ibid*, pp 84 and 85.
37 Following Remiro Brotons, 2002, p 27.
38 (1986) 76 ILR 341, 17 June.
39 Remiro Brotons, 2002, p 28.

response.[40] What is at stake in US and UK declarations of legal policy is something else. It is a reversion to a pre-Charter and a pre-League of Nations situation where a state claims a right to use force to protect its interests which it simply considers injured or even merely threatened. The powers involved simply do not come to the UN for authorisation and do not wish to have their freedom of action limited in any way.[41]

The conduct of the war in Afghanistan, and in particular the civilian casualties – exceeding those of September 11 – the killing of Taliban prisoners, the treatment of some of them as outside the law in the Guantanamo base in Cuba (beyond both US federal law and international law), the special courts martial envisaged (rules on proof, absence of appeal, death penalty), are all understandable responses to the horrors of September 11. However, they also show that liberal legal culture is simply swallowed up in the crises of the national security state. It has no effective way of resisting it.

The tradition which has grown up in the West, at least in the course of the 20th century, of relying on nuclear weapons as the main means of defence and security is quite simply terrorist. This is undisputed. It represents Peace through a Balance of Terror. When the matter came to the International Court of Justice, the UK and US judges were emphatic that law could not question the absolute right of the state to have recourse to nuclear weapons as a final means of defence if it genuinely considered it appropriate. It is also established and common practice for Western states, in particular the US and the UK, to engage in covert assassination of foreign leaders and other figures.[42] Our highest judicial authorities say that those who have the only realistic chance of resisting this activity – those within the secret state apparatus who have access to the necessary information – will hardly ever be allowed to use their advantage to prevent wrongdoing.

The real catastrophe of September 11 is that the white heat of one form of Islamic terror exposes the fine line between a freedom of conscience which respects difference because it knows it cannot understand it and a self-absorbed freedom of conscience which fears difference because it cannot reach out beyond itself.

---

40 Remiro Brotons, 2002, p 29.
41 Remiro Brotons, 2002, p 30.
42 Aldrich, 2001.

References

Aldrich, Richard J (2001) *The Hidden Hand, Britain, America and Cold War Secret Intelligence*, London: John Murray

Ashton, J and Ferguson, I (2001) *Cover-Up of Convenience, the Hidden Scandal of Lockerbie*, Edinburgh: Mainstream

Brierly, JL (1963) *The Law of Nations*, 6th edn, 2001, Waldock, CHM, Oxford: Clarendon

Chomsky, N (2001) *9-11*, New York: Seven Stories

Hobbes, T (1968) *Leviathan*, McPhearson, CB (ed), London: Penguin

Kelsen, H (1920) *Das Problem der Souveraenitaet und die Theorie des Voelkerrechts*, 2nd edn, Tuebingen: Verlag JCB Mohr

Kelsen, H (1957) *Collective Security under International Law*, Washington, DC: US Government Printing Office

Koechler, H (2001) *Report on, and evaluation of, the Lockerbie Trial 2001*, UN Doc E/CN, 4/2002/125

Pfersmann, O (1993) 'De la justice constitutionelle a la justice internationale: Hans Kelsen et la seconde Guerre Mondiale' 16 RFDC 761

Remiro Brotons, A (2002) 'Terrorismo, manteniemto de la paz y nuevo orden', in Revista Española de Derecho Internacional, August

Tournaye, C (1995) *Kelsen et la securité collective*, Paris: LGDJ

Tuck, R (1999) *The Rights of War and Peace, Political Thought and the International Order from Grotius to Kant*, Oxford: Clarendon

Vidal, G (2002) *Perpetual War for Perpetual Peace*, New York: Thunder's Mouth

Cases cited

Her Majesty's Advocate v Al Megrahi (No 4) [2001] GWD 5; [2001] WL 14966 (HCJ); aff'd [2002] JC 99; [2002] GWD 11 (HCJ Appeal)

Legality of the Threat or Use of Nuclear Weapons (1996) 35 ILM 809, International Court of Justice

Lockerbie Case (Interim Measures) [1992] ICJ Rep 3, International Court of Justice

Regina v Shayler [2002] UKHL 11, House of Lords, 21 March; [2002] All ER 47

PART 2

The Ground of Rights

Chapter 5
Cuba and the axis of evil: an old outlaw in the new order

Kim Van Der Borght and John Strawson

In choosing Guantanamo Bay as the site for the United States prison for selected Al Qa'ida and Taliban detainees, the Bush Administration added another dimension to the image of the 'imprisoned island'. The immediate reaction of the Cuban government to September 11 was, however, very much the same as the rest of the world: 'Both for historical reasons and ethical principles,' said Fidel Castro, 'the Government of Cuba strongly rejects and condemns the attacks on aforementioned facilities [the World Trade Center and the Pentagon] and hereby expresses its most heartfelt sympathies to the American people for the painful, unjustifiable loss of human lives resulting from such attacks.' These sentiments, however, were insufficient for the United States to let up its ideological and trade war (pursued inside and outside the World Trade Organization) against Cuba despite the new enemy in Al Qa'ida. In many ways the method of dealing with Cuba prefigured the US attitude to the world after September 11. Cuba was perceived by the United States to be an outlaw state, at the nexus of international terrorism[1] and in need of a 'regime change' for most of the 43 years of the Castro government. In many ways Cuba was Al Qa'ida mark I.

The case of United States-Cuban relations thus offers an instructive case study of how the United States constitutes a legal order for its perceived enemies. The careful colonisation of international law by the United States domestic legal system has created a model that has been much in evidence in the new order. Much has been made of the apparently new and possibly sinister approach of the United States to international law in the wake of September 11. It is true that its opposition to the International Criminal Court has stiffened and that it has questioned the integrity of a whole raft of international agreements, including the Geneva Conventions and the United Nations Convention on Refugees, that perhaps sets a new agenda in international legal discourse.[2] While the comprehensive agenda might be new, this essay explains that in its past treatment of Cuba, this legal discourse had already been established.

American security as international security

In 1996, the Cuban Liberty and Democratic Solidarity (LIBERTAD) Act – otherwise known as the Helms-Burton Act – was passed following the shooting down by the Cuban Air Force of two aircraft from the Cuban-American organisation *Hermanos al Rescate* that had entered Cuban airspace.[3] This incident gave the anti-Castro forces in the United States the extra support they needed to gather the political force to compel President Clinton to sign the Helms-Burton Act. Despite his initial intention

---

1   In the 1960s and 1970s, Cuba was seen by the United States as an organiser of aircraft hijacking. For Castro's response to this see Fidel Castro, 'Eulogy for seventy-five terror victims', 15 October 1978, in Taber, 1981.
2   See generally Vagts, 2001.
3   Cuban Liberty and Democratic Solidarity (LIBERTAD) Act, Pub L N° 104–114 (12 March 1996), repr (1996) 35 ILM 357. Hereinafter Helms-Burton Act.

to end a cold war relic and normalise relations with Cuba, he reinforced the four-decades-old embargo. The original basis for US policy toward Cuba was based on a reaction against the nationalisation of property following the 1959 revolution and the subsequent alliance with the Soviet Union. In 1959, a new Cuban constitution[4] created a legal framework for the revolutionary government's regulation of property and natural resources. One of the first uses of these powers was to bring the largely foreign-owned economy under national control. The Agrarian Reform Law organised land redistribution and provided for compensation of the expropriated landowners.[5] Relations with the US worsened after Cuba imposed a 60 per cent royalty on all oil production and consolidated its relations with the Soviet Union. In 1960, after the US had cut Cuba's sugar quota, Cuba retaliated with legislation that expropriated property belonging to United States nationals.[6] Trade relations were completely severed in 1962 by President Kennedy, who wanted to isolate the Cuban regime to promote national and hemispherical security and thereby reduce the threat posed by Cuba's alignment with communist powers.[7] Kennedy explicitly stated that the US was ready to take all necessary action in accordance with international law.[8]

The Helms-Burton Act brings together all the previous measures against Cuba. It portrays the Castro regime as at the root of 'massive, systematic and extraordinary violations of human rights' that had provoked mass migration and, in general, constitutes 'a threat to international peace and security.'[9] In this context the Jurugua nuclear plant is seen as a particular threat to the national security of the United States, demonstrating the elision between national and international security that is so central to the Act. The significance of these opening passages of the legislation is the way that the text creates a subtle interplay between national interests of the United States and the language of the United Nations Charter. In this manner, threats to United States national security are transformed into threats to international peace and security.

Under any discourse of international law, states are entitled to identify threats to their national security as they see it. The United States cannot be faulted in seeing Cuban communism as such a threat. What is more problematic is the way in which this is internationalised through the appropriation of international legal language. In the United States narrative, international law is deployed within domestic legislation and thus becomes subject to its particular interpretation and application. Within the domestic field this is unexceptional. However, the Helms-Burton legislation has consequences for the international legal relations of the United States and so attempts to extend its reach to other states. This has provoked a fierce reaction from the European Union that questions the legal competence of United States legislation to interfere with what it sees as legitimate trade relations between European companies and Cuba.[10] In general, the international community, beyond the European Union, has adopted a similar stance, seeing the United States embargo as merely a bilateral policy that should have no consequences for other sovereign states.

The legislation is divided into four titles. Title I brings together the existing measures in force against Cuba. Significantly, it places a series of duties on the

---

4 Ley Fundamental de la Republica, 5-123 of February 7 1959, *Gazeta Oficial*.
5 Ley de la Reforma Agraria, May 17 1959, Decreto N° 1426, *Gazeta Oficial*.
6 See Smis and Van Der Borght, 1998.
7 Proclamation N° 3477, 27 Fed Reg 1085 (1962), repr 22 USC § 2370 (1994).
8 *Ibid.*
9 Title I of the Act.
10 Statement by Sir Leon Brittan, Helms-Burton and US National Security, 12 February 1997 (IP/97/120).

President to advocate an embargo in international institutions. At the Security Council, he must propose a resolution for an embargo against Cuba under Chapter VII of the United Nations Charter.[11] In financial bodies, in particular the International Monetary Fund, the International Bank for Reconstruction and Development, the International Development Association, the International Finance Corporation, the Multilateral Investment Guarantee Agency or the International Development Bank, the Executive must attempt to block financial assistance to Cuba. If that fails, the United States must cut its contribution to that organisation equivalent to the assistance provided.[12] Thus the circle of entanglement between international law and American municipal law is complete. The principles of 'international peace and security' are brought within the Act and these are then mobilised so that they become the basis for foreign policy. United States conduct at the Security Council and in the financial institutions aims to create new norms of international law through internationalising the embargo. This is quite consistent with the doctrine of state sovereignty. However, the political position of the United States within the international community necessarily means that it can have a significant impact on the workings of institutions. Using its financial power to punish international institutions that do not follow its foreign policies may appear politically unfortunate to those who disagree, but is hardly inconsistent with a world order where states are the most significant legal actors.

Enforcing democracy

Title II of the Act concerns 'regime change'. Under these provisions the political and economic system to be adopted by Cuba is outlined in some detail. There are few surprises. Cuba must organise free elections, communism must be replaced with a free market system and political pluralism and the rule of law must become part of the permanent environment. In addition, the current political leadership, including Fidel and Raul Castro, are banned from holding office and organisations associated with the revolution (such as the Department of State Security and the Committees to Defend the Revolution) must be disbanded. National legislation supporting the adoption of a democratic regime in a neighbouring country cannot be seen as inconsistent with the international law. Nor is it problematic for a state to tie its foreign and trade policies to the promotion of democracy and human rights. Indeed, that might appear to be entirely desirable.[13]

The problematic area is the means for 'regime change'. In the case of Cuba, military action and covert operations have been regular additional edges to the United States polices. The interesting legal point here is the agency that has the legitimacy to bring about democracy and human rights. In the 1980s, some academics and policy makers did float the idea that there was a duty on states to make democratic interventions against non-democratic ones.[14] Indeed, this idea informed United States policy in Central America at the time, especially in relation to Grenada and Nicaragua. In the immediate aftermath of the cold war, the United

---

11 Chapter VII of the United Nations Charter deals with issues of peace and security, granting the Security Council power to 'determine the existence of any threat to the peace, breach of the peace or act of aggression and ... make recommendations or decide what measures shall be taken' (Article 39). Under Articles 41 and 42 the Council has powers to enforce such decisions through the use of economic sanctions or military means. The last Article of the Chapter is Article 51, which ensures that states retain the right to self-defence.
12 Section 104.
13 See Franck, 1992.
14 See Henkin, 1989.

States appeared to move away from unilateral positions to collective action through the United Nations Security Council, as can be demonstrated in Haiti.[15] In that case the military regime was removed by American forces acting with the authorisation of the Council, and the democratically-elected President restored to office. The agency for the 'regime change' was the Security Council. Significant though that was, it would be an error to regard this single example as either creating a new legal rule or a political model for future action. This is underlined by the fact that the Helms-Burton legislation was being debated while the Haiti mission was being undertaken. Post-September 11, the United States appears to have less confidence in the United Nations system. It would, however, be a mistake to think that United States completely ignores the Security Council, as its discussions of Iraq show. It rather obsessively bases its call for the removal of Saddam Hussein on the famous Resolution 678 (1990) that authorised the use of force over Kuwait. Title II of the Helms-Burton Act demonstrates how the United States deftly weaves an international legal discourse that encompasses both unilateral and collective action, leaving the choice of which option, naturally enough, in the hands of the sovereign state.

American jurisdiction beyond borders

Titles III and IV combine measures relating to the property that has been expropriated from United States nationals. It becomes an offence to deal in any way in these properties. This provision extends beyond United States citizens to any person living in any jurisdiction. The international reach of the legislation invites people everywhere to join the United States in implementing its legislation. However, it also gives jurisdiction to United States courts over any person alleged to have breached the Act. The definition of trafficking for the purposes of this Act is wide.[16] Thus, any person trafficking in such property, even if indirectly, can be charged in a United States court. Title IV provides that people suspected of trafficking may be excluded from the United States. This title further extends the sanction of exclusion to persons with a relationship to the trafficker, such as spouse, minor children or agents.

The degree of economic coercion used by the United States to achieve its foreign policy goals is seen by some as a violation of the objectives and rules of the World Trade Organization, and in some cases of general principles of public international law. The secondary boycott instituted by the Act exposes a contradiction in United States policy. While attempting to impose a universal boycott against Cuba, it actively opposed the Arab League boycott against Israel. The United States argued in that context that it opposed a secondary boycott on the grounds that it might force an Administration to comply with or endorse a foreign state's policy with which it might not agree. This inconsistency, however, reveals the very real sense in

---

15 See Security Council Resolutions 917 (1994) and 940 (1994). The first imposed economic sanctions and the second authorised Member States to create a military force under a united command, to use 'any necessary means' to remove the military government, and to return the deposed elected President Aristide to power.

16 A person trafficks in confiscated property if that person knowingly and intentionally '(i) transfers, distributes, dispenses, brokers, or otherwise disposes of confiscated property, purchases, receives, obtains control of, or otherwise acquires confiscated property, or improves (other than for routine maintenance), invests in (by contribution of funds or anything of value, other than for routine maintenance) or begins after the date of the enactment of this Act to manage, lease, possess, use, or hold an interest in confiscated property; (ii) enters into a commercial arrangement using or otherwise benefiting from confiscated property; or (iii) causes, directs, participates in, or profits from, trafficking [...] without the authorisation of any United States national who holds a claim to the property.'

which the United States has consistently placed itself at the centre of international legal interpretation. The impact of the policy-orientated school of international law is particularly marked here, as what can appear as inconsistent in a purely formal sense can be constituted as legal logic once the objective is clearly articulated. In this account, Israel is a democracy and Cuba is not, and as one of the objects of international law is to promote democracy, all else follows.

The Helms-Burton Act has proved to be controversial in the international community. The European Union requested formal consultations with the United States over the Act under the dispute settlement system of the World Trade Organization. The system provides for two phases, first a diplomatic round of discussion and then, if these do not result in an agreement, a formal stage where the parties argue their case before a panel. However, the United States used the diplomatic phase to explain that if the European Union insisted on its formal right to a panel hearing, it would not attend. The justification was drawn from arguments about national security and the relevant provisions of the GATT/WTO texts.

The United States' arguments against even using the dispute settlement procedures are shockingly logical. First, it makes the substantive case that, under the treaties, issues deemed to be of national security are exempted from the process. As the relevant legislation has been adopted for national security considerations, it simply cannot be regarded as an ordinary piece of trade law. Secondly, matters of national security can only be determined by the state concerned, and this is the intention of the treaties in providing an exception from the dispute settlement process. Thirdly, to allow this dispute to reach a formal panel would simply encourage those (Cuba) who threatened the national security of the United States. The key legal issue is therefore the scope that states have to determine their own national security interests in the framework of the World Trade Organisation.

The United States begins from the proposition that general principles of international law, the United Nations Charter and the treaties that regulate the World Trade Organisation permit states to determine, without international review, their own national security interests. Sometimes called a 'self-judging exception', Article XXI GATT does appear to confirm that states are able to determine their security obligations under Chapter VII of the United Nations Charter. This provision appears to leave it in the hands of states to decide how they implement resolutions adopted by the Security Council under this Chapter. The WTO has no ability to review or to challenge the decisions of states in this area. This is logical as Article 103 of the United Nations Charter creates a norm that in the event of a conflict between an international obligation and an obligation under the Charter, the obligation under the Charter prevails. As such, states merely have to certify that they are acting under a relevant resolution of the Security Council – or, it could be added, any obligation created by the Charter. In addition, clause b(3) of Article XXI allows states to take any measures they consider necessary in the interests of national security in time of war or other international emergency. The origin of this clause lies in the debates that surrounded the creation of the proposed International Trade Organisation. In those debates, the United States was keen to give latitude to states to decide their security interests but agreed that there was a danger of taking this too far.[17] This gives rise to an argument that this clause might be justiciable.[18] However, textual norms even against the background of recorded debates are seen differently in the various international law traditions. While the broadly-speaking

---

17 See World Trade Organization, 1995, pp 600–10.
18 US Department of State, suggested Charter for an International Trade Organization of the United Nations, September 1945 (Commercial Policy Series 93; Publication 2598, reprint).

continental European positivist movement tends to see the text itself as significant, the common law international lawyers have tended to see customary practices that surround the text as constituting a further definition of the norm.[19]

The United States tested out the latter attitude in the cases over its trade relations with Nicaragua. In these cases the United States argued that matters of national security precluded the panel from examining the issue at all. These cases emerged during the GATT period. Both cases concerned the national security exception at a time when tension was high between Nicaragua and the United States. The 1980s were marked by United States military assistance to the Contra rebel movement, who were attempting to overthrow the Sandinista government that had come to power in the Revolution of July 1979. In both *Nicaragua I* (1983) and *Nicaragua II* (1985) the United States successfully used the provision of Article XXI b(3) GATT to prevent adjudication. While in the first case the panel found that there might have been a breach by the United States, the finding could not be adopted by the parties as the Reagan Administration stuck by its view that national security considerations must be beyond the competence of an international body.[20] In the second case, the United States succeeded in inserting the national security issue in the mandate that the panel received. The United States in this case had had the foresight to declare a national emergency.[21] The Administration argued that the panel 'cannot examine or judge the validity or motivation for the invocation of Article XXI b(3) by the United States, [or for] the measures taken by the United States'.[22] The panel, however, asserted that it had general competence under Article XXI to consider the merits of national security, although it was unable to do so in this case as national security had been explicitly excluded from its terms of reference; thus the panel could not give a legal pronouncement *in casu*.

The *Nicaragua* cases

While the United States-Nicaragua trade issues were being argued before the trade panels, the International Court of Justice was hearing the case brought by Nicaragua against the United States over the latter's military support for the Contras[23] and for some direct military intervention against the former. Consistent with its position before the trade panels, the United States argued that the International Court of Justice did not have jurisdiction in the issue, as (a) the dispute between the two countries was political and not legal[24] and (b) under the United Nations Charter the Security Council has the 'primary responsibility for the maintenance of international peace and security'; thus the Charter 'superseded and supervened' all other sources of law on the use of force. The latter argument had a technical aspect as, when the United States had accepted the jurisdiction of the Court in 1949, it had included a reservation that it would not accept jurisdiction in a case involving the interpretation of a multilateral treaty unless all parties to the treaty were joined in the case. Quite apart from the United States' normal position that only states could determine their national security needs, this technical point

19 See Higgins, 1994.
20 See Schloemann and Ohlhoff, 1999, p 434; World Trade Organization, 1995, p 608.
21 Executive Order N° 12, 513, 1 May 1985, 50 Fed Reg 18, 629 (2 May 1985).
22 GATT Doc C/M/196, at 7 (1986).
23 See *Military and Paramilitary Activities in and against Nicaragua (Nicaragua v USA)* (1986) 76 ILR 341, 17 June 1986.
24 Under Article 36 the Court only has jurisdiction over disputes of a legal character, the United States attempted to argue that their conflict with Nicaragua was purely political and thus beyond the jurisdiction of the Court.

aimed at removing the issue from international review. The Court famously rejected the jurisdictional arguments and proceeded to the second, merits, stage of the case, despite the boycott of the United States. When the court handed down its decision in 1986, the United States was found to be in breach of international law for its use of force in Nicaragua. However, while the decision went against it, the judgment contained jurisprudence that would prove useful to the United States in the future.

The *Nicaragua* judgment revolved around an interpretation of Article 51 of the United Nations Charter. This Article had been the heart of the United States' argument. It begins: 'Nothing in this present charter shall impair the inherent right of individual or collective self-defence if an armed attack occurs against a member of the United Nations.' The Court was much concerned to establish what the inherent right was that had not been impaired. It concluded in paragraph 176 of its decision that this right derived from customary international law and that there were thus two parallel and sometimes overlapping sources of law on the use of force: customary law and the Charter. By relying on customary law the court was able to make a decision that the United States' reservation would have been precluded in relation to the Charter. While the United States fumed against the decision, in reality the Court had confirmed the position of the United States on the use of force for much of the cold war period, when it had relied on the customary principles which much of the rest of the world, especially the Soviet block and the non-aligned countries, rejected.

What the United States found most objectionable was the international review of their actions by the Court. Whereas the Reagan Administration had been able to frustrate the trade panels over the issue of national security, it had failed with the International Court of Justice. The status of the court as the principal judicial organ of the United Nations, together with its jurisdiction, is the main reason why the Court was able to proceed to review the United States' actions. It does also highlight the notoriously complex area of national security and the use of force in international law.[25] While the GATT and WTO texts treat wars and other international emergencies as though they are factual situations, international legal doctrine is far more constitutive. Indeed, the International Court of Justice gave a great deal of attention to defining what the meaning of an armed attack might be.[26] Was an armed attack one military assault, or could it be the accumulation of a number of smaller actions? On the whole, the Court thought probably the latter. More complex still is the difference between the triggers for self-defence in the two sources of law. In the Charter, self-defence is a response to an armed attack. Under customary law, the even vaguer criterion of necessity is used.[27] Necessity necessarily has to be determined by the state that perceives the danger. This undoubtedly bolsters at least part of the United States' position, which is to attempt to limit international legal or institutional restraints on states in this area. However, identifying customary law also restores two further criteria that must be used in assessing the justification for self-defence, proportionality and purpose. These concepts impose on states the duty to maintain any force used in proportion to the threat and not to extend the scope of any military action beyond that necessary in military terms. Thus the state relying on self-defence does not have complete discretion but rather has to justify its actions to the international community. Under Article 51, a further procedural duty is imposed that requires states using self-defence to report its actions to the Security Council and to abide by any measures

---

25 See Damrosch and Scheffer, 1991.
26 See above, fn 23, paragraphs 172–94.
27 See Webster's definition of self-defence in the Caroline Incident, 1837–41.

that the Council might take. Thus the Charter creates a forum for international review of the use of force, as it might adopt a resolution calling for any military action to cease. The Council could back this up by using its mandatory powers under Articles 41 and 42 to impose economic sanctions or even to deploy military force to prevent its continuance. However, given that the United States is one of the five permanent members of the Security Council, the veto would give it protection against such a situation occurring.

The effect of this judgment, authoritative although not binding, also complicates the Security Council's position on the use of force. Since the Kuwait crisis, much has been made of the role that the Council has played in authorising the use of force. The first half of the 1990s saw this process in Kuwait itself and then in Somalia, Haiti and Bosnia. At the end of the 1990s, with the Kosovo intervention by NATO, this authorisation was lacking. In the ensuing discussion it became clear that the interplay between the text of the United Nations Charter and the doctrines of customary international law is in fact a conflict between those who think that collective security is possible and desirable and those who believe that, at the end of the day, only sovereign states can decide security interests. The support from NATO for the Kosovo action indicates a diplomatic success for the United States in popularising its legal interpretation. The International Court of Justice's concentration on customary law has therefore armed the United States with a useful tool not only in relationship to Cuba but also for the 'war against terrorism'.

Cuba and the 'war against terrorism'

The US has found a place for Cuba in the post-September 11 world. John Bolton, Under-Secretary of State, has situated Cuba within the axis of the new evil. Cuba is portrayed as a state with its own programme for developing weapons of mass destruction, having a suspiciously sophisticated biomedical industry and having relations with enemies, through regular visits and diplomatic links with certain states – Iran, Iraq, Syria, Libya and North Korea – singled out by the Bush Administration. Bolton attempts to fit Cuba into the perceived policies of these states: '… the United States believes that Cuba has at least a limited offensive biological warfare research and development effort.' He is also suspicious that sales of biomedical products might have a 'dual use' to rogue states and could thus turn into a threat against the United States. Secretary of State Colin Powell did correct Bolton's original comments slightly by saying that Cuba had the 'capacity' to develop such a programme rather than actually being engaged with it.[28]

Inferences are also drawn from the fact that Castro has opposed military action in response to September 11. Castro was one of the few international leaders to openly question the Afghan war. Given the framework established by the United States – that those who are not with us are with the terrorists – such opposition is seen as siding with the enemy. Bolton sees this as a sign that Cuba's disassociation from the attacks is cosmetic and argues that Cuba 'continues to view terror as a legitimate tactic to further revolutionary objectives'.[29] Castro himself, however, has been forthright in his denunciation of terrorism:

> I reiterate that none of the world problems – not even terrorism – can be solved with the use of force, and every act of force, every imprudent act of use of force anywhere is going to aggravate world problems. The path should not be the use of force; … I think this

---

28 'Powell says Cuba has bio weapons research capacity', *International Herald Tribune*, 13 May 2002.
29 Bolton seems to use the concepts 'armed belligerence' and terrorism interchangeably. Belligerents are recognised in international law and have been accorded a specific status. Terrorism is illegal.

unusual event must be used to create an international front against terrorism. However, this international front against terrorism cannot be solved by sanctioning a terrorist here and another one there.[30]

This is quite consistent with Castro's long-held political views. He may have led and supported guerilla struggles but he has never advocated terrorism. Bolton accurately reflects the Bush Administration's amalgamation between terrorism and all other forms of armed force that they oppose. By turning all forms of non-approved violence into terrorism, Bolton can question Castro's sincerity. In this way Cuba neatly finds a place alongside Al Qa'ida, Iran, Syria, Libya, Iraq and North Korea.

Ironically, in the year after September 11, Cuba saw the high profile visit of former President Carter (May 2002). He used the occasion to call on the United States Congress to repeal the embargo and to allow free travel between the two countries. He urged both Cuba and the United States to find a positive and constructive solution to the property disputes. He also argued that Cuba should embrace democracy according to international standards (United Nations and Organisation of American States), but emphasised that he did not want to interfere in Cuba's internal affairs – and Cubans, not foreigners, must decide the future of their country.[31] Carter's views are in sharp contrast with those of the Bush Administration. His comments, however, produced a ringing endorsement of existing policy towards Cuba from George Bush. He saw Castro as a 'tyrant' who employed 'brutal methods' to enforce a 'bankrupt vision' that includes a 'backward economy'.[32] These are interesting images that link Castro to Saddam Hussein and Osama bin Laden, who are also talked about in such terms. Bush's lyrical reference to Castro turning a beautiful island into a prison appears without a hint of irony given the prison that Bush had built at Guantanamo Bay. He underlined his policy, explaining:

> The sanctions our government enforces against the Castro regime are not just a policy tool; they're a moral statement. My administration will oppose any attempt to weaken sanctions against Cuba's government until the regime – and I will fight such attempts – until this regime frees its political prisoners, holds democratic, free elections, and allows for free speech.[33]

President Bush's comments about Cuba reflect the United States' stance in relationship to the rest of the 'axis of evil' states. Legal concepts are drawn from policy objectives that emphasise a particular view of world order in which the United States is the centre not just of economic and political power but also of moral power and democratic values. In a world where the United States perceives itself to be the target of anger and violence from so many undemocratic states and terrorist organisations, international law remains a system to be determined by the United States. This hierarchical view of law means that the United States does not recognise the validity of all sovereign states. The use of the terms 'rogue state', 'terrorist state' and 'the axis of evil' gives testimony to this. To some extent, this is a reconfiguring of the language of the cold war, in which international law for the United States (and for the Soviet Union) could not be a genuinely international system due to the deep and competing ideological conflict. At the end of the Cold War the United

---

30 Speech to United Nations General Assembly, 2001. Were it not for the lack of a common definition, the presidents show a remarkably similar vision: 'We're asking for a comprehensive commitment to this fight. We must unite in opposing all terrorists, not just some of them.' President Bush speaks to the United Nations (10 November 2001).
31 Former President Jimmy Carter Urges Cuba to Embrace Democracy (15 May 2002).
32 Remarks by the President in Recognition of Cuba Independence Day (18 May 2002).
33 See above.

States emerged as the victor, not only with its political values and economic model, but also with its view of international law. This strong connection between political goals and law has been reinforced by September 11. Due to American power, its views of the role of law have an impact on both jurisprudence and procedures. In this vision threats to the national security interests of the United States are constituted as the same as threats to international peace and security. International stability and American interests are fundamentally intertwined in this narrative. The Helms-Burton Act represents in legislative form the way in which the United States constructs itself as the universal. Its legal and administrative system is equipped for a global reach. The history of United States-Cuban relations thus provides a significant backdrop to legal developments after Ground Zero. Cuba provides a useful constant other in the battle that George Bush continues in the new order.

References

Damrosch, L Fisler and Scheffer, DJ (1991) *Law and Force in the New International Order*, San Francisco/Boulder/Oxford: Westview

Franck, Thomas M (1992) 'The emerging right to democratic governance' 86(1) AJIL 46

Henkin, Louis (1989) *Right v Might*, New York: Council on Foreign Relations

Higgins, Rosalyn (1994) *Problems and Process International Law and How we Use It*, Oxford: OUP

Schloemann, H and Ohlhoff, S (1999) '"Constitutionalization" and dispute settlement in the WTO: national security as an issue of competence' 93 AJIL 224

Smis, S and Van Der Borght, K (1998) 'The Cuban Liberty and Democratic Solidarity (LIBERTAD) Act of 1996. Some aspects from the perspective of international economic law' Revue Belge de Droit International 217

Taber, Michael (1981) *Fidel Castro Speeches*, New York: Pathfinder

Vagts, Detlev F (2001) 'Hegemonic international law' 93(4) AJIL 843

World Trade Organization (1995) *Guide to GATT Law and Practice*, Vol I, 6th edn, 1995, Geneva: WTO

Internet sites

Speeches and statements (US)

Statement by the President in His Address to the Nation (11 September 2001): www.whitehouse.gov/news/releases/2001/09/20010911-16.html (last visited 21 May 2002)

Address to a Joint Session of Congress and the American People (20 September 2002): www.whitehouse.gov (last visited 20 May 2002)

President thanks CIA (26 September 2001): www.whitehouse.gov/news/releases/2001/09/20010926-3.html (last visited 21 May 2002)

Transcript of President George W Bush's remarks Thursday at the Georgia World Congress Center in Atlanta (8 November 2001): www.cnn.com/2001/US/11/08/rec.bush.transcript/ (last visited 21 May 2002)

President Bush speaks to the United Nations (10 November 2002): www.whitehouse.gov/news/releases/2001/11/20011110-3.html (last visited 21 May 2002)

President Bush addressing the National Hispanic Prayer Breakfast (16 May 2002): www.cnn.com (last visited 19 May 2002)

Remarks by the President in Recognition of Cuba Independence Day, 18 May 2002: www.whitehouse.gov/news/releases/2001/05/20010518-7.html (last visited 20 May 2002)

Remarks by the President on Cuba Policy Review (President Bush Announces Initiative for a New Cuba) (20 May 2002): www.whitehouse.gov (last visited 21 May 2002)

Secretary Colin L Powell, Remarks with His Excellency Brian Cowen, Minister of Foreign Affairs of Ireland (Washington, DC, 26 September 2001): www.state.gov/secretary/rm/2001/5061.htm (last visited 23 May 2002)

John R Bolton, Beyond the Axis of Evil: Additional threats from Weapons of Mass Destruction, Heritage Foundation Lecture No 743 (6 May 2002): www.heritage.org/library/lecture/hl743.html (last visited 20 May 2002)

US Department of State – International Information Programs, Excerpts: Powell Says Cuba Has Bio Weapons Research Capacity (13 May 2002): http://usinfo.state.gov/regional/ar/us-cuba/02051405.htm (last visited 20 May 2002)

US Department of State – International Information Programs, Text: Former President Jimmy Carter Urges Cuba to Embrace Democracy (15 May 2002): http://usinfo.state.gov/regional/ar/us-cuba/02515501.htm (last visited 20 May 2002)

Speeches and statements (Cuba)

Excerpts from the speech given by the President of the Councils of State and Ministers of the Republic of Cuba, Dr Fidel Castro Ruz at the Reopening Ceremony of 'Salvador Allende' School, Referring to the terrorist acts that took place in the United States, 11 September 2001 (not an official transcript): www.iacenter.org/fidel_onwtc.htm (last visited 20 May 2002)

Statement of the Government of Cuba (11 September 2001) available on the website of the Cuban Ministry of Foreign Affairs: www.cubaminrex.cu/versioningles/STATEMENTOFCUBA.htm (last visited 20 May 2002)

Speeches and statements (other)

Patten, C (European Commissioner for External Relations), How National is the National Interest?, English-Speaking Union – Churchill Lecture, Guildhall, London (30 April 2002): www.europaworld.org/week81/hownationalis10502.htm (last visited 24 May 2002)

White, N, The State of Collective Security, Hilaire McCoubrey Memorial Lecture delivered at the University of Hull Law School (15 May 2002): www.hull.ac.uk/law/docs/mccoubreylecture02.pdf (last visited 14 August 2002)

Discussion forums

American Society of International Law: www.asil.org (last visited 20 May 2002)

Kirgis, F, 'ASIL Insight: Terrorist Attack on the World Trade Center and the Pentagon': www.asil.org/insights/insigh77.htm (last visited 14 August 2002)

Stahn, C, 'Security Council Resolutions 1377 (2001) and 1378 (2001)': www.asil.org/insights/insigh77.htm#addendum9 (last visited 14 August 2002

European Journal of International Law: www.ejil.org (last visited 20 May 2002)

Chapter 6

Al Qa'ida: terrorists or irregulars?
David Meltzer

Introduction

The main contention of this essay is that analyses, for and against, of the American policy reactions to the strikes of 11 September 2001 miss key points. In essence, this 'third way' takes the position that the American approach is worse than a crime; it is a mistake.[1] The current American classification of Al Qa'ida as a terrorist organisation is a mistake on several levels.

Legally ...

Problems of definition

In terms of the strict legalities of war, the notion of a classification of 'terrorist' runs into an immediate problem – the term is nowhere fully defined as a legal term. While there are anti-terrorist laws, these are mainly to do with the granting of powers of search, evidence gathering, arrest and detention rather than a coherent definition of what defines a terrorist, in the way that, say, a rapist can be defined. A terrorist act does not appear to have been satisfactorily legally defined, hence, for example, the skirting around the problem by presuming a person guilty based on certain articles in his possession. The legal vagueness of the word 'terrorist' means that traditional means of determining guilt – guilty acts and thoughts – are useless because the guilty act is so ill defined. In terms of a brief comparison, the latest British legislation seems to draw the definition so wide as to be somewhat meaningless. The earlier European Convention on the Suppression of Terrorism (1977) defines various acts, but only if they are deemed 'unlawful' in their own right.[2] In other words, if a lawful combatant did these things, such acts would fall outside this Convention, and so we are no further forward as this just moves the nebulous issues rather than answering them. More recent attempts by the EC to define terrorism[3] have other major flaws (see below). The UN has had no better success in definitions; the UN GA Resolution 49/60, adopted in December 1994, also relied upon the basis of an act being a crime in most legal systems first, thus murder, kidnapping and arson would qualify, depending on the motive and severity.[4] Again, however, if such acts are legitimately committed by a soldier against the enemy, this is recognised as part of war, so again the issue goes back to the legitimacy or otherwise of the combatants and their cause.

One approach to a legal definition of 'terrorist' is (and here the definition's lawyers' roots are evident) 'one who commits terrorist acts', which acts are then defined as acts whose *primary* intent is to cause terror. To which could probably be added, 'to the citizens of a state at large'. This would seem to satisfy the classification of 'terrorist' those actions, undoubtedly shocking, awful and enraging which are seared on our minds, often in the forms of bombers, suicide or otherwise, killing

---

1   This view has been variously attributed, though I confidently rely on David Chandler who cites it as Fouche's in Chandler, 1994, p 117.
2   Wyngaert, 1996, p 211.
3   From www.statewatch.org/news (visited 7 March 2002).
4   Cassese, 2001, p 259.

ordinary civilians in Omagh, Tel Aviv, Nairobi and, especially, New York. There are, however, two things wrong with this approach, which approach seems to come mainly from the media and politicians, though who is leading whom is unclear. The first problem is that it is, despite the obvious examples, a vague definition. On logical and historical analysis it becomes all-encompassing, contradictory and inefficient. There is, implicit in the examples, an assumption that terrorist groups are non-state ones, and almost by that very fact are outside the laws of war. But this is only an assumption and if the definition of 'primary purpose' is accepted, it enables soundly based accusations of terrorism to be flung back and forth until every country is more or less guilty or none are. More importantly, it could easily become a barrier to swift and humane resolution of conflict – if you can scare your opponent into backing down, you will save lives on both sides. 'For to win one hundred victories in one hundred battles is not the acme of skill. To subdue the enemy without fighting is the supreme excellence.'[5] This was precisely part of the rationale (in that it aimed to avoid an invasion and armed conquest of Japan) of the USA's use of atomic bombs against Japan. Similarly, the Bomber Offensive against Germany was intended to depress morale, which it did as evidenced by the huge losses to production due to absenteeism.[6] In the recent campaign against the rump of Yugoslavia, the broadcasting station was deemed a legitimate target because its loss would depress (an emotion virtually cheek by jowl with terror) the populace.

A further problem with the 'non-state' idea is that history contradicts this by the examples of Resistance to the Axis in World War II (and on which in terms of legal and military details, see below). Despite German fury with irregular fighters, going back to 1870, international law has recognised the rights of combatants outside a state structure. Perhaps the majority of the world's people live in states founded on struggles between the state and others. While it may seem trite to note that one man's terrorist is another's freedom fighter, it also highlights a fundamental truth: that often oppression is only removed by force.[7] Thus the 'state/non-state' sub-argument can be dismissed as illusionary.

The fact is that the introduction of industrialised warfare has transformed the relationship between war and society. The days when civilians could be so far apart from the military that they could take picnic baskets and travel down to Bull Run to watch the battle are long gone – now virtually everyone contributes to a modern nation's military potential and effectiveness and so are legitimate military targets. This has led to pictures of civilians, including children, being caught up in the most heart-breaking ways with war. Such is not proof of an inherent crime – it is proof that now more than ever Billy Sherman's observation that 'War is all Hell' is terribly accurate.[8] The effective interweaving of all parts of a society with its military has

---

5 Sun Tzu, 1994, p 105.
6 Meltzer, 1984. '"Acts or threats of violence the primary purpose of which is to spread terror among the civilian population are prohibited", in para 2 of Article 51 [of the AP I (1977) to the Hague Regulations] … The word "primary" must be noted.' Best, 1994, p 276. Read literally, this would exclude all but true terrorists with no motive beyond creating fear, or, arguably, also those whose objectives beyond this are completely unrealistic, leaving only the terror aspect. Such an interpretation would be in concord with a doctrine of efficacy. In terms of warfare, the methods of guerrilla war are 'not nice. However, there is nothing particularly nice about the methods of conventional war'. Creveld, 1991, p 60.
7 The potential ironies of the situation of 1776, with Americans fighting 'unfairly' (tactically) and with 'improper' soldiers in the cause of religious intolerance and fundamentalism, at least in New England, seems to have been missed.
8 His intention to 'make Georgia howl', because he saw its civilian structure physically and morally as upholding the war (Gray, 1994, p 15) may be open to criticism, but, that accepted, bringing the war home to the population at large certainly coincided with a swift collapse of the CSA, preceded by mass desertions even from 'Massa Bobby' Lee's command.

also led to the expansion of the concept of 'collateral damage'. Much distrusted, especially by those of a certain age and political leaning, this phenomenon does have quite orthodox precedent. The often dreadful impact of sieges and blockades on non-combatants has been accepted in Western law since ancient times. The broadening of this concept has focused on the idea of the primary target being of military significance, and if anything else near such targets was hit, then that was regrettable, but within the law of war. Certainly, in modern war everything is connected in a state to its power to wage war. Again, it would be simply wrong to condemn the strategic bombing of Germany, despite the civilian lives lost, because the net result was to significantly reduce the length of the war, particularly the end game after the Normandy landings. This is of particular importance given that the majority of losses in the war occurred in the last 18 months of the war, and the bulk of those from July 1944. Certainly the majority of Nazi civilian killings occurred in this period. An ability by the Nazis to hold on for longer, with fuel for jet fighters and awesome tanks, and the rail infrastructure to move men and supplies around interior lines, would have meant greatly increased losses, including losses of Germans. The same reasoning and military appreciation holds for the submarine campaign against Japan. This all leads to a central point of the law of war – if it is effective it is legal.

This is where the second major flaw in the argument of 'primary purpose' is revealed. Superficially, it would seem that by focusing on the immediate target we can determine which acts are legal and which are not. In fact, the linking theme with what is and is not acceptable in war is not the target (the status of which may change according to circumstance – a worker producing aspirins may be deemed beyond legitimate attack, but the same person making parts for tanks or even trucks will not be). Nor is it necessarily the weapon – a rifle can be used legally or it can be used to commit a war crime. The common thread is that of efficacy. This provides a logical coherence in determining war crimes and in separating criminal acts from legitimate ones. So chemical and biological weapons are banned not because they are kinds of 'poor man's atomic weapons' but because they are not very effective and as such only add to suffering uselessly, unlike nuclear weapons, which add to suffering but are all too effective. This is also why it is legal to ambush the enemy (he might otherwise do all manner of things that will hurt your effort) but not to shoot prisoners. As prisoners of war, soldiers pose no effective threat, so killing them is useless and not excused by being collateral to some higher purpose. Note that 'efficacy' does not grant a general dispensation to do anything. This proposed doctrine is in addition to established norms of war, perhaps best viewed in seeing the war crimes established in World War II as setting a 'gold standard'. Thus an aggressive war is outlawed in its own right, and it is illegal to take hostages. Going further on this, it is worth noting that it comes back to efficacy anyway. For example, although the massacre at Oradour-sur-Glane by the 2nd SS Panzer Division (10 June 1944) did deter local Resistance fighters for a short time, the overall conclusion from World War II is that such atrocities are counter-productive; such acts were committed almost routinely in the USSR and Yugoslavia, yet these countries produced the most effective partisans by far, the Yugoslavs liberating their country unaided by Soviet ground forces. Similarly, waging aggressive war has become too costly to be effective in terms of a justifiable foreign policy aim – as, for example, Saddam Hussein discovered in his war with Iran and as shown by the inability of Indonesia to hold on to East Timor. Non-aggressive war can sustain these costs precisely because of the legitimacy of the conflict.

This can be morally sustained because effective weapons and methods bring an end to war in the quickest time,[9] and so, most likely, with the fewest casualties. If the primary aim or effect of a weapon or method is gratuitous suffering it is outlawed. Thus one can differentiate between land mines sown to protect a position (as Sarejevo was protected) and those sown indiscriminately – to be legally used, they should be properly marked on the sowers' maps (and, ideally, cleared up afterwards). This is an understood aspect of sea warfare (witness the Americans' clearing of their mines sown in Haiphong harbour after their treaty with North Vietnam). This raises the potential point that the USA has not acted disproportionately in invading Afghanistan, but the mass sowing of mines might be a disproportionate act.

Discussion of 'effective' and 'useful' brings us to examine the legitimate aims of force. Broadly speaking, these are to make a nation change its policy, in part or by a complete change in government or even system. This now traditional explanation of the aim of war comes from Clausewitz, who declared that war is just 'a continuation of political activity by other means'.[10]

This is where the best definition, which comes from the military and war studies rather than lawyers,[11] becomes apparent. A terrorist is one who commits acts of force against a society even though he has no realistic chance of achieving his aims – that is, the government in question will never accommodate or negotiate with the person or group. By this we can define the Baader-Meinhof group, the Red Brigade and the Red Army Faction as terrorist groups – their acts were illegal because they were always going to be ineffective in their aims of changing the targeted societies/ governments. Naturally, ordinary criminals using violence are also guilty, but for other reasons – the point is to define a group of particularly violent crimes just as one differentiates between assault and rape, for example.

There will be some feeling of unease among lawyers because such an approach is not grounded in the basic concept that the law should be predictable and a guide to lawful actions in the future. However, the idea of an expert judging the diagnosis and prognosis of an incompletely understood and unfinished condition is not alien to rational thought. This is precisely what doctors habitually do – most headaches can be cured by two aspirin and signify nothing serious. Simply because some headaches indicate something more serious that develops later is no reason to lose faith in the entire system of diagnosis. In the same way, an expert assessment of the potential of a given group of fighters to achieve their aims can be taken as a guide to their legal position. On the broader scale, as noted, virtually every country is rooted in a period of illegitimacy, so insistence on a continuous legitimacy throughout a struggle is both unrealistic and unhistorical – it is possible to move from illegal to legal. This is precisely what the American Revolutionary forces did during their War of Independence. Other *de facto* regimes have become *de jure* simply by virtue of their continued existence, even though they were termed illegal at first, the prime example being China.

---

9   Such a doctrinal approach of efficacy would also be in accord with the ruling that nuclear weapons are not illegal *per se*, Ticehurst, 1996, pp 107–18, *per* the International Court of Justice ruling (8 July 1996), as well as explaining why, in the same decision, chemical and biological weapons remain illegal.

10 Clausewitz, 1976/1994, p 207. I make no apology in quoting from a collation of military theorists rather than the original.

11 O'Brien, 1981/1994, thinks this is the established case in law anyway – 'The present international-law approach to revolutionary war is essentially one of self-determination by a Darwinian process of armed conflict. Whatever side prevails is legitimate, is the "self" that has been "determined"' (p 181). Similar thinking was shown in *Kawasaki Kisen Kabushiki Kaisha v Bantham Steam Ship Company* [1939] 2 KB 544; McCoubrey and White, 1992, p 190, in which 'war' was held to be a matter of empirical fact.

By this definition it might be argued that a kind of legitimacy is given to highly objectionable people and causes. However, there are precedents for just this aspect, and a fundamental reason for it. During World War II, the Axis powers were required to formally surrender, and the West treated Axis prisoners well, on the whole. This went a long way to enabling new nations to arise from the defeat, by allowing some kind of a line to be drawn, separating the past. Otherwise everyone would become immersed in the past, as with apocryphal family feuds, the cause of which has been forgotten but not the enmity. Freedom to manoeuvre is important to the state when dealing with violent challenges – it is simply bad strategy to needlessly restrict your alternatives, and worse ethics to do so in order for politicians to indulge in macho posturing, refusing to negotiate yet unable to end the violence. Such imprecise use of the word 'terrorist' also hamstrings tactical operations, which have to be conducted as if a series of discrete criminal operations followed each other. Notably, the British government and the SAS were chagrined by the 'Death on the Rock' case,[12] in which the European Court of Human Rights found that the operation had been conducted illegally. Had the Provisional IRA (PIRA) simply been recognised as fighting an irregular war, those resisting them could simply have shot PIRA members without consideration of evidence, crime procedures and maintaining standards, so that the whole criminal justice system would not have become corrupted by the conflict. If captured there would have been no expensive trial process – as POWs they would simply have been incarcerated until peace. This would have given the PIRA a powerful incentive to negotiate rather than fight on. If, under the system of viewing all PIRA (or all Al Qa'ida) as criminal, individuals belonging to these organisations who are locked up will remain so for their sentences (which, especially for Al Qa'ida, generally looks like being for a very long time) regardless of what PIRA or Al Qa'ida do or say, this will cause these groups to be compelled by their own politics to continue fighting. Not to do so would look like betraying those imprisoned. Any attempts to reach peace under such conditions exposes those trying to do so to internal challenges. On the other side, if the prisoners are released, this distorts and brings into disrepute the state's justice. Naturally, even in war there are, as noted, restrictions – if PIRA members had surrendered and were then shot, that would be a crime, but that position would have been far less contentious than the historical record has proved to be. Such comparisons provide powerful arguments for the USA to drop the line of punishing terrorists and proceed as a sovereign state protecting her interests and citizens. By all means bin Laden can be hunted and even tried as a war criminal, but it would be easier and more logically coherent and honest to do so as part of an acknowledged conflict.

The thought of declaring the situation a conflict instead of a criminal manhunt (with an attendant prosecution) brings into focus the target. Striking office buildings literally and metaphorically from out of the blue seems not only unforgivable but also incomprehensible. Yet disrupting an enemy's economic structures, virtual and/or physical, is a long practised legitimate war aim. Fairly recent examples include the Israeli bombardments to prevent the diversion of the Jordan River in 1965 and, arguably, the Anglo-French invasion of the Suez Canal in 1956. If there is a sustainable case that large corporations, based or very active in the USA, are causing hardship in other countries, and/or that the wealth generated by such is being used in part to effectively oppose a nation or group's aims, then it is at least arguable that disrupting that trade is a legitimate aim.[13] The very fact that the

---

12 *McCann v UK* (1996) 21 EHRR 97.
13 This, after all, is the world in which, for example, the TRIPS agreement on intellectual property looks set to render cocoa trees in Ghana, on privately held land, to be the property (via the copyrighting of genetic sequences) of multi-nationals.

attacks on the World Trade Center (WTC) and the Pentagon have produced serious economic consequences in the West is evidence of their effectiveness in achieving what can be surmised as a possible aim of bin Laden, and that effectiveness renders it a legitimate act of war. The WTC was clearly part of the machine of American international power and was a symbol of that power and American society. On the last point, the towers destroyed do count as buildings of cultural significance (like Monte Cassino) because they were of cultural importance nationally, not to the world. As such there is no need for the USA to prove or justify its response to anyone beyond those facts. This line is bolstered by the real possibility that the USA would react to the attacks by withdrawing into, if not isolation, then a very reduced global role. Thus, by attacking those targets in that manner, bin Laden may have achieved something directly analogous to bombing Iraq and imposing sanctions on it – compelling certain behaviour from that government. From this perspective, either both assaults are legal or neither is. If the latter, then virtually every conflict is condemned as illegal, thus making the very search for legitimacy, around which the issue of what is 'terrorism' is based, unachievable.

Strategic issues

This appears to be a problem endemic to legal theory in the realm of warfare – it is often divorced from reality, making for ineffectual law and a weakening of the very rules that are being declared.[14] If legal scholars (and others) persist in pretending that certain military facts do not exist or are unimportant then they have only themselves to blame if the military ignore them. Nor is it clear why self-defence requires a country to allow itself to be fought over in order to be 'proper'. Certainly, the lesson of history that the military (and in particular the American military) have learned, perhaps too well, is that intervention can save lives. If a small act of invasion by the British/French/Belgians in 1936 in response to the re-militarisation of the Rhineland had been undertaken, it would have avoided a world war, or at least rendered that war greatly less destructive.

In making the case for law to recognise the realities of warfare, rather than trying to impose a structure of law that works well for contacts on the battlefield and war-room, the inevitable conclusion is that the USA (and her allies) is involved in a war against Al Qa'ida, and not against 'terrorism'. These realities break down further into considerations of the methods employed and the tactical facts in Afghanistan and possibly elsewhere.

Legitimacy, clear aims (which can be expanded or halted depending on circumstances, as opposed to a vague, unending 'war on terrorism'), strategic options and tactical flexibility can all be achieved, and achieved to a far greater

---

14 An excellent example of such thinking is the assertion by McCoubrey and White, 1992, p 94 that Israel in 1967 always had the options, instead of a pre-emptive strike, of calling upon its allies and 'preparing' to defend on its own territory. Exactly who these allies were, apart from a lack of realistic appreciation of whether they would actually commit troops to Israel, is not explained. In fact the very basis of the Israeli Defence Forces' strategic thinking was that no one could be relied upon to give effective aid. A comparison with Czechoslovakia in 1938 is instructive: by this attempt at legal analysis, all the Czechs had to do was rely on their allies and they would be safe from the full horrors of a genocidal regime. Certainly, if the Czechs had had the capability of defeating the Germans by attacking, according to this assessment, they would have been doing so illegally, purely by the fact of attacking. In Israel's case (apart from the issue of allies) the fact was that modern jets could be over all Israeli cities within about four minutes from the closest Arab airfields and the bulk of the country was within artillery range of installations within neighbouring states. Strategically the country was undefendable, as it was open to being cut apart by limited enemy advances at a number of points. The comparison with Czechoslovakia, surrounded by Germany on three sides after the Anschluss with Austria, and with unfriendly Poland and Hungary on the other side, is striking. Czechoslovakia was, of course, easily swallowed, for all the 'protest' in the West – such can be the value of allies.

extent, by labelling bin Laden and his men combatants (and so the Taliban simply become allies of the enemy) and by declaring that a war is being fought against irregular forces. This might not be immediately politically popular, but it is logically, legally, historically and militarily much more efficient. Finally, it is a recognised war aim to identify one man as the beginning and end of it all – the Allies did exactly that against Napoleon (without for an instant drawing any other comparison between Napoleon or his aims with bin Laden and his objectives).

Methods

The strike on the WTC must be regarded as an act of war. This means a conventional attack on a legitimate target. This can be demonstrated in various ways. Firstly, it was in conjunction with a strike on the Pentagon and the four aircraft hijacked were, apparently, only the precursors of many more across the USA. It is possible to make a case of crimes being committed in the hijacking, but:

- this could be compared to the seizure of enemy shipping in war (although this would be a tenuous claim, ignoring the fact that the passengers were obviously illegally flown to destruction);[15]

- of more moment is the fact that the American reaction has been based not on the hijackings but on the strikes against the WTC and Pentagon.

On this second point it is noteworthy that legal military operations can include acts of war crimes without condemning the whole operation – in 1944 the German attack in the Ardennes included a massacre of prisoners (whose perpetrators were prosecuted later) and the use of Germans in American uniforms. Significantly, some of those so captured were (quite legally) executed, yet the author and commander of the plan, Skorzeny, escaped this charge. By analogy, bin Laden should expect a similar freedom from the death penalty, even if it were adjudged that the attack itself was illegal (ie, even if the aircraft had simply been chartered and flown into the buildings without passengers).[16]

Tactics

The issue of making up the term 'unlawful combatants' has developed with the idea that the Taliban, and especially Al Qa'ida, did not have official uniforms to distinguish themselves as combatants and so simply cannot be prisoners of war. This thinking has serious flaws. First, it ignores the facts of history. On such analysis, the Resistance movements of World War II would all be branded as 'illegal', even 'terrorist', lining up the USA and her allies with the Nazis on this important point simply in the pursuit of legal purity. Such categorisation would hold even more strongly for those movements that fought on despite their government's official surrender, including the French, Danish and Yugoslav movements. The EU has recently attempted to square this circle by excluding as terrorists anyone fighting for democracy or its restoration, thus excluding French

---

15 This is an issue worthy of a paper in its own right. Briefly, on the one hand the civilians can be regarded as collateral casualties, as they were not the prime objective; one might surmise that Al Qa'ida would have been happier if their agents had been the only passengers – the civilians on the hijacked aircraft were superfluous to the plan. On the other hand, these civilians could, once the aircraft had been seized, offer no further resistance, and therefore were entitled to full protection as captives, so flying them into buildings was equivalent to shooting prisoners.

16 Interestingly, there are some analogies between bin Laden and Skorzeny, both playing outside the 'rules' of how to fight and both recording remarkable successes. Quite probably, Skorzeny was not executed because the Americans thought they saw a potential in him in terms of using his talents against the Soviets, while bin Laden received American backing to do just that during the Afghan war against the USSR.

and some other Resistance movements.[17] However, this definition is still seriously flawed because, as noted, the most effective partisans were not the Maquis but those of the Yugoslavs and Soviets, who were most assuredly not fighting for democracy. Yet to class these fighters as terrorists fighting against the Nazis is simply repugnant. The significant contributions made by these groups against Nazi Germany would not only be underestimated but would be (legally) condemned. In fact, in response to the torture and killing of the members of these groups, those responsible were legally found guilty. On the German side, there was recognition of the legitimacy of Free French forces, fighting in uniform but despite their government's surrender.[18] In terms of numbers involved, the actions of SOE in some countries would be indistinguishable from those of a small group of 'terrorists' today. In this, as in the previous examples, it would be a gross distortion of both what was right and what was obviously recognised as the practical realities to insist on artificial legal interpretations of 'lawful combat'. From these historical examples, it seems clear that there is plenty to justify legally categorising Al Qa'ida as a legitimate fighting force. Clearly it was (assuming that by publication the organisation is no more) subject to internal discipline, carried arms openly, and was distinguishable from the general population. These are the key aspects of a fighting force (as opposed to, say, a group of bandits). The clear rule to be derived from experience in World War II and since in numerous guerrilla wars is that even an armband will suffice as 'uniform'.

There is every reason, from military history and in terms of practical application on the battlefield and with regard to the right of a state to go to war, to see the present conflict as a war and Al Qa'ida as lawful combatants.

Self-defence

While it is true that the UN Charter recognises only self-defence as justifying war, this is not the sole source of the international law of war. Accepted practice is arguably far more important (see above), for the very reason that it is generally adhered to. Such practice acknowledges that there are provocations that justify a state going to war (since 1904 the idea of a need to formally declare war has fallen away). These include the blockading of a state, even short of actually firing weapons. The rationale is obvious – if a state can be starved or economically forced into submission, that is what war is all about – making someone else bend to your will. If it is illegal to respond to such actions by force, the whole system falls into disrepute by virtue of being ridiculous.[19] The assault on a group or even an individual may justify a country going to war, the favourite example being the War of Jenkin's Ear.[20]

---

17 At the 16 November meeting of the Justice and Home Affairs Council it was agreed that a Declaration should be added to the Framework Decision which reads: 'The Council declares that the framework decision on the fight against terrorism covers acts which are considered by all Member States of the European Union as serious infringements of their criminal laws committed by individuals whose objectives constitute a threat to their democratic societies respecting the rule of law and the civilisation upon which these societies are founded. It has to be understood in this sense and cannot be construed so as to argue that the conduct of those who have acted in the interest of preserving or restoring these democratic values, as was notably the case in some Member States during the Second World War, could now be considered as "terrorist" acts. Nor can it be construed so as to incriminate on terrorist grounds persons exercising their legitimate right to manifest their opinions, even if in the course of the exercise of such right they commit offences.' From www.statewatch.org/news (visited 7 March 2002).
18 For example, regarding those troops captured in the Gazala battle and in Italy.
19 By analogy with domestic criminal law, it would similarly be ridiculous to deny, as a matter of policy, self-defence against someone threatening with a weapon but not actually using it.
20 While it is true that said ear was actually not cut off, it did serve as justification. The reasoning being that if such actions can be done with impunity there is no end to them; hence, for example, the wars against the Barbary pirates, without whom the Mediterranean is undoubtedly a better place.

A few lines of argument can be outlined regarding the position with the UN. The first is to view the UN Charter as 'superior but not binding', exactly as the European Convention on Human Rights is viewed by British courts. Alternatively, or in addition, the concept of the co-existence of the common law and statute in English law can serve as a template. If it is accepted that UN Article 51 on self-defence takes precedence,[21] that does not preclude other laws of war co-existing, for example, the accepted view that a blockade may be taken as an act of war, even though immediate self-defence seems inapplicable. This would be analogous to the co-existence of the royal prerogative and statute.[22] Again, alternatively or in addition, the term 'self-defence' can be developed. Besides being a reaction to a massive physical invasion, this could also sensibly be applied to blockade or assaults on a society's way of life where such assaults can be directly attributed. Thus the presence of a large number of American personnel may be seen as such an assault on Saudi values, directly attributable to government decisions (Saudi and American). Similarly, attacks such as those of September 11, besides their immediate and economic effects, can be seen, by the resultant reactions, as an attack on the very openness that is the defining characteristic of Western society. By this logic, both bin Laden's attack and the American response can be seen as 'self-defence', thus raising the status of the conflict to one of legitimacy. Note that the presence of, say, McDonalds eateries would be unlikely to justify a claim of self-defence, as the link would be less direct.[23]

There is the further line that would see the events as simply a series of bombings back and forth between the USA and Al Qa'ida, including the bombing of the Tanzanian and Kenyan embassies and attacks on US service personnel and ships, contrasted with the destruction of a Sudanese factory and cruise missiles launched against Afghanistan. Again, this would bring into play questions of whether bombing itself is legal, and the accepted view appears to be that it is, so both sides are legitimate in their methods, in pursuit of the aim of self-defence.

Proportionality

It is, of course, up to the injured or threatened state to decide whether or not to go to war fully, or to simply retaliate at an appropriate level. This is sensible not only for reflecting reality but for actually encouraging a reduction in violence – if it is accepted that acts of violence below a full blown war can redress a situation, then there is less temptation to 'be hanged for a sheep as for a lamb'. Thus raids, 'hot pursuit' operations, blockades (Berlin 1948/9; Cuba, 1962) can be accepted without tipping countries into war. Interestingly, where there is criticism of the USA as acting disproportionately there tends also to be criticism of Israel for reacting in a proportionate, 'tit for tat' way. The rule is that it all depends – in some cases, limited operations back and forth can reduce the violence and its impact on civilians, in others it simply encourages a cycle of violence. For example, when Israel dealt with Hizbollah in the Lebanon as an effective force, capturing POWs for exchange, trading shells and rockets, while newsworthy and apparently alarming, this was a classic case of a limited war, fought in a limited way. In the end the IDF decided that the cake was not worth the candle and withdrew. Similarly, hijackings in the Middle East were greatly reduced after the bloodless destruction of three airliners at Beirut

---

21 Though even this can be contended: '… the UN security council, a body which has as little right to set up a court as to raise taxes …' Laughland, 2002.

22 As confirmed in *R v Secretary of State for the Home Department ex parte Northumbria Police Authority* [1988] 1 All ER 556.

23 On which it is supportive to note the effective boycott by consumers of American companies in Arab countries, as reported in *The Guardian*, 18 May 2002.

(1968), while further attacks like that against the Israeli Olympic athletes (1972) were discouraged by the targeted killing by Mossad of those responsible – both sides played by rough rules in this irregular war, the key being that these rules did achieve some limiting of the violence, both in scope and in those whom it affected. Notably, the assassination policy was ended when an innocent Jordanian was misidentified and killed in Sweden. On the other hand, such an approach cannot work where there is no room for diplomatic manoeuvre, such as in the present intifada: a growing number of Palestinians have nothing left to lose, so the military strategic position clearly indicates war rather than raiding.

Thus, if the USA chooses, it may accept the strikes of September 11 as acts of war, either as being part of a series of strikes and counter strikes (including the previous unsuccessful bombing of the WTC, the bombing of American embassies in east Africa, the cruise missile attacks on Afghanistan by Clinton) or as the first act of a new phase, those preceding being equivalent to raids, just as the Six Day War was preceded by numerous actions by both sides. In terms of a justified war, the US demonstrated its failure to be likely or even able to touch bin Laden while he was in Afghanistan;[24] thus the only way in which Americans could stop his attacks on them, short of complying with his demands, was to invade Afghanistan. Here the obvious comparison with Pearl Harbour is interesting.[25] Even if the Japanese had not attacked Wake, Guam and the Philippines, the US would still have been quite entitled to consider that war had started with Japan, solely on the basis of the attack on Pearl. Moreover, given that the Japanese aim was to neutralise American sea power in the western Pacific rather than conquer the USA, it would not have been far fetched for the Japanese only to attack the US Navy at Pearl. In such cases, it must be up to the attacked country to decide whether or not it has suffered an act of war or a raid. From bin Laden's side, the attacks can be argued as being both legal and practical. Certainly, if 18 dead Special Forces men could trigger a retreat from Somalia (1993),[26] then the wider aims of removing US forces from Saudi Arabia, stopping American support for Israel and halting the bombing of and sanctions against Iraq[27] might well have been achieved by a greater operation in the USA itself. Naturally, the question of bin Laden's legitimacy to wage war single-handedly, especially when his government gave permission to the American forces to be based in Saudi Arabia, must be addressed. Here there is a clear parallel in law (if not, again, in personality, aims or morality). Charles de Gaulle fought against the Germans even though his country's government legally allowed the German occupation of France as part of a peace treaty.

Such reasoning would elegantly combine with an assessment that Al Qa'ida are a legitimate fighting force, whose targets (but arguably not methods) of the WTC and the Pentagon was legitimate. The Trade Center was a legitimate target of war because it played an important role in organising the US economy and especially

---

24 The irony of this lies in the fact that the US contributed to pressure exerted on the Sudanese government to expel bin Laden, thus ensuring that he moved from a state that the US could covertly penetrate to one which they could not. American frustration and ineffectiveness was shown in the cruise missile strikes of 1998, which singularly failed to harm or frighten bin Laden.

25 Quite apart from the coincidences of a sudden strike by air out of a literally blue sky, film footage of the massive explosions (in 1941 a pharmacist caught the first mushrooming explosion aboard the *Arizona*), the losses of life – some 2,000 and some 4,000, as well as the eerie timing of an investigation as to why the *Arizona* went down the way she did, on 11 September 2001 itself to be followed by investigations on why the WTC towers collapsed.

26 There are some indications that bin Laden planned or helped to some degree in the 'Black Hawk Down' ambush.

27 These three aims were aired in a documentary on bin Laden, made before 11 September 2001: *Osama bin Laden*, Biography Channel, screened 9 April 2002.

those multi-national companies being supported by American foreign policy. The very facts that the attack led to fears that it would deepen a recession and/or cause the US to withdraw from foreign affairs into isolationism are proof that it was legitimate – it was important to the economy and its destruction could influence policy (the aim of war, as Clauswitz accurately noted). It is very difficult to see bin Laden's attack as illegal whilst the Dambusters Raid and bombing a country's economy in general are seen as legal.[28]

Weapons of mass destruction

The preceding leads on to a consideration of the latest justification of American actions or proposed actions. Once again, the details of the military hardware seem to escape the notice of both lawyers and the Bush Administration. In such a definition, 'mass destruction' means the destruction of countries, of continents, of species (large in number), of macro ecosystems, even of human (and most other) life on Earth. That this all has realistic application and is not mere hyperbole was demonstrated in the famous TAPPS Report (predicting 'Nuclear Winter' in the event of a major nuclear war). This is in accord with the legal finding that nuclear weapons are not *per se* illegal.[29] Just as one can distinguish between £10,000 and £2,000,000, so there are different classes and types of nuclear weapons, some of which are of mass destruction, others not. The key aims in banning weapons of mass destruction are in keeping with the stated aims of limiting gratuitous suffering and of effectiveness – it is simply ineffective to wage a war of such destructiveness as it inevitably harms everyone, including the perpetrator. As noted, even an unopposed nuclear strike by either superpower (which means thousands of nuclear explosions) would both effectively equal a weapon of mass destruction (the sum of the warheads) and be self-defeating: the resultant destruction of the present climate and the expansion of radiation would simply mean that the 'victor' would enjoy a more prolonged death, both as a state and for its citizens. So the USA is simply wrong to try to justify actions or future actions as against 'weapons of mass destruction' because:

- such do not actually exist in the countries targeted (but they do in the USA);
- simply getting the FBI[30] (tellingly, not a military organisation) to re-classify even conventional bombs as being of 'mass destruction' both brings the attempt into ridicule and makes the legal point meaningless, as all countries have such bombs (if Timothy McVeigh could make one more or less by himself they must be, actually or potentially, ubiquitous).

It is just wrong to try to cover one's errors (a lack of sealed cockpits, proper checks by well paid and trained people, strengthened vital areas in aircraft, accurate

---

28 The ideas of prosecuting Germans, especially Goering, for strategic bombing, and similarly Doenitz, for the U-boat campaign, were dropped for the reason that the allies had found these methods of warfare to be very effective. The argument that there were better charges and evidence is not convincing – the evidence of bombing was indisputable, as was Goering's direct involvement. For example, 'The Commander-in-Chief [Goering] appeared once more at the Channel to be on the spot and to give the order for the beginning of the operation [to bomb London] in person': Galland, 1989, p 46. The same held true for Doenitz, yet in his case there is not even the basis of better charges than that of waging economic war (the main casualties of which are civilians). Despite a U-boat campaign claiming the lives of at least 30,000 merchant seamen (Preston, 2000, p 104), Doenitz was only sentenced to 10 years' imprisonment: Keegan, 1979, p 74. The Allies simply found economic warfare effective, in bombing the Axis, in blockading Germany and in an extremely successful US Navy submarine offensive against the Japanese merchant fleet.

29 Ticehurst, 1996.

30 *The Guardian*, 23 March 2002.

intelligence) with the claim that something only happened because the other side did not 'play fair' and therefore must be a criminal, leading to the logically absurd statement that the 'shoe bomber' had a weapon of mass destruction.

All of the above should satisfy us that the Bush Administration is wrong in law on several counts. It is wrong to classify Al Qa'ida as terrorists or 'unlawful combatants', denying them POW status. It is wrong to declare a war 'on terrorism'. It is wrong to claim 'self-defence' in vague and all-encompassing terms, so that any country could be a target under such a definition. It is wrong to try to justify further moves in terms of acting against possessors of weapons of mass destruction. Critics of the USA are also wrong in condemning it for a lack of proportionality, and for pursuing a war beyond the point of absolute self-defence. The strikes on the WTC and the Pentagon should have been seen as an act of war by a recognised armed force (which does not exclude the possibility of putting individuals on trial for specific war and other crimes, as the Nuremberg and Tokyo trials established). As an act of war the USA did not need, and should not have sought, further justification. Doing so has only undermined its own legal position, the legitimacy of such law in general and has resulted in the USA hampering itself militarily.

Practically ...

While it is tempting for politicians to label opponents as 'terrorists', this being the modern equivalent of 'infidels', worthy of neither respect nor mercy (and damning any who might show such tendencies), the results are not worth the fleeting political advantage.

The first problem is the title. Legal writers have failed to accurately define 'terrorist', reflecting the skirting of this issue by statute drafters (above). Peter Mandelson recently[31] made an attempt, trying to justify treating with the PIRA on the one hand and condemning Al Qa'ida on the other. He argued that the difference lay in the aims of the two: the Irish had a comprehensible political agenda (basically of independence from the UK), but the Arab group was driven solely by 'hatred', and that was not politics – it was simply hatred, with which there is no room for reasoning. In this analysis he was half right. In the absence of a sensible definition from the legal side, it seems fitting to use the definition of a terrorist provided by war studies. In this, the definition is that a group using violence but with no or only remote chances of achieving their aims is a terrorist group. This fits well with the previous empirical approach to the law of war. In short, if they have no chance, then their actions are gratuitous, causing unnecessary suffering. For example, there was no chance that the Baader-Meinhof group could ever cause the destruction of the liberal-capitalist way of life in West Germany in the 1970s. Similar arguments hold for the Angry Brigade, the Red Army Faction, the Japanese Red Army, the Weathermen and the Symbionese Liberation Army. These were tiny organisations with no hope of success, even in their own terms. The same, as was recognised by Mandelson, does not hold true for the PIRA. However, the argument that the same does hold true for Al Qa'ida, and that hatred is 'not politics', does not work. In the first place, there was a very real chance that in reaction to the strikes alone, besides any further operations intended or yet to come, the USA would withdraw from its current interventionist role in world affairs, actively supporting its own version of globalisation. After all, as noted, it took only one real firefight, with the deaths of just 18 servicemen to make them pull out of Somalia, and even fewer casualties to

---

31 *The Guardian,* 29 December 2001 and *The Year the World Changed,* Channel 4, 29 December 2001.

cause a withdrawal from Haiti. Even if Al Qa'ida is totally defeated it cannot be denied that they had a chance.

On the point of 'hatred', Mandelson is surprisingly ill-informed in political history, much of which seems to be about hatred as the guiding light in political affairs. The most obvious example is Nazi Germany, in which the drive of hatred was stronger than anything, even the state's own survival. In short, pure hatred *is* a political creed – it was the Nazi Party's defining aspect, and that certainly was a political party, and one with which the British government negotiated. Nor were the Nazis unique. Hatred was obviously the driving motive behind political forces such as Idi Amin, Pol Pot and Stalin (and is for Mugabe today).

Further, as noted above, bin Laden has not been driven purely by hatred, as Mandelson claimed. Undoubtedly there is much hatred within him, yet his aims are clear and comprehensible ones.[32]

The definition proffered not only avoids the debasement of the term 'terrorist' but also serves to clearly mark out those who fall within its definition. Thus, governments are not left in the position of having to back track on previous tough-sounding statements about not negotiating with terrorists, nor is every failed bank robber afforded the luxury of being classified as a POW (and, his war being over, entitled to release).

The definition holds much greater advantages for the US government, however. If the enemy is not a terrorist but an irregular fighter, then there are great tactical advantages. If the former, he is a criminal, and due process of properly attempting an arrest, assembling evidence and then sentencing, if guilty, to a time of imprisonment – all of which may prove to be too little or too much to fit in with the wider aims of the government. Should the Americans come up behind bin Laden sunning himself on a rock, drinking tea, if he is classed as a criminal they are bound to try to arrest him. If he is classed as an irregular fighter they could do the same, or they could simply shoot him there. While the laws of war forbid shooting POWs, they do not enforce the taking of prisoners of fighters who have not surrendered – in other words, as noted, ambushes are perfectly legal: a surprise attack is perfectly within the rules. If an irregular fighter is captured, there is no need to assemble evidence, or go through a trial. The government could simply keep POWs as long as the war lasts (after which they become an embarrassment anyway). In fact, the government could use such POWs as bargaining chips, increasing its flexibility at strategic and diplomatic levels.

Leading on from this, if the USA were to class Al Qa'ida as an irregular force, it could retain strategic options that are closed as soon as the organisation is classed as 'terrorist'. These would include negotiations over particular issues (like single prisoner exchanges, just as local surrenders and arrangements are agreed in war) up to a general settlement. Alternatively, should it all become too much for the USA, victory can simply be declared and 'the boys brought back home'. This is not nearly as acceptable in terms of a criminal – the police are not supposed to close a case if they know who the guilty party is, especially if there is no statute of limitations on the crime committed (and an example of the tenacity of the police approach was demonstrated with Biggs of the Great Train Robbery). By contrast, Germany and Japan were allies of the USA within some five years of 1945. If this sounds, now, too unlikely, it is worth noting, again, that bin Laden started his military career as an ally of the US, so presumably he could be coaxed back into at least neutrality. If that seems an

---

32 These being, as noted, the removal of US forces from Saudi Arabia, a halt of bombing and sanctions against Iraq, and a withdrawal of US support for Israel, especially in terms of its effects on the Palestinians.

unpalatable option, note that the 'irregular fighter' approach does offer a solution more in keeping with American national myths of a shootout, pure and, as is said, simple (see below).

All these lessons were amply demonstrated in general and in detail in the UK's struggle against the PIRA. In the 'Death on the Rock' case (above), the three PIRA agents were let into Gibraltar because there was insufficient evidence to arrest them at the border crossing. Then a tortuous, and flawed, story was concocted to demonstrate that they could not have been arrested inside the territory. Had they been classed as irregulars, they could simply have been shot in their car at the border – perhaps not cricket, but well within the bounds of warfare. If that was adjudged too dangerous, they could have been shot at any time without the need for an elaborate cover story[33] (which was publicly rejected by the ECHR). Naturally, once they were down and posed no further threat, it would be against the laws of war to continue shooting at them, thus showing the clear boundaries even in such operations. Such a classification would also have the advantage that soldiers would be used as soldiers and not as some kind of super police. As soldiers they can be relied upon to know the rules of war, and if individuals breach these, then their punishment can ensue with the military's co-operation and without prejudicing morale. Strategically, the UK government could have released all PIRA captives without enraging those who saw people convicted of murder serving less than one year. Nor would the situation of any PIRA people captured, convicted, then having served their sentence free to continue their struggle (unless their release was part of a wider diplomatic venture, that is, one controlled by the government and not the courts).

On the issue of POW status and questioning, note that POW status does *not* render the prisoner immune from questioning;[34] it simply limits the answers he is required to give (the famous 'name, rank and serial number'). In fact, this is a position more onerous to the prisoner than is the traditional situation of criminal prisoners, who may maintain absolute silence. Practically, short of torture (and quite possibly not even then), useful information cannot be forced out of prisoners, so a mythical 'right to question' (ie a right denied POWs) is not of much use anyway. However, there are very well known methods of extracting intelligence from POWs. These include putting them together in barracks in order to let them talk (all recorded by electronic bugs) and using 'stool pigeons' (as any devotee of Billy Wilder films could have told the American administration). Clearly, what is not conducive to getting information is to separate the prisoners and to forbid talking. The prisoners may well be determined, dangerous men, but the very fact of their captivity shows there are limits to their abilities – the Americans are the ones with the guns in Guantanamo Bay.

Therefore, far from being a statement of weakness, or of granting bin Laden unnecessary power, classing Al Qa'ida as irregular fighters actually opens up options to the USA, including the freer use of force, legitimately, and with the bonus of being in a consistent position[35] far less susceptible to criticism than the present approach.

---

33 A large part of this cover was that the PIRA agents might have remotely detonated a bomb several miles away. However, the Army well knew that 'A characteristic of fighting in built-up areas is the appalling quality of VHF radio communications': Dewar, 1992, p 85, a point repeated on pp 101 and 106.

34 It appears that a myth circulated that POWs could not be questioned, but this is absolutely not true. Of course, a POW is not bound to give any answer, or even truthful ones, to such questioning. Personal email communications with Tony Rogers, Lauterpacht Research Centre for International Law, University of Cambridge, 14/2/02 and 7/3/02.

35 Even Alexander could not sustain a war with vague aims: his 'ten-year campaign of uninterrupted victories was destined to remain without parallel in history; yet once the question "what for" had been asked, it took only a few days for the campaign to end'. Creveld, 1991, p 188.

Thus, politically and militarily, there are few and only ephemeral advantages to categorising those opposing a government by violent means as 'terrorist'. It should be clear that any POW can still be properly charged with war crimes or other crimes,[36] upon which there seems no reason why such individuals should not go before 'independent and impartial judges'[37] for trial. It seems extraordinary that the principle of an international trial should be acceptable to the USA regarding the Nazis but not for Al Qa'ida and the Taliban. Militarily, strategic and tactical flexibility is lost, while politically, grand strategy and diplomacy are compromised, besides the needless costs to social institutions, as censorship increases and political debate is stifled. In other words, the very freedoms representing the core of Western society are damaged in what are officially operations against crime. Either the response is dangerously out of proportion or the threat is above that of criminals.

By declaring Al Qa'ida an irregular force with which the USA is at war, military flexibility is re-established and a military conflict is not distorted to look like a police operation. It means that there are far more possibilities of disentangling the USA, should that be necessary. It establishes a full and globally recognised set of rules of conduct that the military know and understand, instead of politicians making up 'rules of engagement' on the hoof.

Philosophically ...

Since the end of the certainty provided by Christianity, there has been a search in the West to regain that feeling of security. On occasion this is manifested in the details, such as the absolute belief that DNA evidence can *never* be wrong, and sometimes in a wider perspective. With the latter, the principal idea is that the rule of law can guide and control people's actions. This appears to be especially rooted in the Anglo-Saxon world. For example, the response from Britain to the atrocities of World War II was to push for the establishment of the ECHR. It is incontestable that this was a good thing, but it is only a tool. By itself, the ECHR cannot guarantee good government, contrary to the attitude exemplified by a familiar moan in Britain that 'there ought to be a law against it' – the simple fact of the law will not cure the problem.

This is the first point that seems to have been missed in the declaration of a 'war against terror'. The law is, philosophically, a totem, with only the power invested in it by the people. If some people do not believe in it, then it will have no power over them. As such, it can be a guide for action, but simply declaring an act or person illegal will not solve a problem. The law itself cannot enforce obedience. As a tool, the law must be used wisely, with a conscious awareness of its limitations. In terms of labelling enemies, careful thought must be given, because of the great temptation to call the enemy 'terrorist', particularly for politicians or nations with some insecurity about the legitimacy of their power.

The American legal reaction

Part of the American response has been distorted by the political need to portray Al Qa'ida as completely outside civilised conduct, and clearly this has reached the level of a call for a crusade against Al Qa'ida. Notably, this apparently does not stop short of Al Qa'ida itself but could include its allies and sympathisers. Bush has first accepted much of the narrow legal approach to war in trying to justify his actions, which are guided by the demands of military considerations, resulting in erroneous attempts at legitimisation.

---

36 Apart from domestic crimes such as murder and kidnapping, it is possible that Al Qa'ida forces may be indictable for crimes against humanity. Robertson, 1999, p 294.

37 Robertson, G in *The Independent*, 15 January 2001.

Thus, the USA and her allies need to express a justification beyond an alleged breach of law. Just as religion is interpreted and is not an entity with the power to punish transgressors, so the law is not a separate entity, upon which all can be blamed or justified. To say 'the law requires it' is merely to shift responsibility one step, but not away from human shoulders. There must be a reason why people have decided that that is what the law should be; it did not create itself. So, labelling bin Laden *et al* as criminals is not an explanation of the USA's war aims. The reason why Afghanistan was attacked, and what the USA wants there, and any other campaigns mooted in this war, need to be clearly put and understood. If the reason is to make the world safe for Big Business, then that should be understood, and if it is, the relative costs and benefits may well lead to different conclusions from those brought about by a distortion of the philosophy of law.

Laws must, ultimately, be effective and enjoy general acceptance. The lack of the first has reduced the drug laws in the UK and the USA into causing an incurable ulcer in the body politic. The lack of the latter, apparently, meant that even in Nazi Germany genocide could never be made legal. A combination of both meant that Prohibition in the USA had the reverse effect, on the law specifically and on the role of law in general. Specifically, the consumption of alcohol actually rose during (because of?) Prohibition, while the corruption of and disrespect for the law that it engendered ate into the heart of law enforcement. In addition, it virtually created the Mafia, so the law actually increased the level of law breaking and made society less safe – the reverse of its aims. Therefore, trying to use law as a thing which acts by itself, to hide behind it in terms of a state's aims, risks creating the very opposite result. So the declaration of one side being 'terrorist', while the other side is fighting legally, risks undermining all belief in the war because the distinctions are neither clear nor consistent.[38] Further, trying to justify the war in terms of 'weapons of mass destruction' is wrong because it brings into question the possession by the US government of some weapons genuinely in that category, and when the classification is reduced (see above) in order to be applied in this struggle, it makes the law, and so the justification, meaningless.

The misuse of law, ironically in the name of being bound by it, results in an erosion of international law, when it becomes apparent that it serves mainly as a legitimisation of American interests[39] (as the economic equivalent certainly appears to be). This in turn causes the law to be less effective, and so all lose, again – ironically, the USA most of all as it is the most active global power. Long ago Machiavelli recognised that 'there are two ways of fighting: by law or by force'.[40] This is not to say that war is devoid of laws and rules, but rather that the world of legality and trust should not be conflated with that of the soldier. Yet this is precisely what the Bush Administration appears to be trying to do. In the law of war, a line drawn that is obeyed is better than a more ambitious line that is not. To

---

38 For example, there is the striking case of Otto Reich, the new American Assistant Secretary of State for the Western Hemisphere, who knowingly supports Orlando Bosch, whose activities against Cuba are directly comparable to Al Qa'ida's tactics. *The Guardian*, 18 February 2002, p 19.

39 Dramatically reflecting this is the case of *USA v Brodie, Brodie and Sabzali* Eastern District Court, Pennsylvania, 3 April 2002, in which three people, including a non-US citizen, were convicted (sentencing to come) under the American Trading with the Enemy Act 1917, for selling water purification tablets to Cuba. This ruling came despite the actual availability of American companies' products in Cuba, notably Coca-Cola. Personal communication with Troy Lavers, University of Kent at Canterbury, 10 April 2002.

40 Machiavelli, 1981, p 99. It is possible to go further, noting that he saw 'that the foundation of all states subsists in good laws and good arms, and that the former are dependent upon the latter': Anglo, 1971, p 116. This, at the least, shows the view that the aims and methods of these are distinct, and that warfare cannot be run like a courtroom battle.

achieve this, military realities must be recognised and made part of the law. The more a disobeyed line is insisted upon, the weaker international law will become. In terms of domestic law, the distortions required in order to make these irregulars fit the framework of criminals eat at the heart of the very liberal freedoms upon which modern Western culture, society and economy depend – thus achieving bin Laden's goal. Sweeping overreactions and the desire to find evidence that will survive in court are counter-productive. This has been painfully illustrated several times in the struggle with PIRA, with noted gross miscarriages of justice springing directly from pressure to find criminal proof against someone. The resulting cases, such as the Birmingham Six and the Guildford Four, were not only catastrophic for those incarcerated, but also dealt severe blows to confidence in the justice system. This is what Denning realised when he railed against appeals in these cases – if successful they would reveal the corruption within the system (though he seemed to blame those appealing rather than the system for the no-win situation that it was forced into). On the other hand, if they had simply been detained as enemy soldiers, then they could have been released when the identities of the real bombers became apparent, with the two sets of people simply exchanged, one imprisoned as enemy captives, the other set free. Mistakes in detention occur in war (as, for example, PG Wodehouse found out), but these are of minor embarrassment, if at all, and certainly do not call into question the fairness and reason upon which society is based. Where governments have got such detentions very wrong, notably (and perhaps aptly) the American government's detention of Japanese-Americans during World War II, the focus was on the fairness of the procedure (Italian-Americans and German-Americans were not detained), its reasoning (the infantry regiment of Japanese-Americans finally permitted fought outstandingly) and the conditions of detention. For the purposes of law and national security (mistaken as they were), there was no requirement to impoverish the detainees or to exile them to an inhospitable area with a harsh climate and poor housing. This last point was echoed in the British detentions (though questions of class brought quick improvements to conditions for the Moseleys), and in the sheer idiocy of imprisoning refugees from Hitler's Germany as 'enemy aliens'. However, these clear flaws aside, the basic legality was not overturned.[41] Apart from the specific issues, these cases also demonstrate the flimsiness of asserting that the law is neutral and apart from politics – these decisions were obviously directed by political sentiment. This shows the danger of trying to encompass political aims and beliefs within legal ones – neither side is well served.

In terms of legal battles, the attempt to legitimise everything in terms of being legally justified also causes losses in detail. The 'Death on the Rock' case, already well noted, highlighted this further philosophical problem, in that a specific cover story had to be concocted specifically for the legal position, which then predictably unravelled under the very scrutiny inherent in legal systems.[42]

---

41 In the USA, although compensation has been paid, this was for the unnecessary suffering rather than for an admission that the Act of Congress authorising it was illegal. In fact, '[t]he leading civil libertarian in the [Supreme] Court, Hugo Black, wrote the opinion in *Korematsu v USA* (1944), upholding the constitutionality of the relocation of Japanese Americans during World War II'. O'Brien, 2000, p 281. In the UK, 'in *Liversidge v Anderson* [1942] AC 206, a Defence of the Realm regulation was upheld which allowed a minister to order detention of persons whom he had reasonable cause to believe to be of hostile origins or associations and in need of subjection to preventative control'. Allen and Thompson, 2000, p 444.

42 It is tempting to look on the British government learning, on the international legal stage, the lesson its own criminal justice system routinely delivers to domestic criminals – that feeble alibis and stories will often be pulled apart.

The final lesson is that it is in everyone's interests, especially the USA's, to take responsibility for one's actions, and not to rely on a cloak of legality as allegedly determining those actions. If the USA does not clearly state that it wants bin Laden dead or captured in the interests of the USA, but instead relies on the justifications of self-defence, destroying weapons of mass destruction and acting against 'terrorism', then it risks hampering or even jeopardising its chances of victory, the operations of its troops, the values of its society and the law – both domestically and internationally. It is sufficient to fight, even hate, your enemy; it is not necessary or effective also to try and see him purely as a criminal. Law is not a sensible instrument of war. As Sun Tzu wrote as a conclusion in the chapter 'Dispositions': 'Those skilled in war cultivate politics, preserve the laws and institutions, and are therefore able to formulate victorious policies.'[43]

---

43 General Hanzhang, in Sun Tzu, 1994, pp 88–89.

References

Allen, M and Thompson, B (2000) *Cases and Materials on Constitutional and Administrative Law*, 6th edn, London: Blackstone

Anglo, S (1971) *Machiavelli*, London: Paladin/Granada

Best, G (1994) *War and Law Since 1945*, Oxford: OUP

Campbell, D (2002) 'Friends of terrorism' *The Guardian*, 18 February

Cassese, A (2001) *International Law*, Oxford: OUP

Chandler, D (1994) *On the Napoleonic Wars*, London: Greenhill

Clausewitz, C von (1976/1994) 'Key concepts', from *On War*, Howard, M and Paret, P (ed and trans), Princeton: Princeton UP, in Freedman, L (ed), *War*, 1994, Oxford: OUP

Creveld, M van (1991) *On Future War*, London: Brassey's

Dewar, M, Col (1992) *War in the Streets*, London: BCA/David and Charles

Evans, MD (1996) *International Law Documents*, 3rd edn, London: Blackstone

Galland, A (1989) 'The Battle of Britain', in Young, P (ed), *Decisive Battles of World War II*, New York: Gallery

Gray, W (1994) 'Storm over Georgia' 170 Strategy and Tactics 5

Keegan, J (gen ed) (1979) *World War II*, London: BCA/Bison

Laughland, J (2002) 'This is not justice' *The Guardian*, 16 February

McCoubrey, H and White, ND (1992) *International Law and Armed Conflict*, Aldershot: Dartmouth

Machiavelli, N (1981) *The Prince*, 3rd edn, Bull, G (trans), Harmondsworth: Penguin

Meltzer, D (1984) 'The bomber offensive', unpublished MA dissertation, University of Zimbabwe

O'Brien, DM (2000) *Storm Centre*, 5th edn, New York: WW Norton

O'Brien, WV (1981/1994) 'Just war doctrine and revolutionary war', from *War: The Conduct of Just and Limited War*, New York: Preager, in Freedman, L (ed), *War*, Oxford: OUP

Preston, A (2000) 'The wolf packs unleashed', in Preston, A (ed), *Hitler's War*, London: Quantum

Robertson, G (1999) *Crimes Against Humanity*, Harmondsworth: Penguin

Sun Tzu (1994) *The Art of War*, Shibing, Y (trans), Ware: Wordsworth Reference

Ticehurst, R (1996) 'Are nuclear weapons legal?' 2 War Studies Journal 1, 107

Wyngaert, C van den (ed) (1996) *International Criminal Law*, The Hague: Kluwer

Cases cited

Kawasaki Kisen Kabushiki Kaisha v Bantham Steam Ship Company [1939] 2 KB 544

Korematsu v USA (1944) US Federal Supreme Court

Liversidge v Anderson [1942] AC 206

McCann v UK (1996) 21 EHRR 97

R v Secretary of State for the Home Department ex parte Northumbria Police Authority [1988] 1 All ER 556

USA v Brodie, Brodie and Sabzali (2002) Eastern District Court, Pennsylvania, 3 April

Chapter 7
International refugee law: excluding the Palestinians
Siraj Sait

International refugee law faces its sternest test as the 'war against terror' continues. States can retain their strictest entry controls regarding economic migrants, but the fundamental principle of non-refoulement obliges them not to arbitrarily reject asylum claims from forced migrants. Yet, states 'pay lip service to the importance of honouring the right to seek asylum, but in practice devote significant resources to keep refugees away from their borders'.[1] International refugee law, through a combination of human rights strategies, seeks to balance a state's legitimate security concerns with the protection of refugees fleeing persecution or loss of homeland. What started as a modest Western project, the 1951 Convention on the Status of Refugees ('Refugee Convention'), is being revitalised through some bold new interpretations of its restrictive concepts and supplemented with re-engagement with issues such as gender persecution, internally displaced persons and socio-economic rights. Current research and policy initiatives focus on proactive measures, innovative protection models and durable solutions. But there is little cheer for the estimated five million Palestinian refugees – the largest and longest existing such population anywhere – who have been skilfully kept out of its domain. For the Palestinians, the events of 11 September 2001 could not have come at a worse time and marks a further retreat of international refugee law itself.

This essay will by implication highlight the shortcomings of the international refugee regime[2] and the application of human rights to the Middle East crisis. Its focus, however, will be a reflection on the significance of withholding even the limited levels of available refugee protection from the Palestinian refugees. At least one in every four refugees in the world is a Palestinian, but they are the only group of refugees excluded from the Refugee Convention[3] and the protection mandate of the United Nations High Commission for Refugees (UNHCR). The framers of the Refugee Convention had, justifiably, in mind the Nazi persecution of Jews (1933–45), and the 'the convention's inclusion of persecution for reasons of race, religion and nationality speaks most directly to that experience'.[4] But in choosing 'events occurring in Europe'[5] to be the framework for the Convention, they ignored a more recent refugee producing event – *al Nakba* (the catastrophe) of the 1947–48 war, whereby over 750,000 Palestinians, constituting an overwhelming majority of the population of Mandate Palestine, were forced to leave their homeland. This exclusion of the Palestinians from the global regime and their subsequent allocation to an alternative framework was to create a people displaced from both their land and their refugee rights.[6]

---

1 Hathaway, 1996, p 1.
2 See Tuitt, 1996, p 6; Hathaway, 1990, p 181.
3 See UNHCR, 1992, para 142.
4 See Steinbock, 1999, p 18.
5 Refugee Convention, Article B. The 1967 Refugee Protocol removed the geographical and temporal restrictions without changing the grounds under which a refugee could be accorded asylum. See Hathaway, 1990, p 162.
6 Akram, 2000b, p 4.

In removing Palestinian refugees from its central instrument, international refugee law has configured itself to sustain the marginalisation of the Palestinians through a combination of myths, conditionalities and strategies. Thus, refugees are seen as part of the problem for the stability of the Middle East rather than victims awaiting redress.[7] While refugee camps exist on the map, there is little concern about the fate of refugees living within and their rights are framed as a series of trade-offs with other bands of political issues. Their status is almost interminably 'temporary' and contingent on the creation of a yet unknown form of a Palestinian state as if it has little to do with present day Israel. On the political front, the post-September 11 powerbrokers add several new pre-requisites to the exercise of basic Palestinian refugee rights, including the as yet undefined 'internal reform' of the Palestinian Authority and renunciation of the right to resist Israel. However, this is not a mere political eclipse. The non-recognition of Palestinian refugees by the Refugee Convention in itself may not be fatal, because it is a limited regime that does not address causes, temporary protection or repatriation. But this, added to the lack of protection by the UNHCR, compromises access to general provisions under international refugee law, the application of the relevant UN resolutions and general principles of international law.

September 11 falls in a long line of bizarre events and machinations happening elsewhere which have had the ability to reinvent and rewrite contemporary Palestinian history. Theodor Herzl, considered the father of Zionism, in 1896 influentially canvassed Palestine as a better choice for a Jewish homeland over Argentina, predicting that 'governments of all countries scourged by anti-Semitism [will be] keenly interested in assisting [the Jews] to obtain the sovereignty [the Jews] want'.[8] The treaty between the British Commissioner in Cairo, Sir Henry MacMahon, and Sharif Hussein of Mecca (1915–16) that Britain would support the independence of the Arabs in return for Arab armies fighting for the British against the Ottoman Turkey was only to be reneged. The Sykes-Picot Agreement[9] the same year saw the British and the French carve the lands of the Levant between themselves and set Palestine on course for its subsequent dismemberment. The 1917 Balfour Declaration cleared the way for the 'establishment in Palestine of a national home for the Jewish people'.

American President Woodrow Wilson's 1918 speech that statesmen would henceforth ignore self-determination 'at their own peril' apparently did not apply to Palestine. The brazen 1917 Balfour Declaration, handing over Palestinian lands held in sacred trust for a Jewish homeland to be created, took place several years before the League of Nations validated British administration of Palestine. In 1922, the League of Nations reversed its provisional recognition of Palestine people as an independent nation and issued the British Mandate providing retrospective recognition of the specious Balfour Declaration. Malcolm Yapp notes that the 'principal explanation of how the Declaration was transformed into the mandate lies in the manner in which the mandate was drafted'.[10] While Chaim Weizmann

---

7 Falk notes that 'the term "Palestinian refugee problem" carries the connotation of the international institutions and states "coping with the fact that there are Palestinian refugees", but does not properly include and illustrate the real problems Palestinian refugees face living under harsh and inhumane conditions in refugee camps'. Falk, 2000, p 217.

8 Herzl argued that the new Jewish State would stand as a 'rampart of Europe against Asia, an outpost of civilisation as opposed to barbarism'. Herzl, 1946, Chapter II.

9 The secret agreement between Sir Mark Sykes of Britain and Georges Picot of France was concluded in May 1916 during World War I, between Great Britain and France, with the assent of Russia, for the dismemberment of the Ottoman Empire. It led to the division of Turkish-held Syria, Iraq, Lebanon, and Palestine into various French and British-administered areas.

10 Yapp, 1995, p 15.

and the Zionists played a critical role in the drafting process, there was unsurprisingly no role for the indigenous people and no consideration of the impending mass production of refugees. As John Strawson notes, 'international law is not an innocent bystander in Palestine'.[11]

The Balfour Declaration did note that 'nothing shall be done to prejudice the civil and religious rights of existing non-Jewish communities in Palestine', language reproduced in the preamble to the Palestine Mandate. However, it was naïve to assume that a Jewish political presence would not fundamentally disturb the rights of existing Palestinians. Though the Mandate contains several professions of autonomy and equal rights, it was founded on the basis that there would be mass Jewish immigration into Palestine.[12] The transformation of Palestine into Jewish Israel was managed through domestic laws, which from the vantage point of the 21st century would violate virtually every possible international human rights norm. The Mandate created the basis for a Jewish nascent state in the Jewish Agency while the Palestinian population was forced to react to developments largely beyond their control. With the creation of the State of Israel this process was legislatively managed on a grand scale. Starting from the 1950s, laws such as the Absentee Property law, the Law of Return and the Citizenship Law stripped Palestinians of their property, residency and citizenship while Israel wooed Jews all over the world with promises of unrestricted immigration, settlement packages and automatic citizenship.

Competing narratives regarding the creation of the State of Israel and Palestinian refugees have long obfuscated the core issues of the right of return of Palestinian refugees and the legitimacy of Jewish settlements in the occupied territories, as well as the distribution of responsibilities between Israel and its Arab neighbours. The dominant Israeli discourses on the formation of Israel were built around Golda Meir's infamous claim that 'there is no such thing as the Palestinians'. Israeli propaganda had it that it was created from 'land without a people for a people without land' and the few Palestinians who exited left voluntarily on the orders of Arab commanders.[13] Such a line of argument, influential even today, is apparent in Chaim Weizmann's 1949 letter written to President Truman:

> [The refugee problem] was not created by us. It was not the birth of Israel which created the Arab refugee problem, as our enemies now proclaim, but the Arab attempt to prevent that birth by armed force. These people are not refugees in the sense in which the term has been sanctified by the martyrdom of millions in Europe – they are a part of an aggressor group which failed and makes no secret of its intention to resume aggression. They left the country last year at the bidding of their leaders and as part of an Arab strategic plan. But in spite of all this we are, for humanitarian reasons, ready to contribute as far as we can towards a solution of this problem.[14]

However, there is now abundant archival material to establish that the expulsion of the Palestinians was carried out according to a 'combination of military-strategic, demographic-settlement, and Zionist ideological considerations'.[15] It is no longer merely the Saids, Falks and Chomskys or the Arab writers who challenge the Zionist discourse. Since the 1980s, a group of 'new Israeli historians'[16] including Benny Morris, Tom Segev, Simha Flapan, Illan Pappe and Avi Shlaim have pointed

---

11 Strawson, 2002, p 251.
12 Maslaha, 1992, pp 93–141.
13 However, it is important to recognise that there have been minority voices recognising the refugee problem since the creation of Israel. See Barzilai, 2002.
14 Weizmann, 1949, p 4.
15 Maslaha, 1997, p 8; see also Karmi et al, 2000.
16 See Pappe, 1997; Pappe, 1999; Morris, 2000; Shlaim, 2001; Segev, 2001; Flapan, 1987.

to direct Israeli complicity for the Middle East conflict and the refugee crisis. For example, Benny Morris acknowledges that 'in general, the emigration [of Palestinians] was a direct result of, and response to, specific Haganah (and in small measure, IZL) attacks and retaliatory strikes and to fears of such attacks'.[17] Walid Khalidi quotes Moshe Dayan's rather startling admission:

> Jewish villages were built in the place of Arab villages, and I do not blame you because geography books no longer exist, the Arab villages are not there either. There is not one single place built in this country that did not have a former Arab population.[18]

The Palestinians' protests were in vain as in 1947 the United Nations (UN) sent in the Commission of Inquiry (UNSCOP), who in turn recommended expediting the two state solution. The UN General Assembly Resolution 181 (II) of 29 November 1947 partitioning Palestine nonetheless sought, on paper, parity for the two peoples to establish states on the former mandated territory of Palestine, and the duty of both states to respect minorities while internationalising Jerusalem. Interestingly, the resolution was silent on the issue of the ethnic composition of each state and envisaged no movement of population. Following the exodus of the Palestinian refugees during the Arab-Israeli war, the lobbying of the UN Mediator for Palestine, Count Folke Bernadotte, led to General Assembly Resolution 194 (III) of 11 December 1948 to the effect that:

> ... the refugees wishing to return to their homes and live at peace with their neighbours should be permitted to do so at the earliest practicable date, and that compensation should be paid for the property of those choosing not to return and for loss of or damage to property which, under principles of international law or in equity, should be made good by the Governments or authorities responsible.

Resolution 194 also established the UN Conciliation Commission for Palestine (UNCCP), *inter alia* to extend protection to the refugees and achieve a final settlement for them. This was followed by the creation of the United Nations Relief and Works Agency for Palestinian Refugees in the Near East (UNWRA) on 19 November 1949.[19] While UNWRA continues to provide humanitarian assistance to this day, the UNCCP first had its mandate reduced under General Assembly Resolution 394 (V) of 14 December 1950 and then folded up without much ado. Thus, the Palestinian refugees have not received 'protection',[20] as distinct from material assistance from UNWRA, from any UN agency since the 1950s.

The number of registered UNWRA Palestine refugees has grown from 914,000 in 1950 to more than 3.8 million in 2001, and continues to rise due to natural population growth.[21] These include those living in or around refugee camps within the occupied territories of Gaza and the West Bank (some of which have been transferred to the control of the Palestinian authority) as well as Jordan, Lebanon and the Syrian Arab Republic, but do not include those unregistered or in other parts of the Arab world, in the West and the rest of the world. 'Palestinian refugees', of course, is a general term that covers various categories of refugees with differing

---

17 Morris, 1987, p 52.
18 Moshe Dayan, speaking in 1969, quoted in Khalidi, 1992, p xxxi.
19 See UN General Assembly Resolution 212 (III). Set up as a subsidiary organ of the UN General Assembly, UNWRA's mandate includes programmes in relief and social services, health, and education for registered UNWRA refugees. Its mandate was extended to the children of such persons by UN General Assembly Resolution 2341 of 19 December 1967.
20 See generally Fortin, 2000, pp 548–76.
21 UNWRA Factsheet, *Who is a Palestinian Refugee?*

status and treatment. The term 'refugees', certainly as applied by UNWRA, refers to those Palestinians ejected from their homes in 1948 while 'displaced persons' are those who lost their homes during, and as a consequence of, the 1967 war. Unlike most other refugees who were displaced by conflict in which the UN did not or could not intervene, the Palestinian refugee crisis was a direct result of UN action.

The 1951 Refugee Convention came into force on 22 April 1954, and at present has 140 state parties. These include Israel[22] and Egypt but exclude Jordan, Syria and Lebanon, where almost half of the Palestinian refugee population waits. The reason is obvious: Israel has nothing to answer to the Refugee Convention regarding its responsibilities towards Palestinian refugees, and the Arab countries have nothing to gain by ratifying except to invite scrutiny of its own treatment of the Palestinian refugees. Nor has the Convention been signed by the other Arab countries such as Iraq, Kuwait, Libya, Qatar, Saudi Arabia and the United Arab Emirates, where smaller percentages of Palestinians live, and which also have adopted discriminatory policies towards the Palestinians.[23] Arab host countries, with the exception of Jordan, have refused to grant citizenship to the Palestinians – even to the descendants of Palestinian refugees – on the justification that doing so may 'adversely affect their chances of going home'.[24] The treatment of Palestinians in these countries, and their socio-economic and political rights, have long been a concern of human rights organisations.[25]

The Casablanca Protocol on the Treatment of Palestinians in the Arab States of 11 September 1965 provides them with the right to be employed 'as if they were nationals', and the right to leave and re-enter through travel documents,[26] though this does not create permanent residency rights. There have been continuing efforts to keep Palestinian refugees afloat, creating a permanently temporary status that is, however, not insulated from domestic political dynamics and concerns. The 1992 Cairo Declaration on the Protection of Refugees and Displaced Persons in the Arab World[27] which expresses 'deep concern that Palestinians are not receiving effective protection either from the competent international organizations or from the competent authorities of some Arab countries' is a curious document. The Declaration, emerging out of consultations co-sponsored by the UNHCR, is ambivalent and confused about its relationship with UNHCR.[28] It calls upon Arab States to ratify the Refugee Convention and Protocol 'which constitute the basic universal instruments governing the status of refugees' but does not seek its application to the Palestinian refugees and omits any reference to UNWRA. It recommends that 'Arab States adopt a broader concept of "refugee" and displaced persons' in line with international human rights norms but does not, like African and Latin American initiatives, develop an alternative, broader definition. It calls

---

22 UNHCR does have offices in Israel and co-operates with Israel on refugee matters other than those relating to the Palestinians, much on the same terms as UNHCR works in neighbouring Arab States. Until the beginning of 2002, UNHCR had itself handled asylum claims within Israel.

23 See Shiblak, 1996, pp 36–45.

24 Hammerberg, 2002, p 9.

25 For a review of the situation in individual Arab countries see US Committee for Refugees, country reports at www.refugees.org.

26 'Unified travel documents', issued to the Palestinian refugees pursuant to Arab League Council Resolution 714 of 27 January 1954, are temporary but accord to the holders of these documents the 'same treatment with respect to visas and residence as is accorded to their nationals' (Article 6).

27 See Khadija, 1993, pp 173–75.

28 In para 14 it notes 'with appreciation the humanitarian role of the Office of the United Nations High Commissioner for Refugees in providing protection and assistance to refugees and displaced persons'.

for a future Arab Convention relating to refugees by the Arab League 'within a reasonable time', although this has yet to happen.

According to Lex Takkenberg, it was the Arab States 'who had insisted that the Palestinians refugees be the subject of special United Nations attention rather than being included in the mandate of the UNHCR'.[29] This Arab miscalculation that the Palestinian refugee issue could be sorted out quicker and justly through a stronger specialised alternative arrangement was to play right into the hands of Israel and its backers, who construed the move as placing the Palestinians outside the regular protection net of international law. At the same time, the failure of the Arab League to provide a satisfactory regional refugee regime which could address the Palestinian refugees, more than 50 years after the Refugee Convention had kept them out, has only further reinforced the statuslessness of the Palestinian refugees.

The 'universal' definition of who may be considered a refugee and therefore entitled to international protection and a range of other refugee rights is the lynchpin of the Refugee Convention. It is a definition that states use to grant asylum but, in practice, has implications for access to a broader range of international refugee rights. That formula, in terms of Article 1A, paragraph 2, informs us that the term 'refugee' shall apply to any person who:

> Owing to well-founded fear of being persecuted for reasons of race, religion, nationality, membership of a particular social group or political opinion, is outside the country of his nationality and is unable or, owing to such fear, is unwilling to avail himself of the protection of that country; or who, not having a nationality and being outside the country of his former habitual residence … is unable or, owing to such fear, is unwilling to return to it.

On the other hand, Article 1D of the Refugee Convention stipulates that 'this Convention shall not apply to persons who are at present receiving from organs or agencies of the United Nations other than the United Nations High Commissioner for Refugees protection or assistance'. Assistance is being provided by UNWRA but protection to be guaranteed by the UNCCP has long collapsed with that mechanism. As a result, the next paragraph of Article ID should apply: 'When such protection or assistance has ceased for any reason, without the position of such persons being definitely settled in accordance with the relevant resolutions of the General Assembly of the United Nations, these persons shall *ipso facto* be entitled to the benefits of this Convention.' Palestinian refugees without protection would appear to be covered by the Refugee Convention.

UNHCR, in paragraph 7c of its 1950 statute, states that 'the competence of the High Commissioner … shall not extend to a person: … (c) who continues to receive from other organs or agencies of the United Nations protection or assistance'. The UNHCR handbook further clarifies that only a 'refugee from Palestine who finds himself outside [the UNRWA operating] area and does not enjoy the assistance mentioned may be considered for determination of his refugee status under the criteria of the Refugee convention'.[30] Guy Goodwin Gill, critical of UNHCR's interpretation of Article 1D, opines that the provision is 'not so much an "exclusion" clause, as a contingent inclusion clause, merely postponing the incorporation of Palestinian refugees'.[31] According to Susan Akram, this provision ought to be read not as providing an inferior status under international law but rather a 'heightened protection regime' for Palestinian refugees.[32] The UNHCR

---

29 Takkenberg, 1998, p 345; see generally Chapter II.
30 See UNHCR, 1992, para 143.
31 Goodwin-Gill, 1996, p 93.
32 Akram, 2000b, p 8.

refusal to consider Palestinian refugees as among the rather broad and expanding categories of persons of concern is obtuse. Not only is it aware that UNWRA is not mandated to provide protection, but UNHCR has no objection to any other group of refugees – even if they are also covered by other regional refugee systems such as the 1969 African Refugee Convention or the binding 1984 Latin American Cartagena Declaration.[33]

One explanation of how the Palestinian refugees came to be left out of the Refugee Convention and UNHCR's mandate lies in the chronology of events. The UNHCR was created in 1950 when UNWRA (1949) and UNCCP (1950) had already started operations and it was deemed fit to maintain this division of labour. This, however, meant that the Arab States, or the Palestinians, merely nodded to the continuation of the UNWRA/UNCCP arrangement which was, at the time of UNHCR's creation, still looking promising. Israel and Egypt (and Iran with observer status) were the only states from the region represented at UN Conference of Plenipotentiaries on the Status of Refugees and Stateless Persons, but the exclusion of the Palestinians was not a real issue. The conference did recommend that the Refugee Convention guide those not covered by the convention 'as far as possible'.[34] But at the time, the 1967 Refugee Protocol (which lifted the temporal and geographical limitations of the Refugee Convention) came to be considered, the UNCCP had ceased to exist and, under any formula, the Palestinian refugees should have been included. The UNHCR at that time could also have reviewed application of the Refugee Convention to the Palestinian refugees. However, once the Palestinians were exiled, international refugee law simply did not want them back.

The UNRWA definition is merely an 'operational definition' and does not confer status or rights on the Palestinians but only enables access to its services. It considers Palestinian refugees as those persons whose normal place of residence was Palestine between June 1946 and May 1948 and who lost *both* their homes and their means of livelihood as a result of the 1948 Arab-Israeli conflict. It thus excludes those refugees who did not register with UNRWA as refugees, and those who lost their registration as a result of their changed status (particularly in Lebanon). It also leaves out thousands of rural refugees in Gaza and the West Bank who lost their land and sources of livelihood but who did not lose their residence. The latter includes people who lost access to coastal markets and work sites in pre-1948 Palestine. It certainly has not affected the tens of thousands of refugees inside Israel who lost their properties and residence while remaining in Israel and becoming citizens. At the core of the Palestinian refugee crisis is their ability to produce documents to establish who they were and what they lost. However, even for those Palestinian mothers who still carry the keys of their houses in Israel or pieces of parchment, all this has been merely an academic issue for half a century.

Abandoned by UNHCR, the primary body developing refugee standards, the Palestinians are left to the vagaries of establishing their rights under customary international refugee law but are still mostly invisible within the international refugee legal discourse. The difficulties in getting the international community to systematically discuss Palestinian refugee issues is demonstrated by the experience of the Refugee Working Group (RWG), established as one of the five multilateral committees following the 1991 Madrid conference. The first RWG meeting was boycotted by Israel over the issue of who could be Palestinian representatives. At the second meeting, the Israelis demanded that Jewish and other refugees be included in the mandate of the RWG. Then, Israel insisted that the RWG restrict its

---

33 See Arboleda, 1991, pp 186–205.
34 See Goodwin-Gill, 1996, p 392.

mandate to humanitarian aid issues rather than political issues. Interestingly, the RWG continues its work and has produced a 'vision paper',[35] but initial optimism that the events of September 11 might expedite consideration of the Palestinian refugee issues has waned.

In the absence of a Palestine nationality, with the Israeli refusal to countenance their return, combined with the general Arab refusal to grant them citizenship (with the exception of Jordan), the Palestinian refugees are rendered stateless. Takkenberg argues that 'as there is no State [of Palestine], *ipso facto* Palestinian nationality is also non-existent. Palestinians who have not acquired the nationality of a third state therefore continue to be stateless for the purpose of international law'.[36] Goodwin Gill, however, provides the German example to demonstrate the practical difficulty where third states would entertain asylum applications only if there was lack of protection argued against the state of residency though that state was unwilling to grant them citizenship.[37] Making things worse, the 1954 Convention relating to the Status of Stateless Persons also possesses the exclusion clause, Article 1, paragraph 2, which states that it shall not apply to 'persons who are at present receiving from organs or agencies of the United Nations other than the United Nations High Commissioner for Refugees protection or assistance so long as they are receiving such protection or assistance'.[38] The Palestinian refugees and their descendants are thus mostly condemned to a life in UNWRA camps until political negotiations resume finding homes for them.

The Palestinian refugee inevitably watches the Middle East peace process from the sidelines. Beyond the sloganeering and sympathies lies the 50 year old lesson that their refugee rights are contingent on state building, economic survival and consolidation of the rights of those who remained on Palestinian soil. The Palestinian State may be a pre-requisite for at least part of the repatriation problem, but the refugees are aware that the state might not have a place for them – politically and demographically. The Oslo Declaration of Principles (Oslo 1)[39] was largely concerned about implementation of administrative arrangements (including the creation of the Palestinian Authority) within the occupied territories. The agreement left to the 'permanent status' stage issues at the core of the Israeli/Palestinian conflict: refugees, borders, settlements, water, and Jerusalem.[40] On the ground, control of UNWRA refugee camps was transferred to the PA,[41] while the rights of over three million Palestinians living in the Diaspora were left in abeyance. The 'Quadripartite Committee', comprising the Palestinians, Israel, Egypt and Jordan, envisaged during the Oslo process to discuss repatriation of the 1967 refugees from Gaza and the West Bank has also run aground.

---

35 RWG does not deal with the status of the refugees and is primarily concerned with the living conditions of the Palestinian refugees, particularly those outside the West Bank and Gaza. One success was the question of family reunification with the Israelis agreeing to increase the pre-existing annual quota of 1,000 to 2,000, though this is yet to be fulfilled. See Tamari, 1996, p 4.

36 Takkenberg, 1998, p 351; see generally Chapter V.

37 Goodwin-Gill, 1996, pp 244–45.

38 The 1954 Convention is also poorly ratified by Middle Eastern states, with only Israel and Libya among the 52 state parties.

39 For extensive discussion along these lines with particular reference to the impact of the Oslo framework on Palestinian rights, see Bowen, 1997; Dajani, 1994, pp 5–23.

40 Article V, paragraph 3 of the Israeli-Palestinian Declaration of Principles on Interim Self-Government Arrangements, Washington, DC, 13 September 1993.

41 The Israeli-Palestinian Interim Agreement on the West Bank and Gaza Strip (known as Oslo 2), Washington, DC, 28 September 1995, contains several new items on the status of residency and family reunification that are likely to lead, once Palestinian authority is established in the rest of the West Bank, to important modifications in the status and scope of returning Palestinians.

Oslo was intended as a building block to a 'permanent settlement solution' based on UN Security Council Resolutions 242 and 338,[42] and optimists pointed out that Resolution 242 calls for a 'just settlement of the refugee problem'. Yet, the Oslo negotiations have also been seen as eroding UN General Assembly Resolution 181 (29 November 1947) on partition with equal rights, and Resolution 194 (11 December 1948) on the right of return, restitution and compensation and other important resolutions on Palestinian refugee rights. The Oslo process's official timetable ended in 1999, without a hint of when or in what form a final settlement might come.

The Wye Memorandum (23 October 1998), the Sharm el-Sheikh Memorandum (4 September 1999), the Mitchell Report (30 April 2001)[43] and the Tenet Plan (13 June 2001)[44] are all preoccupied mostly with preconditions for negotiations and are gravely silent on the evaporating Palestinian refugee rights. When the terms of a permanent settlement were discussed at the Camp David talks in July 2000 between Bill Clinton, Ehud Barak and Yasser Arafat, one of the reasons for the breakdown was said to be the Palestinian disappointment with the lack of a 'just solution' to the Palestinian refugees. Frustration with the peace process where Palestinian concessions had brought little movement towards independence or a settlement was already explosive when Ariel Sharon's inflammatory visit to Jerusalem's Haram Al Sharif set off the second Palestinian intifada in September 2000. With Israeli state terrorism and the Hamas, the Al Alqsa brigades and others stepping up their terrorist attacks, the peace process had been decisively transformed into a militarised conflict.

The UN General Assembly had in the past called upon states to combat terrorism,[45] but had been careful to equally promote respect for the Refugee Convention, particularly the doctrine of non-refoulement which guards against arbitrary rejection of asylum claims. The Refugee Convention was seen as possessing sufficient inbuilt provisions to exclude terrorists from the benefits of the Convention.[46] Article 1F states:

> The provisions of this Convention shall not apply to any person with respect to whom there are serious reasons for considering that:
>
> (a) he has committed a crime against peace, a war crime, or a crime against humanity, as defined in the international instruments drawn up to make provision in respect of such crimes;
> (b) he has committed a serious non-political crime outside the country of refuge prior to his admission to that country as a refugee;
> (c) he has been guilty of acts contrary to the purposes and principles of the United Nations.

Moving away from broader conceptions of non-refoulement, which under the 1984 Convention against Torture applied without exception, it was now apparent that after September 11, those accused of terrorism would forfeit their right to be considered for asylum. The charged context after September 11 sidesteps the issue that not only can the label 'terrorist' be speculative, expansive and political, with

---

42 UN Security Council Resolution 338 of 22 October 1973 merely calls for a ceasefire and refers to Resolution 242 with a call for negotiations for a just and durable peace.
43 The refugee issue was raised several times but finds no mention in the Mitchell Report, 30 April 2001.
44 See the Tenet Plan, 13 June 2000.
45 See for example UN General Assembly Resolutions 49/60 of 9 December 1994 and 50/53 of 11 December 1995 on Measures to Eliminate International Terrorism.
46 Note that apart from the 1999 International Convention for the Suppression of the Financing of Terrorism of 9 December 1999, there are a dozen other international treaties that deal with terrorism-related crimes.

the extinction of rights of accused, but that the current discourse 'reinforces the perception that the institution of asylum is somehow a terrorist's refuge'.[47]

In contrast to earlier General Assembly resolutions balancing respect for the Refugee Convention with a call for a vigil against terrorism,[48] the post-September 11 UN Security Council Resolution 1373 (28 September 2001) points the finger at refugees, even though not one of the 19 hijackers was an asylum seeker. It dedicates two paragraphs to call upon states to ensure 'that the asylum seeker has not planned, facilitated or participated in the commission of terrorists acts' or that 'refugee status is not abused by perpetrators, organisers or facilitators of terrorist acts'.[49]

Following September 11, the United States targeted 26 Arab and Muslim countries from where it would not grant visas to able bodied men, and passed the USA-PATRIOT Act[50] which would make asylum more difficult. It also suspended its resettlement program for refugees, under which tens of thousands of people were granted asylum in the country. Attempts to deny or suspend access to asylum procedures are being orchestrated within Europe and across the globe. The UK Anti-Terrorism, Crime and Security Act 2001 requires a low threshold of 'links' with an international terrorist organisation, raising concerns that asylum seekers, themselves often escaping violence, including terrorism, could be deported. Individuals could be penalised merely because they originate in a country of conflict and have political, ethnic or religious affiliations or ties.[51] As stated by UNHCR, 'the fact of membership [of a terrorist organisation] does not, in and of itself, amount to participation or complicity. The decision maker will need to consider whether the applicant had close or direct responsibility for, or was actively associated with, the commission of any crime specified under Article 1F'.[52] The Palestinian refugees are guilty not merely by association but, through a stage managed criminalisation, into a form of collective terrorism.

September 11 was not only an unjustifiable assault on America on the pretext of its Middle East foreign policy, but reverberated to shake the foundations of an already fragile international refugee regime and make it more difficult for asylum seekers[53] – particularly its outcasts, the Palestinian refugees. The Middle East conflict was now perceived as a source of international terror, threatening both the United States and the 'civilised world'. While the Israelis saw the 'international war against terrorism' as a license to crack down heavily on the Al Aqsa intifada, Yasser Arafat was quick to condemn terrorism, and careful not to make the mistake of antagonising America as he done during the Desert Storm operation. He was

---

47 Zard, 2002, p 33.
48 In its 1996 Resolution, the General Assembly asks states to fulfil their obligations under the Refugee Convention whilst at the same time considering whether the 'asylum-seeker is subject to investigation for or is charged with or has been convicted of offences connected with terrorism and, after granting refugee status'. UN General Assembly Resolution A/RES/51/210 of 17 December 1996.
49 See UN Security Council Resolution S/RES/1373, 28 September 2001, paras 3(f) and (g). It does state that this must be done in accordance with international law. Consider also Security Council Resolutions 1269 of 19 October 1999 and 1368 of 12 September 2001.
50 Uniting and Strengthening America by Providing Appropriate Tools Required to Intercept and Obstruct Terrorism Act (USA-PATRIOT), 26 October 2001, not only expands the scope of terrorist-related activity to material support to humanitarian projects that are listed as designated terrorist organisations, but allows for detention and deportation of non-citizens who provide lawful assistance to groups not officially designated as terrorist organisations and scrutinises family reunion. Zard, 2002, p 34.
51 See section 21(2) and (4) of the Act. See Zard, 2002, p 33.
52 UNHCR, *Exclusion Clauses: Guidelines on their Application*, December 1996, paras 40, 45, 47.
53 See Editorial, 2002, p 8.

anxious, too, to counter the isolated but disturbing images of Palestinians celebrating Ground Zero but, given the invisibility of Al Qa'ida, the Palestinian terrorists became the face of the global threat despite no evidence of recent Palestinian terrorism abroad. The American position has hardened and, as Abbas Shiblak finds, the Palestinian refugees are 'at the receiving end of a simplistic and dangerous discourse that sweeps away their aspirations for justice, freedom and peace'.[54]

The cause of Palestinian self-determination has been further undermined by the events of September 11.[55] Antonio Cassese notes that the celebrated Security Council Resolution 242 of 22 November 1967, 'which was intended to establish a framework for peace in the Middle East did not even address the issue of Palestine, nor recognise a Palestinian right to Self determination'.[56] He goes on to review the Oslo Declaration of Principles, which avoids mentioning self-determination and rests on Security Council Resolutions 242 and 338, neither of which discuss Palestinian self-determination.[57] Rather than a solution based on the right of self-determination, the future of Palestinians after September 11 now appears to depend on their renunciation of their resistance and the full cessation of violence by all Palestinians. No promises would be made of addressing central questions, including the plight of Palestinian refugees. Richard Falk argues that the framework of the Oslo 'peace process' did not alter the Palestinian right to resistance 'due to the Israeli refusal to implement the underlying legal directives established by a consensus within the UN'.[58] However, the international legal right to resist foreign occupation[59] virtually evaporates in the post-September 11 drive to make all national liberation groups non-violent. At the same time, it empowers the state to crush every form of dissent that could be labelled as 'terrorist'.

Two-thirds of the Palestinians killed during the first year of the Al Aqsa intifada were refugees, significantly higher than the proportion of refugee to non-refugee residents in the occupied Palestinian territories. By then, 1,500 refugee family houses had been destroyed or damaged. But after September 11, refugee camps had become 'the main targets for the Israeli army, subjected to unprecedented levels of brutality, demolition and destruction'.[60] Apart from the routine UN spectator profusions of sympathy for the Palestinians, it was UNWRA that came out strongly, urging the Israeli government to heed the UN Secretary General's call for an immediate IDF withdrawal from refugee camps in the occupied Palestinian territory and to desist from the Israeli security cabinet policy of targeting refugee camps.[61] Human rights groups from Palestine, Israel and the West have decried the excessive use of force against civilians in violation of international humanitarian law (including commission of 'war crimes'), wanton destruction of homes, schools, crops, religious places, water supplies and infrastructures, such as by-pass roads. Equally disturbing is the Israeli use of Palestinian 'human shields' as well as

---

54 Shiblak, 2002, p 44.
55 See UN General Assembly Resolution 3236 (XXIX) of 22 November 1974, reaffirming the Palestinian 'inalienable right to self-determination'.
56 Cassese, 1995, p 238.
57 Cassese, 1995, p 242.
58 Falk, 2000, p 17; see also Falk and Weston, 1991.
59 See the 1960 Declaration on the Granting of Independence to Colonial Countries and Peoples (UNGA 1514) and the wider 1970 UN General Assembly Declaration on Principles of International Law Concerning Friendly Relations and Co-operation Among States in accordance with the Charter of the United Nations, UNGA 2625 (XXV).
60 Shiblak, 2002, p 44.
61 See UNWRA Press Release, 4 March 2002.

widespread mass round-ups, incommunicado detention, torture and inhumane treatment.[62]

The UN Security Council's response to the Israeli retaliatory and excessive use of force, particularly the 'massacre' at the Jenin refugee camp, holds another clue to the Palestinian refugee's real status under international law. On 12 March 2002, the Council was already aware of the siege of the Palestinian headquarters and in Resolution 1397 called for cessation of 'all acts of violence, including all acts of terror, provocation, incitement and destruction'.[63] It was consistent throughout in condemning all sides but doing nothing more. The approach of the Security Council, post-September 11, can be contrasted with its earlier approaches. For example, UN Security Council Resolution 681 of 20 December 1990 had criticised 'the decision by the Government of Israel, the occupying Power, to resume deportations of Palestinian civilians in the occupied territories and urged the Government of Israel to accept *de jure* applicability of the Fourth Geneva Convention of 1949, to all the territories occupied by Israel since 1967, and to abide scrupulously by the provisions of the said Convention'. After the first phase of the 'war against terrorism' waged against Afghanistan, the rules of engagement with those perpetrating, supporting or harbouring 'terrorists' had changed. The US President George Bush would go on record to say he understood that Israeli actions were in legitimate self-defence and he refused to lean heavily on the Israelis in seeking an 'immediate' end to the incursions into refugee camps.

As the UN and the world media watched, Israel ripped through the Jenin refugee camp, causing unprecedented damage and killing armed militants as well as unarmed refugees – many of them elderly, children and women – who were later found buried under rubble. On 19 April 2002, the Council welcomed 'the initiative of the Secretary General to develop accurate information regarding recent events in the Jenin refugee camp through a fact-finding team and request[ed] him to keep the Security Council informed'.[64] The rest is well known – Israel changed its mind, America did not care and the UN Secretary General, despite Arab protests, disbanded the team. Incredibly, not once does either the UN Security Council or the Secretary General recognise the victims as refugees, although the camp is a refugee camp. Had they been recognised as refugees, the precedent of UN intervention for the Iraqi Kurds during Desert Storm or the action in Kosovo could have been cited. As far as the UN Security Council was concerned, these may have been refugee camps but the inhabitants did not fit the bill as 'their' refugees. Better still if they 'could have been terrorists'. The UNHCR too had other refugees to be concerned about, not these.

While UNWRA does not hold an overall protection brief for the Palestinian refugees, it is concerned about the serious disruption and destruction to its services. In addition to buildings and infrastructure, UNWRA Chief Peter Hansen pointed out that one of his staff had been killed and 185 UNWRA ambulances had been deliberately hit by Israeli fire, killing four ambulance drivers, three doctors and injuring 122 doctors and health workers. Hansen had also been denied access by Israeli forces to camps that he had responsibility for. The World Bank has estimated

---

62 See in particular Amnesty International, 2002.

63 On 30 March 2002, Resolution 1402 again called for 'a meaningful ceasefire and withdrawal of Israeli troops from Palestinian cities, including Ramallah'. It was followed by Resolution 1403 of 4 April 2002 with a reminder that Resolution 1402 must be implemented.

64 See Resolution 1405. The team chosen was former Finnish President Martti Aahtisaari, Cornelio Sommaruga, former ICRC president, and Sadako Ogata, a former UNHCR chief. They were to be assisted by US General William Nash, former Bosnia Commander as military adviser, and former Irish Police Commissioner Peter Fitzgerald as police adviser, along with other experts.

the damage to the Palestinian territories since the start of Israeli incursions at $300 million, including $42 million in the Jenin refugee camp and $111 million in the town of Nablus. This seriously dents UNWRA's capacity to deliver aid, since it was already struggling with a funding gap of $26 million.[65] Given the impoverished conditions in refugee camps,[66] in contrast to the oasis of affluence in surrounding Jewish settlements, this has created a humanitarian crisis. For its criticism of Israeli attacks on Jenin and other refugee camps, UNWRA was vilified as supporting terror, a charge that Hansen, through *Ha'aretz* op-ed (opinion and editorial) and website fact sheets, has sought to counter:[67]

> UNRWA does not run any camps, does not administer them and does not police them for the simple reason that the international community has not mandated UNRWA to do so. … The resolution of the Palestine refugee problem is a matter for the parties involved in the peace process. UNRWA's role, in the meanwhile, is to provide humanitarian services to Palestine refugees.

International legal analysis relating to the repatriation, compensation and restitution which are central to the Palestinian refugee issue is beyond the scope of this article. Yet, despite the abundance of materials,[68] it is plain to see that these rights have been frustrated by the lack of a protection agency which can authoritatively develop or advocate these standards. In repudiating the right of return, Israel not only refers to its security and demographic concerns[69] but takes advantage of what it sees as the lack of authoritative pronouncements in this area.[70] This despite arguments that one's 'own country' refers not only to the state of *de jure* nationality, but also to the state to which the claimant has a 'genuine link'.[71]

Another important area where substantial work has been done is regarding restitution and compensation, assuming that repatriation is not possible or not chosen.[72] Israel is not challenged because the issue remains hypothetical and there is no 'representative for the refugees with authority to take their claims to the international fora, nor is there a forum with jurisdiction over their claims of repatriation, compensation or restitution'.[73] Palestinians are a casualty of law's abdication and face an unfavourable constellation of political stars. Perceptions that the Arab nations must share Israel's responsibilities to the Palestinian refugees are gaining influence,[74] but the Palestinians are caught between Israeli intransigence and Arab wishful thinking. The Palestinian refugees may have justice and truth on their side but law and politics are on the other.

---

65 UNRWA operations are financed almost entirely by voluntary contributions from governments and the European Union, which account for 95 per cent of all income. The Agency's estimated expenditure for the year stands at $311 million. Income forecast for the year stands at $285 million; thus leaving a funding gap of $26 million. Its shortfall means that it now spends only $67 annually for every refugee in its care.

66 Leinwand, 2001.

67 See UNWRA, Fact Sheets-Myths No 6.

68 See for example Palestinian Society for the Protection of Human Rights and the Environment, 2001.

69 Salman Abu-Sitta points out that 78 per cent of Israel's Jewish population lives in only 15 per cent of Israel and proposes that the resettlement of Palestinian refugees could be achieved without any substantial demographic change. See Abu-Sitta, 1999, p 2.

70 See Lapidoth, 1999.

71 Lawand, 1996, pp 532–68. For pragmatic solutions, see Abu Zayyad, 1994.

72 See Hadawi, 1988.

73 Akram, 2000b, p 8.

74 See for example Arzt, 1997.

Conclusion

The argument in this essay was that the Palestinian refugees have been singled out by the Refugee Convention, the Refugee Protocol and the Statelessness Convention for exclusion on the fiction that they are receiving protection elsewhere. The language of Article 1D of the Refugee Convention, however, envisages 'such persons being definitely settled in accordance with the relevant resolutions of the General Assembly of the United Nations'. This implies that a final settlement would respect UN General Assembly Resolutions 181 and 194 (III) guaranteeing refugee rights, choice and the rights to return, restitution and compensation – resolutions which have in turn been reiterated in subsequent resolutions. The American and Israeli strategy, however, appears to be to seek a negotiated political settlement outside the framework of international law, a settlement in which Palestinian refugee rights would be sacrificed at the altar of a truncated Palestinian State. If that happens, there will be no one to speak for the Palestinian refugees, certainly not the disinterested, weakened international refugee law which is equally neo-Orientalist.[75]

The absence of the Palestinians from the Refugee Convention has serious consequences. The ability of some Israeli and Western politicians to characterise Palestinians as terrorists could have been countered to some degree by recollection of their legal status as refugees. This is not a technical 'glitch' but one that has a cumulative effect in crushing all other forms of Palestinian refugee rights, including their right to participate in choosing possible solutions. The Refugee Convention itself does not directly speak of collective rights, as it recognises refugee rights as individual rights. However, there is a significant negotiation of legitimacy that takes place between individually recognised rights and collective rights in mass refugee situations. In the exclusion of the individual, the Palestinian refugees as a whole find that their status is merely politically contingent.

The events of September 11 have brought together the United States and Israel, notwithstanding protests from elsewhere, to demand passivity, reform and further compromises from the Palestinians who have conceded 78 per cent of their territory and are still fighting 35 years of occupation. The status and the future of the Palestinian refugees has become even more tenuous with the onset of the international campaign against terrorism and the terrorist acts and suicide bombings carried out by a militant minority who do not speak for the refugees. The Palestinian refugees may well have to pay for this with their dreams of returning to their homes.

Yasser Arafat, his own position with both the Israelis and Palestinians uncertain, says he understands that the right of return is not absolute[76] and the Saudi peace plan too flags 'a just solution' to the refugee issue[77] – though both reiterate the provisions of UN General Assembly Resolution 194. Ariel Sharon has unequivocally rejected the right of return as one of his basic negotiating positions[78] and brazenly calls for 'realism' in what the Palestinians can ask for.[79] Was it reality

---

75 Akram, 2000a, pp 7–40.
76 'I understand that the right of return [a right guaranteed by international law and UN Resolution 194] … must be implemented in such a way that it takes into account [Israeli demographic] concerns.' See Arafat, 2002.
77 'Achievement of a just solution to the Palestinian Refugee problem to be agreed upon in accordance with the UN General Assembly Resolution 194.' See the Beirut Declaration (endorsing the Saudi Peace Plan), Council of the League of Arab States at the Summit Level, 28 March 2002.
78 Sharon, 2000.
79 'When Israel and the Palestinians eventually re-engage in negotiations, diplomacy must be based on realism.' Sharon, 2002.

or illusion that Ben Gurion's offer of taking into Israel a hundred thousand returnees turned into Yitzak Rabin's reported ten thousand scaled down to Ehud Barak's reported five thousand and now transformed into Ariel Sharon's zero? It is a reflection of the fact that the Palestinian refugees are of diminishing relevance in the region. With their status 'yet to be determined', international law has been deployed to provide that the Palestinian refugees are neither real refugees nor citizens of a state.

When the history of the Palestinian refugees is written, with hindsight, the exclusion of the Palestinian refugees from the Refugee Convention will figure prominently in the list of lapses of international law – as debilitating as the Balfour Declaration or the partition of Palestine itself. International refugee law conspired to strip them of their most obvious status, removing them from law's protection and banishing them forever from their homes. The frustration of Palestinian refugee rights does not derive from cunning political power but is carefully built on the pillar of non-recognition of the Palestinian refugees under international refugee law. Post-September 11, the suicide bombers from refugee backgrounds become a potential symbol of the postmodern outlaw. Palestinian refugees have been placed on the edges of legal exclusion for half a century. The images of the destroyed Jenin refugee camp and the carnage on the streets of Israel must haunt all who have faith in law.

References

Abu Zayyad, Ziad (1994) 'The Palestinian right of return: a realistic approach' 2 Palestine-Israel Journal 77 (Spring)

Abu-Sitta, Salman (1999) 'Palestinians, refugees and the permanent status negotiations', Washington DC: Jerusalem Fund and the Center for Policy Analysis on Palestine: www.palestinecenter.org/news/19991116pb.html

Akram, Susan (2000a) 'Orientalism revisited in asylum and refugee claims' 12(1) Int J Refugee Law 7

Akram, Susan (2000b) 'Reinterpreting Palestinian refugee rights under international law, and a framework for durable solutions' Bethlehem: BADIL: www.badil.org/Publications/Briefs/Brief1.pdf

Amnesty International, 'Israel and the occupied territories: mass detention in cruel, inhuman and degrading conditions', AI Doc MDE 23/05/2002: http://web.amnesty.org/ai.nsf/Index/MDE150742002?OpenDocument&of=COUNTRIES\ISRAEL/OCCUPIED+TERRITORIES

Arafat, Yasser (2002) 'I want to talk peace' New York Times, 4 February

Arboleda, Eduardo (1991) 'Refugee definition in Africa and Latin America: lessons of pragmatism' 3(2) Int J Refugee Law 186

Arzt, Donna (1997) Refugees into Citizens, Palestinian Refugees and the End of the Arab-Israeli Conflict, New York: Council on Foreign Relations

Barzilai, Amnon (2002) 'Some saw the refugees as the key to peace' Ha'aretz, 11 June

Bowen, Stephen (ed) (1997) Human Rights, Self-Determination and Political Change in the Occupied Palestinian Territories, The Hague: Kluwer

Cassese, Antonio (1995) Self Determination of Peoples, Cambridge: CUP

Dajani, Burhan (1994) 'The September 1993 Israeli-PLO documents: a textual analysis' 23(3) J Palestine Studies 5 (Spring)

Editorial (2002) 'The September terror: a global impact' 125 Refugees

Falk, Richard and Weston, B (1991) 'The relevance of international law to Palestinian rights in the West Bank and Gaza: in legal defense of the intifada' 32(1) Harvard ILJ

Falk, Richard (2000) 'International law and the al-Aqsa Intifada' Middle East Report (Winter) 216

Flapan, Simha (1987) The Birth of Israel: Myths and Realities, New York: Pantheon

Fortin, Antonio (2000) 'The meaning of "protection" in the refugee definition' 12(4) Int J Refugee Law 548

Goodwin-Gill, Guy (1996) The Refugee in International Law, Oxford: Clarendon

Hadawi, Sami (1988) Palestinian Rights and Losses in 1948: A Comprehensive Study, London: Saqi

Hammerberg, Thomas (2002) The Palestinian Refugees: After Five Decades of Betrayal – Time at Last?, Stockholm: Regeringskansliet

Hathaway, James (1990) 'A reconsideration of the underlying premise of refugee law' 31 Harvard ILJ 181

Hathaway, James (1996) 'Can international refugee law be made relevant again?', World Refugee Survey: www.refugees.org/world/articles/intl_law_wrs96.htm

Herzl, Theodor (1946) On the Jewish State, D'Avignor, S (trans), New York: American Zionist Emergency Council

Karmi, Ghada, Cotran, Eugene and Gilmour, Ian (2000) The Palestinian Exodus, 1948–1998, London: Ithaca

Khadija, Elmadmad (1993) 'An Arab declaration on the protection of refugees and displaced persons in the Arab world' 6(2) J Refugee Studies 173

Khalidi, Walid (1992) *All That Remains: The Palestinian Villages Occupied and Depopulated by Israel in 1948*, Beirut: Institute of Palestinian Studies

Lapidoth, Ruth (1999) 'Do Palestinians have a right to return to Israel?', Tel Aviv: MFA, State of Israel: www.mfa.gov.il/mfa/go.asp?MFAHOj8r0

Lawand, Kathleen (1996) 'The right to return of Palestinians in international law' 8(4) Int J Refugee Law 532

Leinwand, Ariel (2001) 'The Palestinian poverty problem in the era of globalization' 9 Indiana J Global Legal Studies 325: http://ijgls.indiana.edu/archive/09/01/leinwand.shtml#63fn

Maslaha, Nur (1992) *Expulsion of the Palestinians: The Concept of Transfer in Zionist Political Thought 1882–1948*, Washington, DC: Institute for Palestinian Studies

Maslaha, Nur (1997) *A Land without People: Israel, Transfer and the Palestinians 1949–96*, London: Faber and Faber

Morris, Benny (1987) *The Birth of the Palestinian Refugee Problem, 1947–1949*, Cambridge: CUP

Morris, Benny (2000) *Righteous Victims: A History of the Zionist-Arab Conflict*, London: John Murray

Nicholson, Frances and Twomey, Patrick (1999) *Refugee Rights and Realities: Evolving International Concepts and Regimes*, Cambridge: CUP

Palestinian Society for the Protection of Human Rights and the Environment (2001) 'The dormant right: continuing violation of the right of return': www.lawsociety.org/Reports/reports/2001/dormfoot.html#65

Pappe, Ilan (1997) 'Post-Zionist critique on Israel and the Palestinians, Part I: the academic debate' 26(2) J Palestinian Studies

Pappe, Ilan (1999) *The Israel/Palestine Question: Rewriting Histories*, London: Routledge

Segev, Tom (2001) *One Palestine, Complete: Jews and Arabs under the British Mandate*, New York: Owl

Sharon, Ariel (2000) 'Six red lines for peace' *Jerusalem Post*, 21 July: www.jpost.com/Editions/2000/07/21/Opinion/Opinion.9914.html

Sharon, Ariel (2002) 'The way forward in the Middle East' *New York Times*, 9 June

Shiblak, Abbas (1996) 'Residency status and civil rights of Palestinian refugees in Arab countries' 25(3) J Palestine Studies 36

Shiblak, Abbas (2002) 'Palestinians in the aftermath of 11 September: wishing refugees out of existence?' 13 Forced Migration Review 44

Shlaim, Avi (2001) *The Iron Wall: Israel and the Arab World*, London: Allen Lane

Steinbock, Daniel (1999) 'The refugee definition as law: issues of interpretation, in Nicholson and Twomey, 1999

Strawson, John (2002) 'Mandate ways: self-determination in Palestine and the "existing non-Jewish communities"', in Silverburg, Sanford R (ed), *Palestine and International Law: Essays on Politics and Economics*, Jefferson NC and London: McFarland

Takkenberg, Lex (1998) *The Status of Palestinian Refugees in International Law*, Oxford: Clarendon

Tamari, Salim (1996) 'Return, resettlement, repatriation: the future of Palestinian refugees in the peace negotiations', Beirut: Institute for Palestine Studies: www.arts.mcgill.ca/MEPP/PRRN/papers/tamari2.html#IV

Tuitt, Patricia (1996) *False Images: The Law's Construction of the Refugee*, London: Pluto

UNHCR (1992) *Handbook of Procedures and Criteria for Determining Refugee Status under the 1951 Convention and the 1967 Protocol Relating to the Status of Refugees*, HCR/IP/4/Eng/REV.1 Geneva: UNHCR: www.unhcr.org

Weizmann, Chaim (1949) letter to US President Truman dated 24 June: www.trumanlibrary.org/whistlestop/study_collections/israel/large/folder1/isa24-3.htm

Yapp, Malcolm (1995) 'The making of the Palestine mandate', Middle Eastern Lectures, Tel Aviv: Moshe Dayan Center for Middle Eastern and African Studies, pp 9–27

Zard, Monette (2002) 'Exclusion, terrorism and the Refugee Convention' 13 Forced Migration Review 32

Other documents

MacMahon-Hussein Correspondence, 14 July 1915 to 10 March 1916

Agreement between Sir Mark Sykes of Britain and Georges Picot of France, May 1916

Balfour Declaration, 2 November 1917

British Mandate over Palestine, 24 July 1922

Arab League Council Resolution 714, 27 January 1954

Casablanca Protocol on the Treatment of Palestinians in the Arab States, 11 September 1965

Cairo Declaration on the Protection of Refugees and Displaced Persons in the Arab World, 19 November 1992:
http://pbosnia.kentlaw.edu/services/chicago/legal_aid/treaties/world_arab.htm

Israeli-Palestinian Declaration of Principles on Interim Self-Government Arrangements, Washington, DC, 13 September 1993

Israeli-Palestinian Interim Agreement on the West Bank and Gaza Strip (known as Oslo 2), Washington, DC, 28 September 1995

Wye Memorandum, 23 October 1998

Sharm el-Sheikh Memorandum, 4 September 1999

Sharm el-Sheikh Fact-Finding Committee Final Report (Mitchell Recommendations), 30 April 2001: http://usinfo.state.gov/regional/nea/mitchell.htm#_edn4

Israeli-Palestinian Ceasefire and Security Plan, Proposed by CIA Director George Tenet, 13 June 2001: www.yale.edu/lawweb/avalon/mideast/mid023.htm

Beirut Declaration (endorsing the Saudi Peace Plan), The Council of the League of Arab States at the Summit Level, at its 14th Ordinary Session, 28 March 2002: www.saudiembassy.net/press_release/statements/02-ST-0328-Beirut.htm

Internet sites

ADALAH, Legal Center for Arab Minority Rights: see its Commission of Enquiry into the October 2000 events: www.adalah.org/coi.shtml

Amnesty International: www.amnesty.org

BADIL: www.badil.org

B'tselem, The Israeli Information Center for Human Rights in the Occupied Territories: www2.iol.co.il/btselem/

Forced Migration Review website: www.fmreview.org/2didyouknow.htm

Jerusalem Fund and the Center for Policy Analysis on Palestine: www.palestinecenter.org

Palestinian Society for Protection of Human Rights & the Environment: www.lawsociety.org

US Committee for Refugees country reports: www.refugees.org

UNHCR: http://unhcr.ch

UNWRA: www.un.org/unrwa/refugees/p1.htm

Chapter 8

Islamic feminism, possibilities and limitations
Qudsia Mirza

One of the most striking consequences of the events of 11 September 2001 has been the crude re-staging of the opposition between Islam and the West, an antagonism that has proven historical antecedents and that is perceived by many as the primary characteristic of the relationship between the two. The attacks of last year have provided fertile ground for a re-enactment of the idea that the relationship between these ideological entities is characterised, at best, by mutual incomprehension and mistrust and, at worst, by open confrontation. The representation of the nexus between Islam and the West in these conflictual terms denies the complexity and diversity of both Islam and the West, and reduces the relationship between them to facile polarities: '[f]aith versus scepticism, tradition versus iconoclasm, purity versus eclecticism'.[1] Within this framework, it is the position of Muslim women, whether in the post-September 11 reconstruction of Afghanistan,[2] or the now well-established presence of the Muslim Diaspora in secular Western societies, that has been a key site upon which many of the popular misconceptions and tensions between Islam and the West have been played out. Furthermore, the relationship between Western feminism and the emergence of new, revitalised forms of Islamic feminism also indicates a deepening of the traditional antagonism between the two. It can be argued that the theoretical divergence between Islamic and Western feminism is now even greater than that in colonial times and that this is a development that weakens and disadvantages both systems of thought.

In his ground-breaking analysis of the colonial encounter, Said demonstrates that knowledge of the Orient was constructed and produced by the West[3] as an ideological complement to the exercise of colonial power. Consequently, the European representation of the Orient, characterised as objective, 'scientific' and lacking in bias, nevertheless evinces a 'positional superiority'[4] in which structures of thought were generated as supports of colonial power. The study of the Orient thus contained an ideologically informed depiction of the Orient, one that formed an escort to colonial power. For Said, therefore, Orientalism is the production of a discourse, 'a style of thought based upon an ontological and epistemological distinction made between "the Orient" and "the Occident"'.[5] Thus, by conjoining the operation of power with the production of knowledge as twin, equally weighty aspects of the colonial project, Said's theoretical innovation has been to demonstrate that the success of colonialism was due largely to the consanguinity of these enterprises. And, as Fitzpatrick asserts, '[t]he mythology of modernity is sustained by the experience of imperialism'.[6]

Critiques of *Orientalism* are notable for a recurring focus on certain omissions in Said's analysis.[7] A chief criticism is that Western discourse has been depicted as

---

1 Ahmed, A, 1992, p 5.
2 See for instance *The Guardian*'s report: 'Women lead protests as Afghan warlords muscle in on power', 13 June 2002.
3 Said, 1995, limits his investigation specifically to an analysis of British, French and American Orientalist texts.
4 Said, 1995, p 7.
5 Said, 1995, p 2.
6 Fitzpatrick, 1992, p ix.
7 See Loomba, 1998 for a concise summary of such criticisms.

evoking a fixed polarisation between East and West, a depiction that ignores historical nuances and characterises the relationship between the two as a simplistic and 'fixed East versus West divide'.[8] Allied to this is the critique that Said homogenises the West and that his description of Orientalist knowledge is insufficiently linked to the historical reality of colonialism. Accordingly, in concentrating upon the literary, ideological and discursive dimensions of Orientalist knowledge, Said has suggested that colonialism was predominantly an ideological construct; critics argue that this analysis reduces the importance of the material reality of colonialism. Finally, Said's focus on the exercise of power by the coloniser depicts a schematic view of the colonial encounter by concentrating on colonial authority whilst ignoring the opposition effected by the colonised, most notably, anti-colonial and nationalist struggles. As Perrin contends, the Saidean denial of agency on the part of the colonised results in a fixed view of colonial relations and a position in which the Western production of knowledge becomes equated with the reality of the Orient. In this way, Said 'circumscribes the East's and West's mutual dependency by claiming that the Orient's capacities to resist and appropriate power from the West is always negotiated through the discourses of a superior Occident'.[9] Alternative accounts or descriptions, outside the 'frame of Orientalism'[10] thus become impossible.

The demarcation between Europe and others was essential in allowing Europe to assert its hegemony over colonised lands. The delineation also advanced the idea of Europe possessing a culture, including a legal system, that was inherently more advanced and sophisticated than that of its non-European others. Therefore, the success of the colonial project was firmly based upon establishing a binary opposition: between a refined Europe and an uncivilised Orient, savage, uncontrolled natives and disciplined, sophisticated Europeans, a developed Europe characterised by continuing change, and an immutable Orient, inert and fixed in its primitivism. Thus, the dialectic between Europe and the Orient was central to the conception that Europe possessed of itself as well as the notion that colonising Europe was inherently superior and justified in asserting its power over others. Therefore, 'the West creates those others in simple opposition to which it is created ... the other cannot speak against [this closure] because of the West's arrogation to itself of truth as singular yet universal'.[11] As a result, European identity was equated with a neutral universality and the other defined in a 'fantastic inversion of European identity'.[12]

The imposition and subsequent operation of colonial power was dependent upon an Orientalist construction of colonised peoples. This process was highly gendered as it was by depicting Islam, and its various manifestations, as oppressive to women, that colonial administrators were able to justify the exercise of power over colonised others. The depiction of an inferior Islam was a fundamental part of the European narrative of Islam and the 'peculiar practices'[13] of Islam, particularly such practices in respect of women as veiling, were a central feature of that narrative. In attempting to articulate a nexus between sexual and cultural difference in the discourse of Orientalism, Yegenoglu analyses the trope of the veil in a selection of 18th and 19th century European texts. Her analysis reveals that the colonial feminising of the Orient is crucially dependent upon the figure of the veiled Oriental woman – a figure who is therefore assigned a place at the heart of the

---

8   Loomba, 1998, p 49.
9   Darian-Smith, 1996, p 293.
10 Vaughan, 1994, p 3.
11 Fitzpatrick, 1992, p 30.
12 Fitzpatrick, 1992, p 110.
13 Ahmed, L, 1992, p 149.

colonial enterprise – and demonstrates the metonymic association established between the Orient and its women.[14] The Orientalist production of knowledge of Islam, central to the colonial project, gave rise to particularly insidious and deeply entrenched depictions of Muslim women.

From a different perspective from Yegenoglu,[15] Ahmed suggests that already by the 18th century the Western narratives of women had so far misrepresented the status and position of women in Muslim societies that rebuttals by a number of writers and commentators had very little effect on such entrenched and established narratives.[16] The common perception of Muslim women at this time, therefore, was that such women were unequivocally oppressed and subjugated. By the late 19th century such a view of Muslim women had become deeply rooted in European colonial narratives.[17] The centrality that the issue of women occupied in the colonial narrative of Islam can be attributed to a number of reasons. First, the traditional antipathy against Islam that was, by this time, well established in Western narratives of Islam. Second, the European view that other cultures were to be located as inferior to a refined and advanced culture, an idea that colonialism was founded upon. Third, and as Ahmed asserts, feminism, and, in particular, the notion of female emancipation, 'somewhat ironically',[18] played a central role in the colonial narrative of Islam.

The particular example of Western colonialism that Ahmed investigates is British colonial discourse. An important dimension of the self-perception of British culture as superior to other cultures and as the epitome of civilisation was the position of women in British society. Victorian womanhood and societal mores towards women were viewed as exemplary and the prototype to which other societies must aspire. The rhetoric of colonialism was used to export these values to other societies; the oppression of women by their men was an integral part of this rhetoric, used 'to render morally justifiable [the] project of undermining or eradicating the cultures of colonized peoples'.[19] In this way, the 'new' colonial discourse of Islam was focused predominantly around the position of women. Again, a number of areas were pivotal in this discourse: the use of the veil and the segregation of women.[20] These two visible markers of the deficiency and inferiority of Islam and its societies were ample justification for the mobilisation of colonial civilising forces.[21]

As Ahmed notes,[22] these distorted representations were produced primarily by male colonial administrators. However, as access to Muslim women was prohibited to men, these representations were supplemented by representations produced by women of the colonial age. For example, an analysis of a number of women travellers' texts of this era demonstrates how such texts, perceived as containing a more '"feminine" rhetoric'[23] illustrate the insidious nature of Orientalist women's

---

14 Yegenoglu, 1998.
15 Yegenoglu relies primarily on psychoanalytic techniques in her analysis of the depiction of Muslim women whilst Ahmed's methodology is taken from the sociology of history.
16 Ahmed examines the texts of such writers as Lady Mary Montague, who attempted to refute disparaging accounts of Muslim women in matters such as veiling: Ahmed, L, 1992, p 150.
17 See Timothy Mitchell's account in Mitchell, 1988.
18 Ahmed, L, 1992, p 150.
19 Ahmed, L, 1992, p 151.
20 For other analyses investigating these issues, see Mernissi, 1992; Lewis, 1996.
21 There was a glaring inconsistency in the approach of the colonisers and their view of women. Whilst colonial administrators were convinced that the utilisation of emancipatory principles was essential in the colonial project, their views on the position of women in British society differed dramatically. The emancipation of women in Britain was vehemently opposed, often by the same men who called for the emancipation of women in colonised societies: see Ahmed, L, 1992, pp 243–45.
22 Ahmed, L, 1992, p 243.
23 Yegenoglu, 1998, p 13.

accounts of this time. As figures who were able to gain admittance to the inner spaces of the Orient – closed spaces that the masculine gaze was denied access to – Western women performed an important function, as their accounts filled in the gaps or the lack in the knowledge of the Orientalist male. Such women's texts re-inscribed and endorsed the masculine texts of Orientalism and their depiction of Muslim women. These texts should not, therefore, be viewed as sources of a laudable feminist counter-rhetoric, but rather as closely allied to, and collusive with, the narratives of Orientalist men.

It can be argued that such negative representations of Muslim women did not cease with the end of colonialism and that contemporary Western feminist discourse continues to augment the Orientalist depictions of Muslim women, albeit in a more subtle form.[24] This deficiency in feminist thought may be explained partially by its exclusionary nature and the manner in which it has ignored the concerns of women who do not fall into the paradigmatic norm around which it has coalesced. Much Western feminist thought, until comparatively recently, has been founded upon the implicit basis of women as 'an already constituted, coherent group with identical interests and desires, regardless of class, ethnic or racial location or contradictions impl[ying] a notion of gender or sexual difference ... which can be applied universally and cross-culturally'.[25] Consequently, Western feminist thought has been characterised by a failure to acknowledge differences between women and has cast the experiences of a specific group of women to be emblematic of, or normative for, all women. Thus, the notion of equality contained in feminist discourse was predicated upon a denial of difference and the ethnocentric assumptions of white Western, heterosexual, middle class women. A major issue for second wave feminism has been the attempt to reconcile the twin aims of recognising difference and diversity among women, with the imperative to maintain the impetus and coherence of the feminist movement.

However, the history of Islamic feminism demonstrates that, particularly during the formative periods, many of the critiques of Islamic gender discrimination that were being developed during this time were, to varying degrees, influenced by Western feminism.[26] Throughout the Muslim world, movements for the emancipation of women incorporated various elements from Western feminist discourse in their call for the extension of political and social rights for women. Feminists such as Huda Shaarawi, Saiza Nabarawi,[27] Nawal El Saadawi and Doria Shafiq relied heavily on Western feminist discourse and tailored it to their own needs in developing indigenous programmes for reform. The history of women's participation in nationalist movements in the Middle East and elsewhere also demonstrates how the call for women's rights and gender equality was an integral part of the nationalist struggle, with women incorporating such ideals as the abolition of polygamy, the franchise for women, and equal pay for equal work within their demands.[28] Although all of the early feminists framed their demands within an Islamic framework, this was due either to individual faith and personal belief or, in those cases of 'secular' feminists,[29] because of the need to legitimise their claims. However, what is important to note is that these different strands of

---

24 See in particular Ahmed, L, 1992; Lewis, 1996.
25 Talpade Mohanty, 1984.
26 In general terms, this period covers the late 19th and the first half of the 20th centuries.
27 Shaarawi and Nabarawi are famous for discarding their veils at Cairo railway station on their return from an international feminist conference: Badran, 1993, p 135.
28 These demands were made by women in two congresses, the first in 1930 hosted by Syrian women and the second in 1932, hosted by Iranian women: Ostadmalek, 1988.
29 Where the reforms were more explicitly influenced by Western feminism.

theorisation, with their varying emphases upon Islam as the determining framework, could be combined and could co-exist within the overarching rubric of 'Islamic feminism'.[30] Thus, these early feminist theorisations challenged the Orientalist description of Islam as detrimental and restrictive to women, and as incorrect and misleading.

The contemporary Islamic feminist movement has developed rapidly in recent times as a result of many complex, related factors. The Orientalist depiction of Muslim women – both now and in colonial times – the lack of recognition of diversity in Western feminist thought and the contemporary Islamist revival, have all contributed to the forms of Islamic feminism we see today. The contemporary Islamist revival, allied to the anti-West and anti-imperialist discourses of the 1970s and 1980s has given rise to a number of conservative and orthodox interpretations of Islamic principles. Paradoxically, this Islamist revival has also been the impetus for a greater focus on reform within Islam and, in particular, new feminist interpretations, *ijtihad*, of gender rights. Contemporary Islamic feminism is characterised less by a unified coherence than by a doctrinal diversity which reflects the plurality of Islamic thought within the Muslim world. This diversity is further compounded by great cultural and regional differences. One of the most significant and certainly the most radical, the 'new epistemology' school of Islamic feminist thought which yields revitalised, egalitarian gender paradigms in Qur'anic interpretation, appears to imply a homogeneity and unity in Islamic feminism which is difficult to uphold in the face of the diversity of Islamic feminist approaches. However, before concentrating on this important school of thought, it is necessary to locate Islamic feminism within the wider reform movement and to map the key feminist schools of thought within that broader movement.

As the number and range of reform schools of thought is broad in scope, it is essential to be selective in identifying those schools of thought which have relevance for the re-conceptualisation of gendered legal rights. Hallaq has produced a typology for the wider reform movement in Islam and distinguishes between two main schools of thought: the religious utilitarians and the religious liberalists.[31] However, in one important respect, they have a common foundation in that both are based upon the writings of the Egyptian reformist, Muhammad 'Abduh. In addition, they share the same pragmatic aim of the reformulation of legal theory that produces 'a successful synthesis [of] the basic religious values of Islam, on the one hand, and a substantive law that is suitable to the needs of a modern and changing society, on the other'.[32] However, the difference between these two approaches lies chiefly in the methodology each adopts. The central plank of the religious utilitarian approach lies in the emphasis placed upon the concept of *maslaha* or public interest, which revolves around the notions of need and necessity. Here, the traditional notion of *maslaha* has been divested of its medieval connotations and transformed from being a mere juristic device – a concept of limited application – to a new, expanded concept which constitutes the key element of a revitalised legal theory.

In contrast, the religious liberal view abjures the traditional principles of legal methodology altogether and is predicated upon 'understanding revelation in Islam as both text and context'.[33] The emphasis here is upon a purposive and teleological approach to the interpretation of revealed texts, rather than a narrow hermeneutic that licences a literal interpretation. The development of this hermeneutic is a

---

30 For accounts of the history of Islamic feminism, see: Keddie and Baron, 1991; Kandiyoti, 1991; Badran, 1995; Moghadam, 1993; Tucker, 1993; Ahmed, L, 1992; Kandiyoti, 1996.
31 Hallaq, 1997, p 214. For an analysis of this typology see Khaliq, 1999. See also Peters, 1999.
32 Hallaq, 1997, p 214.
33 Hallaq, 1997, p 231.

distinctly new phenomenon in the history of Islamic legal theory, and, as such, heralds a significant departure from the corpus of established Islamic jurisprudence. This school of thought contends that the traditional readings of texts gives rise to a literal interpretation which distorts the true meaning of Islam and, just as importantly, is insufficiently flexible to remodel legal principles to new, diverse situations. Furthermore, as Fazlur Rahman contends,[34] the principles of need and necessity which form the basis of the utilitarian concept of *maslaha*, result in a form of subjectivism whereby the interpretation of the revealed texts become 'subservient to the imperatives of these concepts'.[35]

For Hallaq, the key indicators to determine the efficacy of any reformist approach include a genuine commitment to Islamic values, and a level of theorisation that is sufficiently sophisticated to produce a cohesive and credible methodology. The religious liberal approach fulfils these two requirements in a far more satisfactory manner than the religious utilitarian approach, as the former produces a set of principles which not only subscribes to a truer and more authentic Islamic value system, but also contains a methodology which offers a more radical and comprehensive challenge to orthodox legal theory. The issue of credibility is significant in another respect. The viability of implementing the precepts of a theoretical approach into a social context is a key dimension which Hallaq also focuses upon. Here, the religious utilitarian approach has been more successful than the liberal approach as many of the principles expounded by utilitarian writers have been implemented by a number of Muslim states in the form of legislative reforms. However, these reforms are limited in scope as they often represent a justification of existing state reforms rather than offering new proposals which would produce radical legal innovations. The more radical proposals are offered by the religious liberals; however, many of the writers working in this area are outside the mainstream of legal thought and peripheral to the centres of power.[36]

In dividing the reformist trend into two schools of thought, Hallaq makes brief mention of various writers who concern themselves with gender issues.[37] However, Hallaq fails to explicitly identify and locate the contemporary feminist trends within either of these reformist schools of thought. Barbara Stowasser, on the other hand, locates Islamic feminist thought firmly within the wider modernist and reformist movement and views contemporary Qur'anic interpretations and the new gender paradigms they are creating as central to this project.[38] In her survey of current feminist schools of thought, Stowasser produces a typology of those writers formulating new Qur'an-based interpretive methodologies which offer progressive readings of those aspects of the Qur'an pertaining to women's rights. Her categorisation is threefold: the modernist movement; mid-century modernism; and, as mentioned above, the new epistemology movement. The first of these categories, the modernist movement, includes writers who assume the right to *ijtihad* which incorporates the right to re-fashion the medieval rationalist tradition in the light of modern society's needs. Despite this reformist stance, a number of writers of this early to mid-twentieth century period still adhere to many of the conservative conclusions of the classical traditionalists, especially in matters concerning women's rights.

---

34 Rahman, 1979.
35 Hallaq, 1997, p 254.
36 Hallaq, 1997, p 254.
37 For example, the critique of 'Abd al-Wahhab Khallaf, who is located within the religious utilitarian school of thought, includes a discussion of how Khallaf's theory fails to deal with the exigencies of modern society such as the shares of women in inheritance, and polygamy: Hallaq, 1997, p 224.
38 Stowasser, 1998.

Mid-century modernism, the second of Stowasser's categories, is characterised by a hermeneutic which regards the Qur'anic text as an 'organic unity'[39] in which the organisation of the chapters, and the verses therein, and their order within the text as a whole, are critically important. Writers such as Mahmud Shaltut[40] advanced the view that the interpretation of the Qur'an should be based on a thematic hermeneutic, stressed the importance of *muamalat* (the rules of social interaction) and the implementation of laws based upon this ideal. Again, emphasis was placed upon a contextual approach to the Qur'an, a departure from the atomistic approach of the classical interpreters. Stowasser's last categorisation is the 'new epistemology',[41] the term she uses to describe a theoretical approach that departs radically from classical interpretations and forms the foundation upon which contemporary feminists base their approach.

Stowasser also views 'Abduh[42] as the founder of Islamic modernism and the base for some aspects of contemporary feminist exegetical work. 'Abduh's innovation lies in creating a new hermeneutic by mapping out a division between the laws of religious devotion, *ibadat*, and those which deal with social interaction, *muamalat*. The former are considered to be immutable and normative whilst the latter, of necessity, must be open to adaptation and innovation in response to the changing needs of society.[43] In addition, Qur'anic verses are to be interpreted in a contextual manner, that is, as a part of the Qur'an as a whole, as well as within the context of a specific time. 'Abduh's analyses of certain Qur'anic verses concerning the rights of women led, in some cases, to radical departures from established interpretations in classical Islamic literature. He advanced the then revolutionary view that the Qur'anic verses regarding polygamy and divorce had been traditionally interpreted in such a way that they had resulted in injustice to women. Polygamy was a practice that should be limited to the context in which it was sanctioned – the original time of Islam's inception – whilst the right of women to demand divorce should be reinstated and men should fulfil their obligations towards their former wives by continuing to maintain them for the requisite period.

However, 'Abduh also interpreted Qur'anic verses concerning women in a conservative manner, thus demonstrating his status as the architect of the more traditional religious utilitarian approach, with many principles from this approach having been implemented in recent times by contemporary Muslim states. One of the most problematic Qur'anic verses is *Al Nisa*: 35, which 'Abduh interprets as sanctioning an inequality between the sexes by virtue of biological and social differences that inhere between men and women. The re-creation of an authentic Islamic society can only be produced by emphasising the role of the family in social life, and, specifically, the role of the woman as wife and mother. Men possess innate leadership qualities and, thus, are enjoined to assert that superiority over women in a benign manner by guiding and directing them towards a correct Islamic life. Therefore, the concept of *qiwama* contained in verse 35 is founded upon an understanding of difference between the sexes; that difference is utilised to explain

---

39 Stowasser, 1998, p 36.
40 See also Zebiri, 1993.
41 Stowasser, 1998, p 38.
42 Hallaq argues that 'Abduh did not develop a new legal methodology but rather 'craft[ed] – or perhaps more accurately reviv[ed] – a theology that was necessary for restructuring and rehabilitating legal ideas': Hallaq, 1997, p 212. Much of 'Abduh's work was given form and content by his commentator Rashid Rida, and it was Rida who was responsible for developing the concept of *maslaha* into a full theoretical approach: see Rida, 1956. See also Kerr, 1966.
43 See 'Abduh, 1927–36 and 'Imara, nd.

and justify the separation of men and women into two distinct functions, roles and domains within society. This separation has been developed by contemporary writers such as Safia Iqbal,[44] who contends that Islam delineates a true equality between the sexes in their temporal lives by enjoining them to inhabit different spheres in life. Indeed, this temporal difference, rather than compromising any equality between the sexes, confirms and strengthens the equality of women with men, whilst also acknowledging and basing itself on the difference between the sexes.

The 'new epistemology' movement, the third of Stowasser's categories, is the latest and most radical approach to Qur'anic exegesis and incorporates the contemporary feminist movement. Stowasser identifies writers as diverse as Fazlur Rahman, Amina Wadud-Muhsin, Mahmoud Mohamed Taha, Abdullahi Ahmed An-Na'im, Mohammed Arkoun and Nasr Hamid Abu Zayd within this category. Although the disciplines they specialise in range from literary criticism and linguistics to human rights law, the underlying theme common to all their work is the advancement of interpretive methodologies which yield authentic constructions of Qur'anic verses, faithful to an ethically correct Islamic impulse. Rahman decried the traditional theorists as he believed that they had developed a methodology which fragmented the Qur'an by delivering interpretations of individual verses without placing them in the context of the Qur'an as a whole.[45] This was particularly apparent in the case of those Qur'anic verses dealing with women's rights as the general ameliorative thrust of the Qur'an in respect of women has been subsumed under an interpretive approach which fragments and diffuses the general reformist impulse of the Qur'an. A related problematic was the limited utility of past interpretations of the Qur'an – interpretations which have fossilised over the years and have not applied Qur'anic precepts to changing social conditions. Rahman, therefore, advances a methodology which directly addresses this problem. The first stage consists of viewing the Qur'an and the Prophetic message as a unity, and in order to do this comprehensively, they must be analysed in the light of the time and location of Islam's inception. An understanding of this background to Qur'anic revelation is necessary in order to universalise it beyond the time of Islam's beginning. The next stage consists of enunciating a general principle from specific verses ruling on particular issues; these verses, Rahman claims, have traditionally been interpreted in a fragmented and particular manner, without placing them in their socio-historical context. Finally, in a 'double movement' which relates to time, the general principles elicited from the specific rulings in the Qur'an at the time of Islam's inception are applied to situations in contemporary times.

The main criticism that has been levelled at Rahman's methodology relates to this final element of the double movement theory. Rahman acknowledges that there will often be a substantial difference between situations in the present and the Prophetic past and addresses this only partially by suggesting that a selection be made to apply those elements of Qur'anic law which are 'worthy of espousing'[46] whilst casting aside those that are not deemed worthy of application in present day situations. However, as Hallaq rightly points out, Rahman does not address the problem of how exactly the general principles surmised from Qur'anic verses are to be applied to the current time. Rahman's solution of selecting principles from those

---

44 Iqbal, 1991. For a similar conservative interpretation see Jameelah, 1990; 1971; 1976.
45 Rahman, 1986. See also Rahman, 1982; 1980; 1983.
46 Rahman, 1986, p 49.

verses which contain some intrinsic worth for contemporary times amounts to a methodology which revolves around the unpredictability of subjective choice.[47]

A writer who has had a noticeable impact in the field of Islamic feminism is Amina Wadud-Muhsin, who falls within the specific category of writers developing new methods of Qur'anic exegesis. Wadud-Muhsin acknowledges her debt to Rahman by reinforcing the method of Qur'anic interpretation introduced by him and the importance of developing a contextual approach to understanding the import of Qur'anic verses.[48] Qur'anic injunctions and *Shari'a* rulings, as interpreted by local *ulama* (jurists), continue to define women's legal status and provide a basis for gendered social and cultural practices. As with many other reformist writers, Abdullahi An-Na'im[49] also advocates a highly contextual approach to interpreting the Qur'an in his quest to reconstruct *Shari'a* to incorporate a viable system of human rights. Implicit in An-Na'im's work is the recognition that the development of a dynamic new methodology is the key to delineating a framework of Islamic human rights, one that locates the idea of gender equality at its very heart. A pivotal aspect of his methodology is the need to differentiate between verses revealed in the Meccan and the Medinan periods, with the former, more egalitarian verses forming the base from which gender equal laws may be formulated.[50]

This approach departs fundamentally from the traditional approach in which the interpretations of orthodox *ulama* have been 'canonize[d] ... into an antihistorical immutability'.[51] This method also requires the jettisoning of much traditional *Shari'a* formulated over the centuries – especially those parts dealing with legal rights for women – as this has been based largely upon the later Medinan verses. This is a revolutionary, and for most orthodox Muslim jurists, unpalatable, proposal as it is predicated upon the abrogation of certain Qur'anic verses: the verses that form the base upon which many of the traditional (conservative) *Shari'a* principles are founded. As far as other contemporary reformist writers are concerned, An-Na'im's methodology in this respect also goes beyond the proposals advanced by them. Thus, by suspending various aspects of the Medinan verses of the Qur'an and the resulting legal rights, a *Shari'a* public law of equal human rights may be created. The contextual specificity that An-Na'im advocates means that the development of the new *Shari'a*, using the earlier Meccan verses of the Qur'an, will now reflect and respond to situations in contemporary life.

Finally, Stowasser categorises Nasr Hamid Abu Zayd in her typology as belonging to the group of writers who, like Mohammad Arkoun,[52] are developing a scriptural interpretive methodology which utilises non-Islamic sources of textual criticism. In particular, Abu Zayd utilises techniques from disciplines such as linguistics and literary criticism to advance the theory that the Qur'an is open to a diversity of interpretations[53] and that the imposition of a univocal interpretation by traditionalist writers has resulted in the distortion of the Qur'anic message as far as gender rights

---

47 For Hallaq, the methodology espoused by Muhammad Shahrur addresses this problem in a far more convincing manner: Hallaq, 1997, pp 245–53.

48 Wadud-Muhsin, 1999. For a concise summary of Wadud-Muhsin's theoretical advances, see Roald, 1998.

49 An-Na'im has developed Mahmoud Mohamed Taha's premise that, in order to initiate a truly reformist approach to Qur'anic interpretation, a distinction must be made between the early Meccan period of Islam in which the liberal and egalitarian verses of the Qur'an were revealed and the second, Medinan period, in which verses were revealed in response to specific social situations as they arose. Taha, 1987 identifies this latter category of verses as enunciating more restrictive principles.

50 An-Na'im, 1990. See also An-Na'im, 1984.

51 Majid, 1998, p 352.

52 Arkoun, 1994.

53 See in particular Abu Zayd, 1990; Abu Zayd, 1994a.

are concerned. In his polemical work, *al-Mar'a fi Khitab al-Azma*,[54] Abu Zayd distinguishes between central or core verses of the Qur'an, which encapsulate the fundamental notion of gender equality, and exceptional verses which discriminate (invariably to the detriment of women) between the sexes. The applicability of such exceptional verses must be limited to particular historical contexts and be viewed as secondary to those core verses which articulate gender equality. It is this latter category of verses which are to have a universal, normative effect.

As mentioned previously, Stowasser's typology is dependent on identifying those writers who are developing a specific hermeneutics based on scriptural, and in particular, Qur'anic, exegesis. Yamani has devised a broader typology of Islamic feminism, bringing together writers from a variety of disciplines including political science, law, sociology, social anthropology and linguistics, categorising them under the terms, 'new feminist traditionalists', 'pragmatists', 'secular feminists', and 'neo-Islamists'.[55] Despite vast differences in the theoretical approach between these schools of thought, all the writers are characterised by 'a common concern with the empowerment of their gender within a rethought Islam',[56] including those writers concerned directly with developing new interpretive methodologies of the Qur'an. Yamani divides the first category of new feminist traditionalists into three further sub-categories: modernists, secularists, and traditionalists.

These sub-categories are not delineated clearly and appear to contain some overlap, but it appears that most of the feminist exegetes developing new interpretive methodologies may be identified as belonging to the modernist sub-category. What differentiates them is the resulting legal rights for women determined by their own particular interpretation. For instance, Raga' El-Nimr, who could also be defined as a new feminist traditionalist in her call for a return to orthodoxy, emphasises the biological difference between men and women. Her contention is that sexual difference is a difference ordained by divine will and that this justifies and explains the resulting inequality that women face. For El-Nimr the advantageous legal rights that men benefit from – the principle of male guardianship, male witnesses possessing greater evidential weight, the male prerogative of polygamy – do not denote a lower status for women but rather confirm their temporal difference from men. However, and this is a significant point, this acknowledgment of difference does not, in any manner, imperil or weaken the notion of spiritual equality between men and women.[57]

In contrast to El-Nimr's traditional approach is the view propounded by Ghada Karmi.[58] As a writer who falls in the modernist or pragmatic category, Karmi is sceptical about the claim that the arrival of Islam led to the introduction of greater rights for women. In her reading of the Qur'anic injunctions on evidence, divorce, custody and polygamy, she finds little evidence of a message of equality and much that points to an explicit scriptural bias against women. Karmi's stance is interesting as it incorporates the notion of re-interpreting the Qur'an but, in opposition to many other feminists offering interpretive methodologies, Karmi's reading of the Qur'an is not predicated upon a belief in the transformative nature of Islam. In other words, Karmi's analysis of women's status at the time of the introduction of

---

54 Abu Zayd, 1994b.

55 Although these terms are, to a large extent, self-explanatory, Yamani fails to define individual writers clearly within each of these categories. As a result, there is some overlap between the categories and a lack of clarity over the exact difference between them (eg what is the difference between 'new feminist traditionalists' and 'neo-Islamists'?): Yamani, 1996.

56 Yamani, 1996, p 1.

57 El-Nimr, 1996. For a similar theoretical perspective see Iqbal, 1991.

58 Karmi, 1996.

Islam demonstrates that Islam had a regressive, rather than an ameliorative, effect on women's rights.

The feminist traditionalist approach in Yamani's typology includes the work of Haleh Afshar, Maha Azzam, Munira Fakhro and Mai Yamani. Here, the emphasis is upon locating women's rights within an Islamic framework and viewing the reversion to an 'authentic' Islam as the means by which an ethically correct gender paradigm and resulting legal rights may be constructed. Many in this school of thought challenge the hegemony of the orthodox interpretive process and offer a clearly defined Islamic agenda for reform. The feminists working on a specifically legal agenda include such writers as Ziba Mir-Hosseini[59] and Najla Hamadeh.[60] Mir-Hosseini analyses contemporary feminist movements in Iran and contends that a number of profound changes are taking place in issues centred around women's rights. Specifically, divorce laws in Iran have been reversed as a result of feminist re-readings of scripture in which a contextual approach has been adopted to 're-interpret' and re-direct the Qur'anic message in favour of gender equality. The significance for Mir-Hosseini lies in the fact that these changes have come about as a result of a feminist discourse that is purely Islamic; the fact that Western feminist language has no purchase within this discourse is critical in explaining why feminist innovations at the theoretical level have been translated into real practical gains at the level of legal change.

Hamadeh investigates Islamic family law, divorce and custody rights in particular, to contend that interpretations of the Qur'an and Sunna have been manipulated and distorted to produce particular laws in favour of men. The laws disadvantage women by diluting, and in some cases denying, the extensive rights they are entitled to if proper constructions of scripture are undertaken and the concomitant legal rights enacted. By highlighting the stagnation of Islamic jurisprudence in this regard, Hamadeh re-affirms the contextual approach adopted by many reformist writers and argues that the implementation of non-discriminatory rights for women entails disregarding outmoded interpretations contained in traditional jurisprudence and in locating the interpretation of relevant Qur'anic verses within the context of contemporary times. Again, her comments, in line with other feminist writers, are founded upon the notion of Islam as a phenomenon which instigated great improvements for women; what is required is simply a reversion to the egalitarian principles of original Islam.

Despite the diversity of approach and emphasis in each of the above schools of thought, it is clear that most Islamic feminists are striving for a re-creation or renewal of gender equality within an explicitly Islamic framework. This has two important implications. First, the idea of equality is one that is assumed, with little or no theoretical discussion of the implications of basing it on the concept of sexual difference or sameness. My main concern is with feminist writers developing new methodologies of Qur'anic exegesis as this is the area in which the most innovative work is being generated. The idea of sexual difference here becomes immaterial when considering the notion of spiritual equality – women and men have corresponding and commensurate spiritual and devotional duties. Therefore, the concept of equality rests upon a 'mirroring' between men and women in their sameness to each other. Second, the feminist rejoinder to orthodox interpretations of the Qur'an has been to highlight the manner in which sexual difference has been deployed to justify the establishment of lesser rights for women. However, feminist

---

59 See Mir-Hosseini, 1996. Also Mir-Hosseini, 1993; 2000.
60 Hamadeh, 1996.

writers have not addressed the question of when and to what extent the idea of sexual difference is acceptable within scripture.

For example, the re-interpretation of problematic Qur'anic verses such as that pertaining to the male right of polygyny[61] revolves around challenging the idea of sexual difference which gives rise to a gender hierarchy in which women possess lesser rights than men in contracting marriages of this kind. The next stage of the feminist argument is directed towards stressing a normative spiritual equality between the sexes and how this should form the basis for equality in marriage. Therefore, this part of the argument hinges on an emphasis on sameness in order to achieve equality. In these cases the concept of equality is used in a 'levelling up' motion which improves the lesser status of women. The more complex questions arise in those cases where scriptural injunctions prescribe certain rights to women in their capacity as wives or mothers. In some cases, these rights may be greater than the ones enjoyed by men and may place a clear and positive obligation upon them. What notion of equality is to be deployed here? Is the normative spiritual equality, implicitly predicated as it is upon the sameness of men and women, to be used as the basis for the elimination of sexual difference in these cases? Or is the conferring of greater rights for (some) women, and the corresponding retention of sexual difference, acceptable if it results in an equality which gives women a superior status in the institution of a new gender hierarchy?

The scepticism about the transformative potential of Islam for women, voiced by Karmi, above, finds a resonance in the work of Haideh Moghissi. Moghissi considers Islamic scripture and teaching as a framework which is based incontrovertibly upon the notion of a gender hierarchy. Consequently, Islam and feminism are wholly incompatible and Moghissi questions the value of developing a programme of social and legal rights for women within a frame of reference which is inherently antithetical to the notion of gender equality.[62] Traditionally, Islam and feminism have been viewed as mutually exclusive ideologies, a schism established and supported by Orientalist and neo-Orientalist renderings of Islam which represent Islam as fixed and immutable and implacably opposed to the extension of women's rights. Conversely, the Muslim world has viewed feminism as an indisputably 'Western' concept,[63] and one that is characterised as secular, individualistic, and critical of women's roles as wives and mothers. This perceived antinomy between the two ideologies has resulted in a denial that feminist activity is taking place in the Muslim world. Although the term 'feminist' may not be used explicitly when describing much of this activity, the proliferation of indigenous forms of endeavour in which the position of women within is being analysed, and in many cases, actively challenged, amply illustrates the importance of feminism within Muslim societies.

The homogeneity of feminist theory has been most strongly challenged from a race perspective, by writers who have critiqued the totalising effects of feminist theory and practice and found that it excluded or marginalised the concerns of black women. The 'gender essentialism' of feminist thought,[64] in which there is an undifferentiated 'women's experience' devoid of any diversity or heterogeneity, is

---

61 *Al-Nisa*: 5.
62 Moghissi, 1999, p 126.
63 This has resulted in Muslim feminists such as Nawal El Saadawi and Fatima Mernissi being branded as 'Western feminists' and therefore being less able to politically influence developments in the Muslim world.
64 Harris, 1991, p 238. Harris argues that, in the US context, gender essentialism has been especially entrenched, making the movement towards recognition of the diversity of women's experiences particularly slow.

at the heart of this critique and has had a significant impact on feminist theory, being one of the main driving forces towards the recognition and implementation of difference. Another important challenge to feminist theory's homogenising tendency has been from 'Third World' feminists, often writing from a post-colonial perspective. Again, critiques have focused on the manner in which the concerns of women in 'Third World' post-colonial societies differ radically from those that are incorporated in Western feminists' agendas. This denial of difference has been detrimental not only because it has ignored the concerns of large groups of women, but also because that denial has been hidden as Western feminism has projected itself as if it has incorporated the concerns and interests of these other women.

The acknowledgment of internal heterogeneity in Western societies and the need to accommodate difference within democratic pluralistic polities has also influenced feminist thought and its belated recognition of difference. In identifying Western feminism, an 'external' site, for the production of difference, and in refusing to incorporate the notion of difference within its own theorisations, Islamic feminism projects itself as truly indigenous and authentic, and untainted by Western concepts. However, in failing to incorporate the notion of difference, Islamic feminism conveniently bypasses the need to take into account the ethnic and religious heterogeneity of Muslim societies themselves, thereby denying the concerns of those women considered to be politically marginal. The need to put forward a coherent feminist position, located within an Islamic framework may well be considered necessary from a strategic perspective. As Hallaq points out, it is the religious utilitarians, the more conservative of the reformist schools, who have had the most political success in translating their theoretical advances into real political gains. Feminists may also feel that it is necessary to advance a homogenised, Islamic framework – particularly in countries in which Islamists wield considerable power – which denies difference, in order to exercise political power for achieving legal and social rights for women.

It may also be true that the emphasis on sameness in contemporary Islamic feminism is a necessary stage in its theoretical development. The focus on a sameness of experience, of culture, and of religion, may be necessary in assisting in the construction of a sense of community and in strengthening theoretical coherence. Nevertheless, there is a danger that this focus on a uniformity of concerns will lead to a 'debilitating ossification of difference'[65] which arrests the development of an internal critique in Islamic feminist scholarship. To some extent, this problematic development is already taking place as there is little internal criticism of scripture-based feminist advances, and the difficulties they pose for women who fall outside their explicitly Islamic framework. Thus, the recognition of diversity among women, and of the concerns of women who are marginalised by current feminist explorations in Islamic scholarship, is essential in opening a new phase in the politics of feminist theorisation in Muslim societies.

---

65 Talpade Mohanty, 1995, p 78.

References

'Abduh, Muhammad (1927–36) *Tafsir al-Manar*, Cairo

Abu Zayd, Nasr Hamid (1990) *Mafhum al-Nass; Dirash fi 'Ulum al-Qur'an*, Beirut: al-Markaz al-Thaqafi al-'Arabi

Abu Zayd, Nasr Hamid (1994a) *Naqd al-Khitab al-Dini*, Cairo: Sina lil-Nashr

Abu Zayd, Nasr Hamid (1994b) *al-Mar'a fi Khitab al-Azma*, Cairo: Dar al-Nusus

Ahmed, Akbar S (1992) *Postmodernism and Islam*, London: Routledge

Ahmed, Leila (1992) *Women and Gender in Islam*, New Haven: Yale UP

An-Na'im, Abdullahi (1984) 'A modern approach to human rights in Islam: foundations and implications for Africa', in Welch Jr, Claude and Meltzer, Ronald (eds), *Human Rights and Development in Africa*, Albany: State University of New York Press

An-Na'im, Abdullahi (1990) *Toward an Islamic Reformism: Civil Liberties, Human Rights, and International Law*, Syracuse: Syracuse UP

Arkoun, Mohammad (1994) *Rethinking Islam: Common Questions, Uncommon Answers*, Lee, Robert D (trans and ed), Boulder: Westview

Badran, Margot (1993) 'Independent women: more than a century of feminism in Egypt', in Tucker, 1993

Badran, Margot (1995) *Feminists, Islam and Nation*, Princeton, NJ: Princeton UP

Darian-Smith, Eve (1996) 'Postcolonialism: a brief introduction' 5 Social and Legal Studies 291

El-Nimr, Raga' (1996) 'Women in Islamic law', in Yamani, 1996

Fitzpatrick, Peter (1992) *The Mythology of Modern Law*, London: Routledge

Hallaq, Wael B (1997) *A History of Islamic Legal Theories*, Cambridge: CUP

Hamadeh, Najla (1996) 'Islamic family legislation: the authoritarian discourse of silence', in Yamani, 1996

Harris, Angela (1991) 'Race and essentialism in feminist legal theory', in Bartlett, Katherine T and Kennedy, Rosanne (eds), *Feminist Legal Theory: Readings in Law and Gender*, Boulder: Westview

'Imara, Muhammad (ed) (nd) *al-Islam wa-al-Mar'ah fi Ta'y al-Imam Muhammad 'Abduh*, Cairo

Iqbal, Safia (1991) *Woman and Islamic Law*, Delhi: Adam

Jameelah, Maryam (1971) *Islam and Modernism*, Lahore: Muhammad Yusuf Khan

Jameelah, Maryam (1976) *Islam and the Muslim Woman Today*, Lahore: Muhammad Yusuf Khan

Jameelah, Maryam (1990) *Islam in Theory and Practice*, Lahore: Muhammad Yusuf Khan

Kandiyoti, D (ed) (1991) *Women, Islam and the State*, London: Macmillan

Kandiyoti, D (ed) (1996) *Gendering the Middle East – Emerging Perspectives*, London: IB Taurus

Karmi, Ghada (1996) 'Women, Islam and patriarchalism', in Yamani, 1996

Keddie, NR and Baron, B (eds) (1991) *Women in Middle Eastern History: Shifting Boundaries in Sex and Gender*, New Haven: Yale UP

Kerr, Malcolm (1966) *Islamic Reform: The Political and Legal Theories of Muhammad 'Abduh and Rashid Rida*, Berkeley: University of California Press

Khaliq, Urfan (1999) 'Coping with modernity? Literature and Islamic legal theories' 20(3) Legal History 115

Lewis, Reina (1996) *Gendering Orientalism*, London: Routledge

Loomba, Ania (1998) *Colonialism/Postcolonialism*, London: Routledge

Majid, Anouar (1998) 'The politics of feminism in Islam' 23(2) Signs: Journal of Women in Culture and Society 321

Mernissi, Fatima (1992) *Women and Islam: An Historical and Theological Enquiry*, Oxford: Blackwell

Mir-Hosseini, Ziba (1993) *Marriage on Trial: A Study of Islamic Family Law in Iran and Morocco Compared*, London: IB Taurus

Mir-Hosseini, Ziba (1996) 'Stretching the limits: a feminist reading of the Shari in post-Khomeini Iran', in Yamani, 1996

Mir-Hosseini, Ziba (2000) *Islam and Gender The Religious Debate in Contemporary Iran*, London: IB Taurus

Mitchell, Timothy (1988) *Colonising Egypt*, Cambridge: CUP

Moghadam, VM (ed) (1993) *Identity Politics and Women: Cultural Reassertions and Feminisms in International Perspective*, Boulder: Westview

Moghissi, Haideh (1999) *Feminism and Islamic Fundamentalism The Limits of Postmodern Analysis*, London, New York: Zed

Ostadmalek (1988) *Hijab va Kashf-e Hijab Dar Iran*, Tehran: Ataii, pp 112–24, quoted in Moghissi, Haideh, *Feminism and Islamic Fundamentalism: The Limits of Postmodern Analysis*, London: Zed

Peters, Rudolph (1999) 'For his correction and as a deterrent example for others: Mehmed 'Ali's first criminal legislation (1829–1830)' 6(2) Islamic Law and Society 164

Rahman, Fazlur (1979) 'Towards reformulating the methodology of Islamic law: Sheikh Yamani on "public interest" in Islamic law' 12 NYU Jo of Int Law and Politics 223

Rahman, Fazlur (1980) *Major Themes of the Qur'an*, Minneapolis: Bibliotheca Islamica

Rahman, Fazlur (1982) 'Towards reformulating the methodology of Islamic law: Sheikh Yamani on "public interest" in Islamic law', in *Islam and Modernity*, Chicago: Chicago UP

Rahman, Fazlur (1983) 'The status of women in the Qur'an', in Nashat, Guity (ed), *Women and Revolution in Iran*, 1983, Boulder: Westview

Rahman, Fazlur (1986) 'Interpreting the Qur'an' 3 Inquiry 45

Rida, Rashid (1956) *Yusr al-Islam wa Usul al-Tashri' al-Amm*, Cairo: Matba'at Nahdat Misr

Roald, Anne Sofie (1998) 'Feminist reinterpretations of Islamic sources: Muslim feminist theology in the light of the Christian tradition of feminist thought', in Ask, Karin and Tjomsland, Marit (eds), *Women and Islamization Contemporary Dimensions of Discourse on Gender Relations*, Oxford and New York: Berg

Said, Edward W (1995) *Orientalism*, London: Penguin

Stowasser, Barbara (1998) 'Gender issues and contemporary Qur'an interpretation', in Yazbeck Haddad, Yvonne and Esposito, John L (eds), *Islam, Gender, and Social Change*, New York: OUP

Taha, Mahmoud Mohamed (1987) *The Second Message of Islam*, Syracuse: Syracuse UP

Talpade Mohanty, Chandra (1984) 'Under Western eyes: feminist scholarship and colonial discourses' 12(3), 13(1) Boundary

Talpade Mohanty, Chandra (1995) 'Feminist encounters: locating the politics of experience', in Nicholson, Linda and Sideman, Steven (eds), *Social Postmodernism: Beyond Identity Politics*, Cambridge and New York: CUP

Tucker, Judith (ed) (1993) *Arab Women: Old Boundaries, New Frontiers*, Bloomington: Indiana UP

Vaughan, M (1994) 'Colonial discourse theory and African history, or has postmodernism passed us by?' 20(2) Social Dynamics 1

Wadud-Muhsin, Amina (1999) *Qur'an and Woman: Rereading the Sacred Text from a Woman's Perspective*, New York: OUP

Yamani, Mai (ed) (1996) *Feminism and Islam: Legal and Literary Perspectives*, Reading: Ithaca

Yegenoglu, Meyda (1998) *Colonial Fantasies: Towards a Feminist Reading of Orientalism*, Cambridge: CUP

Zafrullah Khan, Muhammad (1981) *Qur'an*, translation and commentary, London: Curzon

Zebiri, Kate (1993) *Mahmud Shaltut and Islamic Modernism*, Oxford: Clarendon

Chapter 9
The balancing act: counter-terrorism and civil liberties in British anti-terrorism law

Rhiannon Talbot

Since the attacks on 11 September 2001, Prime Minister Blair has attempted to lead Britain into a major role in the Coalition's 'War on Terrorism'. Militarily Britain's contribution can only be limited in comparison with the resources available to the Americans, but Blair's legal (and diplomatic) efforts could develop a leading position within the Coalition. The Anti-Terrorism, Crime and Security Act 2001 is both part of that endeavour and Britain's response to the United Nations Security Council's call:

> ... on the international community to redouble their efforts to prevent and suppress terrorist acts including by increased cooperation and full implementation of the relevant international anti-terrorist conventions and Security Council Resolutions.[1]

Acts of terror are frequently appalling in the sheer scale of suffering, damage and, in particular, shock they inflict. There is an understandable temptation on the part of politicians and institutions, such as the police, who have to deal first hand with the horror of a terrorist attack, to obtain a plethora of extra, more invasive powers that can prevent the immediate planning and execution of atrocities. When these extra powers are granted the result is often a limitation of human rights and restrictions on civil liberties.[2] Some restrictions on civil liberties, although deplorable, can be very effective in counter-terrorism terms *if* the goals are the aversion of immediate casualties and/or punishing terrorist offenders. Other infringements of civil liberties can have devastating effects in prolonging and promoting conflict. The long term consequence of restricting civil liberties (and human rights) often promotes mistrust and encourages alienation and hostility, thus leading to more violence. The experience of internment in Northern Ireland and the Israelis' recent re-occupation of the West Bank and Gaza Strip are good examples of short term gains actually prolonging the conflict. Anecdotal evidence suggests that disregarding the civil liberties of those who terrorise only encourages more violence in the long term.[3] Consequently, it would appear that for counter-terrorism measures to be successful in the long term and discourage violence, they ought to include a respect for the individual rights of those who terrorise. The ability to balance the demands of counter-terrorism effectiveness with a respect for civil liberties is a precarious one that has rarely been achieved in English counter-terrorism law. This paper will review the Anti-Terrorism, Crime and Security Act 2001 (ATCS) in the light of these two contrary forces, counter-terrorism effectiveness and civil liberties.

Before an assessment of the ATCS balance between these competing factors can be drawn, an outline of the Act and its location within the long history of British anti-terrorism 'emergency' legislation is informative. Specialist counter-terrorism

---

1   Security Council Resolution 1368, 12 September 2001, para 4.
2   I do not equate civil liberties and human rights as the same thing. In this article I am primarily concerned with civil liberties.
3   For example, conflicts in the Middle East, Kashmir, East Timor, Spain, the Philippines, Indonesia and Northern Ireland.

measures in response to modern terrorism in Northern Ireland were first enacted in 1972.[4] In 1996 a government sponsored report by Lord Lloyd of Berwick reviewed all of the counter-terrorism legislation in the light of the peace process in Northern Ireland and considered what laws and powers were required to counter terrorism into the 21st century.[5] The majority of the recommendations found expression in the Terrorism Act 2000 (TA). In contrast to the considered TA, the ATCS was hastily rushed through parliament after the attacks in the United States on 11 September 2001. The ATCS was heralded as necessary to fortify the gaps and weaknesses in the UK's counter-terrorism laws exposed by the attacks in America.

The ATCS is a huge document, containing 129 sections and 8 Schedules. Its provisions range from asylum and immigration law, through bribery and international finance, to police and security service power. It delves into weapons of mass destruction and aviation security. It jumps into hate crimes, paddles in communications and data protection law and ploughs through a variety of institutional changes. It is not possible to review all of the sections of the Act and attention will focus upon those that have introduced the most significant changes. Some of the sections are time limited and after two years the Privy Council must review the whole Act. Any section it specifies will cease to have effect six months later unless parliament chooses to re-enact it.[6] Unlike the TA, the ATCS has been certified by the Secretary of State as complying with the Human Rights Act 1998 and our obligations under the European Convention on Human Rights, although most commentators have been deeply critical of its infringements of civil liberties.[7]

Civil liberties losses to counter-terrorism fervour

Many of the sections within the ATCS have attracted considerable criticism from the civil liberties perspective. Perhaps the most criticised provisions are the extension of police powers, the changes to asylum and immigration law and the retention of communications data.[8]

The retention of communications data

The change to the retention of communications data has been described by Bowden as 'CCTV for the inside of your head'.[9] Under the ATCS the Secretary of State is required to issue a code of practice for the retention of communications data obtained by communications providers, such as postal services, telephone companies and internet services providers.[10] The range of information to be covered is very broad and

> may contain any such provision as appears to the Secretary of State to be necessary–
>
> (a)   for the purpose of safeguarding national security; or
> (b)   for the purposes of prevention or detection of crime or the prosecution of offenders which may relate directly or indirectly to national security.[11]

---

4   This statement is not entirely accurate as the Stormont Parliament in Belfast had passed a number of earlier Acts and statutory instruments, but the 1972 Act was the first major legislative response in Westminster to the conflict in Northern Ireland.

5   *Inquiry into Legislation Against Terrorism* by the Right Honourable Lord Lloyd of Berwick, October 1996, Cm 3420.

6   ATCS 2001, ss 122–24.

7   Eg Tomkins, 2002, pp 205–20; Bowden, 2002, pp 21–24. Editorial, *Criminal Law Review*, pp 159–60.

8   Joint Committee on Human Rights, 2001–02.

9   Bowden, 2002, p 23.

10   This code of practice must be drawn up in consultation with the industry and be laid before parliament, s 103.

11   ATCS 2001, s 102(3).

The definition of communications data in the ATCS is that used by the Regulation of Investigatory Powers (RIP) Act 2000, s 1. In this section, communications data includes all 'traffic data'; who people talk to by phone or email, what they read on website browsers and following where they go by tracking their mobile phones. As Bowden states, 'traffic data constitutes a near complete map of private life'.[12] Most telecommunications companies keep some of this type of information for a limited time for market analysis and billing purposes. It is possible that the ATCS will require telecommunications companies to collect and retain this sort of information on the whole population for very lengthy time periods. Retention and access to this information is not limited to terrorism offences or even activities indirectly linked to national security issues. These are unprecedented surveillance powers, but are there really urgent and pressing counter-terrorism imperatives that require them?

It is difficult to be precise about the threat posed by terrorists using information technology. It appears that Al Qa'ida operatives planned and co-ordinated their attacks through the internet. In the only prosecution for the Omagh bombing, the calls made from a mobile telephone constituted pivotal evidence. Graham Head, Detective Chief Inspector with the National Criminal Intelligence Service (NCIS) and a Europol Liaison Officer for the NCIS, wrote in an article in the *Journal of Terrorism and Political Violence* in 1999 that the new communication technologies, especially the freely available encryption programmes, could be used as an offensive tool by both criminals and terrorists: 'pre-paid mobile telephones, a much sought after product, are very accessible, affordable and a gift to the criminal.'[13] The developments in telecommunications technology's capacity for increasing secret communications between terrorists are clear, as is the law enforcement and intelligence agencies' desire to access this information. In a report leaked to the press, NCIS urged the Home Office to establish a 'traffic data' warehouse to monitor and store just this sort of information on the entire UK population.[14] Although the internet is a potentially powerful tool for terrorists and its use presents minimum risks to their security, the powers granted by the ATCS are deeply flawed as counter-terrorism tools whilst being a very serious infringement on our civil liberties.

Most of the powers granted in the ATCS are concerned with monitoring emails and phone calls, but this information cannot prove who wrote the email or who made the telephone call, even if the communications are sourced to private telephone lines or personal email accounts. Nor can this sort of monitoring prove who actually accessed which internet sites, or that the information gained was intended to be used for harmful purposes. Anyone can easily prevent their 'traffic data' from being monitored by using prepaid telephones and public internet access points, which are not covered by the terms of the ATCS, and the readily available powerful computer encryption programmes.[15] If it is easy for the terrorists to evade successful monitoring or to hide their messages in ways that are almost undetectable,[16] then the provisions are toothless and ineffective in counter-terrorism terms. These provisions, however, have taken a vicious bite out of our

---

12 Bowden, 2002, p 21.
13 Head, 1999, p 23.
14 Gaspar, 2000.
15 Bowden, 2002, pp 21–22.
16 Undoubtedly it is impossible to gauge the extent of this problem, especially when the existence of the message itself may be hidden in an innocuous document such as an image. In his article Graham Head gives two examples where the police, when using 'extremely powerful computers', were unable to decode more than 10 per cent of the encrypted material found on one paedophile's computer and could decode none of the encrypted material on an electronic personal organiser. Head, 1999, p 21.

civil liberties that cannot be justified by reference to preventing or punishing terrorism. These provisions have not balanced our loss of civil liberties with any form of counter-terrorism effectiveness.

The extension of police powers

The Act contains amendments to both the Police and Criminal Evidence Act 1984 (PACE) and the Criminal Justice and Public Order Act 1994. The apparent change in terrorism tactics since 11 September 2001 *may* justify new specialised police powers, but this is not really in contention here as the structure of the provisions means that the most significant changes to police powers that the ATCS has introduced have been to ordinary police activities, not counter-terrorist police powers. Any infringement on civil liberties extends throughout the ordinary law and not just in counter-terrorist circumstances. The ATCS now allows the police to search and examine a person for identifying marks or take a fingerprint for the purpose of ascertaining his identity[17] (this power is also extended to those detained under the TA).[18] The police are also empowered to photograph a person detained at a police station with or without their consent,[19] any identifying mark found on their body[20] and, for the purposes of the photograph, the police can remove any covering from the face or head.[21] These photographs may be 'disclosed to any person for any purpose related to the prevention or detection of crime, the investigation of an offence or the conduct of a prosecution',[22] and the police can retain any photographs.[23] An officer of the rank of inspector or above may in certain circumstances, which are not confined to terrorism, authorise constables within a specified locality and for a maximum of 48 hours to require anyone within that locality to remove any item that the constable believes is being worn wholly or mainly for the purpose of concealing his identity, and that item may be seized.[24]

Whilst some of these powers and their restriction on civil liberties might seem innocuous when compared to preventing an atrocity or prosecuting those who plant bombs designed to murder and maim, the fact remains that they are not purely counter-terrorism measures. They are new powers that the police can enforce against anyone, irrespective of whether terrorism is involved. These powers mean that the police are able to demand a body search in order to identify a person, the removal of items of clothing in public if they conceal their identity, and the retention of photographs and fingerprints will provide the police with a permanent information bank. Ordinary police powers can now override a person's rights to control access to their body. The need to ascertain a person's identity *might* be important for effective anti-terrorism when terrorists are often well trained in counter-interrogation techniques, especially if the authorities are tying to prevent an attack: for example, if the police have intelligence that an imminent attack with potential fatalities is likely to be carried out by a certain individual. However, the provisions in the ATCS are not limited to terrorism in any way or designed to be carefully targeted. These provisions merely present the police with tempting powers that might be convenient and expedient for them, but they are an extremely

---

17 ATCS 2001, s 90. This power can be used either to prove someone's identity or to prove that s/he is not a particular person.

18 *Ibid*, s 89.

19 *Ibid*, s 92.

20 *Ibid*, s 90.

21 *Ibid*, s 92. The person can be detained under the ordinary criminal provisions of PACE 1984; they do not need to be detained under the TA 2000.

22 *Ibid*, s 90.

23 *Ibid*, ss 90, 92.

24 *Ibid*, s 94.

significant extension of power to control the general public and a serious infringement on civil liberties. Like the provisions on the retention of communications data, there is very little attempt to strike a balance between civil liberties and counter-terrorism effectiveness in these provisions because they are not principally concerned with counter-terrorism.

The provisions on asylum and immigration

The changes to the asylum and immigration laws are very significant, and in these provisions the dilemma for the authorities in reaching a balance between civil liberties and effective counter-terrorism measures is acutely demonstrated. It must be noted from the outset that the provisions in this part of the ATCS are limited and expire after 15 months but, of course, parliament has the right to re-enact them if it chooses. The temporality of this part of the ATCS is perhaps its only saving grace. This part of the Act is directed against a perceived problem that foreign nationals involved in terrorism elsewhere in the world are successfully claiming asylum or gaining immigration rights in order to avoid prosecution in their home countries. A potential problem was identified in the UN Security Council's Resolution 1373.[25] Not only are these 'international terrorists' considered to be using asylum claims to avoid prosecution in the UK, they are also thought to be using Britain as a base to organise and promote terrorism elsewhere in the world.

It was these sorts of fears that prompted enactment of an offence of conspiracy to commit offences outside the UK in the Criminal Justice (Terrorism and Conspiracy) Act 1998,[26] the offences of inciting[27] and directing[28] terrorism in the TA, and the widely drafted definition of terrorism that is expressly designed to counter all forms of international terrorism, including acts that are not directed against UK nationals, property or interests.[29] As the information about suspects and their actions generally comes from secretive intelligence sources, it is impossible to assess the accuracy of these fears. There are some clues, however. Firstly, there are governments, for example the Egyptian government, which have been deeply critical of the UK's grant of asylum to some of their nationals who are wanted in connection with terrorist crimes and have been pressing for their extradition. Secondly, the UK government has attempted to return people to whom it had previously awarded immigration or asylum rights because their involvement in terrorism was considered to be a threat to national security.[30] It seems reasonable from these minor indicators that immigration and asylum rights in particular have been at least very occasionally used to shield terrorist activities. Assuming, although this is not actually proven, that this does occur, the question remains whether the powers that have been granted in the ATCS are an appropriate mechanism to counter this activity.

The most sensational development in the ATCS is the introduction of detention without trial for non-UK nationals and is directed at this perceived problem.[31] In

---

25 United Nations Security Council Resolution 1373 (2001), 28 September 2001, para 3 calls upon states to: '(f) take appropriate measures in conformity with the relevant provisions of national and international law, including international standards of human rights, before granting refugee status, for the purpose of ensuring that the asylum-seeker has not planned, facilitated or participated in the commission of terrorist acts; (g) ensure, in conformity with international law, that refugee status is not abused by the perpetrators, organizers or facilitators of terrorist acts, and that claims of political motivation are not recognized as grounds for refusing requests for the extradition of alleged terrorists.'
26 Section 5.
27 TA 2000, s 59.
28 *Ibid*, s 56.
29 *Ibid*, s 1(4).
30 *Chahal v UK* (1997) 23 EHRR 413.
31 ATCS 2001, s 23.

order for a person to be detained, the Secretary of State must have reasonable grounds to believe that the person's presence in the UK is a risk to national security and must suspect that the person in question has been 'concerned in the commission, preparation or instigation of acts of international terrorism',[32] is a member of an international terrorist group[33] or has 'links' with one[34] by supporting or assisting the group.[35] The definitions used for international terrorism and what amounts to being a suspected international terrorist are very broad and a considerable range of people and activities could quite conceivably be caught within these provisions.[36] Certification can only be appealed to the Special Immigration Appeals Commission; there is no judicial review of the Secretary's decision[37] and any periodic review of the certificate is conducted by the Commission.[38] Detention is not the only option open to the authorities. If a certificate is issued, a number of actions can be taken, including refusal of entry or leave to remain, varying limited leave to enter or remain, cancelling leave to enter, removal and deportation.[39]

The UK's experience of the use of internment in Northern Ireland cannot have been overlooked by the government when considering the inclusion of these provisions. It was the Labour government under the same Prime Minister that repealed internment in 1998,[40] describing it as 'a process that is against the rule of law and undermines democratic principles' and stating that 'the government cannot see any circumstances in which they would wish to pursue the power of internment'.[41] They have clearly changed their mind. The last time the British government used internment, in 1971, it was an unmitigated disaster both for those interred and as an attempt to prevent terrorism, because it only encouraged and intensified the violence.[42] If recent history has proven that detention without trial does not prevent terrorism, then why has the government reintroduced it? The likeliest explanation stems from a ruling by the European Court of Human Rights that a foreign national who is a suspected terrorist cannot be removed from the country, irrespective of whether he has arrived legally or illegally, if there is a real risk that he will suffer torture, inhuman or degrading treatment if returned to his own country.[43] It is possible that the government sees detention as the only option since the suspect cannot be deported. Perhaps the government regards detention as

---

32 *Ibid*, s 21(2)(a). International terrorism is as defined in the TA 2000, s 1.
33 *Ibid*, s 21(2)(b).
34 *Ibid*, s 21(2)(c).
35 *Ibid*, s 21(4).
36 For a fuller discussion on the implications and parameters of the definition see Tomkins, 2002, pp 211–12.
37 ATCS 2001, s 21(8).
38 *Ibid*, s 26.
39 *Ibid*, s 22.
40 Northern Ireland (Emergency Provisions) Act 1998, s 3.
41 In the debate on the Northern Ireland (Emergency Provisions) Bill 1998, *per* Lord Dubs, House of Lords, 12 January 1998, col 909.
42 See Hennessey, 1997, pp 194–99; Jackson, 1999, pp 375–76.
43 *Chahal v UK* (1997) 23 EHRR 413. This supposition is supported in the Report submitted by the UK government on its implementation of UN Resolution 1373. In response to para 3(g) of the Resolution, which seeks to prevent the asylum system being abused by terrorists, the UK stated that 'In cases where removal [of terrorists] is precluded by Article 3 of the European Convention on Human Rights, terrorist[s] will be detained indefinitely under the Anti-Terrorism, Crime and Security Act'. Letter dated 19 December 2001 from the Chairman of the Security Council Committee established pursuant to Resolution 1373 (2001) concerning counter-terrorism, addressed to the President of the Security Council, Annex, *The United Kingdom of Great Britain and Northern Ireland, Report to the Counter-terrorism Committee pursuant to paragraph 6 of Security Council Resolution 1373 (2001) of 28 September 2001*, p 12.

the lesser of two evils between letting suspected terrorists organise freely or overriding a fundamental human right.[44]

The irony, however, is that these suspected international terrorists are far from free to organise terrorism. The plethora of anti-terrorism offences available to prosecute people and the breadth of activities and groups that can be caught under the definition of terrorism in the TA and be successfully prosecuted is very wide. If there is enough evidence to justify the deprivation of a person's liberty, then surely there is enough evidence to prosecute them in a court of law? If there is insufficient evidence to conduct a successful prosecution under the huge variety of offences they could be tried for, then the justification for their internment must surely be questioned. The introduction of this power would indicate that people can be interned on the flimsiest of evidence; otherwise why would the government risk the political stigma if it could deprive these people of their liberty through a successful trial that would accord with international legal obligations? The whole concept underlying this provision cannot be justified in any way. There has been no attempt in these provisions to create equilibrium between effective counter-terrorism measures and civil liberties. This section clearly overrides an internationally recognised human right for a very short-term gain, but precedent indicates that the possibility of the long term success of such a policy is almost nil.

Effective anti-terrorism provisions do not have to be developed at the expense of civil liberties. The ATCS has introduced a number of new measures that strengthen anti-terrorism protections, actively work to prevent attacks and should be effective tools to prosecute those who commit atrocities. These provisions have not attracted much attention but they are important, particularly as they reveal that counter-terrorism can be achieved without reducing existing civil liberties. These developments include provisions for controls on weapons of mass destruction and pathogens, aviation security and the disclosure of information between public bodies. Most of these provisions are amendments and extensions of previous legislation. Some of the changes bring to an end lapses in what ought to be basic security. Others are a long overdue establishment of co-operation between the various agencies involved in preventing and prosecuting acts of terror.

In many ways, the gaps in basic national security that the passing of some of the provisions in the ATCS reveals is astounding. It would seem that parliament has been so dazzled by the proposed specialist laws placed before them that they have overlooked some simple safety issues covering aviation, the nuclear industry, and pathogens. The threat from terrorists using weapons of mass destruction, such as nuclear or biological devices, stems from the more recent past. In many ways the new terrorist threats have superseded the expectations of the older legislation. These gaps in security laws should have been a cause for concern, irrespective of any terrorist threat.

No one could truly have anticipated that a hijacked plane could be turned into such a devastating weapon of mass destruction by flying it into a skyscraper. Nevertheless it is well known that terrorists have used plane hijacking as a common tactic. The earliest hijacking of planes took place in the late 1960s, and by the 1970s and 1980s there was a small epidemic of terrorist hijackings, plane bombings and attacks within and around airports. Despite this tragic history and well established legislation to protect civil aviation, it was only in the ATCS that a number of gaps in aviation security were filled. The ATCS now allows a police officer to arrest without

---

44 In order to enact this provision the government have had to derogate from their obligation under Article 5(4) of the European Convention on Human Rights. For a full discussion of the implications in human rights law of the derogation and the provisions, see Tomkins, 2002, pp 214–17.

warrant an unauthorised person who has entered a restricted zone in an airport or on a plane,[45] and allows the use of reasonable force by an officer, or a person acting for the manager of an aerodrome to remove an unauthorised person.[46] It seems to be a strange oversight in security to have restricted zones from which unauthorised persons cannot be removed. The ATCS also provides for regulations to be passed that allow the Secretary of State to maintain a list of persons approved to provide particular airport security services.[47] The regulations will cover how a person becomes registered, including required training or qualifications. This could be considered a restriction on people's freedom to work, but as long as the selection criteria are in the public domain, requiring people to be vetted and pass certain qualifications before allowing them to work as security personnel in a place that is a known target for terrorists is a minimal infringement on civil liberties in comparison to the potential gains in effective counter-terrorism measures.

The first well known terrorist attack using a weapon of mass destruction was the sarin attack carried out by Aum Shrinryko in Tokyo in 1996. Although the Chemical Weapons Act 1996 covered many aspects of chemical attacks, there were still gaps in the security of harmful biological agents and nuclear material. The Nuclear Explosions (Prohibition and Inspections) Act 1998 made it an offence to cause any sort of nuclear explosion but was silent on the matter of the production, possession and transfer of nuclear material. The Nuclear Material (Offences) Act 1983 was only concerned with nuclear material intended for peaceful purposes rather than weapons grade nuclear material.[48] Under the 1983 Act it is only an offence to posses or deal in nuclear material if the person intends, threatens, enables another or is reckless as to its use to commit murder or manslaughter and other violent crimes, theft, fraud or extortion, or intends to compel a state or international governmental organisation.[49] This created a loophole over weapons grade material and possession or dealing in any nuclear material without the required intent or recklessness. This gap has now been filled and any person who develops a nuclear weapon (including any nuclear explosive device that was not intended as a weapon), helps or produces particles for it, possesses a weapon, transfers one or helps to prepare one is guilty of an offence.[50] It is also an offence to assist, aid or incite a non-UK person to commit a biological, chemical or nuclear offence outside the UK.[51]

A similar sort of loophole existed for involvement in the transfer, either by themselves or through another party,[52] of biological agents and toxins. Under s 1 of the Biological Weapons Act 1974 it is illegal to develop, produce, possess, acquire, stockpile or retain biological agents or toxins 'of a type or quantity that has not justification for prophylactic, protective or other peaceful purposes'[53] or any weapon or delivery mechanism that could be used offensively in an armed conflict.[54] Until the ATCS, the storage of pathogens and toxins that were justified, including chemical toxins and pathogens such as the horrifying diseases Ebola, Marburg and even anthrax, were not registered with the Secretary of State. There are now regulations imposed upon those occupiers of premises who keep such

---

45 ATCS 2001, s 82.
46 *Ibid*, s 84.
47 *Ibid*, s 85.
48 Nuclear Material (Offences) Act 1983, s 6.
49 *Ibid*, ss 1, 2.
50 ATCS 2001, s 47.
51 *Ibid*, s 50.
52 *Ibid*, s 43.
53 Biological Weapons Act 1987, s 1(a).
54 *Ibid*, s 1(b).

pathogens and toxins including restricting who has access to them.[55] Filling in these types of gaps is long overdue, and on paper at least these measures increase security against possible terrorist attacks whilst not making serious infringements on civil liberties.

Closing these loopholes and increasing our security laws will not ensure anyone's safety unless those laws can be enforced. The most effective forms of counter-terrorism measures are those that prevent attacks rather than just prosecute them afterwards. Preventing an attack relies on intelligence and information. The ATCS does include a provision on the intelligence services and expands the scope of GCHQ a little, but the most significant changes are the manner in which the different agencies relate to each other. Of all the insights that the events of 11 September and its consequences have revealed, perhaps none is more significant than the need for various agencies concerned with counter-terrorism to co-operate together rather than keep information to themselves. The Americans have recognised this and have created the new National Security Coordination Council within the Department of Justice. This council will convene bi-weekly and includes the Director of the FBI, the head of its anti-terrorism unit, the criminal division, the Office of International Affairs, the Office of Intelligence and Policy, and the Drug Enforcement Agency amongst others.

In ss 17–19, the ATCS attempts something similar but without creating any institutional changes. These sections, which expand upon previous legislation, allow public authorities to disclose the information it holds to another public body, but the disclosure must be proportionate. The range of bodies and information including in the right to disclose is very likely to stretch beyond purely counter-terrorism activities[56] and there is no stipulation within the Act that the disclosure must be dependent upon such an investigation.[57] The principle behind this section allowing increased co-operation between anti-terrorism agencies is potentially a very effective counter-terrorism measure. The information that these agencies hold on the population is a matter of record anyway and the infringement on our right to privacy by disclosing this information to another government agency seems a small price to pay in the balance between effective counter-terrorism measures and civil liberties. However, due to the manner in which the right to disclose has been enacted in the ATCS, the information exchange is not just confined to counter-terrorist operations. The agencies involved and types of information that could be disclosed go far beyond criminal investigations into potential terrorist attacks. Tomkins argues that these sections are potentially in breach of Article 8 of the European Convention on Human Rights, and highlights the Joint Committee on Human Rights' concern over this issue.[58] Such a wide and open ended approach to disclosure seems likely to result in poorly targeted intelligence gathering and hence ineffective counter-terrorism tools. Thus, whilst the principle of co-operation is good, once again the ATCS trounces our civil liberties and does not confine itself in any way to counter-terrorism measures.

This essay might be premature in its criticisms of the ATCS if the Act is required to meet the UK's obligations under international law. On 28 September 2001, the UN Security Council issued Resolution 1373 reaffirming the principle that:

---

55 ATCS 2001, ss 58–75.
56 *Ibid*, Sched 4: the disclosure provisions cover legislative enactments about agriculture, harbours, fisheries, national savings bank, employment, consumer credit, sex discrimination, National Health Service, estate agents, civil aviation, companies, consumer protection, timeshare, the coal industry, pensions, and the Bank of England, to name but a few of the 66 listed.
57 ATCS 2001, s 17.
58 Tomkins, 2002, p 209.

... every State has the duty to refrain from organizing, instigating, assisting or participating in terrorist acts in another State or acquiescing in organized activities within its territory directed towards the commission of such acts.[59]

This Resolution directed all states to introduce criminal offences to prevent and suppress terrorist financing and powers to freeze or seize terrorist property.[60] The Resolution also decided that all states shall introduce measures to prevent attacks by terrorists, block any form of support for terrorist groups, ensure international co-operation and bring those who commit, help or finance terrorist acts to justice.[61] The Resolution called upon all those states that had not yet signed or ratified the 12 international Conventions on terrorism to do so.[62] In Britain's report to the Counter-Terrorism Committee, which had been established under Resolution 1373 to monitor its implementation, the government stated that since September 11 'it was decided to enhance the UK's existing anti-terrorism legislation' which 'resulted in the Anti-Terrorism, Crime and Security Act 2001'.[63] In the report, the government described exactly which pre-existing legislative powers or new legislative innovations satisfy the requirements of Resolution 1373. The ATCS was only expressly referred to in relation to four points in the Resolution; offences for terrorist financing, denying terrorists safe havens, inciting terrorism overseas and preventing terrorists from abusing the refugee and asylum system.

In the report, the UK government said that the expansion of police powers under the ATCS helped prevent incitement of terrorism overseas.[64] However, as the report stated, the relevant section of the ATCS are designed to apply over pre-existing anti-terrorism laws that actually prohibit these activities, and thus in itself it cannot implement the Resolution. From the fact that the police powers merely 'help' to enforce the relevant legislation, it is logical to surmise that these powers are not necessary for the UK's implementation of this section of the Resolution. Moreover, the paragraphs on terrorist financing, one of the main concerns in the Resolution and an issue specifically tackled by the ATCS, has already been widely legislated for. The TA has a long section on terrorist property which enabled the UK to ratify the International Convention for the Suppression of the Financing of Terrorism 1999 in March 2001. The freezing order and seizures of property that took place in response to September 11 and the Security Council Resolutions occurred prior to the ATCS becoming law, indicating that these powers on freezing property in the ATCS could be considered superfluous.

Resolution 1373 requires states to take action to prevent their territories from becoming safe havens and centres of conspiracy. It was claimed in the UK's report that the ability to detain immigrants and asylum seekers without trial implemented the requirement that states deny safe haven to terrorists and prevent people from conspiring to commit terrorist attacks overseas.[65] This power was only one of the range of legislative options mentioned in the report, which also drew attention to the fact that under the Immigration Act 1971 people can be excluded, and conspiring to commit terrorism overseas is a indictable offence under both the TA and the Criminal Justice (Terrorism and Conspiracy) Act 1998. This again raises the question of whether indefinite detention without trial is necessary. The UK parliament has only granted this power against non-nationals who are claiming

---

59 United Nations Security Council Resolution 1373, 28 September 2001, para 1.
60 *Ibid*, para 1.
61 *Ibid*, para 2.
62 *Ibid*, para 3(d).
63 See above, fn 43, p 3.
64 See above, fn 43, p 9.
65 See above, fn 43, p 9.

asylum and any justification for this power through reference to the requirements of the Resolution ought to consider the Resolution's explicit statements on refugee status and asylum law. In paragraph 3, the Resolution calls upon states to ensure that asylum seekers have not 'planned, facilitated or participated'[66] in terrorism, that the refugee status is not abused by terrorists and that asylum claims are not used to avoid prosecution.[67] The Resolution also states that the anti-terrorism measures concerning asylum and refugee status must be 'in conformity with the relevant provisions national and international law, including international standards of human rights'.[68] Indefinite detention without trial under the ATCS has required Britain to derogate from the ECHR, which would seem to contravene the ethos and wording of the Resolution that the measures on asylum and refugees be taken in accordance with international conventions and human rights standards.[69] Thus, the requirements of Resolution 1373 cannot be referred to as a justification for the introduction of indefinite detention without trial.

Even in the few areas where the British government has stated that the ATCS is necessary to meet the requirements of Resolution 1373, it appears that these powers were not strictly necessary. There are others powers under other legislation that satisfy international obligations under Resolution 1373. In the case of indefinite detention, the ATCS might actually be contrary to the intention of the Resolution. The government cannot even claim that the ATCS was necessary in order to implement the other international anti-terrorism laws, as urged by the Resolution, because the UK had already ratified all 12 of the international anti-terrorism Conventions.

The ATCS has not been forced upon the UK by obligations under international law. It is the government's response to what it perceives will be the nature of terrorist threats in the world after September 11. Counter-terrorism legislation is often required to attempt to strike a balance between protecting civil liberties and ensuring that the state has effective counter-terrorism measures. The ATCS frequently fails to strike any sort of balance between these competing needs and it repeatedly sacrifices civil liberties on the altar of anti-terrorism priorities. This does not mean that these policies will actually be effective. Often the powers granted, such as the retention of communications data and police powers, are so wide and vague as to be ineffective as a counter-terrorism tool. Other powers, such as detention without trial, that result in significant human rights abuses can actually be counter-productive in the long term because they encourage alienation, hostility and ultimately more violence. In the long term, these sorts of powers are often highly ineffective as counter-terrorism measures. Paradoxically, the ATCS does demonstrate that counter-terrorism effectiveness does not necessitate significant infringement on civil liberties. Ensuring that there are adequate security measures for places that are vulnerable to attack, that items which could be used as weapons of mass destruction, like pathogens, toxins and nuclear material, are securely controlled is an easy way of making terrorist attacks more difficult without reducing the freedoms that we are supposed to be protecting. Co-operation between the different government agencies that are involved in preventing and prosecuting terrorism has also been shown to be of significant merit in the aftermath of September 11. Unfortunately, although the principle is valid, the ATCS extends the right to disclose so far as to reduce its ability to be effectively targeted against terrorists whilst reducing our civil liberties.

---

66 United Nations Security Council Resolution 1373, 28 September 2001, para 3(f).
67 *Ibid*, para 3(g).
68 *Ibid*, para 3(f).
69 For the full text of these sections, see above, fn 25.

References

Bowden, C (2002) 'CCTV for inside your head: blanket traffic data retention and the emergency anti-terrorism legislation' 8(2) Computer and Telecommunications Law Review 21

Debate on the Northern Ireland (Emergency Provisions) Bill 1998, *per* Lord Dubs, House of Lords Debates, col 909, 12 January 1998

Editorial (2002) 'Anti-Terrorism, Crime and Security Act 2001' Criminal Law Review (March) 159

Gaspar, Roger (NCIS) (2000) 'Looking to the future: clarity on communications data retention law', 21 August, in Bowden, 2002

Head, G (1999) '"The future is bright ..." – but for whom?' 11(4) Terrorism and Political Violence 19

Hennessey, T (1997) *A History of Northern Ireland 1920–96*, London: Macmillan

Jackson, A (1999) *Ireland, 1798–1998*, London: Blackwell

Joint Committee on Human Rights, *Anti-Terrorism, Crime and Security Bill: Further Report*, 2001–02 HL 51; 2001–02 HC 420

Letter dated 19 December 2001 from the Chairman of the Security Council Committee established pursuant to Resolution 1373 (2001) concerning counter-terrorism, addressed to the President of the Security Council, Annex, 'The United Kingdom of Great Britain and Northern Ireland, Report to the Counter-terrorism Committee pursuant to paragraph 6 of Security Council Resolution 1373 (2001) of 28 September 2002'

Tomkins, A (2002) 'Legislating against terror: the Anti-Terrorism, Crime and Security Act 2001' Public Law, Summer, 205

PART 3

Ground Zero's Prospects

Chapter 10
Locating 'Ground Zero': caught between the narratives of crime and war

Keith Hayward and Wayne Morrison

Truth was their model as they strove to build
A world of lasting objects to believe in.[1]

'In the past decade the surge of capital markets has dominated discourse and shaped global consciousness. Multinational corporations have come to seem more vital and influential than governments. The dramatic climb of the Dow and the speed of the internet summoned us all to live permanently in the future, in the utopian glow of cyber-capital, because there is no memory there and this is where markets are uncontrolled and investment potential has no limit. All this changed on September 11. Today, again, the world narrative belongs to terrorists. But the primary target of the men who attacked the Pentagon and the World Trade Center was not the global economy. It was America that drew their fury. It was the high gloss of our modernity. It was the thrust of our technology. It was our perceived godlessness. It was the blunt force of our foreign policy. It was the power of American culture to penetrate every wall, home, life and mind. Terror's response is a narrative that has been developing over years, only now becoming inescapable. It is our lives and minds that are occupied now ... Our world, parts of our world, have crumbled into theirs, which means we are living in a place of danger and rage ...

'... We like to think that America invented the future. We are comfortable with the future, intimate with it. But there are disturbances now, in large and small ways, a chain of reconsiderations. Where we live, how we travel, what we think about when we look at our children. For many people, the event has changed the grain of the most routine moment.

'We may find that the ruin of the towers is implicit in other things ...'[2]

September 11 as the marker of a new epoch?

The events of September 11 gave a profound shock to Western consciousness. At the centre of the events was the symbolic transformation of the Twin Towers of the World Trade Center – the shining embodiment of the financial power of New York and global finance – into 'Ground Zero'. Ground Zero became the site of destruction, loss, mourning and rebirth. But Ground Zero transcended its location. From the moment of impact, images spanned the globe – images of terrorists transforming the use of everyday items, rewriting the symbolism of the Twin Towers of the World Trade Center, showing the weakness at the heart of the military in the attack on the Pentagon, erasing the boundaries of personal security in everyday life. Many found the events hard, almost impossible, to comprehend. How were they to be interpreted and responded to? The range of questions was wide, the impact disorientating.

Were the attacks discrete events – an outrageous crime or a sudden war-like action – understandable on their own terms, or were they evidence of something new in history, even a marker of a new historical period? How could they be located

---

1 WH Auden (1966) 'The history of Truth', in *Collected Shorter Poems, 1927–57*, London: Faber.
2 DeLillo, 2001.

in master narratives so that they can be understood as exceptions to the norm? Was terrorism an exception to the social structure we inhabit or is it so embedded that it becomes a symptom of a normalcy?

Perhaps it is too soon to answer this last level of questions but we know that both the questions and the level of analysis must be global in scope. As shocked Americans asked 'why us … why do they hate us? What do I have to do with Osama bin Laden?' many around the world announced that they shared the pain and the sense of outrage. But as Western politicians announced that 'today we are all Americans',[3] it was obvious they spoke for a particular transnational social grouping. Many others clearly did not perceive themselves as American.[4] *The Economist*, in an edition entitled *The day the world changed*, confidently stated that 'The terror unleashed on America this week is an assault not just on the United States but on civilisation itself', but others saw it as a powerful indictment of the downside of that 'civilisation'.[5] It was clear, however, that the divisions did not run along lines of nationality, nor were the differences a matter of Islam against American values.[6] Did these divisions and fractures in identities, emotions and perceptions reveal the contours of a new social network? A network that rendered obsolete the modernist structuring of social identity and security in terms of the sovereignties and powers of the nation state? This essay will offer some commentary upon this suggestion by attempting to locate September 11 in the two narratives most essentially tied to the power of the nation state: those of crime and war.

---

3 Publicly stated by the British Prime Minister Tony Blair, German Chancellor Gerhard Schroeder, and Peter Struck, German Social Democrat parliamentary leader, among others. There were many displays of international solidarity: the band played the US national anthem during the changing of the guard at Buckingham Palace, Dublin's shops closed for a day of mourning, Canadian stores sold out of American flags and *Le Monde* ran the headline: WE ARE ALL AMERICANS.

4 Four examples of commentary in the UK press that consciously adopted an 'external' viewpoint (all in *The Guardian*, 12 September 2001): Faisal Bidi, 'Yesterday's attacks are the chickens of America's callous abuse of others' human rights coming home to roost'; Saskia Sassen, 'The attacks are a language of last resort for the oppressed'; Martin Woollacott, 'Western policy may have played a part in creating the anger which led to the attacks'; George Gallaway's article was entitled 'Reaping the whirlwind'.

5 *The Economist*, 15–21 September 2001. The Leader asked: 'After this unspeakable crime, will anything ever be the same?'

6 Arab-American and Islamic-American groups were quick to express their horror. The American Muslim Association of North America condemned the 'apparently vicious and cowardly acts of terrorism against innocent civilians' and called for the 'swift apprehension and punishment of the perpetrators', adding that no political cause 'could ever be assisted by such immoral acts'. The Islamic Political Party of America extended condolences to the families of the victims, noting that the attacks were totally indiscriminate and could 'include our own family member, friends and acquaintances'. The acts were 'against our own religious practices' and endangered 'our lives and positions as citizens of this country'. Muslims of America Inc stated that 'as Americans, we are ready to assist in whatever way we can to begin the recovery and healing from these tragedies'. By contrast, white supremacist organisations expressed mixed emotions. American Nazi Party Secretary RJ Frank wrote on an online forum that it was 'thrilling' to hear of 'some of the ZOG [Zionist Occupation Government] machine being taken down', however, to have a foreign power acting on US soil 'really sucks'. Frank expressed his admiration for the effectiveness of the attack: '… while I do not care for the sand niggers, you can't help but admire the military precision, planning, and most of all, dedication they showed. If we had a handful of our people willing to give it their all as they did many of the issues confronting white America would be non-issues today.' The fundamentalist Christian Jerry Falwell, on the 14 September 2001 episode of Pat Robertson's *700 Club* television programme, blamed the American Council of Civil Liberties for the terrorist attacks because they had thrown God 'out of the public square, out of the schools'. He also blamed 'the abortionists', since 'God will not be mocked', and 'abortions made God mad'. Pat Robertson said he 'totally' concurred with Falwell's remarks. President Bush was quick to repudiate their remarks. (Anti-Defamation League, 2001.)

Undercutting security: bringing violence in from 'a safe distance over the horizon'

The World Trade Center and surrounding plaza epitomised the solidity of man's powers of control and ability to design lived space. Violence was designed out – it was a place of work and of urban relaxation. Modernity was founded on violence but gave as its master narrative the removal of violence from everyday life (the civilising drive). The nation state was defined in terms of its having the monopoly on *legitimate* violence (*pace*, for example, the classical positions of Hobbes and Weber or the more contemporary writings of Anthony Giddens). Those who used force or fraud illegitimately within the state were largely recognised through the discourse of crime, while threats and aggression originating through the actions of other states were interpreted through that of war. Locating threats and interpreting events by use of these two narrative traditions gave metaphysical solace and allowed rulers to give an image of rational governance. The discourses of both crime and war were largely the product of the defining powers of nation states.

Modernity was first a grappling for control and second the expression of freedoms and capacities enabled by that control. The pacification of territory was followed by a disciplining of 'subjects', currently understood in criminology as the development of self-control. This rational-legal process required the development of narratives that sought to demarcate acceptable and unacceptable behaviour and then develop administrative means for understanding and reacting to 'deviant' behaviour (criminology and criminal justice). But security within state governed territory was useless without security from without, and this was to be achieved by 'disciplining' the capacity to wage war and constraining the brutality of the effects of war. In light of advances in the technology of war, 'total' war was now a possibility, the destructive force of which was apparent in the 20th century with Europe devastated twice by 'world' wars. The emphasis was on developing 'defensive' pacts (for example NATO, Warsaw pact, SEATO), outlawing 'aggressive war' and allowing only 'just' war (now understood as war as self-defence) that gave security and predictability. War and crime were to be located and institutionalised within a new global social ordering, a Western hegemony that allowed citizens/ subjects to have the space to pursue their diverse strivings for individual happiness. This hegemony came to champion the market and the creation of productive and technological experimentation. But it also denoted social structures with insides and outsides, processes of inclusion and exclusion, realities of freedom (emancipation) and powerlessness. The legitimacy of these demarcations was consequent upon the control of defining what was criminal and what was just war and making those definitions enforceable. [7]

---

7 Crime's inability as a concept to grasp the 'social reality' of events lies in the relationship of crime's ontology to state power. As a concept crime developed in modernity as the product of the power of the sovereign to define, to judge. The ontology of crime was therefore always relative. It was, succinctly put, a question of what the criminal law defined it as. For a brief period after WWII – in the grip of the Nuremberg trials, the passing of United Nations Conventions such as the Genocide Convention and the 1949 Geneva Convention – it seemed as if the paradigm of world politics might turn to an international structuring of Law and Order. But instead, for all that the semblance of a juridification of discourse presented, the reality was the politic of pragmatic state interests. The criminal law linked to progress takes its legitimacy from democratic accountability and debate. But outwith the law lies the shadow of terror. State terror, sometimes in the form of genocide, was called 'legal crime' by Hannah Arendt (1964, p 268); Kelman and Hamiliton (1989) used the term 'crimes of obedience'. Archer and Gartner (1984, p 63) argue: 'The private acts of destructive individuals are treated as illegal violence, while official acts of violence are granted the mantle of state authority, and are thus shielded from criticism and criminal sanctions.' R Lemkin developed a concept of 'genocide'

Violence had been an essential element in the creation of modern nation states. In 18th and 19th century modernity, imperialism extended the grip of largely European nation states globally. The exercise of power in modernity was accompanied by terror and was ruthless towards those individuals and social groupings that did not have a state to defend them. In the course of imperialism, 'native' populations were cleansed from their locality and often extinguished. In the 20th century, as imperialist empires came under pressure, ethnic groups without a state could be culturally and physically decimated.[8]

The 20th century saw vast progress in engineering and technological virtuosity, material production and life chances ... this is the narrative of late modernity as expressive self-creation or self-fulfilment (or at least the ability to go in perpetual pursuit of one's 'true' self). But the 20th century was 'a century of camps', of genocide and where social engineering entailed the denial or trampling upon human dignity. Thus we see the counter-narrative of late modernity as a radically divided globalisation and imbalance of life realities.[9] Moreover, in a century in which scholars could estimate that states deliberately killed some 170 million persons, it was rare for the assertion that such events were 'crimes' to gain state support such that individuals were successfully prosecuted for such events. The dominant narratives of Western modernity created 'states of denial',[10] psychologies that kept violence at a safe distance.

At century's end: a new world order?

Towards the end of the last century there was much talk of a new world order. Its contours were vague but among the phrases used were that of post-cold war (in part induced by the defeat of the Soviet Union in Afghanistan), the end of history, post-modernity, globalisation, free trade and international consumer culture. Instead of the discourses of crime being subjugated to state interests, an

---

to cover the situation where states waged war not on other states but on peoples (often in their own nation state). But the story of the transformation of his ideas into a United Nations Convention was one of negotiating states creating a convention that would not capture their own activities nor handicap their ability to selectively use terror. In situations where killing, raping and terrorising on a massive scale had taken place at the behest of the state – as in East Pakistan – even when a new state was created that could hold the actors who enforced the terror accountable, there were factors at work which ensured that few prosecutions took place. Chief among them were the extra-state considerations of super-state ('super-power') influence and balances of the 'cold war', the 'pragmatic' factors of access to markets and 'economic' stability, and the utilisation of the knowledge and administrative skills of those perpetrators.

8　The destruction of the Hereros of South-West Africa (now Namibia) by the German army, or the Armenians by the New Turks are apt examples. The stateless Jews of Europe suffered a Holocaust at the hands of an expansionist nation state in pursuit of a racial ideology that sought to achieve ethnic purity through the application of modernist technology. In East Pakistan the demands for equality of civil rights and use of language met a military use of terror that was only alleviated by the intervention of another state (India) and the creation of a new state (Bangladesh). While the creation of Israel, itself accompanied by an instrumental use of terrorism (by the Irgun and the Stern Gang), was seen as the only way that Jews would find security in modernity.

9　Rudolph Runnel in *Democide* (1992) and *Death by Government* (1995) estimates that between 1900 and 1987 close to 170 million civilians (and disarmed POWs) were killed by governments and quasi governmental organisations (political parties, paramilitary groups); the vast majority were killed by non-democratic regimes. He defines this as 'democide' (the killing of peoples), while he places 38 million of them as victims of 'genocide' (using the definition within the UN Convention) and nearly 6 million of those were the Jewish victims of the Holocaust. Only a very small number of those responsible for this massive toll were ever prosecuted.

10　The title of Stanley Cohen's book (2001), where he tries to account for the various modes of avoidance used to protect ourselves from what we do not want to know and prevent the violence, atrocities and suffering that our states engage in from penetrating our everyday consciousness.

international discourse of human rights took root, symbolised by the project to create an International Criminal Court (and the *ad hoc* tribunals for the former Yugoslavia and for Rwanda), while the Gulf War and Kosovo indicated a growing readiness to wage war for humanitarian justifications. Political ideologies, we were told, were collapsing, the boundaries between nation states were being redrawn and the power of nation states was becoming increasingly redundant in the face of the globalisation of capital and the new technologies of communication and representation. Post-modern social theory highlighted the role of information and communication technologies where the 'real' was to be understood through its (various) representations and where the knowledge/service economy transformed production capabilities and wealth flows.

Modernist social theory had distinguished the micro and macro, agency and structure, action and context. Developing, in part, from the interactionist tradition, post-modern social theory presented a more fluid and constitutive picture where society was an intersectional accomplishment. People inhabited networks or ensembles of social relationships constituted by the mediation of localised practices by taken-for-granted meanings and collective representations. Power involved the control and manipulation of knowledge of events. In the mass media, world knowledge of the technologies and techniques of representation and communication gave power and acceptance of representation-conferred legitimacy. As children 'lost in the forest of symbols' (Baudrillard) we rely upon the mediation and interpretation of danger: trust becomes a function of the symbolic politics of the media.

The symbolism of Ground Zero: contingency and interconnectedness

September 11 was a real and a symbolic event. Its painful reality was a horror that most affected those personally touched by being there or through loss of family or friends. Its instantaneous presentation in the media made the fear it aroused global:

> The events of September 11 were covered unstintingly. There was no confusion of roles on TV. The raw event was one thing, the coverage another. The event dominated the medium. It was bright and totalising and some of us said it was unreal. When we say a thing is unreal, we mean it is too real, a phenomenon so unaccountable and yet so bound to the power of objective fact that we can't tilt it to the slant of our perceptions.

> First the planes struck the towers. After a time it became possible for us to absorb this, barely. But when the towers fell. When the rolling smoke began moving downward, floor to floor. This was so vast and terrible that it was outside imagining even as it happened. We could not catch up with it. But it was real, punishingly so, an expression of the physics of structural limits and a void in one's soul, and there was the huge antenna falling out of the sky, straight down, blunt end first, like an arrow moving backwards in time.

> The event itself has no purchase on the mercies of analogy or simile. We have to take the shock and horror as it is.[11]

The symbolism of the acts, the use of a mixture of mundane (box cutters and kitchen knives) and the highly sophisticated Western technology (an aircraft) to attack the sites of financial, military and governmental power, was extreme. For the American writer DeLillo the Twin Towers had been a symbol of technological 'truth' itself, a representation of the overcoming of limits.

> The World Trade towers were not only an emblem of advanced technology but a justification, in a sense, for technology's irresistible will to realise in solid form whatever becomes theoretically allowable. Once defined, every limit must be reached. The tactful

---

11 Siri Hustredt, *The Observer*, 10 March 2002.

sheathing of the towers was intended to reduce the direct threat of such straight-edge enormity, a giantism that eased over the years into something a little more familiar and comfortable, even dependable in a way.

Now a small group of men have literally altered our skyline. We have fallen back in time and space. It is their technology that marks our moments, the small, lethal devices, the remote-control detonators they fashion out of radios, or the larger technology they borrow from us, passenger jets that become manned missiles.

Maybe this is a grim subtext of their enterprise. They see something innately destructive in the nature of technology. It brings death to their customs and beliefs. Use it as what it is, a thing that kills.[12]

But the symbolism went further even into the use of the term Ground Zero. The phrase had first gained poetic power in capturing the effects on the area directly under an exploding atomic bomb. Ground Zero first became applied to the World Trade Center towers in the 1993 attack;[13] the first big terrorist attack on American soil when a group of Egyptian, Pakistani and Palestinian terrorists planted a car bomb in the basement car park of one of the Twin Towers. The World Trade Center was a highly symbolic target: unfinished business. This was clearly understood by Benjamin Netanyahu, Prime Minister of Israel for a period in the 1990s. In a 1995 book, *Fighting Terrorism: How Democracies Can Defeat Domestic and International Terrorists*, Netanyahu painted a picture of superpowers subjected to terror at the hands of terrorist networks able to undercut the normal weapons of security and war. 'Such groups nullify, in large measure, the need to have air power or intercontinental missiles as delivery systems. For an Islamic nuclear payload, they will be the delivery system. In the worst of such scenarios the consequences could not be a car bomb, but a nuclear bomb in the basement of the World Trade Center.'

There was also a strange but horrifying irony in the use of the phrase Ground Zero. The commentators were united in drawing parallels to the attack on Pearl Harbour,[14] but did not continue the story of that reaction. But as Arundhati Roy pointed out: 'The reprisal for [Pearl Harbour] took a long route, but ended with Hiroshima and Nagasaki.'[15] The official explanation for the use of the atomic bomb was to shorten the war in the pacific and save American lives. Without the bomb, it was felt, the enemy might not surrender and save themselves (as the Western ethos of liberalism from Hobbes onwards held was the fundamental desire of human nature). They may, instead, choose to fight on, to choose collective suicide. If the Japanese Emperor wished to ask for 'the honourable death of the hundred million', many felt it would be forthcoming. How was this possible, American Defence

---

12 *The Guardian*, 22 December 2001.
13 The reporting was eerily similar: 'Americans were not accustomed to what so much of the world had already grown weary of: the sudden, deafening explosion of a car bomb, a hail of glass and debris, the screams of innocent victims followed by the wailing sirens of ambulances. Terrorism seemed like something that happened somewhere else – and somewhere else a safe distance over the horizon. And then, last week, in an instant, the World Trade Center in New York City became Ground Zero. At 12:18 on a snowy Friday afternoon, a massive explosion rocked the foundation of the Twin Towers of the Trade Center in lower Manhattan … [T]he landmark building near Wall Street seemed chosen with a fine sense of the symbols of the late 20th century. If the explosion, which killed five people and injured more than 1,000, turns out to be the work of terrorists, it will be a sharp reminder that the world is still a dangerous place. And that the dangers can come home.' *Time*, 8 March 1993.
14 'Six decades ago, a generation of startled Americans awoke to discover that their country was under attack. Pearl Harbour changed America, and therefore the world. Now the children and grandchildren of the Americans who went to war in 1941 have suffered their own day of infamy, one that is no less memorable. The appalling atrocities of September 11 – acts that must be seen as a declaration of war not just on America but on all civilised people – were crueller in conception and even more shocking than what happened in Hawaii.' Leader, *The Economist*, 15–21 September 2001.
15 *The Guardian*, 29 September 2001.

department scholars asked: their answer was that the Japanese saw self-assertion as immoral and self-sacrifice as normal. After the bomb, the Emperor asked the nation to endure the unendurable: surrender. In August he toured Ground Zero at Hiroshima, in September General MacArthur arrived with an army of occupation given the task of transforming Japan into the American way: build peaceful technology and play baseball. The bomb brought an end to the war, but ushered in the cold war. The cold war was shortened, many argued, by the American CIA support for Islamic militant (including Osama bin Laden) activities against the Soviet forces in Afghanistan. After the Soviet collapse the mujahedin had turned on each other and the Taliban had assumed 'control'; their honoured guest was Osama bin Laden, who developed training grounds for a new struggle.[16] A struggle in which his weapons included Japanese mobile phones and sturdy pick-up trucks and that now resulted in a new Ground Zero.

But drawing attention to the chains of interconnectedness was not popular, nor, for the time at least, did it appear relevant to the task. The task was, first, to understand the effects of the attack and take measures to alleviate them, and, second, to identify the perpetrators, track them down and punish them.

The effects of the attack were both local and global – who or what was the actual target? As many commentators pointed out, New York was more than American, it was a representation of a truly global city:

Real New York and imaginary New York aren't easily separated. The stuff of a city isn't only material; it's spiritual as well. What is true is that 40 per cent of us are now foreign-born. A few years ago, I read in the newspaper that in a single elementary school in Queens, the children spoke 64 different languages at home. Riding the subway, I routinely see people reading newspapers in Spanish, Russian, Polish, Chinese, Arabic, and other languages I'm too ignorant to identify. New Yorkers aren't bound by a common tongue or by similar backgrounds.

We're everybody from everywhere, and most of the time we tolerate each other pretty well. The people in this city know that in this we are unique. No other place comes close to our diversity. We have our share of ugliness, brutality, and pockets of cruel and stupid racism, but the fact is that if you don't like the hectic jostling of innumerable cultures and languages and ways of being, you wouldn't want to live here. The terrorists were blind. When they hurt New York, they hurt the whole world.[17]

There may be an expression of a new social order in this account. For New York as symbol of a global capitalism and cultural hegemony is also the polyglot New York of a new world order, termed by some as a new imperium (see the concluding section below). The terminology is suggestive, for it is in the nature of empire that its capitals will contain a diversity that the ideology of pure nation building could not stand (the Nazis were not empire builders but ideological purists, as were the actors in many cases of genocide).

Dealing with the perpetrators was more difficult: were they criminals or were they agents of war? Immediate reactions used both terms, almost interchangeably, but although they seemed instinctively to fit and enable the events to be satisfactorily related to achieve a unified response, they were themselves undergoing considerable revision. The concepts of crime and war may themselves no longer hold coherence.

---

16 Osama bin Laden also encouraged collective and individual suicide/homicide killings. In a CNN interview of 1997 he stated: 'Being killed for Allah's cause is a great honour achieved by only those who are the elite of the nation. We love this kind of death for Allah's cause as much as you like to live. We have nothing to fear for. It is something we wish for.' *Time*, 24 September 2001.

17 Siri Hustvedt, *The Observer*, 10 March 2002.

Crime or war? Can the discourse of crime or war be applied to Ground Zero?

The Twin Towers will be replaced. Currently (June 2002) there is a debate as to what will be created to turn Ground Zero into life again. In that ability they are also a symbol of the refashioning of our certainties. Everything now, it seems, is subject to transformation and reconstitution.[18] Even previously stable and seemingly inexorable social components – gender, sexuality, the individual subject, the family unit, the human body, the nation state – have in recent times been rendered mutable. It is the 'truth' of this world that it (unevenly) offers a whole new range of opportunities and possibilities at the same time as it throws up feelings of uncertainty and indeed melancholia as large numbers of people are forced to reconsider their past, present and future. Grand narratives and individual narratives rise and fall together.[19] As all overriding grand narratives are compromised, we experience 'life in fragments'.[20] This has been the stuff of much observation. Giddens,[21] for example, colourfully equates everyday life in late modernity with trying to regain control of an out-of-control juggernaut. In academic criminology Jock Young articulates the dilemma of individual subjectivity:

> We live in a much more difficult world: we face a greater range in life choices than ever before, our lives are less firmly embedded in work relationships, our everyday existence is experienced as a series of encounters with risk either in actuality or in the shape of fears and apprehensions. We feel both materially insecure and ontologically precarious.[22]

Within the context of widespread 'ontological insecurity', crime is doubly implicated. Fear of crime adds to the perception of a risk society, while engaging in crime may be a way of navigating a path through uncertainty. Put simply, many forms of crime are attempts to achieve a semblance of control within ontologically insecure lifeworlds.[23] Settled frameworks and ontologically secure 'social structures' have given way to recognition of the contingency of human ordering. But this ontological difficulty raises a paradox in that it engenders desires to assert confidence in the foundations of identities and institutions just as all narratives that seek to do that can be undercut. It is more difficult to successfully apply labels of criminality and deviancy, just as the power centres believe that they need to rely upon such labels even more.

---

18 As the Twin Towers are being reassessed: '... in the stunned weeks after Sept 11, there was a powerful impulse to simply rebuild the towers, all 110 stories, to show that Americans could not be brought low by terrorists. Then people remembered that however much we love them in retrospect, the Twin Towers were a botch. At their completion in 1973, they were already anachronisms, products of an imperial Modernism that destroyed human-scale neighborhoods and in their place erected mammoth towers on desolate plazas.

'By taking down the towers, Sept 11 blew a hole through the errors of the past. New York's phalanx of city-planning types and regional thinkers has looked through that hole and seen an opportunity. Right away they started dusting off long-cherished schemes, some of which may very well come true. It's likely that any final plan will envision a major new terminal linking the Manhattan subways with suburban commuter rail systems. It will also probably re-establish several city streets that were covered over by the much despised "superblock" of the Trade Center plaza.

'The towers were symbols of "the midcentury arrogance of architects", says architect David Childs of Skidmore, Owings & Merrill. "What they did to lower Manhattan was an act of vandalism just as complete as Sept 11."' (Childs has been commissioned by Larry Silverstein, the developer, to draw up proposals for the Trade Center site, reported *Time*, 27 May 2002.)

19 Lyotard, 1984.

20 Bauman, 1995.

21 Giddens, 1990.

22 Young, 1999, p vi.

23 See Morrison, 1995; Hayward, 2003.

The Culture of Control (2001), a text written by David Garland, a Scottish criminologist living in New York, is a key marker of a new era. That text described a reversal in criminological and penological hegemony over the last two decades. A move from 'understanding' to zero tolerance and control, from treatment to deterrence and incarceration: a society of freedom and the excluded other. The advocates of zero tolerance and of the neo-conservative position called 'right realism' in general depict tolerance towards anti-social behaviour and 'liberalism' as contribute to a new disorder where crime levels rise to high levels and contributing to a fearful society. A central issue is the rise of an underclass, created in part, we are told, as a result of misguided liberal welfare policies.[24] Instead of tolerating crime, war was to be waged against it: consequently crime control became industry and there was a huge expansion in penal expenditure and a borrowing of ideas and concepts from military planning.[25] The rise in imprisonment levels in the US, however, looked to some as if the US was in a state of slow civil war.[26] However, deterrence and incarceration, rather than understanding the causes of crime, was the message put out by both UK and US governments. The overturning of the criminological 'liberal consensus' (at the hands of writers such as Charles Murray)[27] occurred in terms remarkably prescient of much of the reactions to September 11 that blamed the events in part on the lack of resolve and weakness of response (as well as President Clinton's desire for dialogue rather than displays of strength). Bruce Shapiro, for example, described the grounds of 'right realism' in criminal justice policy not in terms of effectiveness but reassurance: 'Zero-tolerance policing unquestionably makes for effective campaign rhetoric, and the original Wilson and Kelling broken window hypothesis

---

24 Some of the writing that sought to encourage understanding of the causes of September 11 and lay out a policy response mirrored 'liberal' accounts of the need to integrate the underclass. For example Jeremy Rifkin in an article entitled 'Dialogue is a necessity to bridge cultural schism': 'We need to begin a cultural dialogue with Islam now, rather than wait until the point of no return. Let me cite just two ticking cultural time bombs. First, in the US, western Europe and other countries, the Muslim populations are young, often unemployed or impoverished, and the subject of growing discrimination. Millions of Muslim youth have been left behind by globalisation. In their desperate search to find identity, purpose and hope, many are being won over to the fundamentalist call for a jihad to recapture the golden age of Islam and reconquer the world for God – a kind of Islamic view of globalisation.

'Second, for most of us who have long accepted the notion of giving private loyalty to our faith and public loyalty to our government, the idea that substantial numbers of Muslims living among us do not share our conviction is unsettling. A *New York Times* reporter recently interviewed young Muslim students in the US and was surprised to learn that some did not think of themselves as Americans, but rather as Muslims living in America. Their bonds are extra-territorial and based on the revival of the Islamic idea of *umma*, the "universal Islamic community". Many young Muslims in Europe and America since September 11 have said they would not fight against their fellow Muslims in Afghanistan if called upon to do so by their own governments. They also view the nation state as a colonial construct imposed on the Middle East and the rest of the world. Add to this the fact that the Muslim diaspora is spreading into virtually every country, and we begin to understand the risk of perpetuating a global ghettoisation of Islam.' (*The Guardian*, 13 November 2001.)

25 As the Norwegian criminologist Nils Christie put it: '… we experience a reappearance of the term "the dangerous classes". We also meet concepts and thinking from the military sector. No longer is there a war against poverty. The war is against crime, against drugs, with ghettos of the inner cities as the battleground. The military men are also mobilised, not only in words. The ministry of justice and the ministry of defence have joint meetings in Washington and elsewhere with the minister of justice conveying to the military people the message, "you won the war abroad. Now you must help us to win the war at home". Slowly, the military industry adapts their production to what is understood to be the needs of law and order.' (1998, p 125.)

26 To quote Christie again: 'In some states [of the US] the proportion of young males in the control of the penal system will be close to 20 per cent, which comes close to a civil war, a civil war where the privileged have created their protected territories, using the state machinery or private police as their soldiers and prisons as places for internment.' (1998, p 126.)

27 Murray, 1984, 1990.

is an easy sell to any society frightened by seemingly uncontrollable crime. On its deepest level, however, it is not about crime at all, but a vision of social order disintegrating under glassy-eyed liberal neglect.'[28] The ex-British Prime Minister Margaret Thatcher's words echoed those of right realism: 'The events of September 11 are a terrible reminder that freedom demands eternal vigilance. And for too long we have not been vigilant. We have harboured those who hated us, tolerated those who threatened us and indulged those who weakened us.'[29]

But it has become difficult to preserve ontological security through the discourse of crime. In part this is because crime has merged with disorder on the one hand and war on the other. Crime mixes with civil disorder (and antisocial behaviour) with the result that it becomes more difficult to demarcate anti-social behaviour from the living out of desires and impulses stimulated by core cultural values (consumption, self-expression, and individual pursuit of pleasure).[30] Certain crimes, such as illicit drug use, normalise. Conversely, authorities declare 'war on crime', often, as in the case of drugs, against the very activity now normalised! As a consequence, we have increased penalisation at the same time as we have normalisation of 'crimes'. This drags into the penal system individuals who would not otherwise have been defined and processed as offenders, and who, having been taken in, become subjects of pressures that encourage further 'criminal involvement'. Crime, disorder and the use of the technologies of para-militarism blur into a continuum inside the nation state. At the same time, state authorities use paramilitary and military 'aid' to combat the production of drugs in countries where drug manufacture is in part a consequence of social disruption and dislocation by previous military involvement.[31] Awareness of the interlocking nature of causal responsibility is kept at bay through the individualising nature of the discourse of crime. The policing function takes on the guise of paramilitary operations whilst the new forms of 'just war' take on the status of police action.[32]

Crime and war are no longer stable categories, nor is terrorism, although there will be those who rhetorically present it as such to galvanise responses. Two texts from the early 1980s are illustrative of the divergent understandings of terrorism. That decade is held out as a time when terrorist activity greatly increased, both at the international level[33] and in various national arenas around the world.[34] The portrayal of the changing nature of terrorist and extremist action during this period,

---

28 Shapiro, 1997, p 6.
29 *The Guardian*, 12 February 2002. Compare Thomas Freidman: 'But the critics [of the American response to September 11] are missing the larger point, which is this: September 11 happened because America had lost its deterrent capability. We lost it because for 20 years we never retaliated against, or brought to justice, those who murdered Americans ... The terrorists and the states that harbour them thought we were soft, and they were right. They thought they could always "out-crazy" us, and they were right. They thought we would always listen to the Europeans and opt for "constructive engagement" with rogues, not a fist in the face. America's enemies smelled weakness all over us, and we paid a huge price for that.' His solution? In part, to be willing 'to restore our deterrence and to be as crazy as some of our enemies'. (Comment, *The Guardian*, 16 February 2002, first published *New York Times*.)
30 See for example Presdee, 2000.
31 Indeed, as the Taliban were swept from power in Afghanistan, the quality British Sunday newspaper *The Observer* entitled a major report 'Victorious warlords set to open the opium floodgates' (25 November 2001).
32 Illustrated by British Prime Minister Tony Blair's speech to the Labour Party Conference, 2 October, reported in *The Guardian*, 3 October under the front page headline of a quote from the speech: 'Let us reorder the world'. On page 3 *The Guardian* asked: 'Can the west really police the world?'
33 See White, 2001 on the general growth of terrorism during the 1980s; and Kurz, 1994 on the expansion and exportation of Palestinian and Lebanese terrorism during the same period.
34 Eg Smith, 1994 on the growth of extremist groups in the United States; and Criss, 1995 on the increased activities of the Kurdish Workers Party (PKK) in Turkey.

and some of the more politically and ideologically infused societal responses to these changes, are tropes of the fears and insecurities of late modernity.

Benjamin Netanyahu's *Terrorism: How the West Can Win* (1986) was an edited collection that included contributions from former US Secretary of State, George Shultz, Yitzhak Rabin and Lord Chalfont. The work aimed, as a 'practical guide', to 'change the course of the war against terrorism'. Terrorism, however, is seen as a strangely uniform phenomenon. Netanyahu asserts that terrorism 'is not a sporadic phenomenon born of social misery and frustration'.[35] He locates it in 'two movements that have assumed international prominence in the second half of the 20th century, communist totalitarianism and Islamic (and Arab) radicalism'.[36] Here, then, is a binary order of terrorism, presented with the type of unashamed absolutism so characteristic of the modernist ideologue.[37] The opinion of many experts on terrorism that, because of its nebulous (even abstract) nature, it is an entity that defies simple definition[38] is casually overlooked. The exclusion is rhetorically understandable, for Netanyahu's writings are more a call to arms than historical or contextual analysis; any suggestion of relativism would compromise the legitimacy of a project aimed at destroying terrorism. Having homogenised, yet universalised, terrorism, we are presented with the remedy: the West must unite in a consolidated, collective effort to defeat terrorism. Again, Netanyahu homogenises, this time the West is presented as a uniform conglomerate of culture and identity. *Terrorism: How the West Can Win* rhetorically (re)presents a monolithic vision of the world (or at least the West), a cohesive society free of diversity, division and conflict: terrorism comes from the 'other' world.[39]

In *The Turner Diaries*,[40] the US white supremacist, William Pierce, presented a very different view of the West from the one posited by Netanyahu. Ostensibly, *The Turner Diaries* is a fictionalised account of the rise of a mythical white terror organisation called The Order and their subsequent involvement in the 'Great White Revolution' that takes place sometime towards the end of the 20th century. However, *The Turner Diaries* also served a second function: among extremist groups in the United States and elsewhere it became known as a veritable 'blueprint for terror':

> For the most part, *The Turner Diaries* is a diatribe against minorities and Jews. It is well-written and easy to read. The danger of the work is that it is correct from a technical standpoint. *The Turner Diaries* is a how-to manual for low-level terrorism. Using a narrative or storytelling format, Pierce describes the proper methods for making bombs, constructing mortars, attacking targets, and launching other acts of terrorism. Anyone of average intelligence who reads *The Turner Diaries* will leave the book with an elementary idea of how to become a terrorist.[41]

---

35 Netanyahu, 1986, p 7.

36 Netanyahu, 1986, p 9.

37 It is interesting to compare the opening sentence of Netanyahu's introduction ('To win the war against terrorism, free societies must first know what they are fighting') with the words of Le Corbusier some 60 years earlier: 'For to plan a large contemporary city is to engage in a tremendous battle, and how can you fight a battle if you do not know what you are fighting for?' (Le Corbusier, 1925.)

38 See Laqueur, 1999, pp 8–10; Schmid, 1983.

39 This structure is largely repeated in his sole-authored book, *Fighting Terrorism: How Democracies Can Defeat Domestic and International Terrorism* (1995).

40 MacDonald, 1985.

41 White, 2001, p 229. It is alleged that several US extremist neo-Nazi groups took their lead from Turner's fictional terrorist organisation, including the notorious Bruder Schweigen (the Silent Brotherhood) (White, 2001, p 230). Famously, when arrested, Oklahoma City bomber, Timothy McVeigh was in possession of a copiously highlighted copy of *The Turner Diaries*. Indeed, there are striking similarities between the bombing of the Murrah Federal Building in Oklahoma City and specific passages in *The Turner Diaries* that graphically depict the gathering and preparation of bomb materials used for a strike against the FBI.

With *The Turner Diaries* (and Pierce's second novel *Hunter*) we see the popularisation of terrorism and extremism within the West (a trend that has continued through the dissemination of terrorist materials on the internet). While Pierce's diatribe appears to represent order, in reality it is illustrative of ontological insecurity and an emotional (perhaps an expression of 'resentment') desire to reassert control and re-establish purity and simplicity. The insecurities of late modern life provide the perfect conditions for the promotion of essentialisms and the spread of fanaticism. Unequivocal beliefs (whether radical or traditional) engender a strong sense of belonging, they help to repel doubts, assuage anxieties and give solidity to chaotic social worlds. We do not wish to universalise, however; some acts of terrorism may thus be both a consequence of and a purported solution to the dislocations and insecurities of an ontologically insecure world order. In reacting and attempting to constrain the effects of September 11, the discourses of crime and war may be intermingled, with a result that is logically unsatisfying but effective in reasserting two traditions of the governing metaphor (and the metaphor of governing). Locating the events in the intermingling discourses of crime and war enables the 'ruler' to reassure the 'citizens' that the ruler understands the events and therefore can mobilise resources to counter the threat and minimise further risk.[42]

Risk and the creation of community

September 11 became the exemplar of a new world order of risk. It illustrated what Beck (1999) has described as the emerging 'global technological citizenship' where the instrument that conferred cultural identification for that citizenship was global television (CNN; CNBC; BBC 24; SKY; FOX). Nowhere was that more evident than in the instantaneous and global presentation of the events of September 11. Through participation in observing the events, audiences divided between a community that saw itself threatened[43] and those who saw the World Trade Center as symbolic of a community from which they were excluded and whose culture seemed devouring.[44]

The reach of September 11 thus displayed the new power and divisions of communication technology.[45] More than 30 years ago Lewis Mumford wrote that

---

42 'The deliberate and deadly attacks that were carried out against our country were more than acts of terror. They were acts of war.' (President Bush, First Address to the Nation after the attacks.)
   '... this new war is for keeps. It is inconceivable that it was unleashed by a few well-financed freelancers. It was done with the connivance or active participation of a state. Unlike individuals who seek martyrdom, states want to survive. Hence they can be deterred. And they will be if the punishment fits the crime. "Rogue states" may be crazy, but they are not stupid.' (Joffe, 2001.)

43 '... the painful lesson I learned was a simple one: that these guys can kill me and my family, and do it very easily, using a couple of cellphones, credit cards, online booking and commercial airlines – deploying Western technology to bury Western values.' (Mark Steyn, *The Spectator*, 22 September 2001.)

44 And the images of that division were another source of threat. As Paul Johnstone put it: '... Islam is notorious for its periodic outbreaks of revivalism, which usually take a militant form, and the world is certainly experiencing one at the moment. Last week's television spectacle of Muslim women weeping and dancing with joy at the destruction of lives in America illustrated, perhaps for the first time for many Westerners, the human depth of the problem we face.' (*The Spectator*, 22 September 2001.)

45 One of the authors [WM] saw the events whilst in Hong Kong, the self-termed 'Manhattan of Asia'. He learnt of it as a business dinner with individuals from Malaysia and Hong Kong broke up and individuals consulted their mobile telephones that had been turned off during dinner. Everyone rang 'home': the Petronas Twin Towers in Kuala Lumpur Malaysia, the world's tallest building, had been evacuated, London had been declared a no-fly zone. Several days of TV channel hopping between CNN, FOX, CNBC, BBC24, French TV, and various channels of Hong Kong, China, Singapore, Australia (SKY), followed. Commentary and analysis varied, but the newscasters, whatever the country of origin, were united in their implicit message that it was their fellow professionals in the World Trade Center and on board the hijacked planes that had died. The international global elite

large scale technological systems were the most influential forms and sources of tyranny in the modern world; he called for modes of democratising technology and communication. For Beck, technological citizenship may be 'enjoyed' and 'risked' at the home, local, state, national or global level. The citizenship is layered and divisions may be horizontal and vertical. Spheres of technological availability and utilisation exist. What 'rights' to technological information and participation exist? Those rights appear governed by the market, not jurisprudentially. And neither the market nor jurisprudence can offer protection from danger resulting from technological malfunction (such as by global warming or Chernobyl-type occasions). There is no global balloting for technological participation, instead immersion in consumer culture serves as the trope of identity.

The political site of what Beck calls 'world risk society' is television. Its political subjectivity lies in the relation of the individual to the staging of cultural symbols in the mass media. Such staging may be the depicting of 'rescue' or aid for victims of famine or of the new 'just war' of Kosovo. Through the staging of such symbols the prospect of a bad conscience at any realisation of the interconnectedness of the new global order is contained.

The imagery of crime, evil and reasserting control

The images of the destruction of the Twin Towers and the damage to the Pentagon were accompanied by images of an empty White House. After the cameras had captured the startled look on Bush's face as he learnt that a second plane had crashed into the World Trade Center he was rushed away and out of sight. Some quickly realised that the image of an American President so obviously lost for words, shuffled from one place to another, unable to return to the White House for more than 10 hours was as dangerous as the images of the actual damage.

In the society of the spectacle, the imagery had to be (re)captured. Explanations were proffered, albeit unbelievable, for the fact that the major leaders had seemingly taken cover.[46] New images had to be created. The first was a mistake. In a staged event, meant to look candid, Bush paced behind his desk during a photo-op phone call with Mayor Rudy Giuliani, accepting the mayor's invitation to tour Ground Zero. His administration fumed that ex-President Clinton, who had been in Australia at the time of the attack, flew back as soon as international air flights, suspended in the wake of the attack, resumed and instantly went to Ground Zero to meet with weeping relatives and exhausted rescue workers. Bush went first to the damaged Pentagon and then, belatedly for many, to Ground Zero.

At Ground Zero, however, Bush found himself. Dressed casually, he fought back the tears, hugged fire fighters and then took a hand-held hailer and rendered an impromptu address. The resultant pictures addressed the mood of the nation.[47]

---

knew they were targeted, whatever their nationality or religion (WM included, as he had had coffee at the Twin Towers while on a visit to New York only in June, some two months previously).

46 'To quiet grumbling about the 10 hours it took for Bush to return to the White House, officials belatedly leaked an account that Air Force One had been targeted. [Vice-President] Cheney vouched for the report. "I got the data, and it was real and credible", he told an aide.' (*Time*, 24 September 2001.)

47 The photos made the front page of all major newspapers and the international edition of *Time* had the subtitle 'America united: digging out – and digging in for war'. In a double page photospread inside, the caption read 'At Ground Zero: Bush mourned, rallied the rescuers and the country, and sent a message to terrorists and the world' (*Time*, 24 September 2001). By May 2002, however, the Republican Party was criticised for now using 9/11 photos in campaign fund raising. *Time*, 27 May commented ironically 'Hey, the "Bush Cowering in Air Force One Toilet" shot should be popular'. In May/June 2002, media attention also focused on whether the White House should have known of the attacks as there were several indications of what was to happen before September 11.

The symbolic fight back had to be resolute: in a posed meeting of his security council, all dressed in casual open-necked shirts and outdoor jackets, Bush clarified the position: 'We're at war' and he would fight for 'as long as it takes'. In reasserting control, knowledge must be claimed. Thus on 20 September, while the FBI were admitting that it was not even sure of the identities of some of the hijackers, President Bush addressed Congress, asserting 'We know exactly who these people are and which governments are supporting them'. To the questioning anguish of a victimised nation he answered: 'Why do they hate us? They hate our freedoms – our freedom of speech, our freedom to vote and assemble and disagree with each other.' On the 21st, in the Washington National Cathedral, Bush drew upon 'a kinship of grief and a steadfast resolve to prevail against our enemies'. The spectacle there was of a united nation and the institutional continuum of authority: Bush sat in the front row next to his wife, his father (ex-President Bush) and mother, ex-President Clinton and his wife Hillary (now Senator for New York). The defeated Democrat candidate, Al Gore, who had actually polled more votes than Bush in the presidential election of November 2000, sat three rows behind him. Bush was, however, still working amidst images of a nation struggling for control, seeking to regain a sense of normalcy. Now the fear was of biological attack. By early November 2001, a number of federal buildings and the Supreme Court had been infected with anthrax spores, the Supreme Court was meeting outside its grand building for the first time in 66 years, Senators were locked out of their offices, and thousands of government workers were put on a regime of precautionary antibiotics.

Beck's question remains: who or what processes discover or invent symbols that disclose or demonstrate the structural character of the problems, as well as creating the capacity for action? Some Americans noted the duality of the communication system.[48] As the British Prime Minister, Tony Blair, implicitly reminded his audience in the UK, the capacity for action should be greater the simpler and neater is the staged symbol. Thus he stressed the need to remember how they felt when they saw the hijacked airliners hitting the Twin Towers, an emotion he harnessed to his pledge not to falter until the Al Qa'ida network had been destroyed. In Cardiff, on 30 October, he warned that the terrorists had one hope. They hoped that the Western democracies were decadent: 'that we lack the moral fibre or will or courage to take them on; that we might begin but we won't finish; that we will start, then falter; that when the first setbacks occur we will lose our nerve.' Reasserting control in this 'war of shadows' depends upon minimising the complications able to be indicated by potential staged protest groups and ensuring that individual spectators can gain a moral identification with the projection (clear his or her

---

48 The American writer Siri Hustvedt, who lives in Brooklyn, a few minutes over the East River from the site of the Twin Towers, contrasted her own experience of watching the events from across the river and on TV and then noted the role the communication network played in the events. 'The problem of direct and mediated images is important to 11 September and its aftermath, not only because most of the world witnessed what happened on TV, but because the terrorists knew that they were staging a spectacular media event. They knew that in the time that elapsed between the first plane crash and the second, television crews would have descended on the scene to record the horrifying image of an airliner entering the second tower, and that the tape would be played and replayed for all the world to see, and they knew, too, that it would resemble nothing so much as a Hollywood disaster movie. A hackneyed fiction remade ad nauseam by the studios was manipulated by the terrorists into grotesque reality.

'At the same time, it must be said that it took very little imagination on the part of screenwriters to take actual events of terror and enlarge on them to fit their own notions of a thrilling spectacle. 11 September was not unimaginable. We could all imagine it. It's the fact of it that annihilated the fantasy.' (*The Observer*, 10 March 2002.)

conscience[49]). Thus the importance of further staged occasions, such as the American President Bush's State of the Union address to Congress and to the United Nations where a doctrine that the real enemy was 'an axis of Evil, aiming to threaten the peace of the world' was drawn out. Represented in the front pages of newspapers and magazines as an image of certainty and strength, Bush announced a clear message: America was at war with terrorism, and the rest of the world had to choose between being 'with us or against us'.[50] It seemed as if the events had stirred the super-power into asserting a dominant sovereignty and redrawing the terms of judgment.

Conclusion: asserting security and avoiding bad conscience in the rise of empire?

> The mad creatures who committed these terrible crimes ... may have hoped to provoke us into mindless revenge in order to create even more devastation, but they are wrong.[51]
>
> I am happy [at the scenes of September 11] not because I support terrorism, I am happy because I hate America.[52]
>
> Our work targets world infidels. Our enemy is the crusader alliance led by America, Britain and Israel. It is a crusader-Jewish alliance.[53]

Those who wish to define the events of September 11 as crimes do so partly to structure the response. Crimes require investigation, perpetrators to be identified, tracked down and held awaiting trial in accordance with their rights, evidence to be collected sufficient to prove the case, punishment should be proportionate to the crime and only those responsible should be punished. The discourse of crime and criminal justice places limits on the power of the state to investigate, and lays out rules to structure the game of investigation and proof.[54] Some of the moves to call September 11 an act of war, and responding to it a state of war, are designed to specifically avoid the rules of criminal justice. There has been concern expressed that many of the measures taken subsequently remove traditional liberties and rights.

---

49 Thus *The Economist* could make its front cover of 3–9 November 2001 a picture of a small Afghan boy carrying an even smaller girl with the title 'A heart-rending but necessary war'. In its Leader, under a section headed 'We all want peace', it counselled that 'in this televisual age, wars come into your living room, bring with them uncomfortable images', but 'patience is certainly required ... In this war, there will be no turning back'. Elsewhere it described the situation as 'a frustrating war against an elusive terrorist enemy'.

50 The cover of *The Economist*, 2–8 February 2002, portrayed a picture of Bush mid-speech beneath the heading 'George Bush and the axis of evil'. The Leader called it 'a memorable phrase', noting that it was 'meant to galvanise support by turning a long and tricky foreign-policy challenge into a simple, moral issue'. The Leader called for Bush's list of 'non-negotiable demands' about values to be defended 'impressive'. This list, 'the rule of law ... respect for women ... private property ... free speech ... equal justice ... religion', was 'admirable' in aim; but *The Economist* warned that 'the application will be harder'. Not only did many countries that America would need on its side not adhere to them, but 'alas, democracies that follow these values are also capable, on occasion, of being in the wrong and even of committing atrocities'. It warned that America would need to listen and engage in dialogue: 'To fight an axis of evil, even a superpower, needs an axis of its own.'

51 Nato Secretary-General George Robertson, quoted *Time*, 24 September 2001.

52 Posting on a Chinese online message board, quoted *Time*, 24 September 2001.

53 Osama bin Laden, *Time* interview, 1998, quoted *Time*, 24 September 2001.

54 Several aspects of America's response fitted this pattern, such as the creation of an 'evidence dossier'. *The Guardian* reported, 3 October, that 'The United States finally showed its Nato allies "clear and compelling" evidence yesterday that last month's terror attacks on New York and Washington were launched from abroad by Osama bin Laden's Al-Qaida network'. The treatment of the prisoners taken to Guantanamo Bay (Cuba) fell between the two discourses. US allies argued that the captives should be treated as POWs under the 1949 Geneva Convention, which authorises detaining them until the end of hostilities. However, the American government refused to accord them that status. While saying that it was providing humane treatment it also denied them the status of suspects to be treated under the criminal law, with the rights that would accompany that status.

The military historian Caleb Carr argues that identifying international terrorism as a type of crime handicapped dealing with the threats.[55] Instead, terrorists must be seen as 'organised, highly trained, hugely destructive paramilitary units that were and are conducting offensive campaigns against a variety of nations and social systems. In truth, international terrorism has always been what its perpetrators have so often insisted: a form of warfare'. Mixing the discourses of crime and war engenders 'confusion and arguments over terms and concepts, goals and strategies'.

Carr sees terrorism as a continuation of a type of warfare practised throughout history (even, he admits, by the United States). He sees terrorism as ultimately unsuccessful, creating resentment, anger and resistance in the target groups instead of capitulation.

It is crucial that the response should not continue the game of terror:

> The successful answer to the terrorist threat, then, lies not in repeated analyses of individual contemporary terrorist movements, nor in legalistic attempts to condemn their behaviour in courts of international law, nor in reactionary policies and actions that punish civilian populations as much as the terrorists who operate from among them. Rather, it lies in the formulation of a comprehensive, progressive strategy that can address all terrorist threats with the only coercive measures that have ever affected or moderated terrorist (or any other military or paramilitary) behaviour: preemptive military offensives aimed at making not only terrorists but the states that harbor, supply, and otherwise assist them experience the same perpetual insecurity that they attempt to make their victims feel. The methods must be different, of course, for, as stated, terror must never be answered with terror; but war can *only* be answered with war, and it is incumbent on us to devise a style of war more imaginative, more decisive, and yet more humane than anything terrorists can contrive.[56]

This is a discourse of a refined 'just war'. Not only is the cause just, but the methodology must be precise and consistent. It is not an approach addressed, as in the analytical part of the discourse of crime (criminology), to the issue of the injustices or grievances that give fertile ground for the sympathisers of Islamic terrorism. Carr's strategy is directed against 'behaviour', terror is to be defeated 'when it is perceived as a strategy and a behaviour that yields nothing save eventual defeat for the causes that inspire'. Other measures must be taken to address political issues. But this is a central problem: what if part of the causes and grievances are justifiable? How is a strategy to work that both wages this new war against terrorist behaviour *and* encourages real political progress? *Moreover, who is to design the rules of such engagements?*

It is here that many worry about American unilateralism. America drew the distrust and hatred of the perpetrators of the September 11 attacks. But was America actually the target, or was it something deeper, something more difficult to reach?

Written self-consciously from the political left, Hardt and Negri's *Empire*[57] postulates that only a concept of a new 'Imperial Sovereignty' is adequate to capture the new world order. There are three tiers to the imperial pyramid of power: the bomb, capital and ether (communication technologies). For these authors, 'the spectacle of politics functions as if the media, the military, the government, the transnational corporations, the global financial institutions, and so

---

55 Carr, 2002, p 9. '... insisting that terrorists are essentially criminals ... generally limits to reactive and defensive measures the range of responses that the American and other governments can justifiably employ. During most of the Clinton administration's eight years, for example, despite the fact that the nature and purposes of such global terrorist organisations as Osama bin Laden's Al-Qaeda were well-known, almost all federal funds for anti-terrorist efforts were targeted at detective and intelligence work, while preemptive military moves against terrorist leaders, networks, or bases were ignored.' (Carr, 2002, p 8.)

56 Carr, 2002, pp 13–14.

57 2000.

forth were all consciously and explicitly directed by a single power even though in reality they are not'.[58] Thus while it has the appearance of domination, the United States is a false target. In their view, 'the United States does not, and indeed no nation-state can today, form the centre of the imperialist project'.[59] Their view might be rather that of a growing international multitude subjected to forms of knowledge, culture, production, and exploitation from the outside. Late 20th century consumer capitalism constituted a global economy whose driving force neither respects nor supports local knowledge or culture, other than as raw material to be fed into the conveyor belts of the products of the world, creating resentment and desires for revenge among those it has not seduced.

While European references to 'America's imperial war' warn that the $48 billion in increased defence spending (agreed as a consequence of September 11) and expanded powers to the military-industrial complex 'now present a threat not just to terrorism but to the world',[60] in America the term 'imperial' is now used admiringly. Conservative commentators are rewriting the history of 19th century imperialism. 'Afghanistan, and other troubled lands today, cry out for the sort of enlightened foreign administration once provided by self-confident Englishmen in jodhpurs and pith helmets … the September 11 attack was a result of insufficient American involvement and ambition: the solution is to be more expansive in our goals and more assertive in their implementation.'[61] A decade ago Paul Kennedy was predicting American imperial overreach, now he notes that American military power far exceeds comparison with the reach of previous empires and asks that it be used. Robert Kaplan[62] argues that only reference to the politics of past empires will give proper guidance to today's leaders.

There will now be great temptations to build a new empire in a narrow sense; the sense of building overwhelming American power and influence. If so, then prospects for an international system of law and government through the United Nations, already under pressure with the reluctance of America to fully participate, will further recede. Moreover, the forces of a military-industrial complex will have strong grounds for dominating the continuing response to September 11. It will not be a simple case of power playing against freedom – for power has long been the preresiquite for freedom in modernity – but of the commodification and packaging of security and displays of might. In this future struggle there will be a need for rituals and discourses of purity. If 'bad conscience' is to be kept at bay, awareness of the contingency and interconnectedness of Ground Zero and our new global citizenship must be constrained.[63] One cannot help but feel that in the new world order there may be little reflexivity and much representation in the system of right and wrong.

---

58 Hardt and Negri, 2000, p 323.
59 Hardt and Negri, 2000, p xiv.
60 Monbiot, 2002.
61 Boot, 2002.
62 2001.
63 To give a flavour of voices that call for greater reflexivity: 'It was stated by the US and the coalition against the terror of September 11 that the response would be military, diplomatic and humanitarian. No question of any effort to deepen an understanding of the roots of fundamentalism; and for a very good reason. If it were our objective to anticipate, and perhaps even to forestall, such developments, this might require an acknowledgement of our own role in the creation of the cycle of hope, disappointment and anger … In the vacuum left by the extinction of socialism and the decay of secular cultural identities, people have found in the disciplined asperities of a regressive version of Islam a hopeful, and sometimes, murderous alternative.

'It seems we are content to rest in an idle laissez-faire of the spirit, which permits events to take their course, and only then to seek to rectify them by intensifying a violence which we have already helped to unleash in the world.' (Jeremy Seabrook, *The Guardian*, 20 December 2001.)

References

Anti-Defamation League (2001): www.adl.org/terrorism_america/saying_091401.asp

Archer, Dane and Gartner, Rosemary (1984) *Violence and Crime in Cross-National Perspective*, New Haven: Yale UP

Arendt, Hannah (1964) *Eichmann in Jerusalem: A Report on the Banality of Evil*, New York: Penguin

Auden, WH (1966) *Collected Shorter Poems, 1927–57*, London: Faber

Bauman, Zygmunt (1995) *Life in Fragments: Essays in Postmodern Morality*, Oxford: Blackwell

Beck, Ulrich (1999) *World Risk Society*, Cambridge: Polity

Boot, Max (2002) 'The case for American empire', quoted *International Herald Tribune*, 2 April

Carr, Caleb (2002) *The Lessons of Terror*, London: Little, Brown

Christie, Nils (2002) *Crime Control as Industry: Towards Gulags, Western Style*, London: Routledge

Christie, Nils (1998) 'Roots of a perspective', in Holdaway, Simon and Rock, Paul, *Thinking about Criminology*, London: UCL Press

Cohen, Stanley (2001) *States of Denial*, Cambridge: Polity

Criss, Nur Bilge (1995) 'The nature of PKK terrorism in Turkey' 18 Studies in Conflict and Terrorism 17

DeLillo, Don, 'In the ruins of the future' *The Guardian*, 22 December 2001

Garland, David (2001) *The Culture of Control: Crime and Social Order in Contemporary Society*, Oxford: OUP

Giddens, A (1990) *The Consequences of Modernity*, Cambridge: Polity

Hardt, Michael and Negri, Antonio (2000) *Empire*, Cambridge, Mass: Harvard UP

Hayward, KJ (2002) 'The vilification and pleasures of youthful transgression', in Muncie, John, Hughes, Gordon and McLaughlin, Eugene (eds), *Youth Justice: Critical Readings*, London: Sage

Hayward, KJ (2003) *City Limits: Crime, Consumer Culture and the Urban Experience*. London: Cavendish Publishing (forthcoming)

Joffe, Josef (2001) 'Asymmetric warfare' *Time*, 24 September

Kaplan, Robert (2001) *Warrior Politics: Why Leadership Demands a Pagan Ethos*, New York: Random House

Kelman, Herbert C and Hamilton, V Lee (1989) *Crimes of Obedience: Toward a Social Psychology of Authority and Responsibility*, New Haven: Yale UP

Kurz, A (1994) 'Palestinian terrorism: the violent aspect of a political struggle', in Alexander, Yonah (ed), *Middle Eastern Terrorism: Current Threats and Future Prospects*, New York: Hall

Lacqueur, W (1999) *The New Terrorism: Fanaticism and the Arms of Mass Destruction*, New York: OUP

Le Corbusier (1925) *The City of Tomorrow and Its Planning*, 1986 edn, New York: Dover

Lyotard, Jean-François (1984) *The Postmodern Condition*, Manchester: Manchester UP

MacDonald, A (William Pierce) (1985) *The Turner Diaries*, Arlington, Va: National Vanguard

Monbiot, George (2002) 'America's imperial war' *The Guardian*, 12 February

Morrison, Wayne (1995) *Theoretical Criminology: From Modernism to Postmodernism*, London: Cavendish Publishing

Murray, Charles (1984) *Losing Ground*, New York: Basic Books

Murray, Charles (1990) 'The British underclass' The Public Interest 99

Netanyahu, B (ed) (1986) *Terrorism: How the West Can Win*, New York: Avon

Netanyahu, B (1995) *Fighting Terrorism: How Democracies Can Defeat Domestic and International Terrorism,* Farrar, Strauss & Giroux, republished Noonday Press, 1997, reprinted 2001

Presdee, Mike (2000) *Cultural Criminology and the Carnival of Crime,* London: Routledge

Rifkin, Jeremy (2001) 'Dialogue is a necessity to bridge cultural schism' *The Guardian,* 13 November

Roy, Arundhati (2001) 'The algebra of infinite justice' *The Guardian,* 29 September

Runnel, Rudolph (1992) *Democide,* New Brunswick: Transaction

Runnel, Rudolph (1995) *Death by Government,* New Brunswick: Transaction

Schmid, AP (1983) *Political Terrorism: A Research Guide to Concepts, Theories, Data bases, and Literature,* New Brunswick: Transaction

Shapiro, Bruce (1997) 'Zero-tolerance gospel':
www.coneworld.orgindexoc/issue497/shapiro.html

Smith, MLR (1994) *Terrorism in America: Pipe Bombs and Pipe Dreams.* Albany: University of New York Press

Thatcher, Margaret (2002) 'Islamism is the new bolshevism' *The Guardian,* 12 February

White, JR (2001) *Terrorism: An Introduction,* Belmont, CA: Wadsworth

Young, Jock (1999) *The Exclusive Society,* London: Sage

Chapter 11
September 11 and American policy in the Middle East

Tareq Y Ismael and Jacqueline S Ismael [1]

In the aftermath of September 11, strident patriotism is the dominant tone and tenor of public discourse in the United States. Unrecorded or unregistered scepticism cowers before strident patriotism; and the outspoken dissent of anti-corporate globalisation protests, environmental concerns, and American foreign policy is muffled by jingoism. On 20 September, US President George W Bush addressed a joint session of the US Congress and told the world: 'you are either with us, or you are with the terrorists!'[2] In effect, this jingoistic discourse has served to disallow questioning of US policy in the Middle East, and US policy makers have essentially narrowed the definition of terrorism to an ethno-cultural term of reference. Terrorism, in other words, means Muslim terrorism and refers to virtually any act of violence, protest, or resistance in the Muslim world.

Following September 11, the subscripts of public discourse on the Middle East are that Islam and the Arabs are the true causes of terrorism; that Israel has been facing such terrorism all its life; that Arafat, Saddam Hussein and bin Laden are basically the same archetype of anti-American foe; and that most of the US's Arab allies (especially Egypt and Saudi Arabia) are corrupt, undemocratic regimes that have played a negative role through their passive support for terrorism.

The subscript of public discourse on the Middle East in the United States is based on a set of myths and metaphors that caricaturise the Arab people along racial lines. In other words, it is a racist subscript. A myth is a partial truth generalised to explain the whole. As a partial truth, there is always plenty of ad hoc evidence to support it so it is particularly resilient to opposing argumentation. A metaphor sets up an analogy that caricaturises links between people and policy makers, institutions and processes, culture and ideology. The classic 20th century racist script in public discourse is represented in German public discourse between world wars. This paper argues that US policy in the Middle East reflects the tension between two inter-twined themes – racism and unilateralism. The purpose of this chapter is to examine how this tension has played itself out in the unfolding of American policy in the Middle East since September 11. It argues that racism reinforces unilateralism in domestic US politics; and it creates obstacles to the acceptance of US unilateralism internationally.

The prism of public discourse

Many academics and intellectuals have moved beyond the monolithic labels of 'West' and 'Islamic world' reintroduced by Samuel Huntington's *The Clash of*

---

1 This paper is adapted from a forthcoming book, *Sanctions and Human Rights: The Iraqi Case in International Politics*. We wish to acknowledge our research assistant, John Measor, without whose wizardry in researching information on the internet this could not have been completed on time.
2 The text of the speech may be found at the White House official website, www.whitehouse.gov; see also 'US strikes at Afghan targets', BBC News, 7 October 2001. By 6 November, Bush had shortened the charge to 'You're either with us or against us in the fight against terror'. See 'Bush says it is time for action', CNN.com/US, 6 November 2001.

Civilizations; in return they sought to better reflect the sophistication of the relationship between societies as diverse as the United States and the Arab states of the Middle East. At the same time, politicians and political commentators have utilised and popularised these terms to frame the discussion of American actions in a classically 'Orientalist' fashion following September 11. Public vetting of American policy options are filtered through the lenses provided by such esteemed pillars of American academia as Samuel Huntington (Harvard), Bernard Lewis (Princeton), and Fuad Ajami (Johns Hopkins University). The lens provided projects an immensely homogenised Islamic Arab 'world' devoid of the humane, enlightened and magnanimous societal achievements of Western – more specifically American – civilisation. The discursive power of this phenomenon allows racist notions to flourish and for tremendous abuses of violent force to be used against the 'other'. Bernard Lewis has advocated a 'get tough' policy with the 'Arab world'.[3]

Arabs are seen as a monolithic community that can only be understood through scholarly analyses of the Qu'ran, the various schools of legal interpretation that have resulted from its teachings, and Bedouin tribal society. Such reductionism was identified by the French scholar Maxime Rodinson as theologocentrism, the referencing of Islamic theology to elucidate any action taken by Arabs.[4] That people living in the Middle East are politically informed, some even motivated to political action ranging from non-violent public demonstrations to the indiscriminate violence of terrorism, through socio-economic forces other than Islam and 9th century Arab tribalism is ignored. Islam and Arab society are rarely portrayed or examined in mainstream English-speaking media, except when terrorism and violence in the Middle East is being examined. Such practices have led to clear connections in public discourse within the English-speaking world equating Islam with terrorism, Palestinians with 'gunmen', and profession of the Islamic faith with 'fundamentalism'.[5]

While religion generally, and Islam in particular, clearly holds a central locus within Middle Eastern culture and political discourse, it would be fallacious to identify any Arab state or political movement as being representative of Islam and its teachings. The discourse promoting a monolithic 'Islam' in conflict with a monolithic 'West' exists in the Middle East in the teachings of many Islamic activists. Osama bin-Laden's statements repeatedly refer to the Christian 'crusaders' who occupy the land of the holy places in Arabia, and to the nefarious actions of the 'West' to deprive the Palestinian and Iraqi peoples of their freedom. This identification of the policies of the governments of the United States, United Kingdom, France etc reflects theologoism successfully transformed into the reactionary political vision of many Islamic political actors who oppose the corrupt and ineffectual Arab regimes and call for the return to a more pious existence. That this has spawned violent action is a tactical decision rather than evidence of any proclivity for violence inherent within Islam. Put simply, the motivations of Islamic activists are political and economic in nature.

Arab regimes make numerous references to their piety and religiosity in an effort to legitimise their rule and increasingly to co-opt the language used against them by political opponents who are largely, if not wholly, informed by religious beliefs and teachings, political forces singularly identified as 'fundamentalist' in the English-speaking media. This singularity has been reinforced as Islamic 'experts' are given

---

3 Lewis, 2001.
4 Rodinson, 1987. For an excellent examination of theologocentrism and its adaptation in the American response to September 11, see Abu Khalil, 2002.
5 See Said, 1997; and Finkelstein, 1995.

pride of place in mainstream media investigations of events as varied as the Gulf War in 1991, the World Trade Center bombings in 1993, and the suicide bombings in Palestine and Israel. The legitimacy conferred on Arab regimes by their leaders and spokesmen is parroted by American calls for a cleansing of Islam from the 'violent' interpretation of opposition movements in countries as diverse as Algeria, Lebanon and Afghanistan. Arab regimes and the people of the Middle East are encouraged to remove the constraints that religion – Islam – has conferred upon their societies.

However, American political leaders, intellectuals, and English-speaking media do not similarly stress the religious orientation or numerous references to the Christian faith by American, British, Canadian or Australian political leaders. Such language and imagery is not seen as bearing on the political decisions emanating from Washington, London, Ottawa or Canberra. Political violence by the IRA, pro-life activists who bomb abortion clinics or assassinate medical professionals are not seen as being archetypal or even representative of the Christian faith. Groups as diverse as the Branch Davidians, the Unification Church, the People's Temple or any other aberrant Christian theological group are dismissed and not given the legitimacy of having their views espoused and analysed by 'experts' who in effect place such groups' beliefs within the cannon of Western Christendom. That Christian phraseology and references are common in American political discourse is not relevant, while religious references by Arab political leaders are stressed within translations by 'experts' within mainstream media.

Moreover, examples of the Christian faith's influence within the political discourse of the English-speaking states are profuse. The United States' national motto, 'In God We Trust', is prominent in both houses of its legislature, inscribed above the speaker's podium on the House floor, and above the entrance to the United States Senate. With the terrorist attacks on New York and Washington, the public display of personal religious faith became both more widespread and conspicuous. As the events of September 11 were unfolding, Senator Joseph Lieberman of Connecticut, who had been Al Gore's Democratic Party nominee for vice-president in 2000, called for prayer as members of Congress were evacuated from the Capitol building in Washington. The following day Congressional leaders and several hundred staff members sang 'God Bless America' on the Capitol steps. A congressional 'day of prayer and reconciliation' – the first since the Lincoln Presidency during the American Civil War, was held on 4 December 2001. Significantly, the resolution affirming this day was passed even before the tragic events of September 11.[6] It called on Americans to 'humbly seek the blessings of Providence for forgiveness, reconciliation, unity, and charity for all people of the United States', and was heralded as evidence of the increasing influence of the religious right in American politics. The two hour meeting included nearly one-quarter of the members of the House and Senate repeating the Lord's Prayer on their knees. This combination of patriotism and religion is not new in the United States, in spite of its profession of adherence to the idea of a separation between church and state. When examining the constitutionality of prayer in government, the US Supreme Court in a 1983 decision found that legislative prayer is 'deeply embedded in [the] history and tradition of this country' (*Marsh v Chambers*).[7]

American theologocentrism has emerged from a long history of similar views in Western Europe that have contextualised Islam as a 'threat' to its civilization. 'Evil' motivations grounded in the teachings of the Qu'ran are seen to imbue the

---

6   H Res 548, 24 July 2000.
7   Russell Chaddock, 2002.

motivations of not only individual but also the collective actions of the Arab Middle East.

September 11 and public discourse

Well before September 11, the themes of Muslim terrorism and Arab terrorism were entrenched in the American media. Since the 1967 Arab-Israeli war, in fact, political violence in the Arab world and politically motivated violence by Arabs anywhere in the world were highlighted more in public media than violence in any other part of the world. The political context of that violence was seldom reported (in contrast, for example, to the political violence in Ireland). Rather, the *Lawrence of Arabia* imagery of the Arab world as a violent place and the Arab people as tribal people, undisciplined and uncivilised, was left to explain the context. Indeed, when the Oklahoma City bombing of 1996 occurred, the initial response in the American media was that 'Arab terrorists' perpetrated it.[8] In this context, the almost immediate ascriptions of September 11's cause to Arab terrorists in the American media raised no eyebrows. On the morning of the attacks, CBS News reported from the Pentagon that the Democratic Front for the Liberation of Palestine (DFLP) had claimed responsibility. When NBC reported that a spokesman for the DFLP denied responsibility, Tom Brokaw, its head anchor, noted that there are always 'claims and counter-claims' in 'situations like these'. Indeed, American news anchors and producers forged within the immediate coverage an image of war rather than tragedy and a search for justice. ABC news anchor Peter Jennings invoked the image of Pearl Harbor and CBS labelled its coverage 'Attack on America'. Over video footage of the second tower's collapse, NBC's Tom Brokaw said, 'The profile of the United States has changed. Terrorists have declared war on the United States' before reporting that Osama bin Laden may have predicted the attacks three weeks previously, when he warned that there would be a future terrorist event in the United States.[9]

This rush to provide viewers with a culpable party, including the repeated (then) unconfirmed involvement of men of Middle Eastern descent, provided a convenient target when calls for revenge emerged shortly thereafter in an emotionally charged atmosphere. On the day of the attacks, former Secretary of State Lawrence Eagleburger stated: 'There is only one way to begin to deal with people like this, and that is … to kill some of them even if they are not immediately directly involved in this thing.'[10] The immediate statements by Arab leaders and prominent Islamic clerics condemning the attacks were ignored by the press and 'expert' analysis on every American network focused on the 'threat' of Islamic fundamentalism emanating from the Arab world. Though threats or responsibility by any Palestinian group remained unsubstantiated, the media made explicit connections between Arab grievances against Israel and terrorism. *New York Times*

---

8   Accounts in the US media for the 48 hours between the bombing and the arrest of Timothy McVeigh were filled with accusations of Arab involvement. Former United States Representative Dave McCurdy of Oklahoma (former Chairman of the House Intelligence Committee) told CBS News that there was 'very clear evidence of the involvement of fundamentalist Islamic terrorist groups'. Speaking on CNN, ATF director John Magaw said: 'I think any time you have this kind of damage, this kind of explosion, you have to look there [Middle East terrorists] first.' Steven Emerson, a self-described 'terrorism expert' employed first by CBS News and then by NBC as well as the *Wall Street Journal*, made claims on CBS News (19 April 1995) in the wake of the 1995 Oklahoma City bombing that the terrorist act quickly found to be conducted by Timothy McVeigh showed 'a Middle Eastern trait' because it 'was done with the intent to inflict as many casualties as possible'.
9   For an excellent synopsis of the reportage of the morning, see Geisler, 2001.
10 CNN, 11 September 2001, as quoted in FAIR, 2001.

columnist Thomas Friedman stated: 'Surely Islam, a grand religion that never perpetrated the sort of Holocaust against the Jews in its midst that Europe did, is being distorted when it is treated as a guidebook for suicide bombing. How is it that not a single Muslim leader will say that?'[11] In reaction to the terrible events of September 11, while addressing the nation, President Bush proclaimed, 'We will make no distinction between the terrorists who committed these acts and those who harbor them'.[12] There was general understanding in the media and the public as to whom he meant and general acceptance of what the threat implied. Rich Lowry exclaimed in the *Washington Post*: 'States that have been supporting if not Osama bin Laden, people like him need to feel pain. If we flatten part of Damascus or Tehran or whatever it takes, that is part of the solution.'[13] Thus, the initiation of air strikes against Afghanistan on 7 October 2001, and the unilateralist direction of policy, were unquestioned in public discourse, as Bush proclaimed:

> Our military action is also designed to clear the way for sustained, comprehensive and relentless operations to drive them out and bring them to justice.

> Every nation has a choice to make. In this conflict, there is no neutral ground. If any government sponsors the outlaws and killers of innocents, they have become outlaws and murderers, themselves. And they will take that lonely path at their own peril.[14]

In the context of American racism,[15] the initial reaction to September 11 and Bush's inflammatory rhetoric of 'crusade' and 'a monumental struggle of good versus evil',[16] was a clash of civilisations backlash. This had two dimensions in the US: widespread acts of racism against individuals and institutions (mosques, Islamic schools) that terrorised people who were or were mistaken for Muslims; and a broad based public outcry by Islamic scholars, intellectuals and Muslim community groups against the vilification of Islam. The White House reacted quickly to distance itself from the clash of civilisations thesis. The overt racism against individuals was condemned, and President Bush made a concerted public demonstration of respect for Islam, consulting Islamic scholars and clerics; hosting a Ramadhan dinner at the White House on 19 November 2001; and on 17 September, visiting the Washington, DC Islamic Center. The media played an important role in highlighting Islam as a major focus in its coverage of September 11 and the 'War on Terror'. Major television programmes – such as *60 Minutes* and *Ted Koppel's Nightline* – featured Islam, dialogues with Muslims, etc. PBS's *Frontline* broadcast *'Muslims': A Clear Picture of Islam*, and specials on the 'nature of Islam' and Arab society dominated media coverage. In its 30 September 2001 broadcast, *60 Minutes* produced an expos on Islam. Host Dan Bradley asked:

> When the suspects in the September 11 bombings were identified as Muslims, people who follow the teachings of Islam, President Bush went to great lengths to point out that the overwhelming majority of the world's more than one billion Muslims are decent, law-abiding citizens. How then is it that a religion that promises peace, harmony, and justice to those who follow the will of Allah can have in their midst thousands committed to terrorism in the name of Allah?

During its 17 December 2001 broadcast, CBS News Correspondent Andy Rooney, after reading the Qu'ran in English, stated that all Americans should read it because

---

11 *New York Times*, 13 September 2001.
12 Statement by the President in his Address to the Nation on 11 September 2001:
   www.whitehouse.gov/news/releases/2001/09/20010911-16.html.
13 *The Washington Post*, 13 September 2001, as quoted in FAIR, 2001.
14 *Op cit*, fn 12.
15 Ismael and Ismael, 1999.
16 See White House official website, www.whitehouse.gov.

'the Koran dominates the lives of 1.6 billion Muslims in the world, many of whom are unfriendly to us', and that 'there's no such thing as separation of church and state in most Muslim countries'.[17]

Visibly ethnic Muslim American spokesmen for the 'American establishment', such as Fuad Ajami (a well known critic of Arab culture in Orientalist studies circles) and Fareed Zakaria (*Newsweek*'s foreign affairs editor), were featured in the media, especially television. The public script of this campaign was the theme of 'saving Islam from the terrorists' but the subscript played on the theme that the Arabs are the bad boys of Islam.[18] This was prominently featured in Fareed Zakaria's feature story on 'Why do they hate us?' in the 15 October 2001 issue of *Newsweek* magazine.

> Only when you get to the Middle East do you see in lurid colors all the dysfunctions that people conjure up when they think of Islam today. In Iran, Egypt, Syria, Iraq, Jordan, the occupied territories and the Persian Gulf, the resurgence of Islamic fundamentalism is virulent, and a raw anti-Americanism seems to be everywhere. This is the land of suicide bombers, flag-burners and fiery mullahs.

In the context of domestic politics, the quick response of the Bush Administration to September 11 represented a virtual *coup d'état* in government. The Bush Administration seized the opportunity posed by the outpouring of patriotic fervor in the wake of September 11 to consolidate and expand executive powers and to override the nation's tradition of civil liberties with draconian legislation. According to a report in *Le Monde Diplomatique*:

> In a spirit of wilful submissiveness, the US Senate (controlled by the Democrats) and House of Representatives passed the USA Patriot Act in late September, relinquishing considerable control. The act grants the executive branch extraordinary powers, including the secret and indefinite detention of 'aliens' (non-citizens) whose status is deemed 'irregular'. An executive order on 13 November created exceptional military tribunals. More than 1,200 people arrested after 11 September were still in custody in December, yet no one knows who they are or what crimes they are accused of.[19]

In the context of international politics, America's war on terrorism initiated a bandwagon which states in the global community with restive minority or border problems climbed aboard to legitimate their efforts to settle their own political scores. Hence, India and Pakistan vis à vis Kashmir, Turkey vis à vis the Kurds, Russia vis à vis Chechnya, Spain vis à vis the Basques, etc, and virtually every state throughout the so-called free world, increased barriers to refugees and asylum seekers as well as travellers from the post-colonial world. On 29 May 2002, *Euronews* reported that since September 11 over 4,500 persons arriving at European airports from the global south were turned away as illegal immigrants due to stepped up border control measures in Europe.

American policy in the Middle East

Ariel Sharon, Prime Minister of Israel, used the opportunity posed by the war on terrorism to initiate a massive Israeli military incursion into the West Bank. Under the pretext of rooting out a terrorist infrastructure – essentially the same pretext the United States used to attack Afghanistan, crush the Taliban and spearhead the invasion of the country – the Israeli army destroyed not only the civil infrastructure of the Palestinian Authority but also the socio-economic infrastructure of

---

17 www.cbsnews.com/stories/2001/12/14/60minutes/rooney/main321447.shtml.
18 Mattson, 2001.
19 Golub, 2002.

Palestinian society. A report in *Le Monde Diplomatique* echoed what journalists were generally reporting in the aftermath of assault: 'During the week we spent in Ramallah, Gaza and Rafah, all we saw was destruction: villages, roads and homes, all demolished. Crops have been burned and public services bombarded. Missiles from helicopter gunships or F-16 fighter planes have destroyed newly completed civilian infrastructure ... Does anyone believe that all these sites were terrorist hideouts?'[20]

Initially, the United States 'watched with detached interest as Sharon dismantled the basic foundations of the Oslo process ... In a December 2002 meeting between Sharon and Bush in Washington, Bush asked only that Arafat not be killed'.[21] While the Bush Administration's call for the establishment of a Palestinian state on 2 October 2001 (and again on 4 April 2002) and its sponsorship of Security Council Resolution 1397 (12 March 2002) were initially celebrated as signs of a more balanced American policy on the Arab-Israeli conflict, in fact they rang hollow against events on the ground. The Israeli carnage of the West Bank intensified in March and April. President Bush dispatched Secretary of State Colin Powell to the region (8–17 April 2002) in an attempt to mollify world opinion in general and Arab opinion in particular. According to Geoffrey Aronson, director of the Foundation for Middle East Peace, 'Powell's itinerary betrayed the aim to isolate the contagion to Israel-Palestine. During planned visits to Morocco, Egypt and Spain, Powell joined in a statement with United Nations, European Union and Russian leaders more aggressive than anything coming out of the White House. It was ignored by Washington and the US press corps ... Israel continued its offensive'.[22]

Colin Powell's junket to the Middle East essentially reflected an American policy of determined inaction on the Israeli-Palestinian front and was in essence an effort at damage control. It was Vice President Dick Cheney's earlier mission in March 2002 – which took him to Britain, Jordan, Egypt, Yemen, Oman, Qatar, Saudi Arabia, Kuwait, Bahrain, the United Arab Emirates, Israel and Turkey – where the Bush Administration's determined course of action on the Middle East was revealed. Cheney attempted to drum up support amongst Arab regimes in Morocco, Jordan, Egypt, Yemen, Qatar, Bahrain, Saudi Arabia, and Oman (as well as Israel, Turkey, Spain and the United Kingdom) for a military build-up in preparation for a ground war in Iraq. CIA officials were reported to have surveyed three key airfields in northern Iraq, much to the embarrassment of Iraqi Kurdish leaders Massoud Barzani, who heads the Kurdistan Democratic Party, and Jalal al-Talabani, the leader of the Patriotic Union of Kurdistan, who both told a high-level delegation from the US State Department visiting in 2001 that the Kurds would not act against Saddam Hussein unless they were certain that the US was determined to overthrow him and had a plan to do so.[23] In early March 2002, the Bush Administration called on Britain to supply a 25,000-man force[24] and US forces began arriving in Kurdish-held areas in the north of Iraq, in support of Kurdish Democratic Party militias.[25] A battalion of 24 Longbow Apache attack helicopters arrived in Kuwait and more than 5,000 US fighting vehicles, mothballed since the end of the Gulf War, were overhauled for use in the event of a ground war. More importantly, the US Central Command moved its service headquarters to the Gulf and US special forces set up a base in Oman. Unconfirmed reports, in the US press and from Iraqi opposition

20 Salmon, 2002.
21 Aronson, 2002b.
22 Aronson, 2002b.
23 Cockburn, 2002.
24 These reports were widespread in the media but dismissed by the Prime Minister's Office.
25 Ahmed *et al*, 2002, at www.observer.co.uk/international/story/0,6903,665083,00.html.

groups, announced a US military build-up in Kuwait of between 25,000 and 35,000 additional personnel.

Saudi government refusals to allow air raids on Afghanistan to be launched from Saudi airfields, as well as unequivocal Saudi opposition to a military campaign to oust the Iraqi regime, saw the United States begin to transfer its forces to more pliable states. In the second week of March, several sources reported that the US Air Force had begun preparations to move its Gulf headquarters from Saudi Arabia's Prince Sultan air force base to Qatar's al-Udeid air base, which has the longest runways in the Gulf.[26] Prince Sultan air force base was reported to maintain a US garrison of some 4,500 personnel as well as an unidentified number of aircraft that patrol the southern no-fly zone over Iraq. To mollify Saudi sensitivities, Saudi Arabia's *de facto* ruler, Crown Prince Abdullah, has been adamant in his opposition to a US attack on Iraq.[27] However, aircraft from Kuwait and US aircraft carriers in the Gulf are used for retaliatory air strikes against Iraq. Although the move was initially explained as a temporary redistribution of American resources to pursue the Afghan war, the leaked request for bids to move sophisticated equipment suggested a more permanent relocation allowing the US to conduct an air campaign against Iraq in the face of Saudi refusals to collaborate. Further, it would alleviate the threat to the stability of the Saudi royal family posed by Sunni Islamic militants for whom the US military presence is a combustible issue. Qatar is seen as a more stable and willing host. Its emir, Sheikh Hamad bin Khalifa al-Thani, has received strong US backing since overthrowing his father in 1995, and he has been a strong advocate of increased Arab ties with Israel. While the deployment proceeded without incident and went largely unnoticed in the Western media, Cheney met unexpected resistance on his visits with Arab leaders.

After hearing objections in every country he visited on his Middle East tour, aside from Britain and Israel, Cheney sought to minimise the difficulties in rallying support for a new confrontation with Iraq.[28] He acknowledged the need for an American role in mediating the increasing Israeli-Palestinian violence for which Cheney succeeded in convincing Saudi Crown Prince Abdullah, the *de facto* ruler of the most important US ally in the Gulf, to announce that he would accept an invitation to visit the US to advance Saudi peace initiatives. Abdullah had rejected an invitation in June 2002 to visit the White House in an exceptional display of solidarity with the Palestinian cause over the Bush Administration's continued refusal to become involved in brokering an agreement. Abdullah's efforts to stall a US attack on Iraq were advanced along with a public overture to break the Israeli-Palestinian stalemate by promising to establish normal relations between the 22-member Arab League and Israel in return for a complete Israeli withdrawal from all land that it occupied in the 1967 war.[29]

In spite of US efforts and public pronouncements to the contrary, the Palestinian and Iraqi issues were increasingly conjoined. Israel's violent repression of the intifada in March and April 2002 and the Bush Administration's determined pursuit of support for its policy of a military response to overthrow the Iraqi regime saw increasing public discussion internationally of the double standard in American policy in the Middle East. In mid-March, Bush even declared that 'all options are on the table – including nuclear weapons – to confront states that

26 Borger, 2002.
27 During Cheney's visit, he declared that Washington 'should not strike Iraq because such an attack would only raise animosity in the region against the United States'. See Borger, 2002.
28 See Schneider, 2002; Sipress, 2002a. For the Israeli perspective see Verter and Benn, 2002.
29 Sipress, 2002b.

threaten to use weapons of mass destruction'.[30] However, the international solidarity afforded to the US as a result of September 11 had dissipated by then and in the face of the Israeli assault on the West Bank, the darker contours of the so-called war on terrorism were becoming apparent and problematic as protests spread across North America and Europe. Nevertheless, on 4 April Bush reiterated his message that 'everyone must choose; you're either with the civilised world, or you're with the terrorists'.[31]

American policy in the Middle East was increasingly criticised by America's allies in the war on terrorism in the spring of 2002 as European politicians sharply questioned the US on diverse issues across the region. On 5 February 2002, Spanish Foreign Minister Josep Piqué, then holding the presidency of the European Union, became the first high-ranking European politician to insist that the European Union would continue trade negotiations with Iran despite the American accusations of Iran's sponsorship of terror.[32] On 7 February 2002, French Foreign Minister Hubert Védrine sharply denounced the unilateral approach taken by the Bush Administration. 'We are currently threatened by a simplified approach which reduces all problems of the world to the mere struggle against terrorism,' he said in an interview with *France Inter*. 'This is an ill-considered conception which we cannot accept,' he declared, and went on to say, 'The Americans are acting on a unilateral basis, without consulting anyone else, and their decisions are guided exclusively by their own individual views and interests.'[33] Chris Patten, EU Commissioner for Foreign Affairs, attacked Bush's 'unilateralist overdrive'.[34] The foreign ministers of all 15 EU Member States assembled for an informal meeting in the Spanish town of Cáceres, 8–10 February 2002. Javier Solana, the high representative for EU foreign policy, joined those cautioning the US against succumbing 'to the dangers of global unilateralism',[35] and German Foreign Minister Joschka Fischer criticised Bush's thesis of an 'axis of evil'. This conception, he said, was 'not in accordance with our political ethos'.[36]

Nevertheless, on his trip to Russia and Europe in May 2002, President Bush in effect raised the barometer of his war on terrorism even higher by calling Iraq a 'threat to civilization' during his speech to the German Bundestag on 23 May 2002. Bush declared, 'we are defending civilization itself' from 'regimes that sponsor terror', who 'are developing these weapons and the missiles to deliver them. If these regimes and their terrorist allies were to perfect these capabilities, no inner voice of reason, no hint of conscience would prevent their use'.[37] Following his speech, Bush and the German Chancellor, Gerhard Schroeder, held a joint press conference at which they stated that they had no concrete plans to attack Iraq.[38] By

30 Milbank and Allen, 2002.
31 Aronson, 2002a.
32 Staunton, 2002; see also 12th GCC-EU Joint Council/Ministerial Meeting – Joint Communique (27–28 February 2002), at
   http://europa.eu.int/comm/external_relations/gulf_cooperation/intro/12thgcc_eu.htm.
33 As quoted by Schwarz, 2002.
34 Freedland, 2002.
35 Everts, 2002; see also 'Peremptory tendencies: France fires a warning shot at the US' *The Guardian*, 7 February 2002, at www.guardian.co.uk/leaders/story/0,3604,646014,00.html.
36 'Germany warns US against unilateralism', *BBC News*, 12 February 2002, at
   http://news.bbc.co.uk/hi/english/world/europe/newsid_1816000/1816395.stm.
37 Speech by US President George W Bush to the German Bundestag, Berlin, 23 May 2002, at
   http://usinfo.state.gov/cgi-bin/washfile/display.pl?p=/products/washfile/geog/
   eu&f=02052321.wwe&t=/products/washfile/newsitem.shtml.
38 'Bush, Schroeder say no concrete plans to attack Iraq', US Department of State, 23 May 2002, at
   http://usinfo.state.gov/cgi-bin/washfile/display.pl?p=/products/washfile/geog/
   eu&f=02052320.wwe&t=/products/washfile/newsitem.shtml.

then, US military and police forces had already been deployed in southern Iraq to enforce sanctions, in Afghanistan (and Pakistan) against the Taliban and Al Qa'ida, in Georgia,[39] Yemen,[40] and the Philippines against Muslim rebels,[41] Pakistan,[42] Uzbekistan, Tajikistan and Kyrgyzstan;[43] and were also being based in Arab Gulf states in increasing numbers to defend US interests in the Middle East and Central Asia.[44] Iran has also come under increasing fire in US public discourse on terrorism and was named the principle sponsor of terrorism in the world.[45] It is likely, in fact, that the Bush Administration's strategy for the Middle East from the beginning included Iran with Iraq. As early as 31 January 2002, US Secretary of Defence Donald Rumsfeld had explained that 'the real concern ... is the nexus between terrorist networks and terrorist states'.[46] Iraq is an easy target for a battle cry, as Saddam Hussain is the West's favourite villain since the 1990–91 Gulf War, and poses no serious ideological challenge to 'American civilisation' (to paraphrase Bush). Iran, on the other hand, poses a real ideological challenge to the American hegemony of Western civilisation and the Israeli hegemony of the Middle East, as it represents a successful model of indigenous political development.

39 Traynor, 2002.
40 Durrani, 2002; see also Agence France-Presse, 2002.
41 'US troops begin Philippine exercises', *BBC News*, 17 February 2002, at
http://news.bbc.co.uk/hi/english/world/asia-pacific/newsid_1825000/1825688.stm; see also:
'Focus on the Philippines: American advisers have raised stakes in troubled area', Pittsburgh Post-gazette, 26 April 2002, at www.post-gazette.com/forum/20020426edphil26p2.asp.
42 Baker, 2002.
43 Kinnane Roelofsma, 2002.
44 'President thanks world coalition for anti-terrorism efforts', 11 March 2002, at
www.whitehouse.gov/news/releases/2002/03/20020311-1.html.
45 In its *Patterns of Global Terrorism 2001* (May 2002), the US Department of State found that Iran 'remained the most active state sponsor of terrorism in 2001'. The seven designated state sponsors of terrorism are Cuba, Iran, Iraq, Libya, North Korea, Syria, and Sudan. See
www.state.gov/documents/organization/10319.pdf.
46 Aronson, 2002a.

References

Abu Khalil, As'ad (2002) *Bin Laden, Islam and America's New 'War on Terrorism'*, New York: Seven Stories

Agence France-Presse (2002) 'Yemen downplays US "experts" role on anti-terror mission', 2 March: www.inq7.net/brk/2002/mar/02/brkafp_3-1.htm

Ahmed, Kamal, Burke, Jason and Beaumont, Peter (2002) 'Bush wants 25,000 UK Iraq force: Britain considers joint invasion plan' *The Observer*, 10 March: www.observer.co.uk/international/story/0,6903,665083,00.html

Aronson, Geoffrey (2002a) 'A sideshow to the conquest of Iraq' *Le Monde Diplomatique*, 17 May

Aronson, Geoffrey (2002b) 'Palestine near and far: a sideshow to the conquest of Iraq' *Le Monde Diplomatique*, 17 May

Baker, Peter (2002) 'For US forces, a secret and futile hunt: local guides describe furtive trip into Pakistan in search of fugitives' *The Washington Post*, 5 May: www.washingtonpost.com/ac2/wp-dyn?pagename=article&node=&contentId=A33591-2002May4&notFound=true

Borger, Julian (2002) 'US paves way for war on Iraq: attack base to be moved into Qatar to bypass Saudi objections' *The Guardian*, 27 March

Cockburn, Patrick (2002) 'CIA survey of Iraq airfields heralds attack' *The Independent*, 18 March: http://news.independent.co.uk/world/middle_east/story.jsp?story=275699

Durrani, Anayat (2002) 'Trooping across the world' *Al-Ahram Weekly Online*, 7–13 March, Issue No 576: www.ahram.org.eg/weekly/2002/576/re74.htm

Everts, Steven (2002) 'Why should Bush take Europe seriously?' *The Observer*, 17 February: www.observer.co.uk/Print/0,3858,4357611,00.html

FAIR (2001) 'Media advisory: media march to war' *Fairness & Accuracy In Reporting*, September 17: www.fair.org/press-releases/wtc-war-punditry.html

Finkelstein, Norman G (1995) *Image and Reality of the Israel-Palestine Conflict*, New York: Verso

Freedland, Jonathan (2002) 'Patten lays into Bush's America: fury at president's "axis of evil" speech' *The Guardian*, 9 February: www.guardian.co.uk/bush/story/0,7369,647554,00.html

Geisler, Jill (2001) 'Minute by minute with the broadcast news', The Poynter Institute, 11 September: www.poynter.org

Golub, Philip S (2002) 'Background to Washington's war on terror: American Ceasar' *Le Monde Diplomatique*, 16 January

Guardian Leader (unsigned) (2002) 'Peremptory tendencies: France fires a warning shot at the US' *The Guardian*, 7 February: www.guardian.co.uk/leaders/story/0,3604,646014,00.html (last visited 14 August 2002)

Ismael, TY and Ismael, JS (1999) 'Cowboy warfare, biological diplomacy: disarming metaphors as weapons of mass destruction' Politics and the Life Sciences, March, pp 16–24

Kinnane Roelofsma, Derk (2002) 'US, Islam, and Central Asia' *United Press International/The Washington Times*, 7 March: www.washtimes.com/upi-breaking/07032002-110409-5870r.htm

Lewis, Bernard (2001) 'Did you say "American Imperialism?"' *National Review*, 17 December

Mattson, Ingrid (2001) 'Saving Islam from the terrorists: American Muslims have a "special obligation"': www.beliefnet.com/frameset.asp?pageLoc=/story/89/story_8987_1.html&boardID=26483

Milbank, Dana and Allen, Mike (2002) 'US will take action against Iraq, Bush says: "All options are on the table" against states that pose threat' *The Washington Post*, 14 March, p A01: www.washingtonpost.com/wp-dyn/articles/A22091-2002Mar13.html

Rodinson, Maxime (1987) *Europe and the Mystique of Islam*, Veinus, Roger (trans), Seattle: Washington UP

Russell Chaddock, Gail (2002) 'A revival of public religion – on Capitol Hill' *The Christian Science Monitor*, 7 January: www.csmonitor.com/2002/0107/p1s4-usgn.html.

Said, Edward W (1997) *Covering Islam: How the Media and the Experts Determine How We See the Rest of the World*, New York: Vintage

Salmon, Christian (2002) 'Palestine near and far: the bulldozer war' *Le Monde Diplomatique*, 17 May

Schneider, Howard (2002) 'Mideast allies warn US not to attack Iraq: leaders of Jordan, Turkey say move against Hussein could destabilize region' *The Washington Post*, 11 March, p A14: www.washingtonpost.com/wp-dyn/articles/A5422-2002Mar10.html

Schwarz, Peter (2002) 'European foreign ministers attack Bush's policy' *World Socialist Web Site News*, 15 February: www.wsws.org/articles/2002/feb2002/euro-f15.shtml

Sipress, Alan (2002a) 'Jordan advises US against a military campaign in Iraq' *The Washington Post*, 13 March, p A24:
www.washingtonpost.com/wp-dyn/articles/A16757-2002Mar12.html

Sipress, Alan (2002b) 'Cheney plays down Arab criticism over Iraq' *The Washington Post*, 18 March, p A10: www.washingtonpost.com/wp-dyn/articles/A42203-2002Mar17.html

Staunton, Denis (2002) 'EU refuses to adopt French Middle East plan' *The Irish Times*, 11 February:
www.ireland.com/newspaper/world/2002/0211/3780008927FR11EUDENIS.html

Traynor, Ian (2002) 'Georgia: US opens new front in war on terror' *The Guardian*, 20 March: www.guardian.co.uk/international/story/0,3604,670542,00.html

Verter, Yossi and Benn, Aluf (2002) 'Israel to US: don't wait for calm here before hitting Iraq' *Ha'aretz* (Israel), 3 May: www.haaretz.co.il/hasen/pages/ShArt.jhtml?itemNo= 151228&contrassID=2&subContrassID=1&sbSubContrassID=0

White House official website: www.whitehouse.gov

Chapter 12
Palestine/Israel: conflict at the crossroads
Rafiq Latta

Of all the fault-lines in world politics highlighted by September 11, none perhaps have witnessed such a dramatic deterioration as the Palestine/Israel conflict. A detailed breakdown of the crisis, or a blow-by-blow account of the horrifying deterioration in the human rights situation since September 11, are beyond the scope of this essay and have been well-chronicled elsewhere. It is hoped rather to develop certain themes that underpin the way in which the conflict has changed since the second intifada, and how these relate to the tragedy of September 11 and the new global order emerging from it.

September 11 had an immediate and profound impact on the Palestinian leadership, which at once grasped the dangers of being identified in any way with what commentators were calling within hours 'a new Pearl Harbour'. These fears were exacerbated by the bogus report of the Democratic Front for the Liberation of Palestine accepting responsibility for the attacks. Having learnt from his bitter taste of life in the diplomatic wilderness following the Gulf War, Palestinian Authority Chairman Yasser Arafat swiftly denounced the attacks, donated blood and mobilised others to join in the universal condemnation.

For many in the United States the scenes of Palestinians celebrating formed one of the enduring images of those days. However, the reaction was far more nuanced than that portrayed by the media. Yes, there was rejoicing in America's pain (free falafels outside the hotel where I was staying, for example), but also a widespread outpouring of sympathy. As Palestinians experienced a rollercoaster of emotions in the hours after the attacks, it was not uncommon to find individuals expressing both moral outrage against the perpetrators and a *schadenfreude* that the mighty US could have been brought so low almost simultaneously. And as the tragedy unfolded on screens across Palestine, both these feelings were joined by fears that Israel would exploit the situation to its advantage. September 11 also sparked hope that the mass slaughter of its own citizens would shock the US into finally reappraising its Middle East policy and taking real action to put pressure on Israel.[1]

The mood soon changed. Bush's clumsy use of the word 'crusade' to describe his war on bin Laden struck a raw nerve in Palestine, where in 1099, knights of the First Crusade described the joys of walking knee-deep in the blood of infidels during the slaughter of Jerusalem's Muslim and Jewish population. Accelerating this shift were the open threat of further action against Iraq, civilian casualties in Afghanistan, the strident tone of a new unilateralist US, and the feeling that the Palestinians were being categorised as belonging to the 'other' side. Arafat's initial reaction was to go all out to placate US public and official opinion, cracking down on an anti-war demonstration at the Islamic University in Gaza at which three students and a child were killed by Palestinian Authority police.[2]

---

1 In common with many of their co-religionists there was also a depressing and widespread inability to accept that the culprit could belong to an Arab or Islamic society. While outside the remit of this study, I believe the phenomenon worthy of further investigation and central to the debate over the clash of cultures thrown up by September 11.
2 Hemmami, 2001b.

On the Israeli side, there was ill-concealed glee at the hoped-for strategic gains to emerge from the war against terror. Benyamin Ben Eliezer, Defence Minister and soon-to-be leader of the opposition Labour Party, told an Israeli reporter soon after the attacks that they were 'from the perspective of the Jews, the most important public relations act ever committed in our favour ... It is a fact we have just killed 14 Palestinians in Jenin, Qabatiyya and Tammun, with the world remaining absolutely silent'.[3] Asked what the attack meant for relations between the United States and Israel, former prime minister Benyamin Netanyahu replied: 'It's very good.' Then he corrected himself: 'Well, not very good, but it will generate immediate sympathy.'[4]

September 11 had the dual effect of crystallising hard-line sentiment among Israel's elite and providing it with justification of its policies. An illuminating article by Dr Gershon Baskin shows how self-conscious and deliberate a process this has been. In December 2001, Baskin attended Kenes Herzliya, an annual gathering of Israel's military and security establishment. Speakers at the conference included Chief of Staff Shaul Mofaz, former Head of Shabak (Israel's internal security service) Ami Ayalon, former Prime Ministers Ehud Barak and Binyamin Netanyahu, Minister of Defense Binyamin Ben Eliezer, Director of the Mossad Ephraim Halevy, Foreign Minister Shimon Peres, and former CIA Director Jim Woolsey.

Based largely on presentations delivered by former Prime Ministers Barak and Netanyahu, Baskin outlined the main planks of the new post-September 11 Israeli strategic consensus:[5]

- For both Barak and Netanyahu 'September 11 marks a change in international relations from which the State of Israel has already benefited from and will continue to benefit. The United States and the Western world today have a clear understanding of the dangers of terrorism and are now leading a world war aimed at wiping terrorism off the face of the planet. The United States has now adopted and supports Israel's position on terrorism'.

- The US will win its war against terrorism and this 'will serve as deterrence for other states that support terrorism and/or give refuge to terrorists'. After Afghanistan, the US will extend the war to places such as Somalia, Sudan, Lebanon and Syria, and especially Israel's arch-enemies Iran and Iraq. 'It is inconceivable that Saddam Hussein will be left in place when the World War against terrorism is completed'.

- As there is no real deterrent against suicide bombers, a measure of deterrence can be created by attacking those states and regimes that support terrorism and encourage terrorism, that is, the Palestinian Authority.

- The Palestinians had two main strategic aims for the intifada; firstly the 'internationalisation of the conflict', and secondly to create splits in Israeli society. Israel cannot allow Arafat or the Palestinian Authority to achieve these goals or indeed 'any political gains as a result of violence and terrorism', as this would be the surest 'guarantee that the violence will only increase'.

- Events since the beginning of the intifada have proved beyond a shadow of a doubt that 'Yasir Arafat is not a partner'. And 'there can be no end to the conflict' until a new Palestinian leadership, 'really willing to accept Israel as a Jewish state and explicitly give up the right of return', emerges.

---

3   MEI No 659, 28 September 2001, 'Peres clings on' by Peretz Kidron.
4   *New York Times*, 12 September 2001.
5   Baskin, 2001.

While much outlined at the conference has long been part and parcel of Israeli security theology, events since September 11 have provided boundless opportunity for the application of this thinking. More importantly, the Kenes Herzliya participants have so far largely been proven right. The attacks on America have given international legitimisation to the doctrine of the iron fist, played out every day in the Occupied Territories and culminating in the mass offensive and occupation of Operation Defensive Wall of April 2002.

Ariel Sharon, the man responsible for putting these ideas into action, came to his job with considerable baggage. An icon of the Zionist right, and ultimate bogeyman for the left and Palestinians, Sharon has elicited strong emotions throughout his career. He came to prominence as the brilliant and unorthodox commander of the 101 counter-insurgency unit in the 50s, gaining notoriety for the massacre of more than 60 civilians in the West Bank village of Qibya in reprisal for the murder of an Israeli woman and two children.[6] A brutal spell as commander of Gaza in the 70s, his glittering if controversial role in Israel's fight back in the 1973 War, his masterminding of the 1982 invasion of Lebanon and the subsequent massacres of Sabra and Shatila have only built on this reputation. Sharon is a proponent of secular revisionist Zionism, with its Greater Israel ideology and single-minded pursuit of settling the 'Land'. In office, Sharon, who sees himself as guardian and heir to this tradition, has tried to carve out for Israel a regional superpower role with influence from the Atlantic to the Gulf, sub-Saharan Africa to the CIS states.

In the 2001 election in which he swept to victory, Sharon exploited widespread anger at the intifada and the Palestinians' rejection of Barak's 'generous' peace offer, to project a caring, sharing father-of-the nation image. This is ironic, for Sharon has made a career out of complete disregard, not only for public opinion, but also for the collective decisions of his peers and orders from superiors, should these clash with his perception of the Nation's higher interests. His railroading of his cabinet colleagues into the invasion of Lebanon 20 years ago is relevant to any examination of present-day relations with his Labour Party coalition partners.

In 1982, Sharon initially presented the 'Little Pines' operation as a punitive expedition against the PLO going no more than 40km into Lebanese territory. Instead, under the pretext of military exigencies, the IDF launched attacks against Syrian forces in Lebanon and pursued the PLO all the way to Beirut, thus laying the foundations of its disastrous occupation of Lebanon. The mechanisms today are essentially the same. Their simplicity and effectiveness are quintessential Sharon: Sharon creates or escalates a situation; opposition to his inevitably draconian prescription is neutralised by accusations of undermining unity at a time of national emergency. However the Sharon of today is a more cautious politician than in his youth. One lesson that the Lebanon War taught him was the absolute primacy of getting the US's blessing for, or at least acquiescence in, Israel's actions. This, as much as the misgivings of his own commanders, accounts for the uncharacteristic delay in kicking off Operation Defensive Wall.

Sharon's policies have led to a Lebanonisation of the conflict, as can be seen by the vastly increased use of such weaponry as F-16s, Apache helicopters and Merkeva battle tanks against largely civilian targets. And reaction of the Palestinian resistance has been strikingly, and indeed intentionally, evocative of Hizbollah; with its embrace of suicide bombings and Islamicist rhetoric. The widespread reports, yet to be confirmed, of Lebanese nationals, presumed to be either former South Lebanon Army or Phalange militia allies of Israel being drafted in to do duty in the

---

6   Morris, 2001, p 278.

Palestinian Territories as IDF security personnel,[7] are disturbing. For Palestinians, with their painful collective memories of Lebanon, this represents the erasure of yet another moral red line. It is as if Sharon were symbolically importing the horrors of the Tel Al-Za'atar, Sabra, Shatila death squads to Palestine.

Sharon thrives on conflict. His Lebanon record suggests that he believes that he can achieve key national security objectives under the cover of military action. That he has failed dismally to deliver on his election promise of restoring the Holy Grail of Israeli security is beyond all doubt, but on his own terms, Sharon may be accomplishing much of what he set out to do. Regarding his core goal of denying Palestinians any sort of viable statehood, Sharon has made no compromise and indeed can be said to be winning.

Sharon's demonisation of Arafat, and declaration that the PA's leader was 'irrelevant' immediately made Arafat the most relevant figure in the region. Arafat's deliberate and daily humiliation by siege and house arrest has only served to restore much needed legitimacy and unite the Palestinians behind their leader. This personalisation of the conflict between the two most talismanic personalities in modern Israeli and Palestinian history has added a further element of intransigence to an already toxic mix.

Sharon's February election victory not only spelt danger for the Palestinians, but should have (and indeed did) set alarm bells ringing for Israelis. In the era of globalisation and the Internet an old battle horse like Sharon should have been yesterday's man. His landslide victory was an expression of a profound disillusionment with the peace process, and jars somewhat with the socio-economic processes that have taken place in Israel and the wider region over the past decade and a half. In a sense, a vote for Sharon was more than just a rejection of the Oslo peace process, it was also an expression of nostalgia – the longing for the old certainties of a military solution. Oslo, with its 'creative ambiguities', 'win-win scenarios', and conflict resolution approach, has been replaced by the zero-sum game. And the result has been a descent into savagery.

Right or wrong apart, the very real democratic, social and material advantages enjoyed by Israeli Jews throws their treatment of the Palestinians into sharper relief. Indeed, juxtaposition may be said to be a defining characteristic of the Arab/Israeli conflict. Nowhere is this more marked than on the settlement issue; sumptuous hillside residences of settlers overlook the barbed-wire enclosed hovels of refugee camps. Each settler is allotted 280 litres of West Bank or Gazan water per day, Palestinians only 93.[8] Soldiers paralyse Palestinian traffic to escort settler children to music lessons, while road closures and the security situation have blocked many Palestinians from getting any education at all. Settlers can whiz along a network of specially built freeways,[9] while the Palestinians' nightmare with transport has resulted in the revival of the donkey as a mode of transport. The five star hotel and 18-hole golf course of the Gush Katif settlement bloc abut the slums of Khan Yunis where IDF marksmen trap and then kill children with silencers.[10]

Since Oslo, every Israeli government has pursued the settlements' cause over the objections of the Palestinians, the international community, and in violation of the Fourth Geneva Convention, and one would have thought their own self interests. According to official figures, the number of settlers, not counting those in East

---

7 Bahour, 2001; Hedges, 2001; Ushpiz, 2002.
8 World Bank, 1993, quoted from Hass, 2000, p 145.
9 The settler road system, 'according to Jeff Halper of the Israeli Committee Against House Demolition, has cost $3 billion and has been funded by the US', quoted in Said, 2002.
10 Hedges, 2001, p 7.

Jerusalem, has increased by nearly 65 per cent from 125,000 to 200,000 since 1993.[11] As well as the settlements themselves, a huge network of roads and checkpoints has been built to improve and protect the settlers' movement and security; these need to be manned by a substantial military force. A spiral has emerged: the settlements' existence and growth provokes resistance, which necessitates security, which in turn justifies the continued occupation, and so on. With their echoes of the Kibbutz movement of the Mandate period, the settlements occupy a central position in the Zionist imagination. Conversely, an immediate halt to them tops the list of Palestinian demands. Settlement was probably the most significant issue fuelling Palestinian lack of faith in Israeli intentions at the time of the 2000 Camp David negotiations – a mistrust that, perhaps more than anything, caused the breakdown of those key talks, thus setting the scene for the outbreak of the intifada.

The growth of the settler/security apparatus asphyxiates Palestinians. It is hard for those who have not been there to appreciate just how palpably claustrophobic existence in the Occupied Territories is. It affects the Palestinians at every level; the personal, the social, the political, the economic, and the cultural. And it exists literally in three dimensions; land, sea and air. Gazan fishermen used to be allowed to fish 20 miles out to sea. After Oslo, this limit was reduced, first to 12 miles and then to six. Needless to say, since the intifada, there has been an upsurge in Israeli harassment, with some fishermen claiming to have been arrested just three miles out.[12] Gaza's port, a cornerstone of Oslo's vision for Palestinian self-sufficiency, remains stillborn. The Strip's long-delayed international airport, another pet project of the international community, has been a favoured target of both travel bans and air strikes.[13]

This strangulation of Palestinian civil society, business activity and personal freedom has largely been achieved by the control of space. These can take prohibitive forms, for example travel, study, fishing bans, etc, but the most significant instrument of control at Israel's disposal is that of the checkpoint. Perversely, these proliferated at first, not so much because of the security situation but as a direct consequence of the peace process and the creation of Areas A, B and C.[14] It is the most damning indictment of Oslo for the Palestinians that the much-heralded agreement not only brought no tangible benefits, but seemed specifically designed to make their lives worse.

Checkpoints envelope the whole of Gaza and the West Bank, punctuating almost every journey of more than ten minutes. While prior to the intifada this made life difficult, the travel situation is now and has been for some time simply intolerable. Getting around has become harder and more dangerous in the post-September 11 climate. While actual shootings at checkpoints have been rare, casual acts of cruelty – the gas bomb thrown in the service taxi, the verbal abuse, and the mass humiliation of queuing for hours – are all too commonplace. Often, the sheer difficulty of getting around has produced scenarios of pure Kafka; for example that of the Saadi family who tried to get to from Ramallah to Tul Karem to see relatives over Eid al-Adha, 2002. Unable to go the direct route, the Saadis came up with the ingenious solution of getting documentation showing they were returning from abroad (and therefore subject to less intrusive security). This involved an arduous journey to Jericho, including a six-kilometre walk, payments to both Israeli and

11 *Settlers: Claiming the 'Promised Land'*, Israel and the Palestinians special report, BBC Online.
12 Levy, 2002a.
13 *The Guardian*, 11 January 2002.
14 The Oslo process created three categories of area in the West Bank and Gaza: Category A under full Palestinian control, Category B under Palestinian civil control only and, by far the largest, Category C under full Israeli control.

Jordanian officials and considerable *sang froid* in riding a cab that was supposed to take them to Jordan in the opposite direction, to Tul Karem.[15] For those unfamiliar with the geography, this would be similar to having to make a detour via Rekjavik, on a London to Paris journey.

The checkpoint system in its present form is not justified or necessary on security grounds, even with the maintenance of the settlements. It is a specifically political instrument, designed to send a strong message to the Palestinian population. A good example of this is the Qalandia checkpoint. Near the site of the refugee camp of the same name, Qalandia is between Jerusalem and Ramallah, on the main transport artery to the north of the West Bank, and it straddles Areas A and B. Travellers are forced to exit their vehicle, walk a distance varying from 400m to 1km (depending on the security situation), get checked/stopped and finally find another vehicle to continue their journey. The result is chaos; queues, traffic jams, dust. The crossing takes two hours on a good day, easily double that on a bad one. The wheelchair-bound, the sick, and the old suffer the same fate as the able bodied. This forced walk clearly performs no security function, and can be easily avoided by any healthy person by taking a simple detour. But the operation demonstrates to thousands of Palestinian commuters daily their political impotence and the price of resistance. Qalandia also effectively severs normal communication between the north of the West Bank and Ramallah, headquarters of the Palestinian Authority, with East Jerusalem, the cultural, religious and symbolic capital of Palestine.

Qalandia is only one of the hundreds of checkpoints that have become part of Palestinians' daily suffering. The degree of pressure on Palestinian society is clearly closely connected with the security situation and/or specific atrocities on Israeli civilians; 55 new checkpoints were added in the West Bank alone since the intifada Al Aqsa began.[16] The situation in Gaza is, if anything, worse. The Erez crossing, the Strip's primary gateway to Israel and the world, functioned in non-closure days very similarly to Qalandia. However, since the intifada, closure has been the rule rather than the exception, bringing economic ruin to the Gaza's population. Roads used by settlers, most notoriously Netzarim junction, location of the infamous Mohamad al-Durra shooting, have become a transport nightmare since the beginning of the intifada, and many Gazans, like their compatriots in the West Bank, have simply surrendered to unemployment rather than brave the gauntlet of checkpoints, searches and harassment.

Many Palestinians have found their own homes turned into checkpoints and have either been made homeless or have had a part of their homes requisitioned. Others have suffered as a result of house demolitions. The house demolitions, some of them large-scale operations, involving air support and considerable military resources, have usually been justified on security grounds; either because they adjoin settlements or are used by fighters. Rafah Camp, bordering Egypt at the south of the Gaza Strip, has been exceptionally hard hit, suffering several pre-dawn mass demolitions. Whether it is the destruction of a dwelling associated with a clan for centuries or a refugee home, the demolitions policy is especially traumatic in a family-oriented culture such as the Palestinians', where the home and the sanctity of private property are sacred.

The methods Israel has used to suppress the intifada has only led to a strengthening of those factors that gave birth to it. It is noteworthy that the principal weapon the Palestinians have chosen, the suicide bomber, precisely aims at creating conditions that mirror their own situation. Through the invasion of

---

15 Levy, 2002b.
16 Hemmami, 2001a.

Israeli public space, the bombing campaign has paralysed social life, disrupted transport and created a feeling of mass helplessness. While the IDF physically controls Palestinian transport arteries and movement, the psychological control exercised through fear of the suicide bombs has been just as effective in dictating many Israelis' movements. This is not in any way to justify the tactic; but to suggest that the adoption of this murderous policy owes as much to the specific nature of Israel's occupation as to Islamic fundamentalist ideology or any imported 'Hizbollah model'. It is instructive to note that Palestinians have reverted to suicide bombings increasingly the longer the intifada and Israeli counter-measures have continued. Beyond arguments about waging an asymmetrical war, this patently counter-productive policy seems more a psychological choice than any realistic military option.

Over the past year, the suicide bomber phenomenon has undergone a transformation from what was a marginal, if horrifying *modus operandi* of Islamic militants into what has become a mass movement. In the six months after September 11, the practice was adopted by most of the intifada factions and won widespread acceptance as a legitimate weapon of resistance from a majority of Palestinians. The wave of suicide bombings dates back to 9 September 2001, when Ahmed Hubeishi blew himself up, killing three people in a crowded railway station in the town of Naharia, and becoming the first Israeli Palestinian to carry out a suicide bombing. The attack underlined just how difficult it was to maintain Israel's security by the tried and tested means of oppression and mass closure, and sparked furious debate in the press over the position of Israel's Palestinian minority. Hubeishi's operation fuelled renewed calls for a mass population transfer of Arabs from within Israel's 1948 boundaries, either as a unilateral ethnic cleansing operation or 'in exchange' for the evacuation of settlements from the Occupied Territories. The attack exacerbated the Israeli Arab community's already vulnerable position. Israeli Palestinians, who make up 18 per cent of the 6.3 million Israelis, have been badly shaken by the ongoing violence. Thirteen of their number were killed in demonstrations at the end of 2000, and the ongoing intifada and attempt to prosecute the Arab Knesset member A'zmi Bishara have further helped to create a sense of being under siege.

On 27 January 2002, the first female suicide bomber struck, killing herself and an Israeli man in a busy West Jerusalem shopping area. Wafa Idriss immediately became an icon of the intifada, her photo plastered on walls throughout the territories.[17] Idriss, a secular young woman, had been a Palestinian Red Crescent volunteer and was described by her family as a cheerful, bubbly character until quite recently, when she had appeared increasingly withdrawn and depressed as a direct result of the political situation. Others speculated that Idriss had been badly affected by specific IDF actions against the Red Crescent, such as the refusal to allow evacuation of the injured and firing on ambulances. Chillingly emblematic of the tragic radicalisation taking place among both sides, the case was, not surprisingly, seized on by the international press corps. Idriss soon had her imitators; for example 18 year old Ayat Akhras, who blew herself up in a Jerusalem supermarket on 28 March, killing two Israelis and wounding 25 others.[18]

Over the past year, the Palestinian groups have targeted the IDF and settlers less and less and focused on attacking Israeli civilians within the Green Line. Most Israelis feel that this is a war against them, their families and the very existence of the Jewish state. What has been taking place is simply unprecedented in the modern

17 Andoni, 2002.
18 BBC, 28 March 2002.

Israeli experience. Horrific as they were, the suicide attacks that followed the Hebron massacre in 1994 and the assassination of Hamas bomb maker Yahya al-Ayyash in 1996 were of short duration. Israelis have now endured months of attacks, with certain 'peak' periods. Some of these attacks have been veritable bloodbaths; notably but by no means a complete list: the Sbarro's pizza restaurant bombing in Jerusalem on 9 August 2001, which claimed 15 lives, the June 2001 Dolphinarium Disco attack in Tel Aviv in which 21 people were killed, the 27 people who died in bombings in 48 bloody hours at the beginning of December 2001 in Haifa and Jerusalem, and the 11 who died in the bombing of the fashionable Moments café near the residence of Prime Minister Sharon. But the single most significant of the attacks has been the murder of 28 people in a Netanya hotel during the Jewish Passover holiday. To those inclined to see it, the fact that the culprit behind the attack, Abd al-Baset Odeh, was a native of Tul Karem which had just suffered from a brutal Israeli invasion, might provide ammunition against an iron fist policy. But for Sharon, in search of a *casus belli*, the fact that Odeh's name had been on a wanted list handed to the Palestinians provided the perfect green light to start Operation Defensive Wall and crush the Palestinians.[19]

The indiscriminate death meted out by the bombings, with Israeli peace activists, not to mention women and children numbered among the victims, has contributed much to the almost total erosion of basic empathy between the two sides. The suicide attacks carry a message of despair, a distillation of hatred. Their fundamental immorality and illegality apart, they do serious damage to the Palestinians. With its resonances with the methods used by the September 11 attackers, the wave of suicide bombings has done more than perhaps any other factor to alienate the Israeli public and the international community. The bombing campaign has skewed the message of the Palestinians' national struggle. Mainstream Israel has increasingly come to believe that the Palestinians are not interested in territorial compromise, mutual recognition or peace – that all Palestinians want is Israel's destruction. Recently, more Israelis have moved to live in the Occupied Territories. This is a result of the change in Israeli public perception. The reasoning has two tracks. Firstly, why not move? Settlements are no less dangerous than anywhere else in Israel. And secondly, why should the settlements be abandoned if peace with the Palestinians is impossible anyway?

The suicide bombing strategy has been instrumental in bringing about a profound change in Israeli political culture. 2001 witnessed a near-total eclipse of Israel's once vibrant peace camp and the emergence of a darker and more radical discourse. 'Reformed' peaceniks have flocked to denounce Oslo, the Palestinians, and the few remaining voices in their society which still call for a real reconciliation with Palestinian aspirations. Ideology is back at centre stage of the conflict. Once the domain of the far-right, the old Zionist concept of transfer has been embraced by many mainstream Israelis. In perfect symmetry, Palestinian calls for the literal application of the right of return for Palestinian refugees and destruction of the Jewish state have grown more strident over the past year or so, leading both sides to accuse the other of acting in bad faith.

This seismic shift encompasses the whole spectrum of Israeli and diaspora society, from prominent liberal historians such as Benny Morris, to Rabbi Jonathan Sacks, head of Britain's Jewish community. It has affected the press, notably the liberal broadsheet *Ha'aretz*, which, I perceive, has modified its editorial stance since the Passover bombing. The same journalistic team still produces its largely excellent coverage and analysis, but there has also been a marked profusion of articles either

---

19 *Ha'aretz*, 28 March 2002.

openly sympathetic to settler/hard-line views or a knee-jerk savaging of any criticism of Israel (even if it is criticism that the paper's line, as a whole, endorses).[20]

Politicians, even on the left, have been quick to grasp which way the wind is blowing, as can be seen by Meretz leader Yossi Sarid's lionising of the ultra right wing Tourism Minister, Rehavim Zeevi after his assassination in October 2001. Zeevi's killing, a reprisal for the murder of Popular Front for the Liberation of Palestine leader, A'li Mustafa, sparked the chain of escalation that would lead to the invasion of April 2002. Another opportunity to see the politics of the new Israel at work came at the rather surreal Knesset ceremony held to honour the War of Independence Zionist leader Avraham Stern 'and his heritage of terrorism'. In this special parliamentary session, Sharon extolled not only the personality of Stern, whose gang pioneered the use of terror in the Arab/Israeli conflict and was responsible for the murder of UN envoy and Holocaust-time saviour of Jews, Count Folke Bernadette, but also his 'path'. Knesset Speaker, Labour leader and former Peace Now activist Avraham Burg said that at his death Stern 'ascended to heaven in a tempest'.[21]

There are signs that Israel is in deep spiritual crisis. The lack of sensitivity demonstrated by the officer who told journalists that in the fight against the Palestinians, Israel must study the Wehrmacht suppression of the Warsaw Ghetto uprising suggests not so much mere callousness, but a wholesale rejection of the Jewish liberal tradition itself. Other examples of this moral malaise include the numbering on the arms of Palestinian prisoners from Dheishe Camp in March 2002, reminiscent of the Nazi treatment of concentration camp inmates; the soldiers who told Israeli television how they loved the smell of dead 'terrorists'; and those others who posed for pictures next to the suicide bomber's corpse,[22] which they had mutilated.

This is not to idealise the past. The Zionist enterprise always has had a dark side and, in common with many nationalist movements, was never conducted according to Marquis of Queensberry Rules. But never has there been a time when Israelis themselves were so aware of the negative impact of the conflict on the values of their society and never have they felt so powerless.

This shift towards the right is reflected elsewhere. Washington's War against Terror does more than suit Sharon's security agenda, it undermines his domestic opponents on the Israeli centre left, who have always looked to the US as a cultural lodestone and believed that a final peace settlement could only come through US mediation/intervention. However, in the US, the vehemence of anti-Islamic feeling, the primacy given to 'security' over all other concerns, and the general post-September 11 jingoism have robbed the Israeli centre left of its terms of reference. A new McCarthyism has begun to emerge in the US, with Palestine occupying the role formerly played by communism. Examples of this include the treatment meted out to pro-Palestinian activist and New York Jew, Adam Shapiro, whose parents were forced to flee their home after receiving death threats, and actor John Malkovich's calls at the Cambridge Union for the shooting of British MP George Galloway and broadsheet journalist, Robert Fisk.[23] In the words of commentator Gideon Samet,

---

20 Eg Tal, 2002. A virulent attack on the whole Danish nation and its 'double standards' after the General Workers Union of Denmark called on Danes to boycott Israeli goods in protest at Israeli military action in Operation Defensive Wall; or Oren, 2002, in which the Vatican's criticism of the IDF handling of the Church of the Nativity siege is dismissed with the phrase 'the Catholic Church up to its neck in the paedophilia scandal is not exactly on a high moral ground from which to preach now'.
21 Tom Segev, Ha'aretz, 12 March 2002.
22 Lavie, 2002; Samet, 2002; Gilmore, 2001.
23 Fisk, 2002.

America has become 'a warm nest for Sharon-style machismo', Americans 'more Israeli that the Israelis'.[24]

The Sharonisation of the US affected debate over the Palestinian/Israeli conflict, but also about the nature of Israeli democracy itself. A law for Israel's domestic security service, the Shin Bet, was passed with almost a complete absence of debate in Israel's normally lively media. The Shin Bet Law, which aims to formalise 'for the first time in the state's history the Shin Bet's authority, function, and mission', completely avoids the controversial issue of interrogations.[25] In a country like Israel where security services are so pervasive, the new draconian prison terms for any present or former Shin Bet employees who reveal classified information could well seriously undermine freedoms. America's refusal to treat its Guatanamo Bay detainees as prisoners of war has been used by Israel's judiciary to refuse release to Hizbollah prisoners after their sentences are up.

The last few years have seen changes in Palestinian political culture too. Years of occupation and failed hopes have not only created the despair that acts as a breeding ground for the suicide bombers, but also the callousness that sanctions them. With the failure of Oslo, political discourse has become more overtly religious and the secular have been forced to moderate their lifestyles to fit in. The endless succession of fruitless peace missions and toothless 'special envoys' contrasts sharply with the vigorous action taken against Osama bin Laden and, in the past, Saddam Hussein, and unsurprisingly this has led to a deep cynicism. It is depressingly symptomatic of the situation that those Palestinians who still retain faith in the international community often come across in conversation as completely out of touch with reality, even deranged.

There is an alternative view of the trajectory of the peace process. This, albeit less heard since Operation Defensive Wall, is one that has the Palestinians out ahead. 'Israel is winning the battle but losing the war and conversely, the Palestinians are losing the battle but they now know that they will win the war'.[26] According to this view, the Israeli public will tire sooner that the Palestinians in this cruel war of attrition. All the Palestinians need to do is to remain *samed* (steadfast) and the Israelis will retreat from most of the territories.

It is a persuasive argument, and indeed there is significant public opinion research supporting this view. It is true that fewer Israelis identify themselves as left wing, and hatred of Arabs, Palestinians and their leadership is at an all-time high. But according to a survey by Market Watch, 45 per cent of Israelis who identified themselves as right wingers backed the establishment of a Palestinian state and the evacuation of some of the settlements. And a staggering 20 per cent of Israelis were prepared to accept the right of return being applied for some of the refugees. The only significant difference between the centre right and the extreme left is that one group wants to make the Palestinians suffer before giving them independence. 'The Israeli consensus today espouses attitudes that the Labour Party did not dare to put forward before Camp David and that the Peace Now organisation hesitated to adopt just a few years ago.'[27]

A seductive argument, but any perceived climb-down in the face of terrorism, let alone the creation of a viable healthy Palestinian state, is almost unthinkable under

---

24 *Ha'aretz*, 8 February 2002.
25 *Ha'aretz*, 29 January 2002; *Jerusalem Post*, 11 February 2002. A notorious court ruling allowed Shin Bet to exercise 'moderate physical pressure' during interrogations. This has been widely condemned as giving *carte blanche* for torture. Ironically, under the new legislation, the press leak by which the outside world came to find out about this would now be illegal.
26 Baskin, 2002.
27 Tamir, 2002.

a Sharon government. These hard-won changes that the intifada is having on Israeli public opinion could have been achieved without resorting to a suicide bombing strategy. And for this the Palestinian Authority and Arafat have to bear a heavy burden of responsibility. Even if documents claimed to be found by Israeli troops during Operation Defensive Wall and showing direct links between the suicide groups and high-level Palestinian officials prove to be false, the reality is that the PA is guilty of a shocking lack of leadership if nothing else. At least at some levels, such as propaganda, the bombers receive official blessing. And in the case of attacks perpetrated by the Al Aqsa Martyrs' brigades, the Tanzim arm of Arafat's Fatah organisation, a more substantial link is suggested.

It should be stressed that calls for Arafat to take decisive and unilateral action against the suicide bombers, possibly from the later half of 2001, and by April 2002, display an almost wilful disregard for the situation on the ground. By then Arafat was besieged in his compound, literally looking down the barrel of an Israeli tank. Water, telephone lines and electricity were cut off and supplies of food and medication dwindled. It had become impossible 'to use a flushing toilet',[28] let alone comply with calls to rein in militants. But, however much one condemns the myriad blatant injustices imposed on the Palestinians, one is still left with the sense that the PA would not have left itself with so little room to manoeuvre, had it invested more energy in establishing truly democratic and transparent institutions, and come up with a creative strategy of its own for combating the occupation, during the five years before the intifada.

The PA's record to date is sadly reminiscent of the PLO's legacy during its sojourn in Lebanon 1971–82. While it built up armed resistance, created fledgling national institutions, and advanced the cause of Palestine in the Arab and international arenas, the PLO also established a culture of nepotism and corruption that it has since imported into the Occupied Territories. This style of rule has hamstrung Palestinian progress and is in sharp contrast to the vibrant civil society that led the first intifada of 1987, changed Israeli and international public perceptions and laid the ground work for Arafat's return.[29] It is illuminating to compare the last major Israeli offensive against the Palestinians, the invasion of Lebanon in 1982 – again masterminded by Sharon – with the 2002 assault on the West Bank. Then, with the exception of a fierce gunfight at Beaufort Castle, Sharon's army encountered scant opposition from regular Palestinian forces in the first days of the war. When they did come up against serious Palestinian resistance, it was not from PLO troops, but from the ordinary refugees of Ain al Helwa camp in Sidon, led by a preacher named Haj Ibrahim.[30] And it is no coincidence that the place that offered the IDF by far the stiffest resistance during Operation Defensive Wall was Jenin, a place that has been outside effective PA control since the beginning of the intifada.[31]

The PA has allowed itself to be manoeuvred into a position of influence without leadership, and responsibility with no control. The present Israeli/Palestinian dynamic of repression, bombings and punishment has crippled initiative and limited the PA's strategic horizons. Given the vast asymmetrical gap in power between it and Israel, the PA was always going to be susceptible to manipulation, but there has also been a disconcerting poverty of vision.

Apologists for the PA argue that criticism of the Authority only undermines its effectiveness and provides ammunition for those who wish to sabotage Palestinian

28 Monbiot, 2002.
29 See Hemmami and Tamari, 2000 for an excellent contrast between intifada Al Aqsa and the first intifada.
30 Schiff and Ya'ari, 1986, p 151.
31 Hemmami, 2001b.

state building. True, it is completely unrealistic to expect the transition from occupation to statehood to be painless. Similar if not worse processes may indeed be common in other cases of decolonisation. However, high levels of education, political activism, the lively internal democracy of the first intifada, but above all the day-to-day effect of seeing how Israeli democracy works (for its Jewish citizenry at least) have made the population that the Authority rules profoundly sensitised to issues of good governance, and oppression, throwing the PA's record (and that of the Israelis) into ever sharper relief.

The escalation that began with Israel's response to the Zeevi assassination, continued with the invasions of the camps and led to Operation Defensive Wall, has rewritten the rules of the conflict. During the operation, IDF troops destroyed faxes, computers, hard disks, and looted safes and offices in every single PA institution and indeed many local NGOs[32] and businesses. Far from wanton, this wholesale destruction of the PA's infrastructure was entirely intentional and had to be sanctioned from the very top. Even vital data, such as that held at the Central Palestinian Bureau of Statistics, and needed to implement a recovery, is missing. The population is now almost entirely reliant on help from the international community.

As well as destroying public institutions, the attacks targeted the Palestinian home and family. Bulldozers ploughed through crowded camps, smashing through the homes that refugees had to spend decades painstakingly building, often giving little or no warning to the sleeping residents. Witnesses tell of Israeli practices that bear little relationship to policing and appear to be a deliberate strategy aimed at crushing the Palestinians' spirit. The smashing of crockery, expensive items like televisions, the *de rigeur* urination and/or defecation on the stairs or in the living room and the humiliation of the senior male family member in front of his children have become well-practised routines. During the invasion, thousands of Palestinian men were taken away for days at a time, held in cold, unsanitary conditions (often in the open), and given little food or water. Many claimed to have been beaten or tortured during interrogations, before being freed to try and return to their homes under threat of being shot for breaking the curfew.

For many refugees, the war against the camps seemed a replay of 1948 and specifically designed to make them leave. While a categorical answer is impossible at this stage, it does appear from the available evidence that there was no massacre of civilians at Jenin Camp in the sense of any numbers of civilians being executed in cold blood; however, the destruction and chilling eye-witness accounts[33] do appear to warrant an independent investigation. The carnage in the camp has become emblematic of Sharon's solution to security. And the battle for the camp, in which 23 Israeli soldiers lost their lives, has already entered the realms of legend as a Palestinian Stalingrad. It is premature to speculate about exactly what demons have been unleashed by the invasions and what the precise effects on the situation will be. But one thing is certain: Operation Defensive Wall has not bought security. After a short pause, the suicide attacks, including one in Rishon Le Zion that claimed 16 lives, resumed. And after all this violence both parties will have to return to the negotiating table and implement an agreement.

The basis for such an agreement, international law, has taken a battering over the past year and a half, with a strengthening of the long Middle East tradition of UN resolutions being honoured in the breach. Tel Aviv differs with the international community's consensus on the Occupied Territories' status; arguing, on the

---

32 Palestine Monitor updates, April 2002.
33 Eg Levy, 2002c.

grounds that they were not administered by the Palestinians prior to the 1967 war, that rather than 'occupied', the territories are 'disputed'. Such sophistry, if accepted, would make void the applicability of the Fourth Geneva Convention, the principal source of international law on occupation, to the conflict. Further weakening the Israeli case is the widespread recognition given to the PLO by both UN member states and international organisations. The Palestinians' case is further buttressed by numerous UN resolutions. Notably, Resolution 242 argues the 'inadmissibility of the acquisition of territory by war' and the precedent of the International Court of Justice's advisory opinion on Western Sahara, that in the case of dispute, it was for the people living on the land to choose sovereignty.[34] But most significant has been the passing of Security Council Resolution 1397 in March 2002, drafted by the United States, and explicitly calling for the creation of an independent Palestine alongside Israel.

The psychological suffering is a vital and relatively little studied aspect of the conflict. But there are frequent glimpses of the vast scale of the problem; that of two peoples under an unbearable, dehumanising strain. There is the increase in bed wetting among Palestinian teenagers; the rise in depression in both societies; the new phenomenon of Israeli road rage; the Gazan psychologist who turns off his fridge because 'every noise now sounds like [an] F18';[35] the Palestinian child who vomits on hearing the sound of a helicopter; the Israelis who fear going out of doors; the middle class Palestinian mother who suddenly wants to become a suicide bomber.[36] On a wider scale, the repeated resort to failed patterns of escalation suggests a cry for help. On a governmental level, no change in either the Israeli or Palestinian leaderships can realistically be expected to break the deadlock. And at an activist level, efforts by local pro-peace groups on both sides have been drowned out by the violence.

It should be clear that the only way to break the Gordian knot at present lies outside the region. A sustained and forceful international intervention, based on UN resolutions and international law, is the sole solution to the crisis. And the US is the only power that can realistically enforce this solution. While recent US administrations have all firmly been in the hands of the pro-Israel lobby, Eisenhower's firm stand during the 1956–57 Suez Crisis shows that there is a precedent for such an action. Israel heeded Washington's call for a withdrawal then and indeed could not afford to defy the US should it decide to do so again. It should be added that many Israelis themselves see a US-imposed peace as the only viable solution; America, with its longstanding strategic and cultural links with Israel, would hardly enforce a situation which would jeopardise Israel's security. To mollify understandable Palestinian distrust of US impartiality, the UN would be given a supervisory role.

At present, any move to implement such a proposal would be met with howls of protest. Israel's supporters like to point out the differences between its behaviour in the Occupied Territories and that of Arab/Islamic regimes towards their respective opposition groups. It is quite true that Israel's human rights infractions do not begin to approach those of the Iraqi Ba'ath, the Syrian, Sudanese or Algerian security services, but this fails to address an important point – several, in fact. Firstly, to condemn the one is not to condone the others. Secondly, Israel derives enormous material, ideological and even cultural benefits from its much-vaunted status as a democracy, and as such can be reasonably expected to behave like one. None of the

---

34 Strawson, 2002.
35 El Serraj, 2001.
36 El Serraj, 2002.

above mentioned regimes gets the billions in US aid, favoured nation trading status with the European Union, the cultural embrace of tournaments like the Eurovision Song Contest or the kudos of playing in the Champions' League that Israel does. There is a sense in which Israel, a creation of the United Nations, has a special responsibility to honour the ideals and norms of the international community.

September 11 has been something of a *diabolo ex machina* for both Palestinians and Israelis, contributing in part to the horrific spiral of violence that the region has witnessed. But the crisis may hopefully carry within it the seeds of its own resolution. There are signs that the nadir which the Palestinians have reached is catalysing a much-needed reform of the PA. More significantly, the conflict's very intractability, and its relevance to the US's national interests, could yet force a fresh and creative realignment of foreign policy priorities.

This relationship between September 11 and the Arab/Israeli conflict is at the centre of controversy; with pro-Arab and liberal commentators arguing that the West's complicity in the tragedy of the Palestinians has fuelled the rise in Islamic terror pitted against pro-US/Israeli analysts. These accuse Arab and Islamic governments of exploiting the plight of the Palestinians to divert attention from their own poor standards of governance and thereby creating a virulently anti-Western political culture; one which both obstructs settlement of the Israel/Palestine conflict and has given birth to the Al Qa'ida phenomenon.

For Muslims throughout the world there is no more emotive issue than Palestine.[37] Standing at the centre of a matrix of ideological and political fault-lines, the fate of the Palestinians goes straight to the heart of the issues thrown up by September 11. For people on both sides of the argument, the Israel/Palestine conflict exercises unique pull, for no other cause is so ideological and on so many levels. Palestine fuses opposing religious loyalties, conflicts of colonial vs Holocaust guilt, North vs South issues, and Islam vs the West.

Palestine was not some problem born in the mists of the 19th century. Israel was created after the Second World War, in the era of decolonisation. But self-determination for the Jewish people came at the expense of that of the Palestinians. However many self-righteous and self-serving arguments are given along the lines of 'the Palestinians never missing an opportunity to miss an opportunity', the fact remains that a serious injustice has been done and that the great Western powers are in no small way responsible. Justice inconsistently applied is no justice at all. At such times of uncertainty, an impartial and effective international legal system is not a luxury but a vital force for global stability. Writing in 1919, British Foreign Secretary Lord Balfour said: '... so far as Palestine is concerned, the Powers have made no statement of fact which is not admittedly wrong, and no declaration of policy which, at least in the letter, they have not always intended to violate.' In the past 80 years such cynicism has been the norm and is deeply dangerous and counter-productive.

It is in everyone's interests to find a just solution to the Palestine issue. There would be no better way to cut the ground from under Osama bin Laden's feet than to start a process that genuinely addresses Palestinian national aspirations. The consequences of not doing so go beyond the physical horrors represented by a September 11-style attack; it threatens the global economy, political stability in the Arab/Islamic world and the very fabric of Western democracies. This may work in

---

37 While the Israel/Palestine issue is of paramount importance in the Arab world, elsewhere in the Islamic world local issues dominate, for instance Kashmir in the sub-continent and the Malukus in Indonesia. However, Palestine typically comes second and over the past year has inspired mass demonstrations in most major cities in the Islamic world.

References

Andoni, Lamis (2002) 'Wafa Idriss, symbol of a generation' Amin.org, 23 February

Bahour, Sam (2001) 'Believe it or not' Amin.org, 24 December 2001

Baskin, Gershon (Dr) (2001) *Barak and Netanyahu – A Look at Mainstream Israeli Thinking*, Israeli-Palestine Center for Research and Information (IPCRI), 19 December

Baskin, Gershon (Dr) (2002) *The Midterm Assessment*, IPCRI, March

Carey, R (2001) *The New Intifada: Resisting Israel's Apartheid*, New York: Verso (New Left Books)

El Serraj, Eyad (Dr) (2001) 'First life' Amin.org, 10 December

El Serraj, Eyad (Dr) (2002) 'Wounds and madness – why we have become suicide bombers' Amin.org, 2 April

Fisk, Robert (2002) 'Why does John Malkovich want to kill me?' *The Independent*, 14 May

Gilmore, Inigo (2001) 'Israelis take "trophy" photos of the dead' *The Telegraph*, 12 October

Hass, A (2000) *Drinking the Sea at Gaza*, New York: First Owl

Hedges, Chris (2001) 'Gaza diary' Harpers.com

Hemmami, Rema (2001a) 'Waiting for Godot at Qalandya: reflections on queues and inequality' 13 Jerusalem Quarterly File

Hemmami, Rema (2001b) *Intifada in the Aftermath*, MERIP Press Information note 74, 30 October

Hemmami, Rema and Tamari, Salah (2000) *Anatomy of Another Rebellion*, MERIP (Winter)

Lavie, Aviv (2002) 'Shots across the bow' *Ha'aretz*, 25 February

Levy, Gideon (2002a) 'Closing the sea' *Ha'aretz*, 15 February

Levy, Gideon (2002b) 'Danger checkpoint ahead' *Ha'aretz*, 1 March

Levy, Gideon (2002c) 'Twilight zone – "I am sorry for your loss" the officer said' *Ha'aretz*, 15 May

McDowall, M (1994) *The Palestinians – The Road to Nationhood*, London: Minority Rights Group

Monbiot, George (2002) 'World Bank to West Bank' *The Guardian*, 9 April

Morris, B (2001) *Righteous Victims – A History of the Zionist-Arab Conflict 1881–2001*, New York: Vintage

Oren, Amir (2002) 'From war to peace in enemy territory' *Ha'aretz*, 23 April

Said, E (2002) 'What Israel has done' Amin.org, 18 April

Samet, Gideon (2002) 'You won't be able to say "We didn't know"' *Ha'aretz*, 28 January

Schiff, Z and Ya'ari, E (1986) *Israel's Lebanon War*, London: Unwin

Strawson, John (2002) 'The Middle East crisis: international law and the Palestinian-Israeli conflict' 36 Student Law Review 50 (Cavendish Publishing)

Tal, Avraham (2002) 'There is something rotten in Denmark' *Ha'aretz*, 22 April

Tamir, Yuli (2002) 'The triumph of left' *Ha'aretz*, 24 March

Ushpiz, Ada (2002) 'Unforgivable, unforgettable' *Ha'aretz*, 24 March

World Bank, 'Developing the Occupied Territories: an investment in peace' Economic and Sector Reports, Washington, 1993, Vol 5, pp 49–50

Internet sites

Al-Haq: www.alhaq.org

Amnesty International: www.amnesty.org

Arab Media Internet Network: www.amin.org

B'tselem Human Rights Centre: www.btselem.org/

Debka.com: www.debka.com

Gamla News: www.gamla.org.il

Gush Shalom: www.gush-shalom.org

Israel-Palestine Centre for Research and Information: www.ipcri.org

LAW: The Palestinian Society for the Protection of Human Rights and the Environment: www.lawsociety.org

Middle East Media Research Institute: www.memri.org

Palestine Monitor: www.palestinemonitor.org

State of Israel, Ministry for Foreign Affairs: www.israel-mfa.gov.il

Tami Steinmatz Centre for Peace Research: www.tau.ac.il/peace

The Atlantic Online: www.theatlantic.com

The Jerusalem Centre for Public Affairs: www.jcpa.org

The Jerusalem Media and Communication Centre: www.jmcc.org

The Palestine Chronicle: www.palestinechronicle.com

The Palestine National Authority www.minfo.gov.ps

The Tzemach Institute of Biblical Studies: www.tzemach.org

Chapter 13
Jirga: power and traditional conflict resolution in Afghanistan
Ali Wardak

Introduction

Conflicts are as old as human societies themselves. Historically individuals, social groups and societies have disputed and competed against one another over scarce commodities and resources – land, money, women, and ideology. They have even fought one another and bitterly sought the elimination and/or subjugation of rivals, in order to control these resources and commodities. But at the same time, human societies and groups have found their own ways and means for averting and resolving conflicts. The existing body of literature confirms that the nature and causes of conflict and the mechanisms for resolving them are deeply rooted in the culture and history of every society; they are in many important ways unique to them. *Pancahiat* in India,[1] Mediation Committees in China,[2] and *jirga* in Afghanistan[3] that operate as informal mechanisms of conflict resolution differ from one another significantly. More importantly, all these traditional forms of conflict resolution are fundamentally different from the ways in which conflicts are resolved in much of the Western world.

These comparative social facts would seem to support the philosophical position of cultural relativists[4] who long argued that the nature of all social phenomena, including conflicts and their resolution, are relative and culturally specific. While this viewpoint has a solid foundation in philosophy and social theory, the nature of human relationships in the 21st century has been radically changing with the increasing globalisation of economic, social, and political relationships among nations.[5] Cultural relativists may need to rethink their position vis à vis the realities of social relationships in the 21st century. Since conflicts are a form of social relationships (though negative), they are bound to become globalised, and so are their resolutions.

Indeed, the complex global nature of the September 11 terrorist attacks in the USA, their global sources and causes and the global efforts to respond to terrorism (and to its causes) confirm this. These developments are certainly pointing to the fact that the time has arrived for different cultures and civilisations to engage with one another as partners in the resolution of their conflicts; and it is time that they learn from one another as equal members of a 'global village'. This paper will focus on examining the institution of *jirga* – a traditional mechanism of conflict resolution in Afghanistan. But first, it is important to place the subject under examination in the general context of the current social and political situation in Afghanistan that has been strongly shaped by the past 23 years of continued conflict in the country.

In the course of this long armed conflict, Afghanistan has been used as a battlefield between competing global and regional powers and groups – a

---

1 Baxi and Gallanter, 1979; Moore, 1985.
2 Li, 1978; Clark, 1989.
3 Elphinstone, 1992; Olesen, 1995; Glatzer, 1998.
4 See Reichel, 1998.
5 Robertson, 1992.

battlefield between the former Communist USSR and the capitalist West (mainly the USA) in the 1980s; a battlefield between Pakistan and the Arab Gulf countries, on the one hand, and Iran and Russia in the 1990s, on the other; and more recently a battlefield between foreign Muslim fundamentalists and a right wing US administration. In this process of rivalry, Afghanistan's main immediate neighbours in particular infiltrated deep into Afghan politics. With competing interests in the county, they created their client factions/warlords and sponsored them militarily, financially and politically. These factions had gradually become so dependent on their foreign sponsors that they saw Afghanistan's interests through the eyes of these foreigners. These neighbours also exploited Afghanistan's existing tribal and religious composition and justified their interventions on the grounds that they had common religious and ethnic ties with their clients. The long civil conflict resulted in a very extensive destruction of Afghanistan's economic, political and social infrastructure. The Western world – particularly the USA, which benefited most from the Afghan-Soviet war, indeed, had lured the Soviets to invade – almost completely abandoned the ruined Afghanistan after the defeat of the Red Army.

The destruction of the country's economic infrastructure in particular provided opportunities for the foreign players and their client Afghan warring factions to exploit the situation for seeking their strategic interests at the expense of the Afghan population. The almost total collapse of the Afghan pre-war economy gradually resulted in the emergence of a 'war economy'[6] – an economic condition that centred mainly on the manufacturing, repair, use and smuggling of weapons and ammunition, on the one hand, and on the production and smuggling of illicit drugs, on the other. What is particularly important to mention is that the 23 year long conflict also resulted in a generation of young people who are largely deprived of educational qualifications and other useful skills. This 'war generation' of thousands of young persons has also been deeply traumatised by the war – many lost their parents, relatives and homes in the war. This situation enabled the warring factions to recruit their fighters from this war generation so that the conflict in which they had a stake continued. Fighting for one or the other warlord provided these young men with a source of income, social status, and a way of channelling their young energies. More importantly, this situation provide the opportunity for foreign Muslim fundamentalist groups – mainly the Al Qa'ida – to use Afghan soil as headquarters for terrorist activities against other nations, and eventually to launch the September 11 terrorist attacks on New York's Twin Towers and other targets in the USA.

The September 11 attacks, which deeply shocked the world, have had a strong impact on global policy, particularly on the US's policy towards Afghanistan. These events convinced US policy makers that the social, political and economic environments that bred terrorism are no longer confined within national boundaries. Instead, the current international military engagement, economic reconstruction plans, and the political stabilisation of Afghanistan are all aimed at the re-integration of Afghanistan into the global community – efforts that provide common ground between the interests of the international community and the interests of the ordinary Afghans. Central to the political stabilisation and to the establishment of social and political order in Afghanistan is the institution of *jirga* – one of the least researched aspects of Afghan culture and society.

This paper will focus on an analysis of the concept and the nature of *jirga*, its different levels and forms, and the social and cultural context in which each form operates as a mechanism of conflict resolution. It is argued that the *jirga* (or its

---

6   Rubin, 1999.

equivalents) as a traditional Afghan social institution is closely bound up with social and economic realities of everyday life in Afghanistan and is deeply rooted in the culture and history of the people of the country.

As a time-honoured mechanism of conflict resolution, at local, tribal, and national levels, it has the potential to act as a powerful means of communication among the various segments of Afghan society, and therefore plays a central role in strengthening national unity and social solidarity among the people of Afghanistan. However, the extent of the effectiveness of *jirga* as a mechanism of conflict resolution depends on the extent to which it is perceived as legitimate. The paper will also examine the continued need for *jirga* to resolve contemporary Afghan conflicts as well as for *jirga* to learn from other societies – to become a traditional institution in a modern setting.

The concept of *jirga*

According to the *Pashto Descriptive Dictionary*, *jirga* is an original Pashto word which in its common usage refers to the gathering of a few, or a large number of people; it also means consultation, according to this source. The word *jirga* is also used in Farsi/Dari. According to *Ghyathul-Lughat*[7] it is derived from *jirg*, which means a 'wrestling ring', or 'circle', but is commonly used to refer to the gathering of people. Other scholars believe that the word *jirga* originates from Turkish where it has very similar meaning to those in Pashto and Farsi/Dari.[8] These meanings of *jirg* and *jirga* strongly reflect the rituals and processes of the Pashtun traditional tribal *jirga* where people gather and sit in a large circle in order to resolve disputes and make collective decisions about important social issues. Rubin, a prominent scholar, describes the institution of *jirga* in this way: 'the *jirga* includes all adult males and rules by consensus. In theory, a *jirga* can be convened at any level of tribal organisation, from the smallest lineage to an entire confederation. *Jirga*s are most commonly held at the lineage level, but there are larger tribal or even inter-tribal *jirgas* as well, at least among the eastern Pashtuns.'[9] While this description depicts almost all the important aspects of this traditional Afghan special institution, Rafi, a contemporary Afghan scholar, has formally defined it and says that *jirga* is 'that historical and traditional institution and gathering of the Afghans, which over the centuries, has resolved our nation's all tribal and national political, social, economic, cultural and even religious conflicts by making authoritative decisions'.[10]

Despite the generality and the generic nature of this definition, it provides a comprehensive framework for the various dimensions of the institution of *jirga*, the different levels at which it operates as a mechanism of conflict resolution, and the kinds of conflicts it is designed to resolve. It is a traditional institution that is more strongly bound up with the tribal economy and society of the Pashtun of Afghanistan who constitute about half of the Afghan population.[11] It is therefore more commonly and effectively used as a mechanism of conflict resolution among the Pashtuns. As the authors of an important field study of 'Contemporary Afghan Councils' say:

> The prototype in Afghanistan, the *Jirga*, is the product of Pashtun tribal society and operates according to the dictates of the *Pakhtunwali*, an inclusive code of conduct guiding all aspects of Pashtun behaviour and often superseding the dictates of both Islam and the

---

7 Gheyathoddin, 1871, p 119.
8 Faiz-zad, 1989, p 5.
9 1995, p 43.
10 2002, p 6.
11 See Dupree, 1980; Canfield, 1986; Hayman, 1992; Wardak, 1998.

central government. Thus, in the tribal Pashtun areas, local *Jirga* settles (nearly) all issues, unless assistance is requested from another tribe or the government.[12]

The *jirga* has, indeed, contributed significantly to the maintenance of social order at local, tribal and national levels in Afghan society. It has, therefore, been considered as a rival to the central state authority by some governments in Afghan history. However, despite attempts by successive Afghan governments to expand their control throughout the country – through the pre-emption of the village *Malik* (a liaison person between the government and the local people) system, introduction of district and rural development councils, imposition of Marxism, and theocracy – the Pashtun social institutions including the *jirga* remained relatively intact. This was particularly the case with those Pashtun areas that had strong tribal structures and that are located far from urban centres. However, in large urban centres where non-Pashtuns and Pashtuns were mixed, or where non-Pashtuns predominated, the central government was able to assert its formal authority more fully. In these parts of the country, most conflicts were resolved by formal agencies of the Afghan state. The Afghan legal system was broadly based on the Western (particularly French) conception of 'legality' and the principles of Islamic jurisprudence.[13]

This examination of the *jirga* may imply that it was an exclusive Pashtun tribal institution that operated as a mechanism of conflict resolution only in non-urbanised (or less urbanised) Pashtun dominated areas in the south and east of Afghanistan. Some warlords and faction leaders who claim to be championing the rights of different ethnic and tribal groups in Afghanistan have particularly promoted this view during the past 23 years of Afghan civil conflict. However, there is emerging evidence which shows that *jirga*, or its equivalents, are used as informal mechanisms of conflict resolution in rural or less urbanised areas where Afghan Tajiks, Hazaras or Uzbaks predominate as the main (or sole) ethnic group.[14] What is very interesting in these accounts is that there are striking similarities between the Pashtun *jirga* and the non-Pashtun *shura(s)*.

Carter and Connor confirm that among Afghan Tajiks, Hazaras and Uzbaks, *jirga*-like councils, which are commonly referred to as *shura* or *majlis*, operated as a mechanism of conflict resolution. These Afghans dealt with less serious conflicts, problems and issues informally through *shura*, which Carter and Connor operationally define in this way: 'A shura is a group of individuals which meets only in response to a specific need in order to decide how to meet the need. In most cases, this need is to resolve a conflict between individuals, families, groups of families, or whole tribes.'[15] This description would seem to indicate that *shura* and *jirga* are fundamentally very similar Afghan informal (non-state) mechanisms of conflict resolution that operate in different social contexts.

Carter and Connor add that unlike the strongly institutionalised and egalitarian *jirga*, the *shura* is more like a short-term advisory council of elders, landlords, *khans* and other influential individuals that does not have clearly defined rules. Also the *shura* often deals with civil conflicts the resolution of which are strongly influenced by landlords, *khans*, and more recently by warlords. More importantly, Carter and Connor's study further reveals that for these reasons and because of Pashtuns' expertise in conflict resolutions, as well as due to their large population size and dispersion through much of Afghanistan, '... it was not uncommon for a non-Pashtun groups to request local Pashtun elders to hold a *jirga* to settle a non-

---

12 Carter and Connor, 1989, p 7.
13 Kamali, 1985.
14 See Farhadi, 2000; Malekyar, 2000; Hashemi, 2000.
15 1989, p 9.

Pashtun conflict, suggesting that the Pashtun *jirga* traditionally had more impact than its non-Pashtun counterpart, the shura'.[16]

This field observation clearly indicates that the fact that Afghans, whatever their ethnic/tribal origin, have over the centuries emulated each others' behaviour – Pashtuns, Tajiks, Hazaras, Uzbaks, Turkmans and other Afghan ethnic and tribal groups all have made their unique contributions to Afghan culture that is more than the total sum of its constituent parts. The contributions of Tajiks to Afghan arts and literature, the Hazaras and Qizelbashs' contributions to civil society and urban entrepreneurship, the Uzbak and Turkmans' contribution to trade and commerce, and the contributions of the other ethnic and tribal groups, have all made what is referred to as Afghan culture and society. This situation has, in turn, contributed to the development of cross-tribal and cross-ethnic national institutions that can only be called Afghan. This is more clearly manifested in the fact that the institution of *jirga* has been translated into the national political life of Afghan society – the two houses of the Afghan parliament have been named as *wolasi jirga* (Lower House) and *mashrano jirga* (Upper House). Thus, whatever the origin of *jirga*, and whatever the extent of its prevalence as a mechanism of conflict resolution among various Afghan ethnic/tribal groups, it has a national currency.

Traditional structures of authority and levels of *jirga*

The notion of 'authority' has been extensively discussed by classical as well as modern social and political thinkers. It has been described variously, depending on the form of authority that is exercised in a specific social situation. In order to understand the meaning of this notion and the ways in which it applies to traditional structures of authority in Afghanistan, it is important to draw on Max Weber, who distinguished three forms of authority: a) 'traditional'; b) 'rational-legal'; and c) 'charismatic' authority. Charismatic authority, according to Weber, is a kind of exceptional (or divine) endowment of grace that is imputed by followers to leaders. Contemporary examples of this form of authority may be the authority of Mahatma Ghandi, Martin L King, and Ayatollah Khomeini. Legal-rational authority, on the other hand, according to Weber is the authority of highly organised groups such as that of the modern state. And finally, traditional authority for Weber is the semi-political decisions made by chiefs of tribes in societies where the modern processes of government are not fully institutionalised. These concepts will be used to theoretically inform the discussion about of the exercise of authority, at various levels, in Afghan society.

Although the main structure of authority in Afghan society include the extended family, the locally based clan (or sub-tribe), the tribe, large ethnic group, and the state, for the purposes of this paper I will focus on the ways in which authority is exercised within local, tribal and national contexts. However, before examining the main social contexts within which public conflicts are dealt with by *jirga*, it is important to mention that most conflicts that are considered 'private' are resolved within the Afghan family that the Pashtun refer to as *kahol* and the Tajik and Hazaras as *khanawada*, or *khanadan*. A great deal of potentially serious conflicts are screened at the familial level; they are dealt with on the spot before becoming a public problem and a burden on other societal institutions – one of these institutions being *jirga*, which is examined at *local*, *tribal* and *national* levels, below.

---

16 Carter and Connor, 1989, p 10.

Maraka – local *jirga*

The concepts of *jirga* and *maraka* (pronounced *mraka*) as informal mechanisms of conflict resolution among the Pashtun of Afghanistan are often used interchangeably. However, some Afghan experts on the subject make an important distinction between the two. Atayee says that 'The difference between MARAKA and JIRGA is that the MARAKA is to investigate and settle problems of small importance. The members of the MARAKA are elders of the various PSHAS (Plarina) of one KHEL. The JIRGA considers and settles problems of great importance and its members are the elders of various KHELS concerned'.[17] The fact that members of *maraka* comprise of elders of one *khel* (often a single village-based kinship group) clearly indicates that it is generally a local village institution. Therefore I will use the term *maraka*, throughout this section to refer to the micro-level village (or inter-village) based local mechanism of conflict resolution.

The social organisation of *maraka* as a local village-based institution will be further examined later in this section, but first it is important to describe the social and cultural context within which it operates as a mechanism of conflict resolution in Afghanistan. The most immediate context in which *maraka* operates is the kinship group that is referred to among Afghan Pashtuns as *khel*. According to Atayee (1979), *khel* is a sub-section of a *tabar*, tribe. A *khel* comprises several immediate kinship groups that are called *plarina* (or *plarganey*). A *plarina* includes several extended families, or *kahols*, that are related to one another by a common ancestor, and whose members have *intense* (as opposed to general) reciprocal relationships among them. Thus the *plarina* represents the smallest unit of tribal formation and the most immediate kinship group of distant relatives, who refer to one another as cousins. Members of several *plarinas* (or a *khel*) usually live in a single *kalay*, village, and normally share public facilities such as the mosque, water spring, mill, and water canals etc. But, members of a large *khel* may live in more than one *kalay*. Occasionally a very large *khel* may comprise tens of smaller *khels*, and therefore form a tribe in its own right, such as the Suleimankhel branch of the Ghalzai Pashtuns. However, what is crucial to the current discussion is that it is the village-based *khel* within the context of which 'public' (as opposed to 'private' matters dealt with by *kahol* and *plarina*) matters are settled by a *maraka*.

Maraka as a local institution of conflict resolution is closely related to the social and economic organisation of the *kalay*. As the overwhelming majority of Afghans are agricultural farmers, it is mainly the agricultural farm, the orchard, the water spring and canal, the water-mill, animal husbandry, vineyard, orchard and the manufacturing of basic agricultural tools around which the *kalay* is socially and economically organised. The average Pashtun *kalay* is a small socio-economic unit that normally consists of several extended families whose members are directly related to a common ancestor. The average size of a *kalay* may range from about 50 to 200 individuals. It is generally a self-sufficient socio-economic unit within which people are not only related to one another through blood ties, but also through *general* reciprocal relationships. They reciprocate agricultural tools, goods, gifts, favours and services. At a *plarina* level the norms of reciprocity are governed by *trabgani*. *Trabgani* refers to the established patterns of behaviour which guide members as to who to co-operate with, who to compete with, who to marry, and in a word how to live as *tarboor* – an equal member of the kin group; it is both a source of cohesion and divisive rivalry among members of a *plarina* in different

---

17 Atayee, 1979, p 39. See also Rafi, 2002.

circumstances.[18] However, at a more general level, it is *pashtunwali* that guides the normative aspects of social relationships (including reciprocal relationships) among members of the *khel*, and constitutes an important aspect of the social order of *kalay*. As will be examined in more detail in the next section, *pashtunwali* refers to the general code of behaviour for a Pashtun as an autonomous and respectable member of society. According to Dupree, 'The values of the Pashtun and the Muslim religion, modified by local customs, permeate in varying degrees all other groups'.[19] This is also confirmed by Newell and Newell, who say that *pashtunwali* 'has influenced other groups within the country who must deal with similar environment and social realties'.[20]

It is this social and economic context of the *khel* and *kalay* within which *maraka* operates as a mechanism of conflict resolution. The existing body of literature shows that *maraka* has not been defined formally. However, looking at the different aspects and elements of *maraka* as outlined in this literature, it may be described as *a local institution of dispute settlement that incorporates a prevalent (time and space-bound) narkh, institutionalised rituals, and a body of marakachian whose prikra about a dispute (or problem) is binding on the parties involved*. This description indicates that *narkh*, institutionalised rituals, *marakachian* and *prikra* constitute the fundamental elements of *maraka*. Thus, an assembly of a *khel*'s members without the materialisation of any of these elements may be considered as an ordinary gathering.

Narkh refers to the centuries-old body of the civil and penal tribal customary 'laws'. While these 'laws' are completely unwritten, they are part of the collective consciousness of a *kalay*. This is summed up in the Pashto proverb '*De watan na wowza kho de narkh na ma waza*', which means, 'you may abandon your tribe/homeland, but you cannot abandon *narkh*'. This implies that these customary laws have profound existence in the minds of local people. However, it is the *narkhey* (expert of *narkh*) who has a detailed knowledge of these laws, applications and their related procedures. According to Atayee,[21] the most well known *narkhs* are the *Ahmadzai narkh* and the *Razmak narkh*. The *Ahmadzai narkh* has two versions, namely the *Esa narkh* and the *Musa narkh*. While the first is considered as strict and precise, the second is more general, but sufficiently flexible to suit different circumstances. Some *khels* and tribes in eastern and southern Afghanistan have developed their own *narkhs* that are more applicable to their social and economic conditions. Nevertheless the *Ahmadzai* and the *Razmak narkhs* are generally followed as sources of reference among Pashtun. At a more general level, *narkh* reflects the fundamental values and norms associated with *pashtunwali*.

However, *narkh* has to be placed in the social context of a specific conflict and thoroughly discussed by *marakachain*. The latter refers to all the *mashran* (elders), *speengiri* (people with grey beards), and *speenpatkian* (people with white turbans, which means *mullahs* here) who form the main body of *maraka*. As mentioned earlier, while *mashran* and *speengiri* represent various *plarinas*, *speenpatkian* join them, in order to bless the *maraka* and to lead the religious aspect of the *maraka* rituals. *Mashran* and *speengiri* are rarely religious leaders, but they often have a working knowledge of 'folk Islam', especially of the general principles that relate to conflict resolution. Although some *mashran* and *speengiri* are normally experts in *narkh*, they may be accompanied by a *narkhey* who often belongs to a different *khel*. This is to ensure that the relevant customary laws are properly and fairly applied.

---

18 *Trabgani* is mistakenly interpreted as rivalry/enmity by some writers, including Rubin, 1995.
19 1980, p 127.
20 1981, p 23.
21 1979, p 67.

Institutionalised rituals form a necessary, but less important, element of *maraka*. The nature and quality of *maraka* rituals vary in accordance with the nature of the issue that is dealt with and with the kind of technique of conflict resolution that is used. For instance, the rituals of *rogha* (reconciliation/mediation) in a criminal case are different from those of a *rogha* in a non-criminal dispute. In addition, since *maraka* deals mostly with civil and relatively less serious criminal matters – such as violations of one's local grazing rights, water rights, disputes over agricultural boundaries, feuds over symbolic resources between members of a *khel*, and relatively minor bodily harm – its related rituals are not as elaborate as those of the tribal *jirga*. Nevertheless, a *maraka* is normally held in a specially designated open and public place or in the village mosque, especially during winter. Only some *marakas* that involve sensitive local issues are conducted secretly without the participation of ordinary people. Some *marakas* are scheduled for the arrival of *eid* (the festival marking the end of *Ramadan*, and the day of pilgrimage of *makka*). Since *eid* is a day of communal joy and celebration, it is a uniquely appropriate occasion for sharing the joy among all members of the village, including the disputants. The *maraka* usually starts by the citation of verses from the holy Qur'an, and ends with *du'a* (prayer) – both rituals are led by the *speenpatkey*.

Depending on the physical location of the place where a *maraka* is held, *marakachian* form the inner circle of the gathering; ordinary members of the village sit at a relative distance in an outer circle. However, the ordinary people are allowed to listen to the proceedings, but are discouraged to get involved. What is crucial is that the ordinary participants are not just spectators. Instead, they carefully observe the *jirga* process, and their presence is a reminder to the *marakachian* that the village is watching what they say and what they decide upon. Therefore what the *marakachian* say and what they decide upon is judged by the public. Thus the *maraka* is a multi-dimensional process of communication between the various parties – it is not only a communication between the disputants, and among the disputants and the *marakachian*, but also a communication among all of these and the apparently silent village. This complex process of direct and indirect communication among members of the village functions as the main source of its social cohesion as a unified community – it reaffirms that the *kalay* has a shared morality the violation of which is not acceptable. It also ensures that the violator must pay the price for his/her violation, so that the actual harm inflicted (on the victim) and the symbolic damage caused to the moral order of the village are compensated.

A very important aspect of *maraka* is *prikra*, which means *maraka*'s final decision about the settlement of a specific conflict. However, the nature of *prikra* varies in accordance with the specific form of *maraka*. According to Atayee (1979) there are two forms of *maraka*. The first one is called *wak maraka*, which is empowered to investigate, discuss and make *prikra* (decision/verdict) about a case in the absence of the disputants. The second is called *de zhabi shorawalo maraka*, which brings together the disputant parties, who present their cases, arguments, and witnesses throughout the process of the *maraka*. In the latter form of *maraka*, the *marakachian* try to find common ground between the disputants and to resolve the conflict in a way that is acceptable to both parties. It is mainly the 'traditional authority' (based on personal qualities, social status and leadership skills) of the *marakachian* which plays a central part in achieving a *prikra* that is satisfactory to both parties. Persuasion through invoking the fear of Allah and threats to the *nang aw namos* – collective honour – and to the unity of the *khel* are used as important techniques in this process. But in *wak maraka*, the *prikra* is final and binding on the disputants' behaviour after it is announced. In this form of *maraka* the disputant parties and the village generally trust the use of what Wrong (1979) calls the 'competent authority' (based on the individual's recognised expertise and skills) of the *marakachian*. Should any of the parties choose not to abide by the *prikra*, s/he may face *ratal* – a collective social boycott by the whole village. In addition, the disobedient may be ordered to pay *nagha* (a fine/compensation) to the other party. Occasionally, their house may be burnt by members of the village.

However, if the disputants and the *khel* see the *prikra* as unfair, it may be rejected. This often happens when a wrong *narkh* is applied. This is called *kog-narkh*, which means dodging the prevalent *narkh* and/or misapplying it to the specific case. In this situation, the dissatisfied disputant must have the support of the *khel* (or at least a majority of it) in order to be able to appeal to another *maraka*. If the second *maraka* proves that a *kog-narkh* has been applied, then the *marakachian* lose their reputation and the right to participate in future *marakas*. They also have to pay *tawan*, compensation, to the parties (especially the dissatisfied party). This clearly shows that the legitimacy of both the processes and outcome of *maraka* is central to its institutional status as a local mechanism of conflict resolution. Indeed, it is central to the social order of the village and to its functioning as a social group. But legitimacy is often subjectively assessed in the wider context of Afghan culture, which is to be further examined in the next two sections.

Qawmi jirga – tribal jirga

As mentioned earlier, *maraka* and *jirga* involve very similar processes and techniques of conflict resolution, and therefore the concepts are often used interchangeably by writers as well as by ordinary people. The fact that the former is often a local, village-based institution means that it deals with less serious, local issues. However, the latter, as a tribal institution, deals with more important issues that are central to the social order of the tribe. Thus, before an examination of the ways in which the *qawmi jirga* operates as a mechanism of conflict resolution, it is important to look at the social context of this traditional institution – the tribe – and how its social boundaries are drawn.

Despite the fact that exploring the nature of the tribe and delineating its social boundaries in the context of the multi-ethnic Afghan society is a highly complex issue, social scientists have attempted to do so. Tapper, a prominent British Afghanologist, describes tribe in the context of Afghan society in this way: 'Tribe may be used loosely of a localized group in which kinship is the dominant idiom of organization, and whose members consider themselves culturally distinct (in terms of customs, dialect or language, and origins) …'[22] While this description outlines key features of the Afghan (mainly Pashtun) tribal formation at a general level, a fuller and more precise understanding of the nature and social boundaries of the tribe is a highly complex issue. This is mainly because the social boundaries of the Afghan tribe fluctuate in accordance with its social position in relation to other tribal, or sub-tribal, units to which it relates as roots of a tree or vice versa. A tribe may have a dozen sub-tribes whose members would see 'themselves' (and be seen by 'others') as members of each of the sub-tribes in different social situations (co-operative, competitive, confrontational) and identify with each accordingly. For example, Kaisarkhel, with an estimated several thousand members in eastern Afghanistan, is a branch of Suliemankhel, which in turn is a branch of the Ghalzai Pashtun tribe. While all members of Kaisarkhel are also Suliemankhels, they are automatically Ghalzais; but the level of their tribal

---

22 Tapper, 1983, p 4.

identification and the manifestation of their tribal loyalty would vary from one social situation to another.

Because of this complex nature and the overlapping social boundaries of the tribe, the term is used, in the present context, to refer to: *any level of lineage based social formation the members of which trace their roots to a common ancestor, see 'themselves' as one unit in relation to 'others' in a specific social situations, but do not necessarily have face-to-face and direct reciprocal relationships.* While this description excludes a local village-based *khel*, it at the same time includes all the various levels of tribal formations, the members of which are able to trace their roots to their various common ancestors and to the founder of the tribe. Of course, this description is not intended to resolve the complexities of the nature and boundaries of the tribe; it only aims at providing a context for the examination of the *qawmi jirga*. Thus, describing the tribe in this way, the *qawmi jirga* may be held at any level of these tribal formations as a mechanism of conflict resolution.

However, before examining the main techniques and processes involved in the *qawmi jirga*, it is important to mention that its main constituent elements – *narkh*, *marakachian*, institutionalised rituals, and *prikra* – are not fundamentally different from those of *maraka*. Because *qawmi jirga* deals with serious and important conflicts within the tribe (such as murder, disputes over land, water canals, water springs, etc) or between tribes (disputes over communal land, mountains, mines, jungle/ woods, and the murder of fellow tribesman by a member of another tribe), and because it operates at a higher level of tribal formation, its social organisation is more structured. For example, all the *marakchain* of a *qawmi jirga*, who are called *jirgamaran* in this context, include prominent representatives of the tribe's various *khels* who have proven qualities of leadership. These qualities include a proven record and reputation of *milmapalana* (hospitality), possession of good family *nang aw ghairt* (honour), a large number of men in the family, bravery in war, political influence within the government, verbal eloquence and regular sound judgments in *jirgas*. Also, the *speenpatkian* in this case must be well known religious leaders rather than local mullahs. Similarly, the other important element of *qawmi jirga* – the *narkh* – is more strictly applied in accordance with the dictates of *pashtunwali*. This Pashtun code of behaviour is described by one pair of Western Afghanologists in this way:

> In addition to the basic requirements of Islam, Pashtuns observe the code of *Pashtunwali*. It is simple but demanding. Group survival is its primary imperative. It demands vengeance against injury or insult to one's kin, chivalry and hospitality toward the helpless and unarmed strangers, bravery in battle, and openness and integrity in individual behaviour. Much honour is given to Pashtuns who can successfully arbitrate the feuds that are endemic among them. Fines and blood money are devices frequently used to limit violence among rival families. *Pashtunwali* is a code that limits anarchy among a fractious but vital people.[23]

This description of *pashtunwali* shows that *jirgamaran* are not only expected to apply the *narkh* fully (especially in cases of murder and other bodily harm), but they should also maintain a good balance between vengeance for injury/insult to one's kin and the collective reputation of the whole tribe as a fair-minded people even against outsiders. Members of the *qawmi jirga* sit in a circle, in a specifically designed place, which may sometimes have a flag. They see each other as equals; there is no hierarchy of speakers and no chairman. As Glatzer put it: 'According to tribal equality, every free and experienced free male person of the tribe has the right to attend, speak and to decide.'[24] The *jirga's prikra* is based on consensus rather than

---

23 Newell and Newell, 1981, p 23.
24 Glatzer, 1998, p 176.

on a majority vote. While this 'make or break' procedure may be a result of the absence of a modern democratic culture and structure in Afghan society as a whole, it sometimes results in accusations and counter-accusations and in bad feelings among those involved. If the *jirga* could not be reconvened in the near future, it shows the inability of the whole tribe to sort out its conflicts, which has serious consequences. After all, the *jirga* is considered by members of the tribe as what Elphinstone (1992) has described as the 'internal government'.

As there seems to be more importance attached to the group than to the individual in Afghan society, the social survival of the tribe often gives a final shape to the *prikra*. In a murder case, for example, *jirgamaran* carefully weigh up the advantages and disadvantages of alternative punishments – *badal* (direct vengeance), *khoonbaha* (blood money), the marriage of a woman from the *par's* (blameworthy/convicted person's) tribe to the victim's close relative. The primary concern in this case is to strike a balance between preventing the conflict from becoming a tribal conflict of revenge killing and the restoration of collective tribal honour. Therefore *khoonbaha*, in most murder cases is preferable to *badal* and is commonly used. It is important to mention that in the case of accepting *khoonbaha*, relatives of the victims are directly involved in the *jirga* process and in pardoning the murderer. This settlement is also encouraged by Islamic law in specific types of murder.[25] One of the main purposes of the involvement of the victim's relatives in the *jirga* decision is to persuade them not to pursue revenge that would inevitably involve the whole tribe. Very interestingly, in the last option of responding to murder, the offender and the victim's relatives (or their respective tribes) are not only reconciled by the *jirga*, but they also have to put an end to their animosity as (new) relatives by marriage. But, the individual – a woman in this case – often pays the price for the tribe's social survival in this patriarchal, group-oriented society.

An important feature of *qawmi jirga*, especially in the case of murder and bodily harm, is the reconciliation of the feuding parties and the re-integration of the offender into the tribe. This is very clearly manifested in *nanawate*. Although the term *nanawate* is described by Dupree as 'the right of asylum and the obligatory acceptance of a truce offer',[26] its more precise meaning is seeking forgiveness/pardon and the obligatory acceptance of a truce offer.[27] This happens when the *qawmi jirga* makes a *prikra* so relatives of the *par* send a *nanawate* to the victim's house. This consists of a group of people that include *speengiri*, *torsary* (female relatives of the offender holding a Qur'an) and *speenpatkian* alongside the offender's close relatives (and sometimes the offender himself), who bring a sheep and flour to the victim's house. The sheep is often slaughtered at the door of the victim's house. Then, members of the *nanawate* ask for permission to enter the house. Once inside the house, they seek pardon on behalf of the offender. As it is against the principles of *pashtunwali* to reject a *nanawate*, the victim's relatives pardon the offender and the two parties are reconciled. This reconciliation is called *rogha*. What is crucial in this ceremony is that the offender is re-accepted into the tribe after he is publicly held responsible and told that what he has done is wrong. This might be an example of what Braithwaite (1989) calls 're-integrative shaming' – a shaming of the offender, which is followed by re-accepting him into the community. Modern criminological literature shows that this form of shaming is more effective in reducing crime than 'disintegrative' shaming, which labels offenders as different, evil, and excludes them from the community.

---

25 A'uda, 1968.
26 1980, p 126.
27 See Atayee, 1979, pp 65–67.

Like the *maraka*, the *qawmi jirga* serves as an important channel of communication, not only between those who are directly involved in the process, but also between the main actors and the whole community of fellow kinsmen. It is a communication that is central to the social survival of the tribe as a cohesive group that is bonded together not only by blood ties, but also by the *pashtunwali* – a code of behaviour that has a profound existence in the collective mind of the tribe, an unwritten constitution. But what is more important about this process is the legitimacy and moral validity of the *jirga*'s *prikra*. The *prikra* is binding on the behaviour of the parties only when it is arrived at fairly and is in accordance to the tenets of *pashtunwali*. However, the *jirga* is not immune from illegitimate and corrupt influences by some *jirgamaran*.[28] This may include nepotism and illegitimate lobbying. In such a situation, the *prikra* is often rejected, and the reconvening of the *jirga* does not normally take place. This has serious consequences for the tribe as a whole, and often results in continued feuding and bloodshed. A continued bloodshed may result in inter-tribal warfare. In such a situation, the central government and its agencies of social control often get involved – a prospect that tribe people fear most. This is not only because the tribesmen do not like officialdom and state interference in their affairs; also, the state justice system is expensive, slow, and corruption is endemic to it. As the state and its role in conflict resolution are issues that lie within the sphere of macro-level national issues, they will be examined in the context of *loya jirga*.

Loya jirga – grand national assembly

Loya jirga is a Pashto phrase that consists of two words – *loya*, which means 'grand', and *jirga*, which means 'assembly' or 'gathering'. So *loya jirga* in Afghan political culture means a 'grand assembly' of Afghan tribal leaders, elders and others who gather in order to discuss vital national issues and make collective decisions. For centuries, Afghanistan has convened *loya jirgas*, and therefore the whole terminology is deeply rooted in Afghan culture and history. The most well known *loya jirga* in Afghan history is the one held in 1747 in Kandahar, during which various Afghan tribes selected Ahmed Shah Durrani (Ahmad Shah Baba) as the first king of modern Afghanistan, who laid down the foundation of the modern Afghan state. Also, the 1964 and the 1976 *loya jirgas* have a special place in Afghan modern history as women representatives, for the first time, participated in them. In 1964, four women were appointed to the advisory drafting committee of the proposed constitution; in 1976 women formed 15 per cent of the members of the *loya jirga*.

Loya jirga is only held periodically, in order to decide on important national issues that are central to the social and political order, sovereignty and national unity of Afghanistan. Roashan[29] lists the following as possible major reasons for the convening of a *loya jirga*:

- Matters related to declaration of war or adoption of treaties of peace.
- Selection of a new ruler.
- Chalking out defending the nation's honours especially religious values and territorial integrity.
- Deciding on the type of government.
- Seeking agreement of the nation to social, economic and political legislation.

---

28 Noelle-Karimi, 1998, p 38.
29 2001, p 4.

- Chalking out programs for social welfare of the country.
- Legitimising actions of the ruling administration.
- Adopting a Constitution for the country or cancelling previous constitutions or laws especially made by the previous king or ruler.
- Trying to convince the world that the society has practised democratic system.
- Deciding on relations with neighbouring countries.
- Deciding the status of the country vis à vis global conflicts and blocks.

Indeed, the chronology of *loya jirgas* in Afghan history shows that one or more of these reasons necessitated the convening of *loya jirgas* in different social, political and economic circumstances. Central to the success or failure of specific *loya jirgas* in Afghan history has been their legitimacy. Legitimacy in this context means the extent to which the Afghan population believed in the entitlement of the *jirga*, as a national political power, to act as their representative and the extent to which its decisions were binding on their behaviour. In the absence of modern democratic culture in Afghanistan, legitimacy often meant 'moral' or 'normative' legitimacy, as differentiated from 'legal' and 'empirical' legitimacy.[30] This is to say that the degree of legitimacy of the various *jirgas* varied in accordance with the extent to which people (subjectively) accepted them as legitimate in different circumstances. It is, of course, very difficult to measure objectively the legitimacy of the various *jirgas* that have been held in the modern history of Afghanistan. But few doubt the legitimacy of the 1747 *loya jirga* in Kandahar, the 1922 *loya jirga* in Paghman and the 1964 *loya jirga* in Kabul, to mention only a few. The source of the legitimacy of these *jirgas* appears to be the 'traditional' as well the 'charismatic' authority[31] of the nation's elders and leaders.

However, not all *jirgas* in Afghan history have been successful in achieving their goals. The *loya jirgas* held by the Afghan Marxists in the 1980s and the mujahedin's *shura – i- ahl al-hal wal a'aqd* in 1992 – lacked legitimacy in the eyes of the Afghan people, and therefore have been massively rejected by the people of Afghanistan. Both the Marxists and the fundamentalist mujahedin attempted to manipulate the *jirga* and to use it as a vehicle for imposing totalitarian governments on the people of Afghanistan. In the case of the mujahedin, they even tried to replace the whole concept of *jirga* by the 'imported' idea of *shura – i- ahl al-hal wal a'aqd*. As the imposition of a totalitarian system of governance is inherently at odds with the nature of the relatively more egalitarian institution of *jirga*, these attempts drastically failed. The failures of the Afghan Marxists and the mujahedin to give the people of Afghanistan the right to choose their rulers have had catastrophic consequences for Afghanistan. Olesen sums this up in this way: 'So far, the "Islamic Revolution" threatens to be as fatal to the Afghan population as the [Afghan Marxist] Saur Revolution was.'[32] Few Afghans, indeed, would doubt this.

The 2002 *emergency loya jirga* (ELJ), based on the Bonn Agreement, is one of the most important events in Afghan history and constitutes an essential first step towards peace and the establishment of a new democratic political order. However, the fact that the ELJ is being held in circumstances in which warlords and faction leaders, who have a well-documented history of political corruption and serious abuses of human rights,[33] dominate military and political power in the country is a source of threat to its legitimacy. There are credible reports which show that these

---

30 Merquior, 1980.
31 Weber, 1964.
32 1995, p 303.
33 Amnesty International's Report on Afghanistan, 2002.

warlords have been making concrete efforts to influence the ELJ process in their favour, so that they stay in power.[34] There is evidence that the warlords have even manipulated the existing demographic data about the population of Afghanistan. While Article 14 of the Procedure of the ELJ explicitly states that those who 'have been involved in spreading and smuggling narcotics, abuse of human rights, war crimes, looting of public property and smuggling of cultural and archaeological heritage … the killing of innocent people' are not eligible to become members of this historic grand assembly, all the powerful warlords occupied the front seats of the *jirga*. The deputy president of the *loya jirga* and the Minster of Women Affairs in Mr Karzai's administration, Ms Sima Samar, told *The Guardian*: 'This is not democracy. This is a rubber stamp. Those with power have already decided every thing. This *jirga* includes all the warlords. None of them has been left out.'[35] The comments by a respected Afghan high ranking woman politician and the unlawful influence of warlords over the ELJ process is a reminder to those in power that the lessons from the history of Afghan *jirgas* must not be lost – successful *loya jirgas* have always given preference to the long-term interests of the Afghan nation over short-term interests of individuals and groups.

In addition to the influence of warlords over the ELJ process, its final outcome regarding the composition of the new Afghan Transitional Administration (ATA) appears to be shaped, to a considerable degree, by the warlords rather than by the other ELJ delegates. The *Daily Telegraph*'s Phillip Smucker reported on the final fateful session of the ELJ, which was to vote on the composition of the new ATA:

> Before delivering his list and asking for the snap show of hands, Mr Karzai sounded almost contrite. 'I am sorry and I hope that you will forgive me – those whose voices have not been heard. I know, I believe that this government will not be acceptable to all of you, but I hope that it will be acceptable to at least some of you.'[36]

But the 'show of hands' instead of voting, and the acceptability of the new cabinet to 'some', instead of at least a simple 'majority' neither represents the traditional *loya jirga* spirit nor the principles of modern democracy. But few would disagree that President Karzai was in a very difficult position in balancing pragmatism and faithfulness to institutional principles and norms. The fragile central government is too weak to withstand pressures from warlords who dominate political and military power in the country – preference of pragmatism over principles will the focus of judgement by the people of Afghanistan in the months and years to come.

Nevertheless, what is important from a sociological point of view is the fact that the ELJ, which brought together hundreds of delegates from the various parts of Afghanistan and the world, in very difficult circumstances, is an important achievement in its own right. This *jirga*, for the first time in the past three decades, provided a channel of communication between the different segments of Afghan society – between warlords and ordinary people; between men and women; between different tribes and ethnic groups; between Islamists and secularists, and between the royalists and their enemies. It provided a forum where the previously silent victims of the conflict were able to express their deeply felt feelings. Jonathan Steele reported from the *jirga* tent in Kabul that 'Taj Kakar and a group of women delegates confronted the former president of Burhanuddin Rabbani. "Why have you killed and raped our women? Why do we have so many widows in this

---

34 Human Rights Watch Report, 2002.
35 *The Daily Telegraph*, 13 June 2002.
36 *The Daily Telegraph*, 20 June 2002.

country?" she asked. The startled political leader of the Northern Alliance whose forces helped destroy large parts of Kabul in the 1990s, had no answer.'[37]

Whether the former president replied to the women delegate's questions or not is of little importance. What is important is that this particular encounter is watched by the people of Afghanistan and by the rest of the world. It is a communication between the female delegates, the former president, and the apparently silent onlookers – the watchful Afghan society and the rest of the world. The fact that this kind of communication has been made possible verbally, instead of through the exchange of bullets, is a significant first step towards the peaceful resolution of conflicts at a national level. This, in turn, is expected to lead gradually to the creation of a culture of tolerance, accommodation and of the rule of law – a culture that the *loya jirga* as an institution is able to provide; it is a culture with which the practitioners of the centuries-old institutions of *maraka* and *qawmi jirga* are not unfamiliar.

However, in this process, the *jirga* has to learn from other cultures. As mentioned in the introduction, in this day and age no nation, including the Afghans, lives in a cultural vacuum. The increasing globalisation of economic, social and political relationships among nations makes Afghanistan as much a part of the 'global village' as any other nation. The Afghan *loya jirga*, as well as other nations, need to engage in dialogue. At this junction of Afghan history, one of the most important historical missions that the *loya jirga* can embark upon is to help to lay down the foundation of an open and inclusive political order in Afghanistan – a political order that represents not only the aspirations of the various tribal, ethnic and religious groups in Afghanistan, but also the aspiration of its most oppressed citizens – Afghan women. Afghan women, who form more than half of the total population of Afghanistan, have not only suffered a great deal in the course of the long armed conflict, they are also the innocent victims of structural and cultural violence. Afghan women's integration into the political life of the new Afghanistan will be a very important step towards the establishment of a fairer and democratic society.

The experience of democratic nations shows that legitimate political opposition and the expression of political opinion help those in power to learn from their mistakes. But, a prerequisite of the new political order is the creation of a social and political environment that is conducive to a meaningful political dialogue among the people of Afghanistan. The new ATA has the historical responsibility to lay down the foundations of a new social and political order – a political order that is acceptable to all Afghans and which will serve as the basis of a fairer and more inclusive Afghan society. The Afghan people have great expectations of the ATA.

Conclusion

The *jirga* is deeply rooted in the culture and history of Afghanistan. It is strongly bound up with the social and economic realities of Afghan society, and is closely connected to the social order of the Afghan village, tribe, and the state. In fact, the *jirga*, and its norms and processes, define the ways in which Afghans resolve their conflicts, and is therefore an important aspect of Afghan national identity. It is an Afghan social institution that has a profound existence in the minds of the Afghan people. Contrary to those who dismiss the importance of *jirga* as an important tool of peace-making in Afghanistan,[38] it is a time-honoured institution that has a

---

37 *The Guardian*, 13 June 2002.
38 Noelle-Karimi, 1998.

proven record of and future potential for resolving conflicts at local, tribal and national levels in Afghan society. The history of *loya jirgas* has shown that the institution is a powerful mechanism for communication of Afghan nationhood among the various tribes, ethnicities and religions of the country – it is a source of national unity and social solidarity.

However, the Afghan *jirga* as a traditional institution at the dawn of the 21st century is entering a new era of national and international transformation – an era of the globalisation of social, economic and political relationships among nations. The *jirga* is no longer only a mechanism of conflict resolution within the context of the Afghan village, tribe and nation. It is also a part of the 'global village' in which different cultures and civilisations today interact. The *jirga* must be prepared to face the challenges of the 21st century and to adapt to the new social, economic and political milieu; it needs to learn from other cultures as much as they need to learn from it. The Afghan *jirga* has the potential to bridge tradition with modernity; it has the capacity to express traditional values in a modern setting.

References

Amnesty International, *Annual Report 2002 – Afghanistan*: www.amnesty.org

Atayee, I (1979) *A Dictionary of the Terminology of the Pashtun Tribal Customary Law and Usages*, Kabul: Academy of Sciences of Afghanistan

A'uda, A (1968) *Al-Tashri'a Al-Jenaiee Al-Islami*, Beirut: Dar Al-Fikr al-Islami

Banuazizi, A and Weiner, M (eds) (1988) *State, Religion and Ethnic Politics: Afghanistan, Iran, Pakistan*, New York: Syracuse UP

Baxi, U and Gallanter, M (1979) 'Panchayat justice: an Indian experience in legal access', in Cappelletti, Mauro and Garth, Bryan (eds), *Access to Justice*, Milano: Giuffer, Vol 3, pp 314–86

Braithwaite, J (1989) *Crime, Shame and Reintegration*, Cambridge: CUP

Canfield, R (1986) 'Ethnic, regional, and sectarian alignments in Afghanistan', in Carter, L and Connor, K, *A Preliminary Investigation of Contemporary Afghan Councils*, 1989, Peshwar: ACBAR

Carter, L and Connor, K (1989) *A Preliminary Investigation of Contemporary Afghan Councils*, Peshwar: ACBAR

Clark, J (1989) 'Conflict management outside the courtroom in China', in Troyer, Ronald (ed), *Social Control in the People's Republic of China*, London: Praeger

Dupree, L (1980) *Afghanistan*, Princeton: Princeton UP

Elphinstone, M (1992) *An Account of the Kingdom of Caubul*, Karachi: OUP (originally published 1839)

Farhadi, R (2000) 'Tajikane Afghanistan wa qadamhaie ashti bain aishan', in *Qadamhaie Ashti wa Masauliate ma Afghanistan*, Falls Church, Va: Kabultec

Faiz-zad, M (1989) *Jirga Haie Bozorge Milie Afghanistan*, Lahore: NFD

Gheyathoddin, Maulana (ed) (1871) *Ghyathul-Lughat*, New Delhi: Kanpur

Glatzer, B (1998) 'Is Afghanistan on the brink of ethnic and tribal disintegration?', in Maley, William (ed), *Fundamentalism Reborn? Afghanistan and the Taliban*, New York: St Martins

Hashemi, M (2000) 'Qadamhaie ashti baine uzbakan', in *Qadamhaie Ashti wa Masauliate ma Afghanha*, Falls Church, Va: Kabultec

Human Rights Watch, 'The warlords are plotting a comeback', 10 June 2002: www.hrw.org

Hayman, A (1992) *Afghanistan under Soviet Domination*, 3rd edn, London: Macmillan

Kamali, M (1985) *Law in Afghanistan: A Study of Constitutions, Matrimonial Law and the Judiciary*, Leiden: EJ Brill

Li, V (1978) *Law without Lawyers*, Boulder, Co: Westview

Malekyar, S (2000) 'Qadamhaie ashti wa solh dar ananaie hazarahaie Afghanistan', in *Qadamhaie Asshti wa Masauliate ma Afghanha*, Falls Church, Va: Kabultec

Merquior, J (1980) *Rousseau and Weber: Two Studies in the Theory of Legitimacy*, London: Routledge and Kegan Paul

Moore, E (1985) *Conflict and Compromise: Justice in an Indian Village*, New York: New York UP

Newell, N and Newell, R (1981) *The Struggle for Afghanistan*, New York: Cornell UP

Noelle-Karimi (1998) 'The loya jirga – an effective political instrument?', in Maley, William (ed), *Fundamentalism Reborn? Afghanistan and the Taliban*, New York: St Martins

Olesen, A (1995) *Islam and Politics in Afghanistan*, Surrey: Curzon

Pashto Descriptive Dictionary (1978) The Academy of Sciences of Afghanistan, Kabul: Government Press

Rafi, H (2002) *Loya Jirga*, Peshawar: Aman

Reichel, P (1998) *Comparative Criminal Justice Systems*, New York: Prentice Hall

Roashan, R (2001) *Loya Jirga: One of the Last Political Tools for Bringing Peace in Afghanistan*: http://home.san.rr.com/roashan/politics/SpecialProjects/LoyaJirga.htm

Robertson, R (1992) *Globalisation: Social Theory and Global Culture*, London: Sage

Rubin, Barnett R (1995) *The Fragmentation of Afghanistan: State Formation and Collapse in the International System*, New Haven: Yale UP

Rubin, Barnett R (1999) 'The political economy of war and peace in Afghanistan', paper presented at the meeting of the Afghanistan Support Group, Stockholm, Sweden

Sumner, W (1906) *Folkways*, Boston: Ginn and Co

Tapper, R (1983) *The Conflict of Tribe and State in Iran and Afghanistan*, London: Croom Helm

Wardak, A (1998) 'The tribal and ethnic composition of Afghan society', in Girardet, Edward and Walter, Jonathan, *Afghanistan: Essential Field Guides to Humanitarian and Conflict Zones*, Geneva: Crosslines

Weber, M (1964) *The Theory of Social and Economic Organisation*, Parsons, T (ed), New York: Free Press

Wrong (1979) *Power: Its Forms, Bases and Uses*, Oxford: Basil Blackwell

Chapter 14
Islamic law and the English press
John Strawson

Edward Said has observed that 'for the general public in America and Europe, today, Islam is "news" of a particularly unpleasant sort'.[1] He could have added that Islamic law is usually extremely unpleasant news. In the wake of September 11, Islamic law became a central issue within Western popular media as societies attempted to grapple with the meaning of the events. Of particular concern was whether or not the attacks on the Twin Towers and the Pentagon were justifiable according to Islamic law. In order to answer this conundrum, politicians and the mass media became taken up with the intricacies of jihad, fatwas and Qur'anic interpretations. A leading figure in this was British Prime Minister Tony Blair, who engaged in well-reported debates on the Islamic legal merits of Al Qa'ida and the Taliban. This essay will track aspects of this popular Western Islamic legal discourse and assess whether this is new or merely a re-run of Orientalist and blood-curdling images of Islamic law from colonial times.

Islamic law has been much affected by the disturbances of colonialism, especially since the British encounter with Islam in Bengal in the late 18th century.[2] Much of the difficulty in establishing answers to apparently straightforward questions about Islamic law and September 11 are to be found in these causes. Islamic law in British and French colonies was reduced in scope while norms were isolated from the jurisprudence and enframed within a colonial legal system and court structure. In addition, Muslim lawyers were drawn within the colonial legal discourses through legal education, joining the new Bars and, in time, the judiciary of the imposed system.[3] During this process the classical structure of Islamic law – resting on diverse sources and with many differing interpretations – was eroded as it became characterised by norms isolated from Islamic methodology, homogeneous and rigidly applied.[4] As the West's power grew during the colonial age, its legal systems were projected as modern and Islam's system was essentially seen as backward. Islamic law, the *Shari'a*, is based on four sources: the Qur'an, the *sunna* or traditions of the Prophet, *ijma* or consensus amongst the jurists, and *qiyas* or analogical reasoning. In addition there exists a further and sometimes more controversial category of *ijtihad*, or independent reasoning, that allows scholars to take new initiatives. This complex structure is sustained by the jurisprudence, *usul al fiqh*, that develops within civil society institutions such as the universities.[5] Colonialism and the general Westernisation of the world (in the Islamic world demonstrated by the decline of the Ottoman and Persian Empires in the 19th century) saw a significant split between the active jurisprudence and an ossified *Shari'a*. This was most marked in those areas of law that deal with the international realm and public law, known as the *siyar* and *siyassa* and thus dealing with issues such as the use of force and human rights. While Islam's international law has a pedigree of over 1,000 years and is thus much older than the Western system – that developed with the beginnings of

---

1   Said, 1997, p 144.
2   See Strawson, 1999.
3   See Strawson, 2001.
4   For a discussion of Islamic legal methodology, see Kamali, 1996.
5   See Hallaq, 1997, pp 1–35.

colonialism – it has been seriously marginalised and largely ignored.[6] It is this history that undermines serious investigations as to Islamic law and September 11.[7] In the immediate wake of the attacks, however, parts of the English press did find the rigid colonial constructions of Islamic law particularly inconvenient and began to challenge some previously firmly held assumptions.

Tony Blair's attempt to reach out to the Muslim world is particularly instructive. According to *The Independent*'s Paul Vallely, Blair is the first British Prime Minister since Gladstone to make a systematic study of Islam.[8] Shortly after the events of September 11, Blair, acting as the intelligent one of an odd couple (Bush-Blair), began to tour the world and engage Muslims in a debate about Islam. It is during Blair's Islamic discourses that he regularly refers to *surat* (verses) of the Qur'an and begins to pronounce on his interpretations of Islamic law. Blair, we are told by the same journalist, packs a Qur'an when he travels. The image of a British postcolonial Prime Minister, Qur'an by his side, striding through the world in multi-cultural mode, strikes an interesting note. Blair as the knower of Islam, able to interpret and to communicate in its language, is perhaps a necessarily comforting figure for a West struggling to size up the strength of post-September 11 Oriental fury. At the same time, such a figure appears to be on the borders of escaping the equally comforting East/West binary divide of Orientalist discourse. The media appears perplexed as to how to deal with him.

Blair has a no-nonsense approach to his topic, he appears generally unconcerned with his location and frees himself from any potential charge of cultural essentialism. He is able to assure us:

> Everyone I have met has told me that these attacks were contrary to all the tenets of Islam and the teachings of the Koran. Everyone wants to see those who carried out the wholesale murder of innocent men, women and children brought to justice.[9]

Blair's comments came after a visit to Oman and Egypt and thus 'everyone' presumably refers to Omani and Egyptian politicians and officials. What makes this statement all the more significant is that the article was written originally for the Muslim media. Blair places himself in a universalist position as he warms to his theme and asks: '… the question Muslims around the world have to ask themselves is: do you want to live under the sort of regime we see today in Kabul? Because that is what Bin Laden and Al Qa'ida want for you.'[10] He answers his own question in the same vein:

> Virtually the only arm of the civil government that functions effectively is the Ministry of Enforcement of Virtue and the Suppression of Vice. This ministry enforces strict observance of all Taliban decrees on social and moral behaviour that bear scant relationship to the teachings of Islam. But they are ruthlessly imposed.[11]

In order to underline the unattractive and un-Islamic character of this he continues:

> Along with terror, this is the kind of intolerant, backward-looking regime Osama Bin Laden wants to export throughout the Muslim world. In permanent conflict with the world and anyone who disagrees; against any form of modernisation and economic progress; ruthless in suppressing any opposition and other ways of life; women treated abominably; denouncing Muslims who live and work in the West as traitors; supporting of the most extreme interpretation of Islamic law imaginable.[12]

---

6   See for example Schacht, 1964, p 112.
7   However, this issue has not been ignored: see Vogel, 2002.
8   *The Independent*, 12 October 2001.
9   'Blair: what will the world look like if we don't stop bin Laden?', *The Independent*, 12 October 2001.
10 *Ibid.*
11 *Ibid.*
12 *Ibid.*

Blair is making an assumption that the Taliban's 'extreme interpretation of Islamic law' bears 'scant relationship to the teachings of Islam'. In this account there must exist another, more moderate and more authentic version of Islamic law. This is an ironic twist to 200 years of Orientalist construction of Islamic law in England,[13] where the emphasis has tended to be the other way around and such extremist interpretations have been portrayed as particularly authentic.[14] In another *Independent* piece, the newspaper questions the status of Blair's Islamic interpretations. Using an interview with the Qatar-based Al Jazeera television station, we find the Prime Minister saying: 'To kill, as these terrorists did, is utterly foreign to the teachings of the Koran ... To justify it by saying such murder of the innocent is doing the will of God is to defame the name of Islam.'[15] And he continues, 'The version of Islam that the Taliban regime and Osama Bin Laden support is a version of Islam a million miles away from reality'.[16] This brings the response from the Al Jazeera journalist, who asks: 'Isn't it the task of the Muslim world to see that, not the Western Christian world?' Unfortunately, *The Independent* does not provide us with Blair's reply. Paul Vallely uses the occasion, however, to offer his readers a lesson in Islamic law and Qur'anic interpretation. Apparently agreeing with the cultural implications of Al Jazeera, he neatly reconstructs the East/West divide:

> But there is a theoretical objection of which most people in the West are unaware. Among Christians, disagreements over interpretation of the bible are common: since the Protestant Reformation, Western culture has put less trust in the idea that interpretation can only be carried out by a single authoritative source.

> But in Islam this breakdown has not occurred. There is a whole Islamic discipline called tafsir whose experts devote a lifetime of study to elucidation of individual verses of the Koran – particularly those that seem to contradict other verses.[17]

This part of the lesson is somewhat obscure and his 'students' may want to ask how it is that while there is a homogeneous version of Islam, at the same time scholars are spending their lives attempting to learn the techniques of interpretation. However, an aspect of the message appears to be that, while the sophisticated West has complex interpretations of its key texts, the East is in some way different and awaiting a Reformation of some sort, indicating that it is backward in this respect. Vallely turns to an Islamic authority to help out on this point. This authority turns out to be none other than George Bush's advisor on Islam:

> For those who are not qualified scholars to fence with quotations from the Koran is, according to Hamza Yusuf, one of President George Bush's advisors on Islam, 'like every American interpreting the constitution according to his whim and expecting it to be as valid as the opinion of a constitutional lawyer with years of training'.[18]

Paul Vallely continues his piece with the argument that there is a chain of authority that can be traced back to the Prophet Mohammad for authoritative interpretations of the Qur'an. Again relying on the authority of President Bush's advisor:

> Over the centuries, tafsir scholars have divided the Koran's verses into categories – general and specific verses, universal and particular, ambiguous and clarifying. Systems have been set in place to make it clear that in Mr Yusuf's words, 'Islam is a holistic tradition in which

---

13 See Strawson, 1999; Strawson, 1997.
14 I am not using 'extremists' in an essentialist way, I hope. This is a reference to the binary system that is set up in both popular and academic Orientalism.
15 'Caution should be the byword when quoting the Koran', *The Independent*, 12 October 2001.
16 *Ibid*.
17 *Ibid*.
18 *Ibid*.

no verse can be taken out of the context as a whole'. Moreover, only those who have a ijaza, a license, to show that they have an isnad, a documented, unbroken chain of authority that can be traced back to the Prophet are considered under Islamic law to have the legitimacy to make such judgements.[19]

The use of the American President's Islamic advisor to trump the arguments of the British Prime Minister is an interesting use of authority and authenticity. The article ends by telling us that whatever Tony Blair's status, Osama bin Laden does not have a license to interpret the Qur'an either.

In the foregoing discussion it is noticeable that several levels of discourse are being engaged with by Tony Blair and his journalist interlocutor. Tony Blair speaks to his Muslim audience in two voices. In the first he articulates the apparently unquestionable truth that there is a singular Islam that is necessarily opposed to any justifications for the September 11 attacks. The attacks are 'utterly foreign to all the teachings of the Koran', everyone he has met in the Middle East thinks that too, and the Taliban and Osama bin Laden are a 'millions miles away from [Islamic] reality'. However, in his other voice, Blair seems to want to shift from this definite position to one where he enters into an argument over the interpretation of Islam. In this voice he asks the questions directly to Muslims, 'do you want to live under the sort of regime that we see today in Kabul? Because that is what bin Laden and Al Qa'ida want for you'.[20] He continues by contrasting the history of moderation of Islam even to the disadvantage of the West: '… historically, Islam has been very tolerant of other religions. The Muslim world was a beacon of civilisation and tolerance when Europe was in the dark ages.'[21] The interplay between both voices, one wanting to articulate a singular authority and the second engaging in a struggle over interpretations of authority, is contradictory. Either Islamic law has a static character or it is a living discourse. Paul Vallely, on the other hand, sets himself up as the authority that tells us that Tony Blair's Qur'anic interpretations may be questionable, lacking as he does a license, and yet so far as we know neither does Paul Vallely have any status in Islamic jurisprudence. His reliance on a Bush advisor merely underlines his curious use of authority. He is also naïve in thinking that Hamza Yussuf's attempted analogy between his view of Islamic law and American constitutional law could be convincing, especially against the background of US civil rights and women's movements that mobilised around activist interpretations of the constitution. He is unaware that by allowing this singular notion of legal interpretation he has undermined his earlier point about the West's centuries of engagement with different meanings of the same text. These two short pieces do raise critical questions about the methodology of Islamic law and how this relates to arguments about the events of September 11.

While Tony Blair attempted to portray a third way *Shari'a*, the popular media was concerned that perhaps the Islamic concept of jihad did legitimise terrorism in general and the September 11 attacks in particular. Within a week of the events, the *Daily Telegraph* carried a piece by Patrick Sookhdeo claiming that Islam sanctioned violence.[22] 'Many horrific acts have been, and continue to be, carried out in the name of Islam, just as they have in the name of Christianity. But, unlike Islam, Christianity does not justify all forms of violence. Islam does.'[23] This sweeping assertion that Islam justifies all forms of violence might appear absurd, and yet the author attempts to justify this by reference to the Qur'an. By turning to Sura 9 (5)

---

19 *Ibid.*
20 *Op cit*, fn 8.
21 *Op cit*, fn 8.
22 'A religion that sanctions violence', *Daily Telegraph*, 17 September 2001.
23 *Ibid.*

we are told that the Qur'an reads, 'then fight and slay the pagans wherever ye find them, in every stratagem [of war]'.[24] This passage, however, comes before a passage (At-Tauba) dealing with enemies who have acted treacherously, and should be read in conjunction with Sura 8 which deals with a balance sheet of the battle of Badr (623), indicating that the text is dealing with very specific circumstances – in particular what to do with the spoils of war. Sura 9 follows these lessons. Sookhdeo does not refer to the paragraph that follows, 'If one amongst the pagans ask thee for asylum, Grant it too him';[25] he no doubt finds this liberal sentiment inconvenient. However he insists that 'the argument that the ... verse was written to refer only to a particular time and people is not valid. The Koran is considered immutable'. No further jurisprudential evidence is provided for this and he concludes his argument in the most contradictory fashion:

> The World Trade Centre attack cannot be dismissed as merely the work of a small group of extremists. The Muslims celebrating the tragedy in America are no doubt recalling the words of the Koran, urging Muslims to 'fight a mighty nation. Fight them until they embrace Islam'. Sheikh Omar Bakri Mohamed, leader of the radical Islamic organisation Al Muhajiroun last week indicated that civilian targets were wrong, but military and government targets were legitimate.[26]

Sookhdeo, described as the 'director of the Institute for the Study of Islam and Christianity', appears unaware that his starting point that Islam sanctions all forms of violence has just been flatly contradicted by one of the Muslims most close to the politics of Al Qa'ida in Britain, Bakri Mohamed. His statement could come straight from a conventional Public International Law textbook. This type of argument about Islam, laced with quotations from the Qur'an and served with an apparently authoritative academic commentary, has a long lineage in popular and academic Orientalism. However, this crude variant is losing favour and September 11 became a moment where a more serious discussion of Islamic law appeared in the media.

Within a week of Patrick Sookhdeo's article, the *Daily Telegraph* published a piece by its Middle East correspondent, Alan Philps, on jihad.[27]

> Jihad, usually translated as 'holy war' is one of the most familiar concepts in the Western world. It conjures up images from the Crusades of Saracen warriors with curved scimitars driving Christendom from Jerusalem. But to Islamic Scholars, the term is much misunderstood in the West, and equally abused for political purposes in the Islamic world. Strictly speaking, it means any effort or struggle.[28]

Philps introduces scholars from Britain and the Middle East to support his view. Zaki Badawi of the Muslim College in London explains, 'Jihad has become an abused term. It does not mean holy war. It means the struggle to do good. It could mean doing your job properly or controlling your anger or appetite'.[29] If this seems tame coming from temperate London, Philps then turns to Zuhair Dubie, a Palestinian cleric based in Nablus.

> Some people in these desperate times think the only way to serve God is to strap explosives to their body and become a suicide bomber. But there are many ways of serving God – I can help the poor, clean the Mosque, plant trees or dress more modestly. This is all Jihad.[30]

---

24 *Ibid.*
25 Qur'an Sura 9 (6).
26 *Op cit*, fn 8.
27 'How God's struggle became a war', *Daily Telegraph*, 22 September 2001.
28 *Ibid.*
29 *Ibid.*
30 *Ibid.*

However, these voices are lost in the rest of the article, which explains that these interpretations have become marginalised as the military version of jihad has come to the fore in the Middle East and central Asia. The article ends by explaining that Afghans became the most successful exponents of the military version of jihad when the mujahedin ('it means those who wage jihad') expelled the Soviets in the late 1980s. The reader might well become confused about jihad; however this more subtle approach at least undermines the homogeneous view of Islam and violence that Sookhdeo's article advanced. Philps does, none the less, work within the East/West binary divide in the way in which he sets up his case. His use of the image of crusades at the beginning of the article becomes a substantive point as he explains that it was the Muslim reaction to the crusades that re-kindled the military interpretation of jihad.

Antagonism between the East and West is a major feature of the media discourse. Italian Prime Minister Silvio Berlusconi's comments on Western superiority as against Islam sparked such a discussion in *The Telegraph*[31] at the end of September 2001. Speaking for the West, Berlusconi reportedly said:

> ... we must be aware of the superiority of our civilization, a system that has guaranteed well-being, respect for human rights – and in contrast with Islamic countries – respect for religious and political rights. Islamic civilization is stuck where it was 1,400 years ago.[32]

The line of the author, Alasdair Palmer, is that 'many people in Britain, Europe and America will secretly agree with him'. Palmer's article is a curious mixture of a crude 'West is best' view mixed with some multicultural sensitivities. He begins to sound like Berlusconi:

> It is not just that the European cultural tradition has richness and variety – from painters such as Michelangelo and Picasso, to the music of Bach, Mozart, Beethoven, Verdi and Wagner – that Islamic cultures cannot match. It is also that extreme fundamentalist Islamist regimes, such as those of Afghanistan are an affront to civilization, women are treated as little better than beasts of burden, they are denied education, property, and even medical treatment ... Men and women have no political rights, there is no possibility of free speech and the country has been impoverished, indeed economically destroyed by the Mullahs' insistence on forcing obedience to Islamic law in every minute detail.[33]

His picture of Afghanistan has, he says, become the 'public face of Islam in the West'. However, he is aware of the dangers of overstating his case and in one short passage argues:

> ... that of course does not mean that citizens of Western countries are superior to Islamic people, or that they are morally better; a quick glance at the history of this century, from Auschwitz to Srebrenica (where 8,000 unarmed Muslims were massacred by Christians), will show that the West has the ability and willingness to wade knee deep in the blood and bones of their enemies.[34]

However, this appears a small matter; the 'point remains [that] the secular societies of the West are more tolerant, more prosperous and more dynamic, and place more emphasis on respecting and preserving individual liberty, than any of their Islamic counterparts'.[35]

In this account we see the problem of the East/West divide conventionally put from the Western, apparently liberal, viewpoint. Berlusconi is pointing to an objective truth; however problematic it might appear, the sub-text is that the West is

31 'Is the West really best?', *Daily Telegraph*, 30 September 2001.
32 *Ibid.*
33 *Ibid.*
34 *Ibid.*
35 *Ibid.*

more advanced. Not only does it have wonderful music and painting but it also happens to possess an equally wonderful legal culture that promotes and protects human rights. There are of course exceptions and the Holocaust and atrocities in the Balkans are footnoted. Palmer does explain that there was a time when Islamic civilisation had something to offer in the form of mathematics and medicine, and indeed Islamic philosophers even 'introduced their Christian counterparts to the learning of the ancient world'. The West has now outpaced these early Islamic contributions and again this is presented as just a fact.

This argument in favour of the West's superiority is constructed without any reference to the actual course of history of Western societies, in which racism, women's oppression and suppression of human rights has been the norm for most of the period since the European Enlightenment. It is unfortunate that Auschwitz cannot be seen as an isolated crime but has to be seen in the context of slavery and colonialism. Western societies, far from being some fortunate beneficiary of human rights culture, are the product of struggles against political systems that justified slavery, colonial conquest and genocide (the Americas, Australasia), racial segregation, discrimination against women and authoritarian rule. Democratic regimes, human rights and rule of law societies are quite new to the West and only really began to be established in the period after the Second World War.[36] September 11 became the occasion, however, for the celebration of the West. It is significant that in this piece Palmer makes explicit the linkages in Western discourses between artistic culture and law. They are indissolubly linked, each refracting light onto the other, constituting a superior cultural and civilisational form.

Muslim voices within the West, however, do disturb the West's superior discourse. Yusuf Islam, the former 1960s rock singer Cat Stevens, argues that he, 'having seen life from both sides – East and West – [is] appropriately placed to confront certain myths' about Islam.[37] He moves between the two locations, explaining how he approached Islam as a Westerner when he embraced it in 1977. In an effort to establish the humanism of Islam, Yusuf Islam emphasises not differences between the Western and Islamic culture but rather commonalities, including those in the Qur'an. He refers to the Qur'an's proposition that 'If anyone kills a person, except [through due legal process] for murder or spreading discord in earth, it will be as if he has killed the whole of humanity'. He also condemns those who interpreted the late Ayatollah Khomeini's fatwa against Salman Rushdie for attempting to take Islamic law into their own hands. Again he uses the Qur'an: 'do not let your hatred of some people cause you to transgress [the law].' On September 11 he is quite emphatic in his condemnation of the attacks and sees the perpetrators as hijackers of Islam.

Yusuf Islam, however, is only one of many Western Muslims who contribute to this debate. Appearing as it were from the other side, Salman Rushdie is quoted as saying that 'world leaders are wrong to say that terrorism and the war against it were not about Islam'.[38] Rushdie's explanation is simple:

> If it isn't about Islam why are there world-wide Muslim demonstrations in support of Osama bin Laden and al-Qa'eda? Why are the war's first casualties three Muslim men who died fighting on the Taliban side? Why does Imran Khan the Pakistani ex-sports [star] turned politician demand to be shown evidence of al-Qa'eda's guilt while apparently turning a deaf ear to the self-incriminating statements of al-Qa'eda's own spokesman?

---

36 For an intriguing analysis of European contemporary history see Mazower, 1998.
37 Stevens, 2001.
38 'Of course this war is about Islam argues Rushdie', *Daily Telegraph*, 3 November 2001.

Why all the talk about American military infidels desecrating the sacred soil of Saudi Arabia if some sort of definition of what is sacred is not at the heart of this present discontent?[39]

Rushdie's almost random questions do fit into the dominant Western discourse and add legitimacy to it through his Muslim credentials. What is more interesting is the way in which the media needs Muslim commentary to sustain its legitimacy. Rushdie, as a very public victim of one version of Islamic law, is able to articulate propositions about Islam that even Berlusconi and Sookhdeo might balk at. 'For the vast number of "Believing" Muslim men,' he writes:

Islam stands, in a jumbled, half examined way, not only for the fear of God but also indicates a cluster of customs, opinions and prejudices and that includes their dietary practices; the sequestration or near sequestration of 'their' women ... and a more particularized loathing (and fear) of the prospect that their immediate surroundings could be taken over – Westoxicated – by the liberal Western-style way of life.[40]

Rushdie's views have been nicely countered by Zaki Badawi.[41] Writing in *The Independent* he argues that:

The pluralistic ideal called for in present-day society was first practised by the Prophet in the first Muslim state in the city of Madina. Muslims, Jews and others were accorded equal rights as citizens. 'The true Muslim,' the Prophet said, 'is the one who hurts no one by word or deed.' Caring for the needy is an obligation. The fundamentals of the legal system, the *Shari'a*, are the protection of the community as a whole, the protection of life, property, honor and sobriety. The Muslim should commit the utmost effort towards self-improvement to be worthy and able to perform these duties. This is called jihad, which in the mind of many people is equated with holy war. Acts of violence are abhorred by Islam. War, a function of the failure of human nature, is only permitted in self-defence, and regulated by strict rule to limit its use ... attacks on civilian targets as took place in New York on 11 September are a violation of the strict Islamic rules and are considered criminal.[42]

Islamic law has thus become much more problematic in these newspaper articles. The singularity of Islam and Islamic law has been contested in a number of ways.[43] Diverse interpretations have been introduced and a quite complex discussion of jihad has been attempted. A small window has been opened on the flourishing of debates about Islamic law and jurisprudence since the end of the 19th century and in particular with the rise to world prominence of political Islam since the Iranian revolution in 1979.[44] In the period since the Iran revolution, arguments about public law, the Islamic state, human rights and democracy have become central within Islamic political circles and within the academy in all parts of the world.[45] In part this is a response to the way in which Islamic law became so narrowly and positively constructed during the colonial period that it almost ceased to exist as a living form of law at all. Western images of Islamic law as being entirely linked to public stonings, amputations of limbs and the oppression of women had a relation to a reality. The revival of debates about international law and the state in part begin to reconnect Islamic jurisprudence to classical works of *siyar*[46] and *siyassa*.[47] The

---

39 *Ibid*.
40 *Ibid*.
41 Badawai, 2001.
42 Badawai, 2001.
43 See Al-Azmeh, 1993; Mallat, 1993.
44 See for example An-Na'im, 1992; Soroush, 2000; Esack, 1997.
45 See for example Moussalli, 1994; Moussalli, 1995.
46 See Kahdduri, 1966.
47 See for example Rushd, 1994.

idea that jihad might not only mean 'holy war' and that there exists a major struggle within Islam over differing interpretations of Islamic law is significant in itself. To a large extent these articles have revealed a surprising reluctance to relate the clash of civilisations thesis to law.[48] However, they also demonstrate how difficult it is to wrench the discourse from the easy stereotype of West versus East. Nonetheless, the fraying at the edges of previously fixed positions has a useful and potentially destabilising influence on attitudes to the centrality and dominance of Western law.[49]

This brief discussion of Islamic law in the English press reveals much about the intricacies of legal Orientalism. Edward Said once talked about the way in which the West in Orientalist discourses constructed Islam, 'represented it and speaking on its behalf'.[50] What we may have learnt is that Western voices come in many tones. Political considerations have somewhat altered the dominant constructions of Islamic law as Tony Blair and other Western leaders want to mobilise Islamic law against the events of September 11. For him *Shari'a* is not an irretrievably backward legal system but on the contrary has progressive features. The desire for an accommodation with Islamic societies and cultures has produced a noticeable shift in the discourse as new images of Islamic law are generated and Muslims are also invited to contribute to this. Yet this is not a radical break within legal Orientalism and it is not new that (post)colonial subjects are invited into its world.[51]

---

48 See Huntington, 1993.
49 See Fitzpatrick, 2001.
50 Said, 1978, p 20.
51 See Strawson, 2001.

References

Al-Azmeh, Aziz (1993) *Islams and Modernities*, London and New York: Verso

An-Na'im, Abdullahi Ahmed (1992) *Toward an Islamic Reformation: Civil Liberties, Human Rights and International Law*, Cairo: American University in Cairo Press

Badawai, Zaki (2001) 'Are Muslims misunderstood?' *The Independent*, 23 September

Bhabha, Homi (1994) *The Location of Culture*, London: Routledge

Esack, Farid (1997) *Qur'an, Liberation and Pluralism*, Oxford: One World

Fitzpatrick, Peter (2001) *Modernism and the Grounds of Law*, Cambridge: CUP

Hallaq, Wael B (1997) *A History of Islamic Legal Theories*, Cambridge: CUP

Huntington, Samuel P (1993) 'The clash of civilizations?' 72(3) Foreign Affairs 22

Kahdduri, Majid (1966) *The Islamic Law of Nations: Shaybani's Siya*, Baltimore: Johns Hopkins

Kamali, Mohammad Hashim (1996) 'Methodological issues in Islamic jurisprudence' 11(1) Arab Law Quarterly 3

Mallat, Chbli (1993) *The Renewal of Islamic Law*, Cambridge: CUP

Mazower, Mark (1998) *Dark Continent: Europe's Twentieth Century*, London: Penguin

Moussalli, Ahmad S (1994) 'Hasan al-Turabi's Islamist discourse on democracy and shura' 30(1) Middle Eastern Studies 52

Moussalli, Ahmed S (1995) 'Modern Islamic fundamentalist discourses on civil society, pluralism and democracy', in Norton, Augustus Richard (ed), *Civil Society in the Middle East*, Leiden and New York: Koln

Rushd, Ibn (1994) *Bidayat Al Mujtahid: The Distinguished Jurist's Primer*, Imran Khan Nyazee (trans), Reading: Garnet, two volumes

Said, Edward W (1978) *Orientalism*, Harmondsworth: Penguin

Said, Edward W (1997) *Covering Islam: How the Media and Experts Determine How We See the Rest of the World*, London: Vintage

Schacht, Joseph (1964) *Introduction to Islamic Law*, Oxford: OUP

Soroush, Abdoolkarim (2000) *Reason, Freedom and Democracy in Islam*, Sadi, Mahmoud and Sadri, Ahmad (trans), Oxford: OUP

Stevens, Cat (2001) 'They have hijacked my religion' *The Independent*, 28 October

Strawson, John (1997) 'A Western question to the Middle East: "Is there a human rights discourse in Islam?"' 19(1) Arab Studies Quarterly 32

Strawson, John (1999) 'Islamic law and English texts', in Darian-Smith, Eve and Fitzpatrick, Peter, *Laws of the Postcolonial*, Ann Arbor: University of Michigan Press

Strawson, John (2001) 'Orientalism and legal education in the Middle East: reading Frederic Goadby's *Introduction to the Study of Law*' 21 Legal Studies 663

Vogel, Frank E (2002) 'The trial of terrorists under classical Islamic law' 43(1) Harvard ILJ 53

Index

Printed in the United Kingdom
by Lightning Source UK Ltd.
101255UKS00002B/61-204